The Soviet Union
and the Challenge
of the Future

The Soviet Union and the Challenge of the Future

Volume 4: Russia and the World

edited by Alexander Shtromas and
Morton A. Kaplan

A PWPA Book

PARAGON HOUSE

New York

First edition, 1989

Published in the United States by

Paragon House

90 Fifth Avenue
New York, New York 10011

Copyright © 1989 by Paragon House

Grateful acknowledgment is made to the following for permission
to reprint previously published material:

Passages from "Gorbachev Without Illusions," by Alain Besançon.
Reprinted from Commentary, April 1988, by permission; all rights
reserved.

Passages from "The Europeanization of Gorbachev," by Jerry F.
Hough, April 8, 1988. Copyright © 1988 by The New York Times
Company. Reprinted by permission.

A Professors World Peace Academy Book

Library of Congress Cataloging-in-Publication Data
The Soviet Union and the challenge of the future.
"A PWPA book."
Includes bibliographies and indexes.
Contents: v. 1. Stasis and change— v. 4. Russia and the world.
1. Soviet Union—Social conditions—1945–   —Congresses.
2. Soviet Union—Politics and government—1945–   —Congresses.
3. Soviet Union—Foreign relations—1945–   —Congresses.
I. Shtromas, Alexander, 1931–   . II. Kaplan,
Morton A. III. Professors World Peace Academy.
HN523.5.S69 1988   306'.0947   87-6904
ISBN 0-943852-37-4 (v. 4)

Manufactured in the United States of America

Contents

PART II

From Crisis to a Post-Soviet Regime

Introduction

Volume 4 is divided into 2 parts: From Current State of Affairs to Possible Crisis; and From Crisis to a Post-Soviet Regime. The editors are aware that the articles included in each section sometimes stray into the area of other sections and, therefore, that the part titles are misleading to that extent. We believed that this material on the whole was so interesting or integral to the chapter that the cost of excluding it would have been higher than the cost of retaining it. We also felt that it was impracticable to ask the authors to separate the elements into individual chapters. We are also aware that we have not included every topic that individual readers would desire to see under the part headings. Even as well-funded and as extensive a congress as ours was runs into limitations. Furthermore, an effort to overcome either, let alone both of the above limitations, would have expanded an already large project to an unmanageable size.

Whether a crisis will develop in the Soviet Union and, if so, what its outcome is likely to be is far more interesting to scholars than the foreign policy consequences of either question; although the latter is likely to be the more important matter from a practical standpoint. The internal consequences of a Soviet crisis are crucial of course to its inhabitants and those of its satellite states. However if a crisis develops, how a Soviet or post-Soviet state responds to its international problems, and how the non-Soviet world responds to a crisis or a succession state will determine whether a war, perhaps a nuclear war, occurs or a more harmonious and peaceful world order emerges. It is difficult to think of more important questions than these.

Every one of the chapters in this volume could have been expanded into a book or at least a large part of one. If it had, there would have been a richer set of data and a more diverse expression of opinions and attitudes. We have attempted to compensate for this to some extent by securing a divergence of opinions among our paper writers. Some sharp differences of opinion do emerge, but these lack the dialectical richness that surfaced during the discussions at the congress. It is unfortunate that these could not have been included, but the result would have been uncommonly long and amorphous.

We believe that the individual chapters speak well enough for themselves and that it is unnecessary to comment upon them. The exception is where one or the other of the editors has a specific critique to make in the context of his own position. Therefore, the failure to comment on some points does not necessarily indicate agreement—indeed, the editors do not agree with each other on many points—but only that we wish to call attention to these particular disagreements.

It is obvious that Shtromas and Vigor are in at least partial disagreement on whether the armed forces might become part of a second pivot during a crisis. Both editors doubt that national interest clashes over Eastern Europe are likely to be as significant as Vigor suggests. And we doubt that the Soviet leadership, as possibly opposed to the ordinary population, really sees a reunited Germany as a military threat or that this would impel a post-Soviet Russia to possess East Europe in order to control a German threat. Russia would still possess nuclear weapons, and even a reunited Germany would be a small and vulnerable nation with little incentive in any event to attack Russia when modern power depends more upon economic productivity. The editors therefore doubt that present Soviet policies would be followed by a post-Soviet regime. And we believe that the expansionist policies of the present Soviet regime (1986) are more a product of a precrisis problem of the *Nomenklatura* than a continuation of traditional Russian foreign policy.

Kaplan has a specific disagreement with Vigor's position on the Soviet military budget. Although he does not advocate spending the Soviet Union into crisis, he does believe that the Soviet regime is close to the limit that it can extract from its population without a decrease in production because of despair, illness, and sabotage. Furthermore, unlike Vigor, he does not take at face value Soviet comments on ABM and SDI. The Soviet Union has long been working on such weapons systems. What it does not want to see is a vigorous American effort that would force it to intensify those efforts over the short term or to face American superiority in the intermediate term. Perhaps there is a low-cost method of defeating SDI, but if the Soviet Union were confident of this it would wish to see us wasting our resources and would make no effort to pursue this path itself. Does Vigor really believe that the Soviet Union would be trumpeting, as it is, the ease of defeating SDI by countermeasures if it were confident of this? This reminds me of those RAND scholars who used content analysis to prove Stalin and Mao were uninterested in nuclear weapons at the very time that they were expending extremely scarce resources to produce them.

The major disagreement the editors would like to stress in the case of Dr. Pick's chapter deals with his assertions about Cuba and Nicaragua. The United States did not initiate a quarrel either with Castro or the Sandinistas. In fact, United States influence played an important role in the decision of both Batista and Somoza to leave the country and in the decisions of the army and national guard respectively to stand aside when the takeover occurred. Fidel Castro specifically instructed the head of the Bank of Cuba not to discuss economic aid from the United States, when it was ready to offer it. It is true that the show trials in the stadium quickly cooled off American public support for Castro and that the prejudicial manner in which Castro's expropriations were carried out alienated the American government. But it seems clear that Castro, for whatever reason, desired the quarrel. Moreover, in an interview with *Figaro* in 1986, Castro asserted that he had been a Marxist-Leninist before the revolution but had hidden that fact for tactical reasons. In addition, in a letter written in 1958 from his guerrilla hideout, Castro wrote, "When this war is over . . . I'll start a much longer and bigger war of my own: The war I am going to wage against the Americans. I realize that will be my true destiny."[1] In the case of the Sandinistas, the Carter administration had an initially favorable attitude toward them and extended substantial economic assistance. It was only after the Sandinistas created conditions under which the democratic elements in the regime had to leave and its newspapers expressed support for the Soviet invasion of Afghanistan that the Carter administration began to understand the character of the Sandinista regime. Later, with the capture of the minutes of the New Jewel Party of Grenada, we learned of the Cuban strategy of initial pluralism, while seizing the levers of power, to fool the West and of the linkage of the Nicaraguan regime to Russian western hemisphere strategy. In any event, the evidence of the Marxist-Leninist—and pro-Soviet—commitments of the Sandinista leadership is so abundant that it cannot be denied.

Furthermore, Dr. Pick asserts that the New Peoples Army (NPA) in the Philippines is relatively independent of the Communist Party. That is incorrect. It is led by members of the Communist Party, although some leaders of the Party such as Jose Maria Sisson are not in the field. My long conversation with Sisson made it clear that it is the Soviet Union to which he is looking for leadership and not China.

Kaplan finds Tang's comments on Mao's sycophantish support for Stalin misleading. And he thinks he overstates, or at least somewhat misrepresents, Stalin's support for the Chinese CP after World War II. He believes that Stalin did not want a unified China, that he supported the Chinese CP only partially and even that he did not expect, let alone want, a Chinese CP victory.

Kaplan agrees with many of the interpretations of the rules of the game in Soviet foreign policy that both Kintner and Gress delineate, and particularly with respect to the meaning of peaceful coexistence. However, he does not believe that Soviet policy necessarily follows the path they suggest. There is opposition to particular gambits in the Soviet command. After all, the decision to invade Czechoslovakia in 1968 was made by a one-vote majority. Some extensions of Soviet power are merely targets of opportunity and not necessarily part of a design of world conquest.

Moreover, Soviet leaders may believe that their system is effective in making the Soviet Union a world power, but they can hardly have failed to note its economic defects or the strain that their present course of world empire is placing on the Soviet system. Gorbachev's variation on Kaplan's proposal for a troop drawdown from the Atlantic to the Urals may be partly propagandistic. But it would be a mistake to ignore entirely the possibility that it may be an opening in the exploration of alternative courses of foreign policy for the Soviet Union.

Kaplan's major disagreement with Berton lies in his belief that national welfare now lies primarily in economic development. Military expenditures are counterproductive. Moreover, there are ecological problems that will soon be pressing the Soviets and that will require a cooperative international solution. Particularly if the Soviet-style incentives for external aggrandizement are absent, Kaplan believes, the *realpolitik* incentives for conflict will be reduced significantly.

In short, Kaplan would emphasize the role of American and Western policy in the determination of Soviet policy. Although the Soviets think in terms of conflict and inevitable change rather than in terms of harmony and concordance, tactical agreement with them under some circumstances can help to shape a world more favorable to American and Western values. Although the differences between Kaplan on the one hand and Kintner and Gress on the other in terms of analysis are subtle, they can be important in terms of orientation.

These comments conclude the major disagreements between editors and authors that we see some reason for calling to the attention of the readers. We are satisfied that the authors did well, particularly those authors who had the burden of dealing with difficult speculative issues. The editors do not, and we are confident that the individual authors do not, regard these speculations as predictions or even necessarily projections. They are heuristic devices that permit us to think about possibilities that we may have to confront, to understand the major factors that may influence developments, and that may assist us in interpreting and responding to them should they occur. We also believe that they will be useful to students and of assistance in teaching them in relevant courses.

Addendum

Except for a new chapter 12, which includes recent appraisals of Soviet foreign policy by Jerry Hough and Alain Besançon, the book stands as it was written in early 1986. The reader can compare what we said then with this addendum, which takes into account the most recent developments in October 1988. The Soviet Union is evacuating Afghanistan although it is threatening to delay its withdrawal unless Pakistan changes its policy toward the guerrillas. Most observers believe that this is primarily a bargaining position designed to prevent a quick collapse of the Soviet-imposed government, a conclusion that the editors believe is more likely correct than assertions that this is evidence of Soviet trickery.

The Soviet Union has been reducing its forces on the border with China and is moving toward a political summit with China. We believe this represents a desirable normalization of relations rather than momentum toward reestablishment of an alliance. It has offered a compromise to Japan on the northern islands, although it has not yet made an offer that Japan could consider seriously. It has been modestly helpful with respect to Cambodia, although not to an extent that would jeopardize its association with Viet Nam. It has offered to shut down the Cam Ranh naval base if the United States gives up its Philippine bases. This is either a bargaining ploy or propaganda because the geopolitics of the contemporary world system makes a peripheral power such as the United States much more dependent on far-flung bases than is a central power such as the Soviet Union. It has pursued possibly helpful policies in the Middle East and Africa. On the other hand, it has been no help with respect to Nicaragua.

Except for Afghanistan and the insufficient proposal to Japan, these are moves that could have been engaged in by any predecessor Soviet government. The latter two moves are unprecedented in the absence of massive external pressure. Retreat except under great pressure would have introduced fear of massive instability under leaders prior to Gorbachev. Even more striking was the speech of the new chief of ideology, Vadim A. Medvedev, who was promoted to the Politburo on September 30 after the "coup" by Gorbachev, a coup that some regarded as preemptive. Medvedev said that Communism was in a period of worldwide crisis. He rejected the idea of a worldwide struggle with the West based on class analysis. He called for a new concept of socialism that borrowed political and economic ideas from other countries, capitalistic as well as socialistic. He supported the idea of a market-oriented economy and spoke of the private ownership of property, and not only in small-scale industry.

These are truly radical ideas. If they are ever effectuated, we may have to revise substantially our concepts of relations with the Soviets. But we must remember that Gorbachev's reforms are popular primarily with the intelligentsia. Party conservatives do not like them although they are temporarily outflanked. The ordinary Soviet citizen is unsettled by changes that thrust initiative upon him and that threaten unemployment. He regards a bad day's work for a bad day's pay as akin to a natural right. Moreover, Perestroika, which so far has been more slogan than accomplishment, has been accompanied by increasing shortages and rising prices. Glasnost was not been too popular with Gorbachev when he was been questioned about shortages in Siberia. Severe nationality problems in the Baltic states and the Caucasus overhang the regime. Although we believe that forces have been set in motion that in the longer term will have revolutionary impact on the Soviet Union—short of war or the Finlandization of Western Europe—the shorter-term game has not been played out. It is not entirely unlikely that unrest and instability may call a halt to this particular phase of reform and its foreign policy implications.

A straight-line Soviet policy is unlikely even in the present phase. Gorbachev's present power is based upon temporary alliances we do not adequately understand. But we should make modest attempts to shape the future. Kaplan in particular would like to emphasize his proposal for advocating an end to the division of Europe. Shtromas agrees. Unfortunately, political circles in the West still seem to support either negative reiterations of strength—a line we agree with provided that it is complemented by more constructive proposals—or idealistic proposals that would do more to provide an ambiance for provocations by Soviet conservatives than to solve any problems.

Alexander Shtromas and Morton A. Kaplan

Notes

1. Frank Calzon, "Go Beyond the Embargo," *The New York Times*, September 10, 1986.

FROM CURRENT STATE OF AFFAIRS TO POSSIBLE CRISIS

1

Soviet Foreign Policy Alternatives Under Gorbachev

Decision-Making Context and Prospects

R. JUDSON MITCHELL

The election of Mikhail Gorbachev as General Secretary of the CPSU in March 1985 clearly marks a major turning point for the Soviet political system. After several years of general drift in both foreign and domestic affairs due mainly to leadership instability, the Soviets can look forward to an extended period during which formation of coherent policy will probably not be strongly inhibited by uncertainties concerning the regime's configuration of power.

This dramatic turnaround in the Kremlin obviously confronts Western decision makers with a vastly different context for the formulation of their own policies. It is assumed by most observers that the Soviet Union will pursue a more activist course in world affairs under Gorbachev than was the case during the brief tenures of Andropov and Chernenko. But the general thrust of Soviet policy in the Gorbachev era remains very much an open question. The new leadership faces difficult choices in the establishment of priorities and in the selection among available policy options. This decision-making process will be heavily influenced by perceptions of recent changes in the world "correlation of forces."

The decade of the 1970s was marked by consistently optimistic Soviet appraisals concerning the external environment. Acknowledgement of the

USSR's superpower parity with the U.S. at the 1972 Moscow summit was hailed as a decisive step in the "diplomatic struggle of the two worlds" but the Soviets quickly escalated to claims of a qualitative change in the world "correlation of forces" tending toward superiority for the "socialist camp." This appraisal was articulated quite bluntly by Foreign Minister Andrei Gromyko in September 1975:

> The present marked preponderence of the forces of peace and progress gives them the opportunity of laying down the direction of international politics.[1]

This sanguine view was echoed repeatedly by Soviet spokesmen during the remainder of the decade. Detente, or *razriadka*, was described as the rational acceptance by the "imperialists" of the inexorable shift in the world "correlation," and successes achieved by Soviet proxies in the Third World lent powerful encouragement to Kremlin boasting about the progressive "restructuring of international relations."[2] Discounted by some in the West as Soviet posturing or rhetoric for domestic consumption, Moscow's claims of advance toward world hegemony nevertheless correlated rather precisely with observable levels of aggressiveness in the USSR's external behavior. The supposed foundation for this favorable Soviet position in world affairs was the growing might of the "socialist camp," featuring principally the enhanced military capability of the USSR.[3] But this absolute increment in Soviet strength is consequential for the "correlation of forces" only in relation to "imperialist" capabilities and intentions. As Adam Ulam has observed:

> . . . . It has been Moscow's reading of the strengths and weaknesses, and especially of the degree of cohesion, of the entire community of democratic nations that has been mainly instrumental in shaping the U.S.S.R's foreign policy.[4]

From the onset of Watergate to the invasion of Afghanistan, Soviet policymakers confronted weakness and vacillation in the Western alliance, especially at its center, the United States. The real key to the "restructuring of international relations" was the perceived Western impotence in resisting carefully calibrated Soviet advances, which accordingly entailed little risk. The American response to Afghanistan wrote finis to general East-West detente, at least for the short run, but had little perceptible effect on Soviet appraisals of the overall world "correlation of forces."

The Soviet view of the international balance began to change with the advent of the Reagan administration in 1981. The projected American buildup of forces combined with Washington's reversion to militant anti-

Communism meant the end of the USSR's "free ride" in expansion of its influence. But the acid test was Western determination to restore the strategic balance in Europe. When the Soviet diplomatic and propaganda offensive failed to halt the installation of Pershing and cruise missiles, the Kremlin leadership was evidently caught off base and the USSR temporarily retreated into an isolationist stance reminiscent of the early years of Stalin's dictatorship. Western staunchness on the missile issue and concerns about Reagan's "Star Wars" initiative, with its implicit technological challenge on terms unfavorable to the USSR, soon brought the Soviets back to the conference table. During this period, the Soviet policy-making process sometimes appeared to be caught in immobility or inconsistency reflecting leadership disarray in the Kremlin. Nevertheless, the general outlines of policy were consistent with perceptions of an unfavorable shift in the "correlation of forces."

In the first half of this decade, Soviet spokesmen avoided explicit admission of a downturn in the world balance, but acknowledged it obliquely. They no longer advanced claims of growing Soviet superiority. Rather, they concentrated upon an alleged American drive for supremacy, a goal said to be impossible of attainment.[5] While maintaining that the U.S. lacked the means to produce such a radical transformation of the "correlation," the Soviets explicitly identified the NATO missile program as a "qualitative threat" to the USSR's security and implicitly acknowledged that the world balance could be tipped in the "imperialists' " favor by two means, the buildup of strategic military arms and ideological offensives.[6]

Perhaps the most interesting aspect of these Soviet assessments, both during the era of detente and since, is the emphasis upon what the Soviets call the "subjective factor."[7] Neither of the competing camps holds a decided preponderence in objective resources; therefore, the advantage goes to the side which can most effectively organize its resources and summon the will and rational judgment to pursue its aims successfully. Emphasis upon the "subjective factor" coincides with a downgrading of class and economic determinants of political change; international politics is increasingly regarded by the Soviets as an open-ended struggle between competing power blocs. With the erosion of historical determinism, legitimation of the Soviet system is tied precariously to continuing success in the world arena, and success is largely measured in terms of the extent of national power, i.e., the Soviet Union's status as a superpower. This has profound implications for the formulation of Soviet policy in the Gorbachev era.

The apparent decline of ideological commitment, sometimes admitted by authoritative Soviet spokesmen, and the theoretical revisions that have largely drained the conviction of inevitability from official doctrine do not mean that ideology can be dismissed as a determinant of Soviet behavior.

Ideology retains its salience in the analysis of Soviet policy-making for three reasons. First, an ideology is a language of discourse and Soviet pronouncements on world affairs are communicated in the peculiar language of "Marxism-Leninism," which provides the exclusive framework for analysis. Soviet international relations doctrine is permeated with images of conflict: "two camps," "diplomatic struggle of the two worlds," revolutionary violence, "imperialist" aggression, and so on. Given the fact that all public discussion of international relations is confined to this procrustean bed, it would be surprising indeed if much of this imagery were not internalized in the mental processes of the actual policymakers, notwithstanding the indubitable fact that Soviet leaders arrive at the top as a result of highly pragmatic behavior in the performance of their assigned functions. Western observers who expect or hope for a fundamentally different outlook from Gorbachev may justifiably be asked this question: where could the new General Secretary have obtained, within the range of his experience, an alternative worldview? Further, these ideological images of conflict are buttressed by centuries of Russian national experience vis-à-vis the outside world; this may well be the feature of official ideology that the average Russian takes most seriously.

Second, the ideology is an essential element of cohesion for the bureaucratic structure that governs the Soviet Union. The political leadership must set the agenda for systemic action; the agenda is invariably justified in ideological terms; the ideologically sanctioned legitimacy of set goals precludes overt conflict over objectives and integrates supportive domestic activities into the framework of external policy planning.[8]

Third, and perhaps most important, the one-party system and the monopoly of state power by the elite of the *Nomenklatura* are crucially tied to these images of conflict. Absent the vision of an unavoidable conflict against an external foe, what would be the justification for the coercive role of the KGB? Or the special status accorded the military? Or the oppressive weight of the legions in the ideological sectors of Party and state apparatus? In short, these images of conflict serve a positive function in holding together an entrenched system of power. Acceptance of an alternative, less militant view of the world is incompatible with maintenance of the state bureaucratic regime created by Stalin, the structure of which his successors have tinkered with but have not fundamentally altered.

Since the imagery of conflict is deeply embedded in the belief system or, at the very least, in the language of discourse and since it serves important integrative and system maintenance functions, I think we may assume that the basic Soviet approach to world politics will continue to be centered on the concepts of polarization and competition between systems in the short run and probably also far into the future.

The first concern here must be this: the short run is likely to be somewhat prolonged. Given the track record of Soviet extended leaderships, if Gorbachev's physical vigor remains relatively undiminished (he appears to be much healthier than any other recent Soviet leader at time of accession), the probability is high that the Gorbachev era will last into the twenty-first century. Even a tenure of ten years for Gorbachev would almost certainly coincide with changes of leadership in every other major nation of the world. Constitutional norms and the actuarial tables both conspire to yield an important advantage to the Soviets. Western decision makers may usually be forced to respond to Soviet initiatives, rather than the other way around, given Moscow's expected advantage in leadership stability.

There are some indications that Soviet foreign policy decision makers act much like their Western counterparts in particular cases, pragmatically seeking to reduce problems to manageable proportions. Long-range planning may be sacrificed to the pressures of short-run decision making just as much as in Western systems.[9] Nevertheless, even if behavior is comparable in this respect, it does make a difference if one side has a more settled frame of reference for general policy than the other, thereby relatively diminishing the *ad hoc* character of specific decisions. Stability of leadership appears to be the crucial variable in the forging of such settled frames of reference. Exploration of Soviet foreign policy alternatives requires initial consideration of this question: to what extent is the political leadership free to define alternatives and set systemic goals?

If the political leadership is relatively free to set the general framework of policy, it still faces the monumental task of sorting out the complexity of variables impinging upon the decision-making process. It must be assumed that decision makers select a few key variables as paramount foci in the formation of general policy. These variables presumably are evaluated under the general rubric provided by "correlation of forces" analysis. Proceeding under these assumptions, we must make some judgments concerning the saliency of variables. Both Western and Soviet analysts assign preeminance to questions of the strategic and overall military balances. Next, attention on both sides tends to focus upon two sets of variables, those pertaining to technological and economic factors and those relating to the geographical distribution of world power. There is, of course, an overlapping of variables among these three main fields of analysis. Detailed examination of the existing strategic and overall military balances is beyond the scope of this study. But these balances are ultimately contingent upon specific political and economic factors; accordingly, they are considered here in relation to those factors. Following an examination of the leadership factor, this study will move to a necessarily brief exploration of technological, economic, and geographical factors. The final section will posit general alternatives in relation to the preceding analysis and offer tentative conclusions concerning the probable contours of the new leadership's world policy.

Soviet Political Leadership

Recent Soviet history strongly supports the assumption that the USSR's external behavior will tend to be erratic under conditions of unstable leadership. Fragmentation or debility of the leadership is not associated with any particular orientation toward major events requiring responses by decision makers. In the three major crises confronting the USSR during the succession imbroglio of 1979–85, the leadership was in turn aggressive, vacillating, and inept.[10]

Such erratic behavior should be less likely under conditions of stable, extended leadership because the domestic political context is more conducive to consensus and consistency in the formulation and execution of policy. But the conventional wisdom based upon Soviet history is that Party leaders, in the early years of their tenures, are inclined to be extremely tentative in external policy pending their consolidation of domestic authority. How does this square with the impression conveyed by Gorbachev of a remarkably confident new leader, ready to move swiftly in both domestic and foreign affairs?

An answer to this question requires that we take into account the peculiar characteristics of the most recent succession crisis. Prolongation of this crisis over a period of six years, during which two transitional leaders appeared in the absence of obvious "traditional" candidates for the top post,[11] yielded an outcome unique in Soviet history: the real succession crisis, i.e., the working out of the configuration of power among system interests pointing toward an extended leadership, mainly occurred prior to, rather than after, the election of a "full term" General Secretary. The crucial elements in this outcome were the reassertion of authority by the central Party leadership and the substantial turnover of personnel in key Party and state positions, under Andropov.

The election of Gorbachev allies or clients Viktor Chebrikov, head of the KGB, and Party secretaries Yegor Ligachev and Nikolai Ryzhkov to full Politburo membership barely a month after the new leader's accession was unprecedented, giving him a commanding majority of supporters on the supreme policy-making body, a condition achieved by Khrushchev and Brezhnev only after four and six and one-half years, respectively, of their tenures. Contrary to Western expectations concerning a young, relatively inexperienced leader, Gorbachev, as of June 1985 appeared to have established a commanding position unmatched by any previous leader, not excepting Lenin, in the period immediately following formal installation as the regime's top man.

This dominant position is based upon the earlier installation of clients and allies of Andropov and Gorbachev in key posts in the Secretariat and Central Committee apparatus, in the Party Control Committee, and in major regional secretaryships. The result has been a highly impressive "organizational tail" for the new leader and deep roots in the Party's "levers of command." But what of Gorbachev's relationship with the major functional interests that flourished under Brezhnev's politics of consensus building and "depoliticization" strategy,[12] the Foreign Ministry, the KGB, and the defense establishment?

The Foreign Ministry has evidently achieved in recent years an unprecedented degree of independence and the relative autonomy enjoyed by the denizens of Smolensk Square became even more apparent during the tenures of the transitional leaders. This suggests the possibility that foreign policy decision making may be regarded as an essentially separate function, largely immune to changes in the domestic constellation of political forces. Against this, one must question the institutionalization of this apparent autonomy. This independence seems to reflect no institutional trends but rather the personal political authority of Andrei Gromyko.

In the first weeks of Gorbachev's tenure, Gromyko seemed to have emerged as the number two man in the regime. In addition to the clout derived from his seniority in the hierarchy, he had apparently formed the same sort of tutorial relationship with Gorbachev on matters of foreign policy as he had with Brezhnev, shrewdly identifying both men prior to their accessions to the general secretaryship as future holders of power, taking them under his wing to fill in their experiental gaps.[13] Notably, for several years prior to his election as General Secretary, Gorbachev had regularly headed the delegations welcoming Gromyko at the airport upon his return from foreign travels.

The elevation of Gromyko to the presidency and the appointment of Eduard Shevardnadze as foreign minister in July 1985 occasioned much surprise among Western observers in view of the previous Gorbachev-Gromyko relationship. There was some speculation that Gromyko might continue to dominate foreign policy from the presidency. However, subsequent events, especially the November 1985 Geneva summit, indicated that Gorbachev had taken personal command of foreign policy. The diplomatic establishment clearly had not salvaged much independence from the political transition. But the change at the foreign ministry appeared to involve more style than substance. Gromyko's legacy of pragmatism and realism, most clearly indicated by his stout defense of negotiations ("the future belongs to detente") in the well-publicized 1983 debate in official journals over diplomatic as opposed to other means in foreign policy,[14] appeared to be strongly reaffirmed.

Unlike the foreign ministry, the KGB exerts a highly institutionalized influence in both domestic and foreign affairs and its functional role in both areas has clearly expanded in recent years. The promotion of Chebrikov to full Politburo rank may be regarded partially as a reward for KGB support in the succession, but Gorbachev's ties with the KGB seem to be quite deep, deriving from his clientage relationship with Yuri Andropov. Gorbachev appears to have already established a relationship with the KGB at least comparable to that achieved by Brezhnev after only two and one-half years in the highest office.

There may be some problems, however, in this relationship. if, as seems certain, Gorbachev gives fresh impetus to Andropov's campaign for "discipline" and drive against corruption, he will be heavily dependent upon the KGB in domestic affairs. This dependence may serve as something of a check upon the continuing revival of central Party authority, which should otherwise be assured by the actuarily dictated cadre renewal. At some point, the KGB may be perceived by Gorbachev as posing a threat to his hegemony. But any conflict between Gorbachev and the KGB would figure to strengthen elements less favorable to the General Secretary, such as the military chiefs and the governmental bureaucracy. Account must also be taken of the fact that the KGB is the one Soviet institution whose only rationale for existence is polarized ideological struggle. This presumably should have some impact upon the general approach of a leader strongly backed by that organization. However, this does not necessarily imply any built-in preference for particular policy options. During the era of detente, the KGB was able to utilize fears about the dangers of ideological subversion under conditions of increased contacts with the West to justify expansion of its domestic power. Whether the overall Kremlin approach is detente or confrontation, the KGB is likely to maintain its functional role and high visibility.

Gorbachev's relations with Frunze Street are quite different from those with Dzerzhinsky Square. He is the first long-term successor in Soviet history without previous ties to the military. It might be expected that the marshals would be lukewarm toward an agricultural specialist with no background in the military-industrial complex as General Secretary but much more than personal preference seems to be involved. The dismissal of Marshal Nikolai Ogarkov as chief of staff and first deputy minister of defense in September 1984 represented a clear warning to the military against political involvement and probably solidified Gorbachev's standing as heir apparent. Ogarkov's dismissal followed public controversy over military allocations but this issue was probably not the sole determinant of the dramatic move. Ogarkov had gained a reputation as an outspoken "political" general, with a record of frictions in his relationship to the Party leadership.

Defence Minister Dimitri Ustinov had probably played a major role in Ogarkov's ouster, but the former's incapacitation in late September and his death in December 1984 yielded no recovery of influence for the uniformed military leaders. The flamboyant Ogarkov was succeeded as first deputy minister by the lackluster 73-year-old Marshal Sergei Sokolov, who subsequently moved up to replace Ustinov. At the time of Chernenko's funeral, Sokolov was reportedly ill but, remarkably, there was a total absence of military figures atop Lenin's Mausoleum for the main ceremony.[15] When Chebrikov was promoted to full Politburo membership in the following month, Sokolov was given only candidate membership, although two Party secretaries were advanced to the ruling body without having served in candidate status. This chain of events clearly indicated a limited role for the military leadership in the succession decision and its subordination to the political leadership. Perhaps more importantly, the KGB appeared to have gained significantly from the political downgrading of the military leadership.

Well before the dismissal of Ogarkov, there were hints of tension between Frunze Street and the Andropov-Gorbachev elite group. The public criticism of the military by *Pravda* editor Viktor Afanasyev,[16] reportedly close to both Andropov and Gorbachev, and by commentator Fedor Burlatsky[17] in the fall of 1983, at a time when Gorbachev was Andropov's right-hand man in the Secretariat, raises the possibility of a persistent hostility between the service chieftains and the new General Secretary. In any case, there can be little doubt about the recent diminution of the military's direct political influence and this is necessarily related to the political ascendancy of Gorbachev.

For the long run, Gorbachev's route to power may foreshadow problems. Ultimately, the central role of the Party in the system is dependent upon maintenance of a balance between the major coercive forces. The present apparent imbalance may be incompatible with the continuing drive to reassert central authority upon which Gorbachev's dominance depends. Further, the armed forces cannot be lightly dismissed as a domestic political factor. The military can claim credit for the rise of the USSR to superpower status and this is probably the principal source of contemporary popular legitimation for the regime. Moreover, the pervasive militarization of Soviet society, a crucially important element in regime control of the populace, assures the armed forces a continuing special domestic role.[18]

For the short run, this imbalance may dictate a heightened aggressiveness in the political leadership's approach to external affairs. Both the support of the KGB and the acquiescence of the military may hinge upon Gorbachev's demonstration of toughness in foreign policy. He may feel impelled to show that, in Gromyko's colorful phrase, he is a man with "iron teeth,"[19] in order to gain the freedom of action he requires in domestic affairs to consolidate his authority over the Party organization and the economy. Conceivably, such a stance dictated by the imbalance between the coercive agencies could be highly dysfunctional for the achievement of a wide range of strategic, political, and economic goals.

The structural framework of the Soviet system thus imposes certain inhibitions upon Gorbachev. Nevertheless, as compared with the recent past, the new leadership should be relatively freer in the formulation of a general foreign policy agenda. The outlines of that agenda will surely be manifest in the new Party program, to be adopted at the XXVII CPSU Congress in February–March 1986. The crucial advantage for Gorbachev in the implementation of an agreed foreign policy agenda is the probability of an extended stable leadership, an advantage that cannot be matched by any potential adversary of the USSR

Technological and Economic Factors

For some 30 years (since Khrushchev's enunciation of the rationale for "peaceful coexistence") Soviet analysts have given priority to questions of the strategic nuclear balance. Soviet policymakers have clearly acted in accord with such a priority since the Potsdam conference of July 1945. And the Soviets have demonstrated an ability to attain nuclear parity, if not superiority, under conditions of decided technological inferiority. Nevertheless, that technological inferiority is highly important.

At the heart of the current Soviet campaign against "Star Wars" is the assumption that in any no-holds-barred technological competition with the West, the USSR would probably lose. The Soviets' opting out of the race for the moon, in 1964, was based precisely on such calculations. While Western scientific and political opinion is sharply divided over the viability and usefulness of the Strategic Defence Initiative (SDI),[20] one fact is starkly evident: the Soviets are acting as if the successful development of SDI cannot be excluded. They would hardly transform SDI into the most controversial international issue if they concluded that the proposed application of American resources was irrational from the standpoint of U.S. interests or irrelevant to the world "correlation of forces."

Given this perspective, the Soviets face difficult choices. Assuming even the probability of development of SDI as a partial defensive shield,[21] if the U.S. proceeds, the Soviets must respond, certainly at enormous strain to the domestic economy, although the effort might be made less burdensome by the fastest growing Soviet industry, the theft of Western technology. A negotiated pause or cessation of SDI or a slowing down of the U.S. program via internal political pressures in the Western countries would lessen the pressure upon Soviet resources. But in circumstances of a political defeat or check of "Star Wars" on the American side, if there is a probability or even possibility of its technical feasibility, the domestic pressure for a sustained drive toward Soviet development of such a defense would be overwhelming.

In this, as in other matters related to the military component of the "correlation of forces," the Soviets face a continuing dilemma ultimately rooted in the endemic condition of technological inferiority. The USSR is hard-pressed to provide existing levels of sustenance for its military machine and the accompanying imbalances are dysfunctional for general Soviet economic development. Yet Soviet world power is primarily a function of the country's military strength and its capability of projecting that force beyond the USSR's borders.

Over the last two decades, the USSR has progressed in absolute terms across the board of economic categories. But relative to the West, the Soviets have fallen further behind in consumption, productivity, and technological competence. This situation is rather openly acknowledged by Soviet leaders and the shortcomings of the Soviet economy have sparked a significant ideological debate over the "contradictions of socialism" relative to practical questions of economic organization and management. Many Western observers consider the crisis of the Soviet economy as so acute that Gorbachev must give absolute priority to its resolution, irrespective of foreign policy goals.

Domestic consumer satisfaction is unlikely to be a primary consideration as the new leadership addresses this problem, although mass discontent may pose a long-range threat to the leadership if present trends continue. But Soviet world power is ultimately dependent upon the overall strength of the USSR's economy. The long-standing precedence for military production and the extreme compartmentalization of the economy into defense and civilian sectors have served to sustain the USSR's massive accumulation of armaments but this is a dangerously flawed approach, even from the narrowest policy standpoint. A generally inefficient economic mechanism cannot operate at optimal efficiency even in the military sector.

The two principal reasons for Soviet technological inferiority, the absence of a market mechanism and ingrained cultural attitudes, obviously are highly resistant to change. Recognizing this, Soviet leaders have considered two alternate solutions, reorganization of the economy and importation of Western technology. Brezhnev's policy of technological cooperation with the West, a cornerstone of detente, was partially motivated by the desire to avoid difficult reform of the domestic economy. The results of Brezhnev's economic opening to the West were disappointing, apparently strengthening opponents of detente within the leadership. Nevertheless, the need for Western technology will continue to strongly influence the making of general Soviet policy.

These technological considerations and the diminishing Soviet potential for economic growth make it difficult to envision a lengthy period of heightened international tensions without a further reallocation of resources to the military sector. The first alternative noted above, reorganization, has been tried on a limited scale on numerous occasions, most recently with the modest experimentation since 1983. There are indications that Gorbachev would prefer to pursue this approach, striving for rationalization of both agricultural and industrial production via decentralization of the economy. Perhaps Gorbachev will have the political clout to force a sweeping reorganization of the economy upon reluctant bureaucrats, but this is most doubtful. Andropov's tentative moves along this line, in 1983, set off a remarkable public debate between him and Gosplan head Nikolai Baibakov.[22]

The hidden rationale for such measures as Andropov's "discipline" campaign of early 1983 and the current drive against alcoholism is that any success in these endeavors increases efficiency while diminishing the pressure for reform of management and provision of more positive incentives. Such measures touch the raw nerve of those ingrained cultural attitudes associated with Soviet backwardness. But enforced cultural reform is obviously viewed as less hazardous to the leadership than fundamental structural reform of the Soviet system. Gorbachev and his associates are surely aware of the narrow parameters of permissible restructuring. And however successful specific domestic policies of the new leadership may be, I think we must assume that the condition of the Soviet economy will remain, at least for the balance of this century, the primary negative factor for the USSR in the world "correlation of forces."

The Geographical Distribution of Power

The notion of "encirclement" has figured prominently in Soviet international relations doctrine from the outset of the regime. Stalin explained that "capitalist encirclement" was not a geographical concept; it referred to the overall unfavorable balance between systems. This usage has been consistently maintained, especially by Khrushchev when he related the end of "capitalist encirclement" to the impossibility of a "bourgeois restoration."[23] The implication of a developing "socialist encirclement" of capitalism under the impact of a qualitative change in the world "correlation of forces" during the 1970s was expressed in similar terms.[24]

The overall "correlation" is supposedly a resultant of the political, economic, and military factors that underlie the power of competing systems. The second, more operative, level of analysis, that of the regional "correlation of forces," is also keyed to these determining factors but the relationship between the various regional "correlations" and the global "correlation" is characteristically expressed in purely geographical terms.[25] Moreover, the decisive empirical proof for the heralded "restructuring of international relations" has been, for the Soviets, geographical detachments from the "imperialist camp" that effect qualitative changes in the regional "correlations."[26]

During the heyday of detente, when the overall "correlation" was claimed to be increasingly favorable to the Soviets, this sanguine general assessment coexisted with frequently expressed fears of a specifically geographical encirclement of the USSR, featuring a ring of hostile states around the country's borders, with the Sino-American relationship particularly emphasized. Indeed, over the past 20 years, an abiding central concern of Moscow's policymakers appears to have been the exigency of tipping the overall "correlation" in the USSR's favor by leapfrogging unfavorable or problematic situations on the periphery of their "empire" to project Soviet political and military power in distant corners of the world. Such projection eases the pressures upon the boundaries of the empire and facilitates detachments from the opposing camp. The capability of projecting Soviet power on a global basis is crucial to superpower status but that projective capability may be limited in the foreseeable future by the USSR's domestic problems, the incohesion of its base bloc, and intractable dilemmas related to the Soviet empire's periphery, such as Afghanistan.

The four major geographical areas of Soviet concern, all of which attracted Gorbachev's public attention during the early weeks of his tenure, are Eastern Europe, Western Europe, China, and the Third World. It can be assumed that the Soviets will do whatever is necessary to maintain at least current levels of influence over the Warsaw Pact countries, which constitute the USSR's base bloc. Moscow's facedown of Erich Honecker in 1984 over the issue of normalization of GDR-FRG relations is the most recent significant indicator of this constant objective. But, under prevailing circumstances, the choice of means employed to insure control of the base bloc must be conditioned by East European economic dependence upon the Western European economies; at the same time, that condition of economic dependence compounds the problem of political control.[27]

The Soviet approach to Western Europe must be formulated in the shadow of the most significant Soviet diplomatic setback since the Cuban missile crisis: the failure of varied pressures to forestall NATO missile deployment, a gambit that, if successful, would have radically transformed the regional "correlation" and, probably, the global "correlation" in Moscow's favor. Further, the USSR is constrained in this area by its own technological dependence upon the more advanced Western economies. On the other hand, there are some favorable aspects: the predominant West European preference for "normal" economic relations with the USSR and its bloc; widespread support for a revival of detente; the continuing, if diminished, influence of "peace" movements; and the pronounced leftward turns of the German Social Democrats and the British Labour Party.

Since the accession of Andropov, the Soviets have pursued a limited normalization of relations with China, a process briefly interrupted early in Chernenko's tenure, and this approach has meshed with the People's Republic of China's (PRC) aim since 1981 of achieving a more balanced relationship with the superpowers. Thus far, the normalization has been mainly economic and very limited, as reflected in the modest agreements signed by First Deputy Prime Minister Ivan Arkhipov in Peking, in December 1984. Prospects are dim for resolution of the three major issues identified by the PRC leadership: the massive Soviet military presence on China's borders; Afghanistan; and Southeast Asia.

Soviet success in the Third World, so pronounced during the 1970s, appears to have run out of steam and even existing commitments may impose an unacceptable burden upon the strained Soviet economy. This difficulty produced a rare note of levity in international affairs when the Soviets exported aerobic dance instructors rather than food to Addis Ababa during the tragic Ethiopian drought. But, whatever the current limitations, Gorbachev's reception of Nicaraguan leader Daniel Ortega and promises of economic support in May 1985 indicate that the new leadership has not forsworn attempts to alter the world "correlation" via support for "national liberation movements."

For the immediate future, there may be little prospect for a decisive breakthrough in these four general areas of foreign relations or, indeed, for a fundamental revision of any particular regional "correlation." But maintenance or enhancement of the USSR's superpower status dictates continued Soviet involvement and pressure in all major areas of concern, thereby diffusing effort and scarce resources.

Alternatives and Prospects

Bruce Parrott, in an article written several months before the accession of Gorbachev, outlined four general policy options available to the Soviets:

(1) A "soft" option, entailing acquiescence in American geopolitical primacy, reduced commitments in the Third World, and, possibly, acceptance of unfavorable outcomes in Poland and Afghanistan;

(2) Attempted revival of the "two-track" approach, i.e., a combination of detente and expansionism, under the assumption that the international trends of the early 1980s are temporary and that the United States can be pressured to return to policies more "equitable" from the Soviet standpoint;

(3) A short-term confrontational stance, downgrading bilateral negotiations and emphasizing efforts to match Western military deployments, in order to induce the West to accept terms more favorable to the USSR in subsequent negotiations;

(4) A long-term policy of heightened confrontation, involving a great acceleration of the Soviet military buildup and reduced reliance on East-West negotiations, under the assumption that detente with the United States is irretrievable.[28]

There can be no quarrel with Parrott's conclusion that the first option has been definitively rejected. In his view, extensive debate within the Soviet leadership had not, at mid-decade, resolved questions concerning viability of the other options. Parrott produces ample evidence from Soviet sources to demonstrate that the debate over policy, 1983–84, was conducted within the frame of reference of these indicated options. However, it cannot be assumed that this compilation of general options is exhaustive. The unexpectedly rapid assumption of power by a new leadership in Moscow alters in important ways what Morton Kaplan calls the "situational components of policy,"[29] enhancing the potential viability of other alternatives. I think that at least two of these must be seriously considered.

Option (5) would involve a sequential approach, with Soviet strategy geared to expected differences in relative leadership stability. Unlike Parrott's option (3), in which the sequence is a function of the strategy, here the strategy would be a function of a particular time frame. There would be an emphasis upon negotiations in the very short run, under the assumption that this would offer the best hope of decelerating Western rearmament during the balance of the Reagan Presidency. The Soviets would attempt to match any further Western military buildup, with the aim of holding the line until Reagan's departure from the scene, but would not try for superiority. Soviet decision makers would anticipate greater Western malleability on policy after 1988, making possible the next stage of strategy, a renewal of the drive toward a standing as the number one superpower. Such an approach would imply a judgment by the Soviet leaders that, in the short run, the best they can hope for is to prevent a further deterioration of the Soviet position in the world "correlation of forces." If successful, it would have three distinct advantages:

a) It would prevent a further downturn in the "correlation" for the USSR.

b) It would provide maximum latitude for the consolidation of domestic power by the new leadership and for dealing with pressing domestic problems.

c) It would enable the Soviets to approach the end of the decade with a settled long-range policy and a well-established leadership, precisely at the time when the West will have a new leadership mix and, as a consequence, probably unsettled policies.

Option (6) would involve a "three-track" approach, with strategy segmented in accord with varied expectations concerning principal international actors. Here the emphasis might be focused upon manageable levels of confrontation with the United States, general detente with Western Europe, and, possibly, a strategy designed to draw the most important developing countries, China and India, further away from the Western alliance. Under this approach, the Soviets could pursue Third World competition with the United States, but negotiated settlements on Afghanistan and Cambodia might be necessary to appease China and India. However, such a partial reversion to a "soft" option might not be essential; a quick and complete Soviet triumph in Afghanistan would present China and India with a fait accompli, perhaps effectively removing Afghanistan as a negotiable issue. In any case, the Soviets could hope to maintain at least some measure of rapprochement with China and a strong influence upon India. Implicit in option (6) is a particular variation on the oft-expressed Soviet concept of the "divisibility" of detente.[30]

The most desirable alternative for the Soviets, if successful in policy execution, would probably be Parrott's option (2). Although disappointing on the economic side, detente coincided with substantial gains for the USSR in the world "correlation of forces." The passing of detente was not the preference of the Soviets; it faded because the Western powers finally concluded that the "two-track" approach was unacceptable. A reconstruction of detente totally excluding the second track would mean acceptance of the "soft" option, which has been ruled out by the Soviets. A total reliance upon Parrott's option (4) is unrealistic in view of the limitations upon Soviet resources and the continuing dependence upon Western technology. Only in circumstances of total diplomatic failure could this option be accepted and then only out of necessity.

The Soviets can scarcely afford to place all their stakes upon a single policy option. One reason is that superpower status requires expenditure of resources upon diverse goals, some of which may be secondary. Additionally, account must be taken of "friction," the intrusion of unexpected events and the unanticipated consequences of policy initiatives, both one's own and those of adversaries. Nevertheless, priorities must be established and an agenda must be set for the system that facilitates coordination of behavior in accord with those priorities. In that process of agenda setting, the Soviet leadership must give precedence to these overriding considerations:

First, the world "correlation of forces" is considerably less favorable for the Soviets than it was ten years ago, but this may be a temporary phenomenon. If, as seems certain, the Soviets are unwilling to accept the current state of the "correlation," the problem becomes: how to manage a favorable adjustment in the "correlation" and how to do it most economically?

Second, while the recent track record of Soviet diplomacy has not been scintillating, Soviet gains in the superpower era have been often associated with skillful negotiations by the Soviets to obtain a maximum of unilateral advantage. Gromyko's expressed preference for diplomatic over other tools is likely to figure prominently in Soviet foreign policy during the early Gorbachev years. From a public relations standpoint, Moscow cannot afford to disdain negotiations over nuclear weaponry. More importantly, the Soviets must seek to obtain the best deal possible on both strategic arms and economic matters.

Third, the buildup of military power has been the one really successful area of Soviet activity, providing the objective basis for the domestic legitimation associated with superpower status. If Gorbachev downgrades the military role, then presumably he must find some other area of success to provide a practical substitute legitimizing factor. Whatever the degree of internal reform that might be achieved, prospects for such a substitution are not promising. Moreover, if the new leadership were to succeed, for example, in substantially raising Soviet living standards, the ensuing "consumerism" would mesh poorly with requirements for elitist political control of the society. But some solution of endemic domestic problems is a matter of urgency: maintenance of even the present Soviet standing in the world "correlation of forces" is incompatible with indefinite continuation of the current stagnation in the domestic economy.

Fourth, only a supremely successful outcome of negotiations and/or an incredible turnaround in Soviet economic efficiency could obviate the probable necessity for a reallocation of resources affecting the military. Under conditions of heightened international tensions, the proportion of Soviet resources going to the military could conceivably increase but the constituent elements of the military's allocations would necessarily change. If negotiations fail to halt the spiral in strategic arms, then there must be some deemphasis of conventional weaponry. Marshal Ogarkov, in 1984, called for an acceleration of conventional arms development and he presumably lost the debate. The main point here is ultimately a political one: Gorbachev appears to be better positioned than any Soviet leader since Khrushchev in the late 1950s to impose a reallocation of resources upon the military.

Fifth, if the present overall "correlation" is unacceptable to Moscow under circumstances of heavy Soviet involvement in Afghanistan and extensive influence in Southeast Asia, it is difficult to envision a major Soviet overturning of the balance via gains in peripheral areas over the next few years. Total conquest of Afghanistan by the USSR and/or further expansion of Soviet influence in Southeast Asia would affect the world balance only marginally and might trigger countervailing responses that would cancel any gains. The Eastern Mediterranean and the Middle East offer some hope of a breakthrough but expansion of Soviet influence in Greece and Syria would be principally related to diplomatic initiatives. Given the multiple pressures and demands facing the Soviets, they would do well to hold on to what they now have in terms of the geographical distribution of world power. Soviet capacity for military interventions either on the system periphery or in distant areas will probably be maintained but subject to severe restraints. In the potentially most explosive areas, Africa and Latin America, the Soviets will no doubt continue to support revolutionary movements but will probably be constrained to avoid direct involvement. Accordingly, improvement for the Soviets in the global "correlation" in the short run is likely to hinge upon policy at the center of the international political system, i.e., the success of initiatives by the USSR designed to improve its military, economic, and diplomatic positions vis-à-vis the United States and NATO.

The conditions and pressures indicated above point toward a mixed strategy, perhaps a combination of options (5) and (6) and some early actions by the new leadership suggest at least tentative movement in this direction. It seems likely that the new leadership will pursue a sequential approach, with a short-run combination of negotiation and militancy, pointing toward a period after 1988 when it might be anticipated that American leadership would be more accommodating to Soviet interests.

Even if such a sequential approach fulfills expectations, the Soviets cannot expect the United States to acquiesce quietly in any thrust by the USSR toward world hegemony or even a substantial shift in the world balance of power. Accordingly, option (6) may offer greater potential. The May 1985 visit of Indian leader Rajiv Gandhi to Moscow and the economic aid package agreed upon then accord with the "three-track" approach set out in option (6). But here the most important area is Western Europe.

The strategic and economic factors involved in detente with Western Europe are obvious. Less obvious is the connection between bloc control and the framework of Soviet relations with the major West European states. The attraction of the West is a more troublesome problem under conditions of East-West polarization. Normalization of relations with West Europe eliminates much of the political leverage that satellite leaders can exercise vis-à-vis Moscow; the relative stability of the bloc for several years after the initiation of detente with the FRG in 1970 is highly instructive on this point.

"Finlandization" of Western Europe is probably unrealistic, but a partial neutralization may not be. Opposition to NATO objectives in the Netherlands, Spain, and Greece must provide continuing encouragement for Moscow. But in major Western countries, the leftist proclivities of broad segments of supposed decision-making elites—clergy, academicians, media personalities—has paralleled an underlying, apparently growing, general conservatism of the masses, a phenomenon affecting both middle and working classes. The pronounced leftward swing of the British Labour party offers no immediate solace for the Soviets; that party's penchant for self-destruction will probably keep it out of power for the remainder of the century. But in democratic societies, the eventual alternation of power between parties must be assumed; therefore, the orientation of parties of the left toward Soviet policies makes a great deal of difference.

The most tantalizing prospects for Moscow in this area are no doubt concentrated in West Germany. Despite the abysmal failure of the heavy-handed Soviet attempt to influence the outcome of the 1983 elections, the FRG is still the country with the greatest potential for any Moscow policy aimed toward a separation of Western Europe and the U.S. The peculiarities of the West German electoral system make it possible for the SPD to obtain sole power with a minority of the popular vote. If the Greens hold on to five percent of the "second ballots," an SPD-Green governing coalition in 1987 is a distinct possibility. Under present conditions, either outcome could entail the effective dismantling of NATO. Whether the Soviet leadership would be flexible enough on European and world policy to facilitate such a denouement is, of course, another question.

Adoption of a defensive, as opposed to the prevailing offensive, military strategy in Europe by the Soviets would no doubt be conducive to the neutralization of West Germany and general detente with Western Europe and would lessen the economic pressures faced by the Soviet leadership.[31] Such a reversal in Soviet planning is highly unlikely but is not absolutely essential for a European-oriented strategy of "divisible" detente.

Should the Soviets opt for a "three-track" policy, this would probably have a pronounced short-run impact upon the location of international conflicts. In any case, such a strategy would be consistent with apparent Soviet perceptions that the regional "correlation of forces" in Europe is the most crucial one for the near future.

While a mixture of sequential and "three-track" approaches appears to be the most rational course for the Soviets, and there are indications that the new leadership tends in this direction, there can be no guarantees concerning actual Soviet policy.

What we can be reasonably sure of is that the Soviets will continue to view the world in terms of polarized conflict. While that perspective serves important functional purposes for the regime, it has never corresponded very well with objective reality, except perhaps in some measure as self-fulfilling prophecy, and may possess even less empirical salience in the future. For the long run, the best hope for the non-Communist world may lie in the further diffusion of power among major components of the international system. For the short run, one aspect of Soviet "correlation of forces" analysis is surely accurate: the most important element of resistance to "restructuring" on Soviet terms is the strength of, and application of the "subjective" factor by, the United States. When American leadership is weak or vacillating, the USSR scores its greatest gains.

Whatever options the USSR pursues in the coming period, the new Soviet leader's brief in foreign affairs will be restoring the momentum of "restructuring" in the world "correlation of forces." Given the existence of seemingly intractable domestic problems, the long-range prospects for Soviet hegemony in world affairs are rather bleak and there are indications that the USSR has passed the peak of its influence as a superpower. But the Soviets possess enormous untapped material resources, an awesome arsenal of armaments, and a political control structure that promises to tighten, not loosen, its hold upon the Soviet citizenry. The critical condition of the USSR's economy does not assure a continuation of existing trends in world affairs unfavorable to the Soviets; technological backwardness has not prevented the expansion of Soviet influence in the past. And given the nature of the regime, we can be certain that the Soviets in the future will exploit every opportunity to expand their influence. Much will depend upon how well Western leaders and publics have learned the lessons of detente and its breakdown.

The favorable upsurge in world politics for the USSR during the 1970s was based, as the Soviets candidly admit, upon the vast expansion of Soviet military power. This was paralleled by a measure of unilateral military disarmament on the part of the West, particularly the United States, a trend conditioned by a preceding psychological disarmament. The recent downturn for the Soviets derives from a number of causative factors, principally Moscow's mistakes on policy, the succession crisis, domestic social and economic problems, and the revival of American morale and military power under a more vigorous leadership since 1981. Absolutely crucial during the next decade will be the extent to which the West can maintain political cohesion, permitting technological superiority to exert its force as a restraining factor upon the Soviets.

The USSR is surely burdened with serious liabilities in the exercise of its superpower role and in the further expansion of its influence in the world. On the other hand, the Soviets possess, at the outset of the Gorbachev era, what is probably the most vigorous, and perhaps the most cohesive, leadership of their system in more than three decades. Just as the Soviets are aware that their "free ride" came to an end in 1981, so the West must recognize that its relatively inexpensive passage of the early 1980s has ended and is unlikely to recur in the twentieth century.

Notes

1. Andrei A. Gromyko, "Programma mira v deistvii" [The peace program in action], *Kommunist*, no. 14, September 1975, p. 5.
2. See R. Judson Mitchell, *Ideology of a Superpower: Contemporary Soviet Doctrine on International Relations*, Stanford: Hoover Institution Press, 1982, pp. 54–70.
3. See Andrei A. Grechko, "Glavnoi roli KPSS v stroeni armiie razvitie sotzialisticheskem obshestve" [The main role of the CPSU in building the army of developed socialist society], *Voprosy istorii KPSS*, no. 5, April 1974, pp. 34–35, 37, 41, 43 and Aleksei A. Yepishev, "Vooruzhennie sili obshenarodnogo gosudarstva" [The armed forces of a state of the whole people], *Kommunist*, no. 2, February 1979, pp. 60–61.
4. Adam B. Ulam, *Dangerous Relations: The Soviet Union in World Politics, 1970–1982*, New York: Oxford University Press, 1983, p. 314.
5. See Grigori Romanov's Bolshevik Revolution Anniversary speech, *Pravda*, November 6, 1983, p. 2, and Andrei Gromyko's Bolshevik Anniversary speech, *Pravda*, November 7, 1984, p. 3.
6. V. Kortunov, "The Ideology of Peace versus the Ideology of War," *International Affairs*, no. 11, November 1983, pp. 9, 11.
7. For the official Soviet view of the "subjective factor," see A. Viktorov's lengthy commentary on the XXV CPSU Congress, *Pravda*, March 27, 1976, pp. 2–3.
8. Arthur J. Alexander, "Modeling Soviet Defense Decisionmaking," in Jiri Valenta and William Potter, eds., *Soviet Decisionmaking for National Security*, London: George Allen and Unwin, 1984, p. 17. Alexanders's analysis of the role of doctrine in the functioning of the defense establishment can be

usefully applied to all structures engaged in fulfillment of foreign policy goals.

9. See Arkady N. Shevchenko, *Breaking with Moscow* (New York: Alfred A. Knopf, 1985), p. 160.
10. The three crises concerned Afghanistan, Poland, and the KAL airliner incident. For a stimulating, albeit highly speculative, analysis of the effect of leadership disarray upon decision making on the invasion of Afghanistan, see Vladimir Solovyev and Elena Klepikova, *Yuri Andropov: A Secret Passage into the Kremlin* (New York: MacMillan, 1983), p. 183.
11. On "traditional" candidates for the leadership, see Grey Hodnett, "Succession Contingencies in the Soviet Union," *Problems of Communism*, XXIV, 2, March–April 1975, pp. 1–21, and Seweryn Bialer, *Stalin's Successors: Leadership, Stability and Change in the Soviet Union* (Cambridge: Cambridge University Press, 1980), p. 77.
12. Gail Warshofsky Lapidus, "The Brezhnev Regime and Directed Social Change: Depoliticization as Political Strategy," in Alexander Dallin (ed.), *The Twenty-Fifth Congress of the CPSU: Assessment and Context* (Stanford: Hoover Institution Press, 1977), pp. 26–38.
13. On the pre-1964 relationship to Brezhnev, see Shevchenko, *op. cit.* p. 149.
14. Bruce Parrott, "Soviet Policy Toward the United States: A Fork in the Road?" *SAIS Review*, 5, 1, Winter–Spring 1985, pp. 115–116; Andrei Gromyko, "V.I. Lenin i vneshniya politika sovetskogo gosudarstva" [V.I. Lenin and the Foreign Policy of the Soviet State], *Kommunist*, no. 6, 1983, pp. 11–32.
15. *The New York Times*, March 14, 1985, pp. 1, 6.
16. BBC broadcast, September 18, 1983; FBIS Daily Report, September 19, 1983.
17. *Literaturnaya gazeta*, November 23, 1983, p. 4.
18. See Dimitri K. Simes, "The Military and Militarism in Soviet Society," *International Security*, 6, 3, Winter 1981–1982, pp. 123–143.
19. Dusko Doder, " 'A Nice Smile, But Iron Teeth': Gorbachev's Smooth Rise," *Washington Post*, March 17, 1985, p. 1.
20. Dr. George Keyworth, Director of Science and Technology Policy for the Reagan administration, emerged in 1984–85 as the principal proponent of the argument that SDI is both practical and essential. However, Keyworth left this government post in late 1985 to enter private business. ABC News, November 29, 1985. For a detailed negative assessment of "Star Wars" from a technological perspective, see Sidney D. Drell, Philip J. Farley and David Holloway, "Preserving the ABM Treaty: A Critique of the Reagan Strategic Defense Initiative," *International Security*, 9, 2, Fall 1984, pp. 51–91.
21. If, as some critics of SDI maintain, it will be an "umbrella" suitable for a "mild drizzle" but not for a "torrential downpour," the strategic balance could conceivably be rendered noncompetitive in some measure without negotiation. If both sides possessed the certain capacity to destroy a few missiles, this would be the surest guarantee against accidental occurrence of nuclear war, the most probable scenario for its inception.
22. *Pravda*, August 16, 1983, p. 1; *Izvestia*, August 18, 1983, p. 1.
23. *Pravda*, January 28, 1959, p. 9.

24. See Boris N. Ponomarev, "Neodolimost osvoboditelnogo dvizheniya" [Invincibility of the liberation movement], *Kommunist*, no. 1, January 1980, p. 23.

25. Michael J. Deane, "The Soviet Assessment of the 'Correlation of World Forces': Implications for American Foreign Policy," *Orbis*, 20, 3, Fall 1976, pp. 625–636.

26. See Supreme Soviet campaign speech by Boris N. Ponomarev, *Pravda*, February 13, 1979, p. 2.

27. Vojtech Mastny, "Eastern Europe and the Future of the Soviet Empire," *SAIS Review*, 5, 1, Winter–Spring 1985, pp. 142–143.

28. Parrott, *op. cit.*, p. 109.

29. See Morton A. Kaplan, "Changes in United States Perspectives on the Soviet Union and Detente," in Kaplan (ed.), *Great Issues of International Politics*, 2nd Ed., Chicago: Aldine Publishing Co., 1974, p. 217.

30. Hannes Adomeit, "Capitalist Contradictions and Soviet Policy," *Problems of Communism*, XXXIII, 3, May–June 1984, p. 5.

31. Richard Ned Lebow, "The Soviet Offensive in Europe: The Schlieffen Plan Revisited?" *International Security*, 9, 4, Spring 1985, pp. 44–78, esp. 69–78; *Cf.* P.H. Vigor, *Soviet Blitzkrieg Strategy*, New York: St. Martin's Press, 1983, esp. chs. 1, 10, 12–14.

2

Arms Control and U.S.-Soviet Relations

JOSEPH L. NOGEE

There is a general belief that domestic reform heads the agenda of the Gorbachev administration.[1] Internal problems facing the Soviet regime are so serious as to bring into question not just the stability but the survivability of the Soviet regime as we now know it.[2] If the assumption of the primacy of domestic issues is valid, we can expect the Kremlin to avoid initiatives or drastic changes in foreign policy until it has begun its program of domestic reform. Of course, unexpected foreign policy crises may force the attention of Gorbachev whether he is ready for them or not. No great power can isolate itself from the demands of balance of power politics for any length of time, particularly one—like the Soviet Union—committed to expanding its global position.

Whatever his priorities Gorbachev will be compelled to give concerted attention to relations with the United States. It is probably no exaggeration to say that for both the superpowers the problems of foreign and domestic policies are inextricably linked. By that I mean that the character of domestic changes will be significantly influenced by the degree of tension which exists between the United States and the Soviet Union and the extent to which resources must be committed to achieve foreign policy objectives. It is not simply a "guns versus butter" question—although that is part of it—but also the direct impact of foreign events upon domestic politics. That impact may impede the mobilization of political and bureaucratic forces supporting change or it may intensify the pressures for change. Gorbachev warned party and government leaders last June that "external circumstances" increased the "need to accelerate socioeconomic development."[3]

United States-Soviet relations have been in a state of protracted crisis since the collapse of detente at the end of the 1970s. It is difficult to categorize Soviet-American relations in the 1980s. Are we in a new Cold War? Did the Cold War ever really end? What are the essential differences in Soviet relations with the West between the current and earlier periods of conflict? It has been observed that for several years we have been experiencing tension without crisis.[4] That is to say, unlike the pre-1980 period there have not been any major United States-Soviet confrontations comparable to the Berlin, Cuban and Middle Eastern crises that threatened to involve the superpowers in a military conflict. Whatever impact such events as the Soviet invasion of Afghanistan, the Korean airline incident or subversion in Central America have had in embittering Soviet-American relations, they have produced no lethal confrontation.

The primary issue dominating United States-Soviet relations over the past half-decade has been arms control. The rise and fall of prospects for an agreement, stalemates, deadlocks, walkouts and resumption of negotiations have served as a barometer of superpower relations. A central reason why these relations have been cool to frigid is that on the whole arms control efforts in the 1980s have been a failure. It is not at all self-evident that the collapse of arms control has been the cause of Soviet-American tensions. One could well argue that the poor state of Soviet-American relations is itself the reason for the inability of both sides to agree on an arms control treaty. No one, for example, doubts that the failure of the United States to ratify the SALT II agreement was precisely because Congress (and the American public) were angered by Soviet behavior in Afghanistan and elsewhere in the Third World. Indeed, the traditional view of arms races and disarmament efforts is that arms buildups are the result of underlying political conflict, and that the way to disarm is first to remove the source of the conflict. That done, so it is argued, disarmament will follow.[5] In other words, in the relationship between arms buildups and political conflict it is the latter which is the independent variable.

That relationship and that theory may not apply today. It is an argument of this paper that the state of the strategic balance today is itself both a cause and an effect of Soviet-American relations; that not only are the superpowers engaged in a strategic competition for arms because they fear the political objectives of the other, but that the possession of these strategic weapons *ipso facto* creates fear and suspicion on both sides. This observation in and of itself is hardly new. But the present period in U.S.-Soviet relations is unique in the extent to which political relations have been directly dependent upon the strategic balance and the failure of arms control efforts to moderate the arms race in strategic weapons.

Thus, arms control today is the central issue governing superpower relations, in effect the surrogate for Soviet-American relations in general.[6] It is the only important issue currently negotiable between the two powers. If the superpower relationship is to change in any significant way, it will almost certainly be reflected in the state of arms control negotiations. An agreement may or may not restore detente, but inevitably a continuation of the deadlock or a breakdown in the negotiations will be accompanied by a state of tension and an atmosphere of crisis. Some issues like trade or scientific and cultural exchanges may be negotiable, but these pale in importance in Soviet-American relations to the arms race. Other issues, like the competition in the Third World, are of vital importance but they are not negotiable. Indeed, the fundamental political and ideological struggle between both sides is beyond negotiation.

Arms control is an extraordinarily complex subject. The scientific and technical dimensions are understood by only a small, highly trained cadre of personnel. Much of the information about weapons development, force structure and strategic targeting is classified secret. The policy-making process is complicated by vast political and bureaucratic forces which must be accommodated prior to any agreement on policy decisions. Before the two governments can even begin talks, a complex negotiation must be worked out between the civilian and military bureaucracies of each side.[7] Adding to these complexities is the dynamic of constant change: growth in technology, modernization of weaponry, change in military strategy and doctrine, the emergence of new leaders and administrations and the vagaries of public opinion (at least in the West). Finally because weapons are so central to the balance of power, and because of the profound conflict between the Soviet Union and the United States, the struggle through arms control diplomacy to retain an advantage or to avoid a disadvantage is powerful.

Soviet objectives in arms control since 1979 have shifted with circumstances. Since the leadership changed so often during this period, one might expect arms control policy to have changed with each new leader. But it did not. Between the four oligarchs who dominated the Politburo in this period there was more continuity than change. When policy did change it reflected external rather than internal developments. Since 1979, Soviet arms control policy falls into three distinct periods: (1) 1980–1983, (2) 1984 and (3) 1985.

1980–1983—The Propaganda Battle

The negotiations that took place in the first period were intended less to reach an agreement than to influence political forces beyond the bargaining table. Moscow and Washington both sought to achieve their objectives by means other than through an agreement. Not since the late 1950s had arms talks become so totally a propaganda slugfest. The central issue under debate was NATO's decision to modernize its theater nuclear forces. In the 1970s Moscow began to replace its missiles targeted against Western Europe (the SS-4's and SS-5's) with a newer, longer range, more accurate, more powerful and less vulnerable missile, the SS-20.[8] To counter that weapon NATO decided in 1979 to deploy 572 Pershing II and cruise missiles beginning in 1983, unless a lesser number, coupled with restraint in the SS-20 buildup could be negotiated with Moscow. Because the NATO decision was a reaction to the Soviet action the central question became whether or not NATO would proceed with the deployment in 1983.

Negotiations were slow in getting started because a new U.S. administration was elected in 1980, and it needed time to formulate a position. When announced in 1981 Reagan's policy became known as the "zero option": the United States would forgo the missile deployment only if the Soviet Union disbanded all of its intermediate nuclear forces (INF) in Europe.[9] It was a tough position, requiring the Soviet Union to give up what it already had in place for a United States commitment to in effect do nothing.

Moscow's response was equally hard. While agreeing to accept some limits on its own missiles, the Kremlin refused to consider the deployment of a single Pershing II or cruise missile on European soil. As the discussions proceeded it became increasingly clear that both sides had taken nonnegotiable positions. Washington had determined that NATO cohesion required the missile deployment while Moscow refused to concede even the symbolic deployment of a single new missile. At heart what was at stake was the solidarity of the North Atlantic alliance. Europe (particularly West Germany) had asked for the American missiles in the first place in order to be assured of American involvement in Europe's defense should the Soviet Union invade Western Europe. The theater nuclear missiles were intended to "couple" Europe's defense with U.S. strategic forces. Each year after 1979, as the NATO decision was reaffirmed by the governments involved as well as the electorate which supported the candidates of political parties that endorsed the decision (notably in Britain, West Germany and Italy in 1983) the question increasingly boiled down to whether or not Europe's democratically elected governments could pursue a prolonged coherent defense policy.

Moscow's overriding objective in the Pershing II-cruise missile debate was to undermine NATO unity and to separate the United States from its allies. The Kremlin made a calculated—and not totally unreasonable— gamble that a combination of pressure and manipulation would force Western Europe to back down. The pressure consisted of warnings that the

Soviet Union would take retaliatory measures as well as the threat to walk out of the talks if NATO deployed the INF missiles. Moscow also warned Washington that the use of Pershing II or European-based cruise missiles against Soviet territory would inevitably lead to retaliation against the territory of the United States. Potentially more devastating, however, was the attempt to manipulate European—and to a lesser extent, American—public opinion to force their governments to abandon or delay the deployment. On both sides of the Atlantic powerful antiwar movements developed to freeze nuclear weapon growth and to stop the deployment of new missiles in Europe. During 1982 and 1983, rallies involving hundreds of thousands of demonstrators protested the stationing of American missiles in Europe. Even before the negotiations began the Dutch government, responding to an antinuclear rally of between three and four hundred thousand people in Amsterdam, decided to defer its decision to station nuclear armed missiles on Dutch soil.

The greatest pressure was against West Germany, on whose territory would be located the entire force of 108 Pershing II missiles (The 484 cruise missiles were scheduled to be stationed in Britain, Italy, West Germany, Belgium and the Netherlands). Brezhnev and Andropov both devoted particular attention to influencing the West German government and Social Democratic Party, a large segment of which opposed the NATO modernization. Brezhnev visited Bonn personally to pressure Chancellor Helmut Schmidt. He proposed a mutual freeze on the deployment of new weapons. Later, with SS–20 production around the 300 level Brezhnev announced a moratorium on the construction of new missiles. Public opinion polls gave the Soviet leadership grounds to believe that it might be possible to force NATO to stop the deployment altogether or to postpone it while negotiations were proceeding. In 1982, 61 percent of West Germans preferred a postponement and a year later over 70 percent opposed deployment while the negotiations continued.[10]

Stopping the NATO missiles became Andropov's primary foreign policy objective. Scarcely a month passed during his brief administration that did not witness some new proposal or public announcement on the subject. Shortly after taking office he stated the Soviet Union's willingness to retain in Europe only as many missiles as possessed by Britain and France, then numbering 162 combined. Britain and France had always considered their nuclear weapons to be national rather than NATO forces and thus not subject to the calculation of the NATO-Warsaw Pact balance. Moscow's insistence upon counting these weapons in the balance had the dual advantages of serving as a driving wedge between the United States and its two European allies as well as appearing plausible in the court of public opinion since, after all, they were theater weapons on European territory capable of hitting the Soviet Union. Gradually Andropov reduced the number of Soviet missiles demanded by Moscow as its concession for a backdown on NATO INF deployment to 120, a figure that would have reduced the Soviet intermediate missile force to its smallest level in some 20 years.

The INF struggle dominated U.S.-Soviet relations for almost two years. In its intensity and scope the effort to block the INF was comparable to the previous campaigns by Moscow to defeat the European Defense Community (EDC) in the 1950s and the Multilateral Nuclear Force (MLF) in the 1960s. In both previous struggles the Soviet Union was successful, even if only temporarily in the EDC fight. In again seeking to limit Western Europe's capacity to organize its defense, Moscow relied heavily on appeals to public opinion accompanied by a complex diplomacy that included both threats and inducements. The West German Bundestag's approval of the NATO deployment in November 1983 followed by the first shipments of missiles to Germany, Britain and Italy constituted a major defeat for Andropov's foreign policy.

November 1983–November 1984— ## The Collapse of Negotiations

Moscow's decision to break off the INF talks was part of a general strategy that involved the termination of all arms control negotiations. On December 8, 1983, the Soviet Union ended the strategic arms talks and a week later those on conventional force reductions in Europe.

The Strategic Arms Reduction Talks (START) were the successor to the strategic arms efforts that began in 1969 and culminated in the SALT I agreement and the unratified SALT II treaty. From the beginning the START talks took a back seat to INF. They were slow in getting started not only because the U.S. administration was new, but because it was internally divided over what should be contained in the United States proposals. From the American point of view the most pressing concern was to reduce the substantial Soviet superiority in land-based ballistic missiles—particularly the heavy ones—which when MIRVed with accurate warheads posed a potential first strike capability against the American ICBM's. When the START talks began in 1982 the Soviet Union had 1398 ICBM's (including 308 of the heavy SS–18 missiles) to 1,052 for the United States. Basically what the United States wanted the Soviet Union to do was to restructure its strategic triad so as to put more forces either in submarines or long-range bombers, as was the case with the U.S. strategic deterrent. Toward that end, Reagan proposed a plan limiting ICBM's to a total of 850 and reducing the total number of strategic warheads from the approximately 7,500 possessed by each side to 5,000, of which no more than half could be carried on ICBM's. These were "deep cuts" with a vengeance. Like Reagan's "zero option" for the INF this was a position that Moscow would not likely accept. Just before the Soviet walkout of the START talks Nikolai Ogarkov, then chief of the general staff, stated in a press conference that "Washington wanted cuts in the Soviet land-based missile force that would force a fundamental restructuring of the Soviet armory costing billions of rubles."[11]

Notwithstanding these objections, there is good reason to believe that the Soviet Union was prepared to make significant concessions to the American demand for deep cuts in land-based missiles. Moscow's counterproposal called for a total of 1,800 missiles and bombers with sublimits for putting multiple warheads on different categories of launchers.[12] The 1,800 figure was well below the SALT II limit of 2,250 launchers and surprisingly close to the figure proposed by President Carter in 1977 and vehemently rejected by Brezhnev. The offer of a reduction to 1,800 launchers was, however, made conditional on progress on INF. In other words, the deployment of Pershing II or cruise missiles in Europe meant that Moscow would not agree to deep cuts in ICBM's. In view of the secondary importance of START to INF in Soviet priorities it is difficult to know how serious Moscow's intentions in strategic arms were at that time.

In retrospect it is clear that the Kremlin's decision to terminate arms talks was a blunder. Why did Andropov do it? Partly because he had threatened a walkout if the INF deployment took place as scheduled. The American action forced some response if only to maintain Soviet credibility. Furthermore, the walkout was consistent with Soviet diplomatic style which often displays a rather heavy hand. Moscow, of course, could have made its point without such a categorical rupture. It might, for example, have left open the possibility of a resumption of negotiations if the deployment of new missiles ceased after the arrival in Europe of a small—perhaps symbolic—number. But Andropov insisted that a condition for the resumption of talks be the restoration of the *status quo ante*, meaning the removal of all missiles. "If," he said, "the US and the other NATO countries show their readiness to return to the situation that existed before the deployment of the American medium-range missiles in Europe began, the Soviet Union will be prepared to respond in kind. In that event, the proposals we submitted earlier on questions of the limitation and reduction of nuclear arms in Europe would regain their force."[13] That is the position he held to his death.

At the core of the Soviet strategy to torpedo the arms control talks was its assessment of Ronald Reagan and the question of whether he would be in power for only four years or perhaps eight. It is somewhat ironic that the Kremlin initially cautiously welcomed Reagan's replacement of Jimmy Carter in 1980. However, within a short period of time Soviet leaders began to voice strong criticism of the American President. In 1981 Marshal Ogarkov warned that U.S. policy was pushing the world toward "the brink of war." Defense Minister Dmitri Ustinov claimed in *Pravda* in May 1983 that certain hotheads in the West by their "insane actions have brought the world to the brink of a universal nuclear catastrophe." In June of that year Konstantin Chernenko used virtually identical language on the danger of war with Reagan in the White House before a plenum of the Central Committee.[14] A comprehensive indictment of U.S. policy was published in 1984 under the title *Whence the Threat to Peace*, a 96-page slickly printed monograph filled with facts and pictures. The first paragraph read:

> The Reagan Administration's nearly four years in office have shown just how dangerous the course of whipping up the arms race is for all nations. The policies of this Administration, which has openly committed itself to the achievement of military superiority (in effect, world domination), to the use of force as the chief means of gaining its ends worldwide, have led to a steep rise in international tension and increased the threat of war.[15]

Though intended for propaganda, there is good reason to believe that Moscow took its own words seriously. Thus, it is highly likely that the Soviet leaders saw little prospect of success in continuing arms control negotiations.

Indeed, it is probable that Andropov came to the conclusion that arms control negotiations actually facilitated Reagan's arms buildup. While the negotiations were going on, the American President worked diligently to obtain congressional approval of several new strategic systems for the 1980s and 1990s, among which were the MX and Midgetman ICBM's, the Trident I C–4 and Trident II C–5 SSBM's, and the B–1 and Stealth bombers. Initially Reagan had strong support in Congress for his military buildup, but increasingly he had to rely also upon a number of congressmen who were willing to vote for military systems only if they were assured that serious efforts were being made to limit the buildup through arms control.[16] So long as the talks proceeded Reagan could point to such efforts. The Kremlin undoubtedly saw some advantage in ending even the facade of serious arms control negotiations.

Presidential politics played its part also. Moscow would have liked to see Reagan repudiated at the polls. Certainly it wanted to avoid any step that might benefit the Republicans. Rarely does Moscow openly voice its support for one side or the other in American presidential elections, but in 1984 it made no attempt to conceal its preferences. *Isvestiya*, the official government newspaper, observed in March: "But on the whole, the Democrats are countering R. Reagan's bellicosity and adventurism with a foreign policy that is based on common sense and an understanding that America will be secure only when the Soviet Union is secure."[17] One of Reagan's campaign claims was that he knew how to deal with the Russians since they understood and respected strength. Andropov and Chernenko both sought to disabuse the American public of that belief, and terminating the arms talks was one means of making that point.

Whatever its goals, the Kremlin's tactic of the walkout was a failure. Instead of hurting Reagan's presidential candidacy, it probably aided him. Soviet propaganda disingenuously sought to portray the United States as the party responsible for the stoppage of talks, but it is difficult to imagine that many were so persuaded. By taking on the opprobrium for terminating negotiations, the Soviet Union seriously undermined the anti-American peace movement in Europe. Though demonstrations and rallies continued during 1984, they were nowhere near the size of those in 1983. It was difficult to blame Washington for the failure of arms control when Moscow refused even to meet with the Americans. The Republican presidential candidate stressed this point often during the campaign. Indeed, Reagan took advantage of Soviet discomfiture by taking a more conciliatory posture toward the Soviet Union as indicated by his address on January 16, 1984, urging a return to nuclear arms negotiations as part of a larger Soviet-American dialogue. Moscow, now locked into its rejectionist posture could only respond by calling the speech "propaganda."

It fell to Andropov's successor, Konstantin Chernenko, to execute the Soviet policy of no negotiations. Either there was division within the Politburo or Chernenko was himself uncertain about the course U.S.-Soviet relations should take, for throughout most of 1984 Soviet behavior fluctuated, sometimes rather sharply. For example, in his first major speech after taking office Chernenko urged a renewal of the U.S.-Soviet dialogue. At the Geneva disarmament conference, the Soviet Union agreed in February to allow continuous inspection of chemical weapons as part of a future arms control accord. But in March, Chernenko snubbed a high-level U.S. group with a personal letter from Reagan. That month East-West talks on reducing armed forces in Central Europe resumed in Vienna. In May, Moscow announced a boycott of the Summer Olympics in Los Angeles, a new deployment of intermediate missiles in East Germany and an increase in the number of nuclear submarines off the United States coast. In June, Moscow formally proposed negotiations on banning space weapons, and in July the United States and the Soviet Union agreed to modernize the "hot line" between Moscow and Washington. In August, an American Marine was beaten by Soviet police at the U.S. consulate in Leningrad.

The fall was a period of unusual gyrations in Soviet behavior. East German leader Erich Honecker and Bulgarian leader Todor Zhivkov were forced to cancel visits to West Germany. At the United Nations Foreign Minister Gromyko delivered a harsh attack on U.S. foreign policy, repeating the Soviet demand that the United States remove the INF missiles in Europe before arms control negotiations could resume. Yet that same month Gromyko met (for the first time) President Reagan in the White House, an event even shown on Soviet television. In October, Chernenko gave an interview with a *Washington Post* reporter in which he notably omitted the demand for the removal of U.S. missiles in Europe as a precondition for a resumption of talks. Finally in November (after the American elections), the United States and the Soviet Union announced that George Shultz and Andrei Gromyko would meet in Geneva early in 1985 to establish the basis for a resumption of arms control talks.

These and other actions betrayed an uncertainty and some inconsistency in Soviet policy toward the United States. Perhaps this was inevitable during a period of transition such as was taking place within the Kremlin leadership. From the moment he assumed power, Chernenko was confronted with a basic paradox: he was obliged to pursue the policy of nonnegotiation inherited from his predecessor. On the other hand, that policy became increasingly unproductive, even counterproductive. Nonnegotiation undermined the Soviet propaganda campaign, but even worse it denied the Soviet Union the opportunity to achieve the benefits that could come with an arms control agreement with the United States. It became increasingly apparent that an unconstrained arms race posed for Moscow substantial costs. The massive Soviet advantages resulting from its military buildup in the 1970s were now threatened by Washington's own military buildup, and the combination of Soviet economic paralysis and U.S. technology made the benefits of arms control look increasingly good to the Kremlin.[18] One issue in particular which appeared menacing to the Soviet leadership was the prospect of an arms race in space. The genesis of that threat was President Reagan's Strategic Defense Initiative (SDI) proposed in a televised speech on March 23, 1983.

1985—The Struggle Over Space

One of the oddities of contemporary arms control is how quickly one issue—strategic defense in space—has come to dominate the arms control debate. From the time Reagan made his proposal that the United States develop a space-based antiballistic missile (ABM) system capable of destroying Soviet missiles before they could reach their targets, until the Soviet walkout of the arms control talks, SDI took a back seat to INF. It was only after the INF issue was settled, with the U.S. deployment, that SDI emerged to its current position of prominence. Sometime during 1984 the Politburo decided to reinstitute negotiations, with the primary objective of stopping the United States from proceeding with research, development and ultimately deployment of a space-based ABM system. Exactly when this decision was reached is not known, but the jockeying over the resumption of negotiations that began in June 1984 was likely the beginning of a new Soviet approach.

On June 29, the Soviet government proposed negotiations to begin in September "to prevent the militarization of outer space." Specifically, it sought a prohibition against space-based ABM defense weapons and antisatellite weapons. Also proposed was a moratorium on the testing and deployment of such weapons while negotiations for an agreement took place.[19] The inclusion of the moratorium indicated that Moscow was engaged in a propaganda ploy, because the U.S. would never have accepted a moratorium before anything of substance had been agreed upon, and certainly the Kremlin understood this.[20] Moscow must have been taken aback by the speed and perhaps the disingenuousness of the American reply. On the same day, Washington agreed to the proposal with the addendum that it would also want to discuss the reduction of all nuclear arms, not just the banning of defensive weapons in space. In other words, Washington was taking advantage of the narrow Soviet proposal to reopen the broader issues of arms control. TASS rejected the American reply as "totally unsatisfactory." "By linking questions of nuclear arms to the problem of preventing the militarization of space," said TASS, "the American administration is seeking to avoid talks on space."[21] Both governments were engaged in a classic negotiating ploy. Each sought a different agenda: Moscow wanted to talk about SDI and Washington wanted to discuss strategic weapons. Both wanted to pin the blame on the other for the failure of negotiations to begin. For weeks a kind of diplomatic minuet ensued in which Washington tried to persuade Moscow and the public that it had accepted the Soviet offer of negotiations and Moscow to convince everyone that Washington had not. The Soviets "have been having a great deal of trouble taking yes for an answer" chided Secretary of State Shultz.

Moscow's decision to say yes came grudgingly but inexorably. The United States held firm to its position that any resumption of arms talks had to include all nuclear arms, not just space weapons. President Reagan, speaking before the thirty-ninth General Assembly of the UN offered a formula of "umbrella" talks as a solution to the procedural impasse. Soviet ambassador Anatoly Dobrynin called the umbrella suggestion "unprecedented" and worth studying. A breakthrough was revealed on November 22, when both governments announced that negotiations for controlling nuclear arms would take place in 1985. Shultz and Gromyko were scheduled to meet in Geneva on January 7–8 to set an agenda. Nothing was said about a moratorium on testing space weapons while the talks were in progress.

The working out of a framework for a resumption of talks did not come easily. President Reagan resisted opening the issue of space defense to negotiation, even though that was the price the United States had to pay for a resumption of arms control talks. According to Andrei Gromyko, his discussions with Secretary of State Shultz were very acrimonious. "We spoke firmly," the former foreign minister has stated, "and—I am ready to use the word—sharply."[22] The joint Soviet-American statement that resulted from the Shultz-Gromyko meeting was a carefully crafted document which made it possible for both sides to claim that the negotiations would focus on the issue of greatest importance to each. The critical sentence read: "The sides agree that the subject of the negotiations will be a complex of questions concerning space and nuclear arms, both strategic and medium range, with all these questions considered and resolved in their interrelationship."[23] Moscow got its desired talks on space weapons while conceding to Washington a resumption of nuclear arms negotiations. The Soviets sought to downplay the fact that they were resuming nuclear arms talks without any removal of NATO INF missiles by claiming that the impending talks had no connection with the earlier negotiations. "These are to be truly new talks," said *Pravda*, "Not a return to the table of the former negotiations in Geneva that were torpedoed . . . by the deployment of new American nuclear missiles in Western Europe. What is new about the talks . . . is the fact that the talks will be conducted on the entire range of issues relating to the nonmilitarization of space and the reduction of strategic and medium-range nuclear weapons."[24]

The "militarization of space" whose prevention has become the central object of Soviet arms control policy does not, as an expression, have a single or precise meaning. Since ballistic missiles go beyond the atmosphere in their trajectory, the demilitarization of space could mean a prohibition of ICBM's and SLBM's. Or it could mean the prohibition of earth-orbiting satellites which obviously have military utility. But current Soviet policy seeks neither of these goals. In January, 1985, Andrei Gromyko was asked by a *Pravda* correspondent "What, specifically, is meant when the Soviet Union resolutely calls for preventing the militarization of space?" Gromyko replied, "We mean that weapons intended for use against objects in space should be categorically banned. Also, weapons intended for use from space against the earth as a planet should be categorically banned. In other words, weapons intended for use against objects on the ground, in the sea and in the atmosphere."[25] Currently that formulation encompasses two distinct programs: (1) the antisatellite (ASAT) weapon, and (2) the proposal to create a space-based ballistic missile defense (BMD). The latter program is the one associated with Reagan's SDI, popularly known as "Star Wars."

However, the SDI concept itself has been used to mean more than one kind of a missile defense. American proponents of SDI now speak of two different types of programs. One is President Reagan's original vision of a defense system that could protect the entire population of the United States (and its allies) by intercepting and destroying Soviet ballistic missiles upon launch or in flight. The technology to do this involves lasers, particle beams, sensors and other forms of directed energy which are today only partially developed. The other is a partial defense to protect American strategic weapons such as missiles or bombers.[26] Though both are essentially defensive in nature, they differ substantially in their objectives, costs and technical feasibility. The goal of the larger program is to eliminate nuclear weapons entirely and thus replace the strategy of nuclear deterrence with one of absolute defense. The lesser program would enhance the strategy of retaliation by guaranteeing that an enemy would suffer a devastating retaliation, if it committed nuclear aggression. Moscow's criticism of the idea of strategic defense fails to distinguish between these variations. It resolutely opposes all forms of ballistic missile defense in the name of preventing the "militarization of space."

What are the objectives of Moscow's campaign against the Strategic Defense Initiative? In considering this question one must keep in mind that diplomacy may yield two types of benefits: those that accrue without the necessity of an agreement and those that are explicitly a part of an agreement. Propaganda is a good illustration of the former. For Moscow the opportunities are many in attacking a program that has incurred widespread opposition in the United States and abroad. Domestic opposition to SDI focuses upon its cost, its technical uncertainity, the possibility that it would stimulate a Soviet offensive capability to overcome it as well as a Soviet program to acquire its own BMD, and the negative impact of SDI on arms control and Soviet-American relations in general.[27] In Europe, the SDI issue has replaced INF as the principal means of encouraging anti-American sentiment. The Soviet media frequently use the expression "Star Wars" with special emphasis on the term "War" to describe the essence of Reagan's plan.[28] The United States is portrayed as willing to sacrifice Europe in pursuit of its own aggressive aims. "Essentially," warned *Izvestiya*, "it (SDI) boils down to protecting oneself while using Europe as a staging ground for a nuclear attack on the USSR. . . ."[29] One measure of the potential appeal of Moscow's message is the rather limited response by European governments to the United States call for its NATO allies to join in a joint research effort for SDI.

Soviet opposition to BMD, however, is more than just propaganda. It genuinely seeks to prevent an all-out race with the United States for a strategic defense against ballistic missiles. Before taking up the reasons for current Soviet opposition to BMD, I want briefly to review the role of BMD in Soviet doctrine and practice. It should be noted that historically Soviet thinking about strategic defense has been open-minded, i.e., there has not been an orthodoxy for or against the idea of BMD. Throughout the nuclear age Soviet strategists have argued on both sides of the issue.

There is considerable irony in the fact that today Washington is trying to convince Moscow of the blessings of ballistic missile defense, for less than 20 years ago United States officials were trying to persuade skeptical Soviet leaders that defense against missiles undermined mutual deterrence.[30] Soviet interest in BMD goes back to the 1950s. General N. A. Talensky, an editor of *Military Thought*, a classified journal of the Soviet General Staff, was an important theoretician of missile defense. In one of his influential articles he attacked the Western argument that BMD undermined deterrence, arguing that "the creation of an effective antimissile defense system by a country which is a potential target for aggression merely serves to increase the deterrence effect [of its retaliatory forces] and so helps to avert aggression."[31] An additional consideration for some Soviet strategists was the belief that BMD could mitigate damage in the event that deterrence failed. In 1958 the Soviets created an independent BMD organization within their air defense command. In the 1960s they began construction of the Galosh ABM system to protect Moscow. Their ABM network probably became fully operational by the early 1970s, but Galosh was never as large as originally planned. From the original 128 planned interceptor missiles Galosh was progressively cut to 96 and then to 64. Soviet enthusiasm for BMD waned as the cost rose and the limitations of missile defense became more apparent.[32]

By 1968, when the Soviet Union decided to participate in strategic arms limitations talks, it had come around to the U.S. position that a comprehensive BMD was neither stabilizing nor cost effective. When the negotiations actually began in 1969, Moscow actively pushed for an ABM treaty. Whether or not they were persuaded by the theoretical arguments about the destabilizing character of BMD, Soviet leaders understood very well that the American Safeguard ABM embodied substantially more sophisticated and powerful technology than anything available to them. Undoubtedly too, they were influenced by the capability of the U.S. missiles armed with MIRVed warheads to overwhelm their own limited missile defense. The ABM treaty that emerged from SALT I in 1972 met Moscow's (and the U.S.'s) desire to prohibit a territorial BMD while at the same time permitting Moscow to retain its partial BMD around Moscow.

The ABM treaty is important to Moscow for two reasons: the constraint it imposes on missile defense and its value as a symbol of detente. That symbol retains its validity notwithstanding the collapse of detente. The Kremlin recognizes that Soviet-American relations have deteriorated sharply from what they were a decade ago, but it continues to describe the restoration of detente as one of the goals of its foreign policy. A report of the Soviet Academy of Sciences in 1984 stated: "In the minds of people the [ABM] treaty is tightly associated with the possibility of detente and mutually, beneficial cooperation. The ABM treaty is a strategic and political 'anchor'. . . ."[33] In June 1985, Marshall S. Akhromeyev, Chief of the Soviet General Staff, wrote in *Pravda*:

> Accords between the USSR and the US based on equality and equal security are an important contribution to lessening the threat of war. The achievement of more reliable international security depends to a significant extent on whether or not we succeed in strengthening the international-treaty basis of arms limitation—on whether or not we preserve, not destroy, what already exists in this field and conclude new agreements. At the same time, preserving the treaty between the USSR and the US on the Limitation of Antiballistic Missile Systems from destruction is of enormous importance.[34]

SDI as proposed would be impossible without either abrogating or radically amending the ABM treaty. Article V which reads: "Each Party undertakes not to develop, test or deploy ABM systems or components which are sea-based, air-based, space-based, or mobile land-based."[35] clearly precludes carrying through with SDI in any of its currently proposed variations.

The objections that Moscow had to BMD at the time of SALT I have not lessened in the 13 or so years since. Although we cannot be sure of the exact ranking in Soviet calculations, we can identify five important reasons for Soviet opposition to President Reagan's SDI today.

1. As was the case in the early 1970s, so today the Kremlin does not wish to become involved in a space race with a nation whose technological and economic resources are greater than those available to it. Soviet officials can no more foresee the outcome of such a race than can American scientists, and it is the very uncertainty of the enterprise which is so troubling to many. An element of the problem is the cost, which at this stage can only be a matter of speculation. Figures discussed in hearings before the U.S. Congress range between five hundred billion to a trillion dollars.

2. Soviet scientists are doubtful that a foolproof space-based defense

against missiles is possible. A report prepared in 1984 by a group of Soviet scientists led by Ronald Z. Sagdeyev, director of the Space Research Institute of the Academy of Sciences and Andrei A. Kokoshin, deputy director of the United States and Canada Institute concluded that the proposed SDI would be vulnerable to countermeasures. It acknowledged that elements of the SDI system were technically feasible but that the proposed space stations could be put out of action by small ballistic missiles, orbiting space mines, high-power, ground-based lasers or clouds of chaff.[36] The availability of this report in English suggests a propagandistic motive in publishing it, yet the basic argument is fully consistent with the fundamental judgment of the Soviet military that "in general, the offense will overpower the defense."[37]

3. One might wonder: if Moscow really considered SDI an unattainable objective, why be so determined to stop it? Indeed, might there not be some benefit to the Soviet Union for the United States to engage in building an unworkable, flawed and costly system? That is not how Soviet leaders calculate this issue. Perhaps their greatest fear is that out of SDI will come a partially effective defense which could be effective against "a ragged retaliatory strike" and which when combined with a fully modernized offensive missile force would give the United States a real first strike capability.[38] In other words, Moscow looks at SDI not as an isolated development but in conjunction with a general posture of the United States which it sees as menacing. This concern was expressed by Andropov within days of Reagan's original proposal:

> At first glance, this may even seem attractive to uninformed people—after all, the President is talking about what seem to be defensive measures. But it seems so only at first glance, and only to those who are unfamiliar with these matters. In fact, the development and improvement of the U.S.'s strategic offensive forces will continue at full speed, and in a very specific direction—that of acquiring the potential to deliver a nuclear first strike. In these conditions, the intention to obtain the possibility of destroying, with the help of an antimissile defense, the corresponding systems of the other side—i.e., of depriving it of the capability of inflicting a retalitory strike—is designed to disarm the Soviet Union in the face of the American nuclear threat. This must be seen clearly if one is to correctly appraise the true meaning of this "new concept."[39]

Konstantin Chernenko, just weeks before his death repeated the Soviet view that there was nothing defensive about the SDI. In an interview published in *Pravda* he said:

The use of the term "defense" is playing with words. In essence, this concept is offensive—more precisely, aggressive. The aim is to try to disarm the other side, to deprive it of the possibility of delivering a retaliatory strike in the event of nuclear aggression against it. More simply, the task is being set of acquiring the possibility of delivering a nuclear strike with impunity, covering oneself from retribution with an antiballistic "shield." This is the same old line aimed at achieving decisive military superiority, with all the consequences ensuing therefrom for the cause of peace and international security.[40]

4. In addition to the negative impact strategic defense would have on U.S.-Soviet political relations is the destabilizing effect it would have on U.S.-Soviet military relations. Soviet spokesmen contend that a competition to develop strategic defense in space would stimulate an all-out arms race. In the interview quoted above, Chernenko also noted, "The militarization of space would not only mean . . . the end of the process of the limitation and reduction of nuclear arms, it would be a catalyst for an uncontrolled arms race in all areas."[41] An all-out arms race would spell the demise of arms control probably for a long time. According to some analysts, the SALT I agreement was an indication that Moscow had come to accept many of the basic premises held in the United States on the stabilizing virtues of arms control. Even military spokesmen, who are less impressed with arms control in the USSR than are civilians, express concern about a total collapse of constraints. *Red Star*, the official organ of the Ministry of Defense, has warned of "an endless escalation of measures, countermeasures, and counter-countermeasures which would be more and more difficult to halt" if the BMD is pursued.[42]

5. Destabilization can result from causes other than just the growth in the numbers of weapons. Another problem is the complexity of command and control over these systems. Strategic defense would be so complex and would have to operate so quickly that it could only be controlled by a computer system vastly larger and more complex than anything now in existence. It is estimated that the software would involve a program containing roughly 100 million lines of code. Such a program would presumably have to operate correctly the first time without ever having been tested in real world conditions. Soviet scientists—and many of their American counterparts—question whether it is prudent to rely upon untestable systems and whether the dependence upon computers and speed removes the human element in decisions that could affect national (and perhaps global) survival. A prominent Soviet spokesman voiced this concern:

. . . an arms race in space can only lead us to a point at which decisions regarding the use of weapons will be even more divorced from living decision makers and delegated to computers of extreme sophistication and rapid operation. As forecast in some of the world's more nightmarish works of fiction, decisions literally involving global life or death will be wrenched from human hands. The destruction of civilization will then become not just probable but almost certain.[43]

Formal arms control negotiations were begun (or resumed) on March 12, 1985, in Geneva. In accordance with the Shultz-Gromyko plan the three basic issues—space, strategic weapons and medium-range theater weapons—are being considered separately by a trio of subgroups. As expected, the early rounds of talks produced no agreement. Through the summer of 1985 both sides were jockeying for diplomatic advantage. Also as expected, the central focus of discussion was strategic defense. Moscow has taken the hard line that an agreement prohibiting defense weapons is a prerequisite to an agreement on offensive weapons. More than that, it has insisted that such an agreement preclude not just the development and deployment of space weapons but research as well. That dubious position will guarantee stalemate because U.S. officials have publicly stated that the American negotiators are under instructions not to accept restrictions on research on SDI.[44] The basic fact is that research per se cannot be monitored or verified, and it has been a long-standing position of the United States not to accept any arms control or disarmament constraint that cannot be verified. Moscow understands this. Soviet arguments to the effect that research (as opposed to development or deployment) violates the ABM treaty are clearly disingenuous. Admittedly, the language of the treaty is vague on the subject, but neither party to the ABM treaty ever considered its provisions to preclude research. Soviet Defense Minister Andrei A. Grechko stated before the Supreme Soviet during the ratification session that the treaty "does not place any limitations on carrying out research and experimental work directed towards solving the problems of defense of the country against nuclear missile attack."[45] In fact, Moscow itself is engaged in an active research program whose spending is roughly comparable to what the Reagan administration seeks from the Congress.

In July, newspaper reports claimed that some Soviet negotiators informally said that Moscow was prepared to accept some SDI research within an arms control agreement. A distinction would be drawn between laboratory and scientific which would be permitted and development and testing which would be prohibited. Although these reports were subsequently denied by Soviet spokesmen, the form of the denial suggested that Soviet authorities were more concerned about the publication of the reports than their validity.[46] At some point the Kremlin is going to have to take a more realistic position on the subject of research.

Conclusion

A central thesis of this paper is that the arms race and efforts to limit it through arms control are today a major determinant of Soviet-American relations. The crisis in Soviet-American relations following the failure of SALT II in 1979 was reflected in the sterility and then collapse of arms control negotiations from 1979 through 1984. During this period, Moscow sought to achieve its objective by means other than through a negotiated agreement. In part, its policies reflected the belief that conditions in Washington were inhospitable toward an agreement because of the commitment of the Reagan administration to a military buildup. In part, the Kremlin was persuaded that domestic pressures in Europe and the United States might achieve its ends without concessions having to be made.

Moscow's arms control diplomacy during the period from 1979 through 1984 was a failure. It failed to stop the deployment of the American Pershing II and ground-launched cruise missiles in Europe. Nor did it succeed in getting the United States to reverse that action by terminating talks in 1983–84. Throughout this period the leadership in the Kremlin was weakened by the infirmities of the incumbents and the struggle for power taking place among the ruling oligarchy. The Kremlin's poor performance in this period almost certainly was linked to the problems of leadership change coupled with intractable difficulties with the economy.

In 1984, Soviet tactics shifted when it agreed to resume arms control talks without preconditions. The one factor most critical in bringing Moscow back to the negotiating table was Reagan's program for strategic defense in space. That and the continued buildup of American offensive strategic forces likely to take place in a second Reagan administration posed for the Soviet leaders the unpalatable prospect that their own massive buildup of the 1970s might be negated, and they could be forced into a ruinous arms race in space.

The Soviet Union is now unequivocally committed to stopping strategic defense. But it remains to be seen how this can be accomplished. Filibustering at the negotiating table or appealing over the heads of negotiators to public opinion will likely be no more successful with SDI than it was with INF. If Moscow is serious about bottling the SDI genie, then it will have to bargain it away. The question is: how much is it prepared to pay? One obvious concession would be in the area of greatest concern to the United States, namely a substantial reduction in the number of Soviet land-based ICBM's. The Kremlin understands this and is prepared to make a deal. In January, 1985, former Foreign Minister Gromyko was asked by a commentator from *Pravda*, "What prospects would be opened with respect to the reduction of strategic arms if an accord is reached on preventing the militarization of space?" He replied:

I would say that the prospects that would open up would be more favorable than they have been up to now. As I have already said, the banning of strategic arms cannot be considered in isolation from space. But if the problems of space are considered from the proper angle and if accords in this field make an appearance, it would be possible to make progress on questions of strategic arms as well.

The Soviet Union is ready not only to consider the problem of strategic arms, it would also be ready *to reduce them sharply.* . . .[47]

However, it is uncertain that the United States will agree to a ban on strategic defense whatever Moscow's concessions or that both sides can agree on an acceptable level or composition of strategic forces. Also, there remains the problem of the balance of intermediate nuclear forces in Europe. So long as Moscow continues to insist that any nuclear weapons based in Europe or in European waters be counted against its own INF forces, they will require a larger SS–20 inventory than is acceptable to NATO. One could list a large number of difficult issues that remain to be resolved via arms control.

Perhaps the most difficult problem facing arms control is the separation that exists between strategic and strictly military issues and Soviet-American political relations. What is notably lacking in current U.S.-Soviet relations is a general incentive to come to some kind of a political settlement with the other. SALT I was possible because it was part of the larger policy of detente. There is no detente today. It may not be possible to separate the nuclear competition of the Soviet Union and the United States from the basic rivalry that motivates both sides as arms control today seeks to do. We began with the observation that the differences over arms control were fundamental to the current Soviet-American antagonism. We may be faced with the paradox that that very antagonism is a major barrier to overcoming the deadlocks in arms control. Certainly the summit meeting in Geneva between Reagan and Gorbachev did little to dissipate that antagonism.

Notes

This article was written at the U.S. Army War College where the author was a visiting faculty member. He wishes to thank the Department of National Security at the War College and its chairman, Col. Keith Barlow for support in the preparation of the original draft.
1. Elizabeth Teague, "Gorbachev Picks Up Where Andropov Left Off," *Radio Liberty*, RL 78/85, March 14, 1985, p. 1.
2. R. V. Burks, "The Coming Crisis in the Soviet Union".

3. *The New York Times*, June 11, 1985, p. A9.
4. See, for example, Leslie Gelb in the *New York Times*, October 26, 1984.
5. For descriptions of the traditional theory of disarmament see Hans J. Morgenthau, Revised by Kenneth W. Thompson, *Politics Among Nations, the Struggle for Power and Peace*, 6th ed. New York, 1985: Alfred A. Knopf, Chapter 23 and Inis Claude, Jr. *Swords Into Plowshares, the Problems and Progress of International Organization*, 4th ed. New York, 1984: Random House, Chapter 13. It is important to note that the traditional theory of disarmament is not applicable to arms control because there are important differences between arms control and disarmament. The latter applies to measures to reduce or eliminate weapons. Arms control refers to measures to stabilize the deterrent relationship between the superpowers and may or may not involve an actual reduction in weapons inventories.
6. For current analyses supporting this argument see William Hyland, "The Gorbachev Succession," *Foreign Affairs*, Spring 1985; Arnold Horlick, "U.S.-Soviet Relations: The Return of Arms Control," *Foreign Affairs*. Vol. 63, No. 3 and Michael R. Gordon, "U.S.-Soviet Arms Control Negotiation: Nuclear and Space Weapons," *AEI Foreign Policy and Defense Review*, Vol. 5, No. 2, 1985.
7. A thorough description of these negotiations within the American government during the first Reagan administration is contained in Strobe Talbott, *Deadly Gambits, the Reagan Administration and the Stalemate in Nuclear Arms Control*, New York: Alfred A. Knopf, 1984. Unfortunately, there is not a comparable expose of Soviet policymaking.
8. For background on the SS–20 see Raymond L. Garthoff, "The Soviet SS–20 Decision," *Survival*, Vol. XXV, No. 3, May/June 1983.
9. Theater missiles are long-range weapons able to strike deep into the territories of the Soviet Union or Western Europe as opposed to "tactical" weapons which are intended for battlefield use. Strategic weapons are intercontinental. For a summary of the debate over NATO nuclear modernization see Joseph L. Nogee and Robert H. Donaldson, *Soviet Foreign Policy Since World War II*, New York: Pergamon Press, 1984, pp. 318–322; Lawrence T. Caldwell, "Soviet Policy in Nuclear Weapons and Arms Control," in Dan Caldwell, ed. *Soviet International Behavior and U.S. Policy Options*, Lexington: D.C. Heath, 1985.
10. *Strategic Survey 1983–1984*, London: International Institute of Strategic Studies, p. 37.
11. *The New York Times*, December 6, 1983, p. A9.
12. The term "launchers" comprises ICBM and SLBM missiles and manned bombers capable of delivering strategic nuclear weapons.
13. *Pravda*, November 25, 1983, p. 1.
14. The Ogarkov, Ustinov and Chernenko statements are from Caldwell, *op. cit.*, pp. 228–229.
15. *Whence the Threat to Peace*, Moscow, 1984, p. 3.
16. See, for example, Strobe Talbott, *op. cit.*, pp. 272, 305–7, 330ff.

17. Quoted in Joseph Nogee, "Soviet Foreign Policy since Brezhnev," in *Soviet Politics, Russia after Brezhnev*, New York: Praeger Publishers, 1985, p. 228.
18. See Arnold Horlick, "U.S.-Soviet Relations: The Return of Arms Control," *Foreign Affairs*, Vol. 63, No. 3, pp. 526–534.
19. *Pravda*, June 30, 1984, p. 1.
20. Additional confirmation of the propagandistic character of the initiative was the fact that the text was made public two hours after delivery of the note by Dobrynin to Shultz.
21. *Pravda*, July 7, 1984.
22. *Pravda*, January 14, 1985, p. 4.
23. *The New York Times*, January 9, 1985.
24. *Pravda*, January 6, 1985, p. 4.
25. *Pravda*, January 14, 1985, pp. 4–5.
26. *The New York Times*, March 8, 1985, p. A14.
27. For a critical look at SDI by American scientists see Union of Concerned Scientists, *The Fallacy of Star Wars*, New York: Vintage, March 1984.
28. See *Radio Liberty*, March 20, 1985.
29. *Current Digest of the Soviet Press*, April 18, 1984, p. 21.
30. See David B. Rivkin, Jr., "What Does Moscow Think?", *Foreign Policy*, No. 59, Summer 1985, p. 86.
31. Quoted in Raymond L. Garthoff, "BMD and East-West Relations, in Ashton B. Carter and David N. Schwartz, eds. *Ballistic Missile Defense*, Washington: The Brookings Institution, 1984, pp. 292–293.
32. Sayre Stevens. "The Soviet BMD Program," in *Ballistic Missile Defense*, pp. 198–200 and Garthoff, *op. cit*, 300.
33. Quoted in Michael Gordon, *op. cit*, p. 38.
34. *Pravda*, June 4, 1985, p. 4.
35. United States Arms Control and Disarmament Agency, *Arms Control and Disarmament Agreements, Texts of Histories and Negotiations*. Washington, 1984, p. 140.
36. *The New York Times*, January 8, 1945.
37. Stevens, *op. cit*, p. 188.
38. Raymond l. Garthoff, *Detente and Confrontation, American-Soviet Relations from Nixon to Reagan*, Washington: the Brookings Institution, 1985, p. 1027; Rivkin, *op. cit*, pp. 95–96.
39. *Pravda*, March 27, 1983, p. 1.
40. *Pravda*, February 2, 1985, p. 1.
41. *Ibid*.
42. Garthoff, "BMD and East-West Relations", p. 326.
43. Genrikh Trofimenko, "Challenges to Global Stability in the 1980s: A Soviet View." in Adam M. Garfinkle, ed. *Global Perspectives on Arms Control*. New York: Praeger, 1984, p. 42. American scientists are skeptical about the possibility of producing software that would be error free. See *New York Times*, July 12, 1985, p. A6.
44. *The New York Times*, January 6, 1985, p. 10.

45. Quoted in Stevens, *op. cit*, p. 209.
46. *The New York Times*, July 9, 1985, pp. A1, A7, and *Ibid*. July 11, 1985, p. A6.
47. *Pravda*, January 14, 1985, pp. 4–5. Underlining added for emphasis. His sentence continued "needless to say, while adhering to the principle of equality and equal security."

3

Soviet Policy with Regard to Revolutionary Movements: Past Experience, Current Costs, and Future Prospects.

OTTO PICK

Almost seven decades after the Russian revolution, the revolutionary blueprint drawn up by Marx remains in the realms of theory. Capitalism has undergone many cyclical economic crises, as he predicted, but it has survived and is moving, though not without difficulty, from the smokestack age into a new postindustrial era. The rise of the welfare state in the West has not only ameliorated the condition of the working class, but it has raised living standards to unprecedented levels. The structural unemployment, which currently afflicts the Western economies poses a set of problems which lie largely outside the Marxist analysis. The Soviet Union has developed in a manner which would have horrified Marx and Engels. Instead of fading away, the state has become omnipotent; a privileged bureaucracy has simply replaced the former ruling classes and nationalism has not been submerged by the spirit of proletarian internationalism.

The "revolutions" in Eastern Europe after the end of the last war were carried out because and with the direct or implied support of Soviet military power. The attempts at Communist revolutions in Germany and Hungary in the aftermath of the First World War failed. Since then, the proletariat of the industrialized countries has largely relegated Communist parties to a minor role. The exceptions are France and Italy, but even here where the Communist parties play a credible role within the structure of liberal-democratic states, their electoral support has been declining.

The monolithic threat of international Communism has become a thing of the past. Many Communist parties in the West have been split into contending factions by the Sino-Soviet dispute and the conflict between Moscow and Peking has, at the same time, provided nonruling parties with an opportunity to increase their ideological independence from the Soviet Union. The last Communist attempt to seize power by revolution in Europe was in Greece in 1944 and in the civil war which dragged on until 1949. But even that revolution was only possible in the aftermath of war, and it certainly did not have the full support of the Soviet Union. It was left to the electoral process many years later to bring a different brand of socialism to power in Athens.

The large Communist parties in France, Italy, Spain and to a lesser extent Portugal have come to behave like ordinary political parties competing for votes and their function as instruments of Leninist revolution has been eroded by economic and social developments unforeseen by Marx and Lenin. They have enthusiastically followed the line laid down by Khrushchev in 1956 that each Communist party should follow its own path towards "socialism." As they try to gain power legally and without violence, they have to be viewed primarily in the context of their own national perspectives because they have to pursue policies attuned to the situation in their respective countries. Some West European Communist parties have distanced themselves from the Soviet position on Czechoslovakia, Poland and Afghanistan, and the Italian and Spanish Communists have explicitly rejected the Leninist model as irrelevant to the contemporary condition of sophisticated Western societies. Indeed, at the 1974 Congress of the Italian Communist Party it was even asserted that adherence to Marxism-Leninism had become optional for its members.

Communist parties in the West pursue their own interests, which may not be at all identical with those of the Soviet Union. They have to produce political programs likely to appeal to their electorates, and the slogan of Leninist revolution does not attract many votes nowadays. Or as Proudhon said: "Universal suffrage is counter-revolution."

This trend was very marked at the international Communist conference held in East Berlin in 1976, where some of the West European comrades spoke up for cooperation and dialogue with "progressive" non-Communist parties and movements—a policy which would have been anathema to Lenin. Indeed, there have been signs of a desire to return to the good old days before Lenin divided the international socialist movement. As a leading Italian Communist has put it more tactfully: "The principal question concerning internationalism in Western Europe today, in my opinion, is whether we shall succeed in bridging the historic gap opened up by the split provoked by the First World War."[1] Perhaps this was what Eurocommunism was all about.

There is some evidence that this approach has now found favor in Moscow. Memories of the Popular Front of the 1930s are very much in the air. The contrast between the decisions of the Seventh Congress of the Comintern in 1935, which were basically dictated by Stalin to serve Soviet security interests, and the largely self-generated attitudes of some West European Communists is, of course, ignored by Soviet commentators. Be that as it may, special attention is being given to courting West European Social Democrats. In May 1985, after Willy Brandt's and Bettino Craxi's visits to Moscow, *Pravda* argued that "the continued development of contacts between the Soviet Communist Party and the Socialist International, and Social Democratic and Socialist parties, in particular with the SPD, is taking on considerable significance."[2] Gorbachev's intention to visit President Mitterrand of France before his meeting with President Reagan was given much publicity in the Soviet media. The fiftieth anniversary of the 1935 Comintern Congress and the proclamation of the Popular Front policy was marked by a feature article in *Pravda*, which drew an analogy between the common struggle of socialists and Communists against Hitler with the "present threat of nuclear cataclysm" which "demands a global response: united action by all those who speak out against the militarists." The paper concludes: "A major role in the defense of peace belongs to the joint actions of Communists and Social democrats."[3]

Blatant Communist fronts, like the World Peace Council whose chairman, Romesh Chandra, proclaimed ten years ago that the WPC "reacts positively to all Soviet initiatives in international affairs"[4] are more willing tools of Soviet policy than Western Communist parties, but they cannot be said to correspond to Lenin's blueprint of a revolutionary elite. The much more broadly based "peace" movements in the West, which played a prominent part in the Soviet attempt to prevent the modernization of NATO's theater nuclear forces and which are likely to figure again in the opposition to President Reagan's Strategic Defense Initiative, are also not the stuff revolutions are made of. They are loose coalitions of sincere pacifists often moved by their religious beliefs, professional protesters and left-wingers of various hues including, of course, Communists. But though their efforts may serve the purposes of the USSR at times, they are not a structured instrument of Soviet policy, and certainly they are not revolutionary movements in the Leninist sense. They have been critical of Soviet actions in Poland and Afghanistan and their activities have had an undesired spillover effect in Eastern Europe, notably in East Germany, where a religiously inspired "peace" movement has developed partly in response to the deployment of Soviet nuclear missiles there.

It has been argued that revolutions do not necessarily have to be violent and that a revolution by stealth is actually taking place before our eyes. The electoral position of Communist parties is said to be irrelevant as Communist influence has penetrated the intellectual climate of the West— academics, journalists and other opinion makers, as well as non-Communist parties of the left and various mass movements, have become the unwitting agents of this process which, in the end, would simply transform Western decision making, relating it more closely to Soviet goals and aspirations. This scenario ignores both the strength of the liberal democratic tradition and the influence of conservative and neoconservative intellectuals in the West. Even if it were to correspond to reality, it certainly would not represent a revolution as Lenin understood the term, although it might play a significant role in helping to create a revolutionary situation.

It is however certain that the prophecies of Marx have been overtaken by the evolution of Western societies.

Lenin, on the other hand, has proved to be a more reliable prophet. It can be argued that the Chinese and Cuban revolutions related in some aspects to Lenin's prediction, quoted below, and that the progress of the ex-colonies to some extent corresponds to his analysis. Mao, for example, also telescoped the bourgeois and socialist revolutions into a single phase: "The Chinese revolution as a whole involves a twofold task. That is to say, it embraces a revolution that is bourgeois-democratic in character and a revolution that is proletarian-socialist in character. It embraces the twofold task of the revolution at both the present and the future stages. The leadership of this twofold revolutionary task rests on the shoulders of the party of the Chinese proletariat, the Chinese Communist Party, for without its leadership no revolution can succeed."[5]

Both at the present time and for the foreseeable future, it would appear that the only prospect for revolution lies in the application of the Leninist theory of national liberation, and that the Third World provides the only possible arena for it.

National Liberation

The Soviet Constitution currently in force states in Article 28 that the goals of Soviet foreign policy include "supporting the struggle of people for national liberation and social progress." The same article also states that the foreign policy of the USSR "is aimed at ensuring international conditions favorable for building Communism in the USSR," and "safeguarding the State interests of the Soviet Union." By definition, therefore, there is no dissonance between the Soviet national interest on one hand and support for national liberation movements on the other—on the contrary, the two goals are complementary in so far as the strengthening of Soviet power also serves the cause of world revolution. There has always been a conceptual and practical overlap between Soviet national interest and the progress of Marxist revolutions and even the experience with China and Yugoslavia has not affected this linkage in the thinking of Soviet decision makers.

Official Soviet foreign policy doctrine relies on the concept of the "correlation of forces," a variation of balance of power theory. The determinist philosophy, developed by Marx and applied by Lenin to international relations, holds that, because of the intrinsic deficiencies of the capitalist system, "socialism" must inevitably emerge as the accepted solution to society's social and economic problems. After the outbreak of the First World War, Lenin argued forcefully that the downfall of capitalism would not be inevitably brought about by internal proletarian revolutions, but could also be effected by the collapse of colonial rule spilling over into the capitalist states and turning the workers there into revolutionaries. In 1919, Lenin claimed that "the socialist revolution will not be solely, or chiefly, a struggle of revolutionary proletarians against their bourgeoisie—no, it will be a struggle of all the imperialist-oppressed colonies and countries, of all dependent countries, against international imperialism . . . the civil war of the working people against the imperialists and exploiters in all the advanced countries is beginning to be combined with national wars against international imperialism."[6]

As it became increasingly clear in 1919–1923 that revolutions in advanced countries would either not take place or would fail because of insufficient support among the proletariat, the emphasis of revolutionary theorizing and Comintern activities shifted more and more towards the colonial struggle against international imperialism. Developments in Asia, and to a lesser extent in Africa, began to assume major significance in the interpretation of the "correlation of forces."

The theory has provided its practitioners with a conceptually flexible tool enabling them to pursue and rationalize their policies simultaneously at the levels of ideology and national interest. Opportunism is built into the concept. If the victory of "socialism" is ultimately inevitable, then the long-term configuration of the correlation of forces is predestined. In the meantime, Soviet policy must accelerate and manage this inexorable process by seizing every available opportunity which can be exploited to some advantage. There have been occasions when this opportunism appears to have collided with ideological precepts, but as all policies are regarded as a means towards a defined end, they can always be justified.

Soviet policy in Africa, Asia and Latin America has fitted in with this pattern with a considerable degree of consistency. Indeed, the Third World has offered an almost ideal opportunity for combining the pursuit of national interest with the teachings of revolutionary theory. At the 1920 Congress of the Comintern, Lenin stressed the links between the revolutionary struggle of the proletariat and the fate of the colonial peoples. "It is unquestionable that the proletariat of the advanced countries can and should give help to the working masses of the backward countries, and that the backward countries can emerge from their present stage of development when the victorious proletariat of the Soviet Republics extends a helping hand to these masses and is in a position to give them support." He went on to apply the experience of Russia's "single-phase" revolution to the colonial areas—what had been done in Russia, could be achieved there:

> Not only should we create independent contingents of fighters and party organisations in the colonies and the backward countries, not only at once launch propaganda for the organisation of peasants' Soviets and strive to adapt them to pre-capitalist conditions, but the Communist International should advance the proposition with the appropriate theoretical grounding, that with the aid of the proletariat of the advanced countries, backward countries can go over to the Soviet system and, through certain stages of development, to communism, without having to pass through the capitalist stage.[7]

In fact, Lenin laid here the ideological foundations for the Chinese, Vietnamese and Cuban revolutions. During the years of Stalin's dictatorship, this aspect of revolutionary activity was pushed into the background, as the policy of "socialism in one country," which had to be pursued in the interests of industrialization and Soviet security, led to a Soviet form of isolationism, which really precluded the international Communist movement from undertaking more than token schemes of revolutionary activity in the colonial territories. The Stalinist emphasis on the orthodox Marxist progression towards socialism, i.e., by way of capitalist-induced industrialization, really placed national liberation into cold storage—a situation, which served Stalin's purpose at the time. The Soviet Union returned to this revolutionary task only after his death, when it had become obvious to his successors that the policy of containment, reinforced by nuclear deterrence, had thrown up an insurmountable barrier in Europe. Opportunities to adjust the correlation of forces had to be sought elsewhere.

In Soviet national liberation theory, the process proceeds roughly in two stages. The first stage consists of the beginnings of the struggle against the colonialist oppressors. The fight of the colonial peoples begins to converge with the revolutionary movement of the working class in industrialized societies, which has either already achieved the overthrow of the capitalist system or whose efforts in that direction are reinforced by the anticolonial battle. At this stage, it is accepted that in the absence of an industrial proletariat in the backward countries, the national liberation movement must be led by a nationalist middle class, which, in these special conditions, can only be regarded as being progressive. As Lenin put it, with some reservations:

> It is beyond doubt that any national movement can only be a bourgeois-democratic movement, since the overwhelming mass of the population in the backward countries consist of peasants who represent bourgeois-capitalist relationships. It would be utopian to believe that proletarian parties in these backward countries, if indeed they can emerge in them, can pursue communist tactics and a communist policy, without establishing definite relations with the peasant movement. . . . [w]e, as Communists, should and will support bourgeois-liberation movements in the colonies only when they are genuinely revolutionary, and when their exponents do not hinder our work of educating and organising in a revolutionary spirit the peasantry and the masses of the exploited.[8]

Or as he told the Second Congress of Communist Organizations of the East more bluntly in 1919:

> You will have to base yourselves on the bourgeois nationalism which is awakening, and must awaken, among those peoples, and which has its historical justification. At the same time, you must find your way to the working and exploited masses of every country and tell them in a language they understand that their only hope of emancipation lies in the victory of the international revolution, and that the international proletariat is the only ally of all the hundreds of millions of the working and exploited peoples of the East.[9]

After 1956, the USSR applied these principles with determination and vigor, causing some Western observers to interpret support for "bourgeois" elements, like Nkrumah in Ghana or Nasser in Egypt, as evidence that under Khrushchev the Soviet Union had abandoned ideological doctrine as a guide to policy. Nothing could have been further removed from the truth. Both the role allotted to the national bourgeoisie by Lenin and the opportunism implied by the theory of correlation of forces led directly to the policies followed by Stalin's successors. Indeed, the post-1917 record is equally pragmatic: in its early days the Soviet state was quite prepared to support nonproletarian nationalists like Amanullah in Afghanistan, Kemal Atatürk in Turkey, or Chiang Kai-shek in China.

The second stage in the process of national liberation is reached when the colonial regimes have been overthrown and when the liberated colonial peoples proceed to socialize their societies and ultimately merge with the world socialist camp. The experience of the USSR itself is quoted to support the validity of this thesis. The victory of the 1917 revolution in Russia helped the colonial peoples of Central Asia to achieve their national liberation and ultimately to become part of the socialist Soviet Union.

However, the postwar experience has shown that decolonization by itself is not the end of the struggle. Nominal political independence is not enough. The capitalists have simply changed their methods of oppression and exploitation, and, according to the Soviets, only socialism offers a long-term, viable alternative to neocolonialism. At the XXV Congress of the Soviet Communist Party in 1976, Brezhnev described the national liberation movement as part of the international class struggle. Addressing a plenary meeting of the Central Committee in April, 1985, Mikhail Gorbachev said: "The exploitation of the countries of the newly liberated world is being intensified and the process of their economic decolonization blocked."[10] Immediately after his election as General Secretary, on 11 March, 1985, Gorbachev delivered his first policy statement to the Central Committee, stressing, *inter alia*, that "The Soviet Union has always supported the struggle of peoples for liberation from colonial oppression. And today, our sympathies go out to the countries of Asia, Africa and Latin America which are following the road of consolidating independence and social renovation. For us, they are friends and partners in the struggle for a durable peace, for better and just relations between peoples."[11]

There is another aspect to the Soviet relationship with the developing countries, of which, however, less has been heard in recent years. The problematic performance of the Soviet economy and the consequent constraints on Soviet economic aid have cast a shadow over the claim that the Soviet Union represents a uniquely valid model of economic development. The Soviet argument is that since 1917 the USSR has raised itself from being an underdeveloped country to the status of an industrialized superpower by transforming the economic and social character of its society. The developing countries could do the same by following its example, especially as now they can count on the support of the socialist camp. However, the nature and extent of this support raises problems.

Economic Policy

"Even if the USSR were to double or treble its trade with the Third World every five years, it would be 1990 before this would show any significant change in the percentage of world trade among major groups."[12] Between 1955 and 1980, Soviet economic aid to Third World countries, excluding the client states of Cuba, North Korea and Vietnam, amounted to just under $20 billion, with another $9.8 billion coming from the other East European countries.[13] From 1945 to 1979, U.S. aid totalled over $107 billion.[14] Soviet bloc trade accounts for about eight percent of LDC turnover.

These are the key facts concerning Soviet economic relations with the Third World and the magnitude of the economic drive behind Soviet policies there. The state of the Soviet economy has continually limited the scope of Soviet economic support to less developed countries. This has inevitably led to a policy of concentration on specially selected target areas, either because they are Communist client states, like Cuba, Mongolia, Afghanistan, Ethiopia or Vietnam, or because they offer especially favorable opportunities for the future.

Apart from support for North Korea, the first major step was a six million dollar loan to Afghanistan in 1954, the year which marked the beginning of a reinvigorated Soviet interest in the potential of the Third World. By 1983, turnover of aid and trade between the members of the Warsaw Pact and developing countries had grown to a mere $40 billion.[15] The statistics do not include subsidies provided by means of special pricing agreements concluded within the Council for Mutual Economic Aid (CMEA) providing, in the past, for cheap energy supplies for Cuba, Vietnam and Mongolia, and artificially high prices for Cuban sugar and nickel.

Soviet bloc aid programs are marked by very specific characteristics. On the whole, they are almost entirely conducted on a bilateral basis, although some eight years ago a vocal group of younger Soviet economists tried to project a different approach. They based their recommendations on the recognition of the global character of the world economy, having jettisoned Stalin's concept of two separate economic systems with its implied intention of incorporating the Third World into the socialist camp in a fully economic context. Experts like L. A. Fridman, G. Mirsky and Academician A. M. Rumyantsev argued that Soviet policies should be founded on purely economic self-interest, and relations with the less developed countries should be aligned within a global framework, which would take the capitalist world's policies and interests into account in a reasonably objective manner. The new pattern of aid policy would also include joint enterprises with the LDCs and even specific project cooperation with capitalist countries. The theoretical debate arising from these proposals went on for some time, but, apart from taking steps towards a greater degree of multilateralism within CMEA, these proposals seem to have had little impact on actual policies.[16] Bilateral aid is still the predominant mode adopted by the Soviet bloc; specially favoured recipients are given grant aid, i.e., grants and loans on specially favorable terms and long-term credit, and the political motivation continues to play a significant role, as in the case of India, where the USSR is determined to maintain and extend its influence. Trade and arms sales, however, are also used to earn hard currencies whenever possible.

By contrast, Western aid patterns are very different. About a third of OECD development assistance is provided multilaterally. It is difficult to compare Soviet disbursements to developing countries with Western practice, because the yardsticks of definition are not the same. For example, preferential pricing agreements within CMEA represent a special case, which does not fit in with generally accepted international statistical criteria. In 1983, net Soviet aid ($2.6 billion) to developing countries amounted to less than one tenth of that provided by OECD countries. In terms of GDP, the USSR disbursed 0.21 percent of GDP to developing countries, including its Marxist clients, as against 0.36 percent for the OECD.[17]

Furthermore, Soviet "aid" consists largely of weapons deliveries which, unlike the West, the USSR can usually supply from stock. About 40 percent of Soviet exports to the Third World is made up of arms. Although the motivation here is mainly political, concentration on Middle East recipients produces welcome hard-currency returns,[18] and, with some exceptions, Soviet credit terms for arms purchases have become less advantageous since 1974. Soviet client states—Angola, Afghanistan, Ethiopia, Vietnam and Cuba—have had to be reequipped, and since 1980 Nicaragua has been added to the list. Many developing countries depend exclusively on Soviet bloc arms supplies, with obvious political consequences. The presence of large numbers of Soviet military advisers in Third World countries and of trainees from states buying Soviet equipment in the USSR is also significant in the political context.

The balance sheet of Soviet bloc economic relations with the Third World is by no means entirely one-sided, even if the political gains are discounted. In some cases, particularly from arms sales, there are hard currency returns, as has already been pointed out. Eastern Europe is also able to dispose of manufactured goods which cannot find a ready market elsewhere and it obtains access to relatively cheap sources of raw materials. It is obvious, that Soviet bloc aid policies amount to much more than investment in revolution and support for "revolutionary" regimes. Apart from hard economic advantage, the principal goal is to achieve levels of political influence in areas of interest to a global superpower—a policy more easily understood in terms of power politics than of revolutionary rhetoric. The ideological emphasis may be useful as a rationalization of policies, which may not be popular with the comparatively hard-pressed consumer in the USSR and in Eastern Europe. It may also represent an almost Pavlovian reaction on the part of the Soviet leadership. It cannot, however, obscure the prime significance of the power-political factor. In this connection, the mounting emphasis on Soviet bloc military "aid" and the large presence of Soviet and Cuban military personnel in many parts of the Third World represents a potentially destabilizing influence, and provides further cause for concern. And again, aid recipients have to pay the expenses and salaries of Soviet aid personnel in hard currencies.

However, as is evident from a comparison of Western and Soviet bloc aid disbursements, the USSR suffers a major constraint upon its ability to deploy economic resources in the Third World—the state of its own economy. Help to revolutionary movements abroad is not really affected by this, as the totals are relatively insignificant and the USSR can fulfil its role as patron by dispensing arms, of which it has more than enough. Here the restraints are of a purely political rather than an economic nature.

The Military Factor[19]

In contrast to its economic debility, the USSR now disposes of great military power. After decades of theorizing about national liberation and Leninist revolution, the Soviet Union has acquired the means of lending its practical and physical support to revolutionary movements and regimes in other continents. The achievement of nuclear parity with the United States has also released conventional capabilities for use as instruments of foreign policy outside the direct area of East-West confrontation. The use of military power, as in the Horn of Africa in 1977–78, serves to transform the correlation of forces and can also support the extension of ideological influence.

The most visible aspect of the expansion of the Soviet Union's global reach has been the growth of Soviet naval power and the increase in its airlift capacity. Admiral Gorshkov, whose has stood at the head of the Soviet navy for a quarter of a century, is a convinced advocate of the peacetime use of naval power to extend the state's political influence and to increase its freedom of action.[20] The buildup of the Soviet merchant marine, fishing fleet and oceanographic capabilities has added to the USSR's ability to project its presence in distant waters and, incidentally, to reinforce its military operations. It is of course true that the naval power of the United States continues to outmatch that of the Soviet Union, but it is the USSR which has, on the whole, shown greater willingness to apply military force as an instrument of policy. The reinforcement of the Ethiopian armed forces in 1978 and the invasion of Afghanistan have demonstrated this quite clearly. The U.S. appears to be still inhibited by the experience of Vietnam, for with the exception of the minor operation in Grenada, there has been a marked reluctance in Washington to indulge in gunboat diplomacy, despite the assertive rhetoric practised by the Reagan administration. Furthermore, the USSR has been able to move quickly, with no prior warning. Although in Afghanistan the military calculation seems to have gone wrong, the operation in the Horn of Africa was almost a textbook example of effective planning and logistics.

Again with the exception of Grenada, the USSR has made plain its determination and ability to support distant regimes, which claim to be sympathetic to its ideological principles. Support for the Sandinistas in Nicaragua, the lavish subsidies granted to Castro's Cuba, the intervention on behalf of Mengistu in Ethiopia, Soviet and Cuban actions in Angola and even the invasion of Afghanistan are seen by Third World elites sympathetic to the Soviet Union as proof of the USSR's commitment to defend and support its friends, in sharp contrast to the fate suffered by the late Shah of Iran, Emperor Haile Selassie, and even Somoza in Nicaragua and Batista in Cuba. On the other side of the ledger, there is the irrelevant British operation in the Falkland Islands, U.S. intervention in Grenada and Chinese action in Cambodia.

However, from the Soviet point of view, a more significant factor has emerged in the shape of "national liberation" movements directed against Marxist regimes, which enjoy the support of the USSR. While so far no Marxist regime has been overthrown by a guerrilla campaign, the panoply of superpower weaponry, which the USSR has acquired, is of little use in these kinds of situations. This, at least, has been the American experience. In June 1985, representatives of the Nicaraguan contras, the Afghan mujaheddin and the Laotian tribes opposed to Communist rule journeyed to Jamba, the stronghold of Dr. Savimbi's UNITA movement, which has been fighting the Angolan government for more than ten years, for a conference of movements struggling against "Soviet colonialism." The Jamba meeting[21] could not issue a ringing declaration denouncing Communism as such, because the insurgents in Laos and Afghanistan rely to some extent on Chinese support. UNITA and the Afghan mujaheddin represent the most serious challenge to the regimes they oppose. Savimbi has maintained control of large parts of Angola for many years. His forces have captured East European experts and technicians engaged in Soviet bloc aid programs in Angola, and East European governments have had to negotiate with his movement to obtain the release of their nationals. In Afghanistan, the rebels have held their own in a direct confrontation with Soviet military power with some success. While Soviet propaganda tries to explain these facts by reference to traitorous movements supported and kept going by American imperialism and South African racism, they represent a novel and serious challenge not only to Soviet power, but also to Leninist ideology. If, as Lenin and his successors have argued, the peoples of the "backward" countries want nothing better than to be given the chance to start out on the road to "socialism" with the support of the fraternal Soviet Union, why do so many of them turn against the "national liberation" movements.

Cuba, the Caribbean and Latin America[22]

Cuba is often regarded as an almost classic case of Soviet investment in revolution. Soviet subsidies to Castro, including free arms supplies, are said to amount to well over $4 billion a year.[23] However, the Cuban revolution was more a typical Latin American *coup de main* than a realization of Lenin's blueprint. When Castro descended from the mountains in 1959 to oust Batista, his movement appeared to be a characteristic Latin American insurrection, compounded of the usual mixture of justified social discontent and dislike of North America. This dislike derived from identification of the U.S. with the corrupt and oppressive regime currently in power, reinforced by the customary degree of intellectual frustration and simple machismo. There was little trace of any ideological commitment to Marxism-Leninism or even to the concepts of Leninist liberation theory. Castro's public declaration that he was a Marxist came in 1961, long after he had won control over Cuba. He may, of course, have become sincerely confirmed in his ideological profession, but in many ways this conversion is typical of the motivation of other self-proclaimed Third World Marxists. To be a Marxist represents a bid for Soviet support. In many cases these so-called Marxists have little understanding of what is, after all, a complex ideological structure based on essentially European experiences. To someone like Mengistu in Ethiopia, who might have some difficulty with the dialectic or the theory of surplus value, it also offers a useful rationalization of relentless totalitarianism. While this is not necessarily true of Fidel Castro, his adoption of Marxism must have been influenced by the the deterioration of Cuba's relations with the U.S.; in 1960 he could turn towards the USSR to avoid isolation.

In 1960, the USSR obviously welcomed the opportunity for establishing a foothold in the western hemisphere. Yet, with the exception of Khrushchev's reckless missile adventure in 1962, the USSR proceeded with considerable caution in Latin America, partly because of resource constraints, but mainly because it recognized the exceptional sensitivity of the area from the American point of view. This analysis was amply confirmed by President Kennedy's reactions and actions during the Cuban missile crisis of 1962.

Latin America has only recently moved to the forefront of Soviet concerns. Between 1918 and 1950, 17 Communist parties were established in the region, but they were divided by factional disputes and attracted little attention and few members. The First Congress of Latin American Communists took place in Buenos Aires in June 1929, and the South American section of the Comintern was set up in the same year. At this time, the USSR was simply concerned to win the allegiance of South American Communists and incorporate them in the Third International. The reorientation of Soviet policy towards the Third World after 1956 led to a more structured approach to Latin American issues. The Latin American Institute of the Soviet Academy of Sciences was established in 1961, and in 1969 it began publication of the journal *Latinskaya Amerika*, which has become one of the main sources of information about Soviet attitudes toward this region. Nevertheless, Soviet policy in Latin America in the 1960s proceeded with its customary caution, although in deference to Castro, guerrilla actions in certain specified countries were endorsed, and in 1965 the Venezuelan police captured two Soviet couriers carrying cash for the leftist guerrillas in the country.[24] Generally, Moscow tried to restrain Castro's enthusiasm for exporting his revolution, fearing perhaps that encouragement of violently revolutionary movements in the western hemisphere might prejudice the process of detente. The USSR was clearly unhappy with the resolutions of the 1965 Tri-Continental Conference held in Havana, which declared its support for revolutionary movements in Latin America. Ché Guevara's abortive foray into Bolivia in 1967 received no encouragement from Moscow. The differences with Cuba came to a head in 1968, when the USSR used its position as Cuba's only source of oil to persuade Castro to moderate some of his policies. In November, 1968, *Pravda* complained about "anti-Marxist groups of adventurists" in South America whose platform had "nothing in common with Communism and coincides completely with the platform of Trotskyite groups." The Soviet Party newspaper went on to complain that these ultraleftist groups had "completely discarded" Marxist-Leninist theory in their belief that "armed struggle can be called into being artificially any time in any country, regardless of conditions."[25] In fact, *Pravda* had put its finger on one of the main problems facing the Soviets in South America. Castro's "revolution for export" does not correspond with any degree of precision to the Marxist-Leninist blueprint. He has been remarkably eclectic in his choice of causes to sustain, perhaps regarding revolutionary activity as a military operation, deserving support provided it conformed with vaguely "anti-imperialist" criteria. Reading some of Castro's speeches, one feels that he has an almost emotional compulsion to extend the success of the Cuban revolution to other spheres. In the 1960s, Cuba supported Ben Bella in Algeria, Nkrumah in Ghana and various regimes in the Congo, as a prelude to its subsequent major involvement in Africa.

In retrospect, the *Pravda* article quoted above was strikingly prophetic about the evolution of revolutionary movements in Latin America. Generally, the Latin American revolutionary tradition offers little ideological comfort to Moscow, although it, of course, affects the correlation of forces in the area to the disadvantage of the United States. In most cases, revolutionary movements in Latin America, though they may include Marxists, are not led by copybook Communist parties and some of the ultraleftists, who lead them, have long ago outpaced the Marxist-Leninist model. Intellectually they owe much more to the dependency theories of Galtung and his South American disciples[26], whose analysis of the economic dependence of nonindustrial societies on industrialized states as the prime cause of their unfavorable condition can, in fact, be applied to Cuba's relationship with the USSR. In their book, dependency is brought about *inter alia* by reliance on exports of primary products (frequently single crops like Cuban sugar) to a predetermined market, dependence on foreign capital for development and the tendency of indigenous elites to act as proxies for the dominant foreign power.

After 1973, Soviet policy underwent a change and moved closer to Castro's ideas. The seminal event, which brought this about, was the fall of the Allende government in Chile. The electoral victory of the Popular Unity Coalition, led by Salvador Allende in 1970 appeared to support the then prevailing Soviet view that socialism in South America could be brought about by peaceful, legal means, somewhat in consonance with the views expressed by Khrushchev at the XX CPSU Congress in 1956. The Allende victory was certainly interpreted in this manner at the XXIV CPSU Congress in 1971. After the violent overthrow of Allende by a reactionary military putsch in 1973, Moscow was forced to reassess its position.[27] It also became increasingly obvious that far from leading to the establishment of socialist regimes, left-wing violence merely served to unleash a right-wing backlash, bringing extremist dictatorships to power. The experience of Uruguay was a case in point.[28]

Furthermore, for the Soviets nothing succeeds like success, and Castro had certainly showed his capacity for achieving success. He had survived in the teeth of U.S. hostility, and he had begun to play a very significant part in the nonaligned movement. It is debatable whether Cuba's move into Angola was the result of a largely Cuban decision or whether it arose from a Soviet initiative. The massive buildup of Cuban forces in Africa and their introduction into Ethiopia certainly depended not only on Soviet agreement with Cuban policies, but on concrete Soviet logistics support. Generally, Castro's role has led to new thinking about the uses to which client states could be put in the Third World in support of Soviet policy goals.[29]

Yet opportunism has continued to be the dominant feature of Soviet policy in Latin America. In South America, the USSR has maintained its habitual caution, preferring to extend its influence by developing diplomatic and economic links. Thus, for example, it gave diplomatic support to the Argentinian junta during the Falklands crisis, though it stopped short of using the Soviet veto in the UN Security Council on Argentina's behalf. The right-wing character of the Galtieri regime did not inhibit this policy, especially as Argentina must be regarded as a major source of grain supplies should the need arise. The main thrust of the new policy came in Central America as opportunities there were opened up by local conditions and American incompetence.

In El Salvador, the U.S. decision to back the centrist Duarte against extremists of the right and left limited some of the damage. However, as the situation in Central America as a whole continues to be extremely volatile, mainly because of the potential crisis over Nicaragua, nominal support for the left-wing guerrillas opposed to the Duarte government has become a matter of course for the USSR. Practical assistance from Cuba and Nicaragua to the guerrillas in El Salvador has been provided, but it would appear that Duarte probably faces a more dangerous challenge from the right than from the left.

The major battleground lies in Nicaragua. There the revolution has enjoyed Cuban support from the very beginning. Although there are superficial similarities between the two revolutions, there are some fundamental differences. The Nicaraguan revolution seems to have been much more broadly based than Castro's insurrection. The Somoza regime was much more corrupt and rapacious than Batista's rule in Cuba, and seems to have united many more people in opposition to its excesses. The original revolutionary movement in Nicaragua covered a wide political spectrum, although as the Sandinista Marxists began to push policies increasingly to the left, the initial revolutionary consensus became eroded. The contras, who have gone to war against the government in Managua, now contain many supporters of the original revolution as well as men who had been linked to Somoza. Nevertheless, a "national liberation" movement, which includes Roman Catholic priests among its leaders, makes a strange bedfellow for Castro and the Kremlin. It would be fascinating to know what Lenin would have made of liberation theology. He would have probably classed its proponents as members of the "progressive" national bourgeoisie.

On the other hand, in two essentials the Nicaraguan revolution ran parallel to that in Cuba. It stemmed from a widespread revulsion against an inefficient, blatantly corrupt and oppressive regime, and it quickly adopted an anti-American position. The miniscule Nicaraguan Communist Party had played no significant part in the Sandinista revolution, and the anti-Americanism displayed in Managua therefore soon assumed the character of a populist and indeed popular trend. Washington's intransigence, especially after Reagan's arrival in the White House, only made matters worse. Castro had assisted the revolution in Nicaragua from the very outset, and from 1980 onwards the Soviet Union began to deploy its resources on behalf of the Sandinistas. The Soviet attitude to armed action veered towards that held by Castro. In March 1980, S. A. Mikoyan, the editor of *Latinskaya America*, wrote: "up to now only the armed path has led to revolutionary victory in Latin America."[30] The Sandinistas, in their turn, proclaimed their intention to transform their movement into a revolutionary party of the Leninist type, though nothing was said about the role allocated in this evolution to the Nicaraguan Communist Party. Soviet aid to Nicaragua began to increase from 1981 onwards and included grain shipments, which the USSR itself had to import. Aid agreements with several East European countries followed. East German and Cuban specialists were enlisted to train the Nicaraguan police, and by 1982 the presence of Soviet military advisers was reported. Considerable quantities of Soviet military equipment were shipped to Nicaragua, mainly through Cuba. In other words, the USSR appears to have made a full commitment to the Nicaraguan revolution, despite, or possibly because of the Reagan administration's obvious determination to destabilize the Managua regime, if only because of the assistance it gives to the left-wing guerrillas in neighboring El Salvador. It would certainly appear that Nicaragua is being used by the USSR and Cuba to transship material aid to the guerrillas in El Salvador, whose intention to pursue the course of armed revolution was firmly endorsed by the Salvadorian Communist Party as early as 1980.

The policy of supporting armed uprisings in Central America, while continuing to rely on more peaceful methods of extending Soviet influence in Latin America, has survived the recent change in leadership in Moscow. The head of the Nicaraguan revolutionary junta, Daniel Ortega, was received by Gorbachev in April 1985. A new loan to Nicaragua was agreed upon and the Soviet Union promised to meet most of Nicaragua's oil requirements following the imposition of U.S. sanctions.

The Soviet position on Central America can, of course, be interpreted simply in terms of the theory of the correlation of forces. Opportunities for action presented themselves and were used. The advantages to the Soviet Union, which would derive from a reversal of the status quo in the area are obvious. The proximity to the United States and the extent of American investments in Central America make it a manifest target. In case of war, the Caribbean basin would be a major transit area for U.S. shipments to Europe, and finally continuing problems on America's doorstep would distract American attention from Europe and could easily add to the differences between the U.S. and its NATO allies.[31]

On the other hand, the balance sheet of Cuba's and the Soviet Union's intervention in Grenada has been entirely negative. Grenada, insignificant as it may be, provides a well-documented example[32] of a revolutionary situation which has gone wrong, because of internal dissensions within the revolutionary movement, which ran out of control, and ultimately because of U.S. military intervention. The correlation of forces may not have been strongly affected by the change which occurred on an island of 344 square kilometres, inhabited by just over 100,000 people, but the psychological impact of the American action was considerable at the time. Grenada provides the outstanding example of a Soviet failure to sustain and save its clients, perhaps because they were intent on murdering each other. While factional quarrels are endemic within Latin American revolutionary movements, military action by the United States, such as it took in Grenada, could hardly be applied elsewhere in Central America or the Caribbean without major international repercussions simply because it would take longer, cause much greater bloodshed and Congress would not permit it.

In its clearly Marxist orientation from the very beginning and in its aping of the structures and usages of ruling East European Communist parties, the New Jewel Movement in Grenada was certainly not typical of revolutionary movements in Latin America. Furthermore, Grenada cannot be taken as representative of developments in Latin America. As a former British colony, it shares with many of the other Caribbean territories a political culture and colonial inheritance which differs fundamentally from the Latin American tradition. Poverty is distributed more equally than was the case, for example, in Nicaragua, militarism is unknown and the interaction between the churches and society is on a very different level. In one respect, there was a similarity between the situation in Grenada and other Central American territories: the revolution was provoked by and directed against an almost irrationally corrupt and dictatorial regime. The overthrow of the Gairy regime in 1979 followed an established pattern. However, the goals of the revolutionary New Jewel Movement were defined quite clearly. In September 1982, Maurice Bishop, the leader of the NJM, declared that its aim was to "ensure the leading role of the working class through its Marxist-Leninist Party backed by some form of the dictatorship of the proletariat."[33] Bishop's personal friendship with Castro was reinforced by overt and covert formal links with Cuba and the USSR. Quantities of Soviet bloc weapons out of all proportion to the island's size or normal needs were shipped to Grenada. The Grenadian leadership was keen to export its revolution to neighboring islands, partly believing that success in this respect would raise its status in the eyes of its Soviet allies. The course of Grenada's policy was established very firmly by Maurice Bishop, and his fall and death at the hands of his comrades in the autumn of 1983 was caused not only by conflict of personal ambitions, but also by disputes over policy within the NJM. There is no evidence that he had lost the confidence of the Russians or the Cubans—on the contrary, Castro was quick to express his condemnation of events in Grenada. What makes the Grenada experience interesting is the determination of this small group of revolutionaries to turn their tiny country into a Leninist outpost in a very sensitive area and the encouragement which they received from Cuba, and more surprisingly from the USSR. The documents captured by the Americans after their invasion of Grenada provide a unique insight into the *modus operandi* of a somewhat megalomaniac "national liberation" movement, its Cuban sponsors and its Soviet allies. The available material, however, adds little that would affect the bases of analyzing Soviet behavior patterns with regard to the western hemisphere in particular and the Third World in general.

Africa

Postcolonial conditions in Africa south of the Sahara did not reflect any of the major prerequisites for the application of national liberation theory, except that in some areas the anticolonial movement was led by representatives of a "national bourgeoisie." But even this middle class lacked an economic base, except in Nigeria and Ghana, and it had strong cultural ties with the metropolitan power. The landless peasantry, which should have provided the revolutionary mass, did not exist. The successor states to the colonial empires based their frontiers and claim to sovereignty on the territorial arrangements made by the European powers at the end of the nineteenth century, and were thus largely artificial creations. Their frontiers cut across tribes and even divided villages. The new rulers were therefore faced with the task of establishing national identities in the territories they controlled. They had little use for Leninist theory in this context. Their chosen instruments were extreme nationalism, tinged with antiwhite racial feeling, and personal charisma, which enabled them to usurp the traditional role of the chief in African society.

In the 1960s, the rallying point for the new countries south of the Sahara was opposition to the apartheid policy pursued in the Republic of South Africa and hostility to Portuguese colonialism. South Africa, the only country which has a large black industrial proletariat, contains some of the elements required to create a revolutionary situation in the Marxist sense, but even here the issue is greatly complicated by questions of race, on which neither Marx nor Lenin had much to say.

The relationship of the former colonies to the West was ambiguous. Despite cultural and economic ties with the former colonial powers, there was in many cases strong anti-Western feeling, accentuated by the economic dependence of these countries on their former masters and on the multinationals. It was in this area that the Soviet Union sought, and in some cases found, an entry point. Yet in many respects the foreign policy of the new African states developed in ways with which the USSR had some difficulty. The East-West confrontation was regarded by them as largely irrelevant to their own situation, although they were not averse to playing both sides against the middle in order to obtain economic advantages. The Organization of African States (OAU) was conceived as an agency to protect the status quo. It has consistently, though with little success, condemned all policies aiming at subverting existing regimes and it is a staunch defender of the established frontiers between states in Africa, which have been inherited from colonial days.

As the dust of decolonization began to settle, the "democratic" constitutions drafted by the former colonial powers began to collapse all over Africa. They were replaced by more or less benevolent despotisms, and in some deplorable instances by personal dictatorships of the worst kind. The Soviet Union was left with the option of fishing in troubled waters. It tried to do so in the Congo in 1960, but could not save Patrice Lumumba from his tragic fate. "National-bourgeois" regimes, which had enjoyed Soviet support included Guinea, but this did not stop Sekou Touré from expelling a Soviet ambassador who had meddled too openly in the country's affairs, and Ghana and Mali, where the Soviet Union could not prevent the overthrow of its friends, Nkrumah and Keita, by military regimes in the mid-1960s.

The emergence of military regimes in many parts of Africa south of the Sahara has presented the USSR with a new set of problems. They all claim to be anti-imperialist, whatever that may mean to them. They are basically of three types: the bloody personal dictatorship of men like Idi Amin in Uganda, which embarrasses all those connected with it; groups of officers who have grown impatient with the inefficiency and corruption of civilian governments and who genuinely try to improve things before becoming corrupt themselves; and soldiers, who claim to be Marxist-Leninists because this represents a bid for Soviet support and lends some credibility to their regimes. The dividing lines between these three types of military government are flexible and ambiguous, but in all cases the officers emerge as the arbiters of national policy mainly because the armed forces are in some instances the only organized power structure capable of translating policy into action. These men do not fit any of the categories devised by Lenin. Only states, like Tanzania or Zambia, which abandoned the Westminster model early on in favor of establishing one-party states, have managed to find alternative solutions. The introduction of single-party systems, however, contributed to the radicalization of African politics.

The USSR has had to come to terms with its self-styled friends. The emergence of a group of states claiming to be revolutionary in the Leninist sense, and in some cases even moving to form a "vanguard" party on the Leninist pattern, has provided not only opportunities for Soviet intervention, but also the somewhat loosely interpreted need for ideological commitment. The turning point came in 1974, with the collapse of Portuguese colonial rule and the overthrow of Haile Selassie in Ethiopia. The long struggle against the Portuguese had inevitably radicalized the national liberation movements in Angola and Mozambique. In Angola, the Soviet-backed MPLA faced a twofold challenge from groups which had participated in the war against the Portuguese—the FLNA, supported by China, and UNITA. From 1975 onwards, the USSR became the MPLA's main source of weapons to counter U.S. and Chinese support for UNITA and the FLNA, respectively. Since then, the Cuban military intervention in Angola, undertaken with full Soviet support, has succeeded in maintaining the MPLA in Luanda and parts of the country, although about a third of the country is controlled by UNITA. The FLNA has faded away. Its allegedly socialist character as a vanguard party has not prevented the MPLA regime from entering into business arrangements with capitalist enterprises like Gulf Oil, probably using its revenue income from these sources to pay for the Cuban soldiers on whom its survival depends.[34]

The Angolan developments highlighted Sino-Soviet rivalry in Africa, but this has by no means been confined to Angola. In the Nigerian civil war, the USSR joined Britain in backing the central government, while China supported the secessionist Biafran regime. In Rhodesia, now Zimbabwe, the Chinese for once backed a winner by aligning behind Robert Mugabe, while the USSR maintained links with his more senior, but much less Marxist rival, Joshua Nkomo. In the event, Mugabe won Zimbabwe's first elections, and in the early months of his rule displayed marked coolness towards the USSR.

The situation in the Horn of Africa was much more complex. Moscow sees the extension of its influence here as beneficial from a purely strategic viewpoint, as the expansion of Soviet naval activities in the Indian Ocean turned the Red Sea into a strategically significant area. The initial points of penetration were Aden and Somalia. When the former British colony of Aden achieved independence as the People's Democratic Republic of Yemen, the dominant National Liberation Front began to introduce the trappings of a "socialist" state; it had to rely on economic aid from some of the Arab oil states and from the Communist countries. Major Soviet interest in South Yemen developed in the mid-1970s, after the reopening of the Suez Canal. In 1976, the USSR overtook China as a provider of economic aid to the Aden regime; Soviet assistance was again increased after the crisis in the Horn of Africa and the installation of a firmly pro-Soviet leadership in Aden.[35] The PDRY has remained loyal to its ties with the Soviet Union.

The relationship with Somalia developed much less smoothly. Following a military coup in 1969, General Siad Barre came to power with a strong commitment to pursue Somalia's irredentist claims against Kenya and Ethiopia, by force if necessary. His attempts to obtain weapons from the West, notably from the United States, failed because the U.S. was at that time firmly committed to Emperor Haile Selassie of Ethiopia and because the West certainly had no desire to increase the likelihood of war in the Horn. Barre promptly embraced "scientific socialism" and turned to the USSR, which responded to his needs by generous supplies of arms and by sending out advisers in considerable numbers to train the Somalis in their use. The revolution in Ethiopia in 1974 transformed the political environment totally. Initial Western sympathies for the soldiers, who had overthrown a corrupt feudal regime, were soon dissipated by the violent excesses of the new rulers in Addis Ababa. After Colonel Mengistu emerged at the head of the Ethiopian junta, the regime engaged in a ruthless but initially futile attempt to exterminate the guerrilla groups in Eritrea, who were fighting to secure some measure of autonomy for this former Italian colony incorporated in Ethiopia after the last war. In May 1976, the United States refused to consider further aid if it were to be used against the Eritreans. Mengistu thereupon turned towards the USSR, even though vast supplies of Soviet arms were by then pouring into Somalia.

The Soviet Union thus found itself in a position of backing two adversaries neither of whom was prepared to yield an inch, for the military regime in Addis Ababa was resolute in its determination to maintain the country's territorial integrity. Perhaps the Soviets hoped to impose a *Pax Sovietica* on the Horn with the intention of strengthening their position there. However, they found themselves captive to a local situation which they could not control. The Somali attack on Ethiopia in 1977 forced them to take sides and they chose Ethiopia, a much larger country than Somalia, with considerable though unrealized economic potential. The Soviet operation undertaken to supply and reinforce the Ethiopians and to introduce large numbers of Cuban troops into the area needs no recapitulation here; its success, however, has had a marked effect on the USSR's position in the Third World as it demonstrated the extent of the USSR's global reach and its commitment to those it supports. Mengistu willingly fulfilled his side of the bargain by proclaiming his regime to be fully and scientifically socialist, proceeding to form a revolutionary vanguard party and aligning his country firmly with the USSR.

Barre in Somalia also reacted predictably by expelling all Soviet advisers from the country, abrogating the Soviet-Somali treaty and depriving the USSR of naval facilities on Berbera and at Kismayu. It was a price the USSR must have expected to have to pay, but on the whole it emerged from the 1977–78 crisis with both its position and prestige enhanced. The loss of naval facilities in Somalia was not too serious, as Aden continues to be available, and there have recently been reports that Ethiopia is prepared to replace the onshore support lost in Somalia.

The details of Soviet involvements in Africa have been summarized not because this would throw new light on actual Soviet policies, but because they illustrate the fundamentally power-political and nonideological caus- ation of Soviet actions. In the former Portuguese colonies the Soviets saw an opportunity to extend their influence, particularly after the adoption of the Tunney amendment by the U.S. Senate signalled American reluctance to become involved. The USSR's interest in the Horn of Africa centers primarily on the need to obtain local support for its naval presence. Gen- erally, the theory of correlation of forces requires that opportunities to diminish American or Chinese influence should be used to advantage.

The ideological nexus is slight. The self-styled Marxists of Benin, Ethio- pia, or even Angola and Mozambique are not very credible from the ideological point of view, as their Marxism appears to be essentially opportunistic. The Soviet Union looks after clients who can be useful in the pursuit of Soviet national interest. Even the most assiduous professions of ideological commitment offer no guarantee of Soviet support, as Barre found out. In Ethiopia, the Soviets condoned the extermination of the Marxist Ethiopian People's Revolutionary Party and went on to endorse the Dergue's own "Leninist" vanguard party. They also assisted in the destruction of another Marxist group, the Eritrean People's Liberation Front—an enterprise in which the Cubans refused their participation.

The notion that the peculiar role played by Marxism-Leninism in Africa south of the Sahara could be explained by the evolution of a brand of Communism special to the continent is rejected by the Africans themselves, perhaps because they are determined to stay as close as possible to the Soviet model in view of their complete dependence on Soviet support.

Thus Samora Machel of Mozambique: "We reject the idea that there can be an African socialism or Mozambiquan socialism; we consciously affirm that there can be no socialism other than scientific socialism."[36] Machel is right. The doctrinal basis for Afro-Communism does not exist.

Although the USSR has some justification to be sceptical about the Marxist convictions of its African friends, the encouragement and support accorded to the "national-bourgeois" leaders in the years after decolonization, and more recently to various Marxist regimes can, of course, be easily reconciled with national liberation theory. However, what really matters is the national interest of the Soviet Union—power politics lead and Leninist theory follows.

The Middle East

In the Middle East, the USSR has also been successful in utilizing the opportunities which presented themselves in consequence of local conditions and Western errors. The crucial political development in this area was the creation of the State of Israel in the teeth of Arab opposition and with vital and indispensable American support. The revolutionary situation, which developed in the Arab countries, owed as much to frustration brought about by the dismal failure of the *anciens regimes* against Israel as to popular discontent with social conditions. The anti-Israel policies, which the USSR adopted in the early 1950s and which were reinforced by periodic bouts of officially sponsored anti-Semitism, formed the spearhead of Soviet penetration. U.S. support for Israel had turned the USSR into a friendly power in the eyes of most Arabs. The West's reluctance to supply arms to the Arab states which could be used against Israel, cleared the way for Soviet initiatives. Indeed, it has become obvious that the supply of arms has become the Soviet Union's principal instrument for maintaining its influence in the Middle East. Whenever Soviet enthusiasm for the Arab struggle against Israel appears to have waned, Arab leaders reacted strongly as did Sadat in 1972 and Assad in 1978.

Soviet policy has had to concentrate on exploiting the anti-Western attitudes of the "bourgeois-democratic" leaders which emerged in the Arab world in the 1950s as Arab politics grew increasingly radical, mainly because of the total failure of the campaign to destroy Israel. The showcase of this era of Soviet policy was Nasser's Egypt. Cairo's decision to turn to the Soviet bloc for arms in 1955, and John Foster Dulles' subsequent refusal to provide finance for Nasser's Aswan High Dam led to the dispatch of large numbers of Soviet technicians; after the USSR had decided to step in where the West had feared to tread. The USSR strongly supported

Nasser over the nationalization of the Suez Canal, and provided diplomatic comfort during the military action taken against Egypt by Britain, France and Israel in 1956. Nasser's almost simultaneous drive against the Egyptian Communist Party and his leading role in the formation of the bloc of nonaligned states, which expressly tried to keep the Third World at a distance from the East-West confrontation, did not appear to worry the Soviets unduly. As Khrushchev himself said in 1957: "many Arabs . . . are very remote from Communist ideas. In Egypt, for instance, many Communists are held in prison. . . . Is Nasser a Communist? Certainly not. But nevertheless we support Nasser. We do not want to turn him into a Communist and he does not want to turn us into nationalists."[37]

The Soviet presence in Egypt became increasingly significant with the acquisition of naval facilities at Alexandria. On the ideological front under Nasser's successer Anwar Sadat, the "Arab socialism," which had become the official ideology of the new Egypt, was allowed to fade into the background. When Brezhnev, presumably in his determination to maintain East-West detente, tried to restrain Egypt from moving against Israel, Sadat responded by expelling 15,000 Soviet technicians and military advisers in 1972. Israel, and not socialist revolution, was his first priority. The Israeli victory in 1973 convinced him that the military option against Israel had to be abandoned—Camp David was the result. The USSR's hostility to the Egyptian-Israeli agreement showed its desire to keep the Middle Eastern pot boiling, but it confirmed Sadat in his belief that the Soviet Union was merely pursuing its selfish interests in the area. In 1976, he abrogated the Soviet-Egyptian Treaty of Friendship and deprived the Soviet navy of its facilities at Alexandria. The Soviet Union's Egyptian policy was in ruins and even Sadat's death has made little difference. As in the case of Somalia, Moscow had become the victim of local conditions and attitudes, which were beyond its control and which were not amenable to manipulation by means of volumes of revolutionary rhetoric.

Elsewhere in the Arab world, the USSR has also faced considerable problems, though nowhere has the outcome been as disastrous as in Egypt. However, the primacy of considerations of purely great power interest has been the most significant feature of Soviet policy in all cases—the Leninist concept was relegated to relative insignificance. In Iraq, the USSR maintained its position by acting as the country's main supplier of arms until 1981. The war between Iran and Iraq has again faced it with having to make choices. The virtual suppression of the Iraqi Communist Party and the execution of 39 Communist officers and soldiers in 1978 led to protests throughout the Soviet bloc, but did not materially affect Soviet arms deliveries, which were resumed in 1982.

Syria is certainly the most potent of the Arab states which still cling to a policy of direct confrontation with Israel. The amount of Soviet weaponry in Syrian hands is considerable, but Assad has pursued his own designs during the Lebanese crisis and in his attitude to Israel. By no stretch of the imagination could he be described as a Soviet proxy in the Middle East, even though Syrian and Soviet interests on certain issues are parallel. Perhaps the USSR's general commitment to the Palestinians stems from a vestigial loyalty to Leninist principles, but in Lebanon where the Palestinians have become a pawn and victim of the contending factions and of Syrian *Realpolitik*, the USSR has neither been willing nor able to do anything for them.

Libya is another major Soviet customer for arms, buying much more than it could legitimately absorb. Quadaffi propagates his own ideology: "after all, his system is not Communism and Qadaffi is its prophet."[38] The Soviets do not seem to care what happens to the arms after they are delivered to Libya. They are content to be paid in hard currency and to emphasize Libyan dependence on Soviet arms and expertise.

Iran, though not an Arab country, plays a seminal role in Middle East and Persian Gulf affairs. Russia has long-standing interests in Persia and after the last war the Soviets tried to establish puppet states in northern Iran. They were persuaded to withdraw by the firm stand adopted by the United States. Iranian resentment at British domination of the oil industry led to the ascendancy of Dr. Mossadegh's nationalist National Coalition Front, which became increasingly penetrated and influenced by the Iranian Communists—the Tudeh party. The Soviet Union welcomed the Mossadegh regime and its propaganda machine was suitably outraged by the coup, which overthrew Mossadegh and brought back the Shah in 1953.

The United States proceeded to build up the Shah as the force of order in the Gulf to replace the former British presence there. Although a Tudeh conspiracy was suppressed by the Shah in 1954, he was not averse to developing close commercial ties with the USSR, and he went to Moscow in 1956 to negotiate a new trade agreement. But in military and security matters the Shah aligned his country firmly with the West and for this policy he was continually attacked by Soviet and Arab propaganda. His ill-judged domestic policies led to the revolution of 1978–79—originally a movement inspired mainly by social discontent and violent nationalism, but soon taken over by Khomeini's Islamic fundamentalists.

Moscow, like Washington, was initially confused by events in Iran. It had little sympathy for the mullahs and their theocratic doctrines, but as the Shah's doom appeared to be sealed, the Soviet Union began to voice its support for the Khomeini regime and in February 1979 it recognized his Islamic Republic. The Soviet position in relation to Iran has not been made easier by the destruction of the Tudeh party. Its services to the 1978 revolution in mobilizing Tudeh supporters in the oil fields were ignored by the mullahs who sat in judgment on its leaders. Some of the Tudeh leaders on trial were forced to confess in public that they had plotted with the KGB against the Islamic Republic, charges which were indignantly rejected by the Soviet media.[39] Other anti-Soviet moves by the Khomeini regime include the decision to cancel the second pipeline project which would have carried Iranian natural gas to the USSR to replace Soviet gas exported to Europe, the expulsion of 18 Soviet diplomats from Tehran in 1983 and the support given by the Islamic Republic to the rebels in Afghanistan.[40] Yet the USSR continues to find itself in an ambivalent position. The fall of the Shah obviously shifted the correlation of forces against the West. But the religious fanaticism of the new rulers of Iran and their eagerness to export their revolutionary wares must be a cause of concern to the Soviet Union, which after all contains millions of Moslems in its Central Asian republics. Some revolutions are obviously not entirely beneficial from the Soviet point of view.

As regards the Middle East, Stalin and his successors succeeded where the Tsars had failed; they established Russia as a major power in the Middle East and the Mediterranean. They did this by exploiting the political situation in the area and by a display of military power—exactly the methods Catherine the Great and Nicholas I had used to less effect. The historical analogy could be pressed too hard by comparing how the USSR has used Marxism-Leninism as an ideological tool to attract support and subvert the status quo in the Near East with the Tsars' manipulation of Orthodox Christianity as an instrument of Russian foreign policy. At any rate, Arab Communism is largely moribund,[41] as the "national bourgeoisie," on the whole, has succeeded in suppressing or controlling it. The key to the ideological understanding of the Middle East is Islam, but Communism was on the decline long before the Islamic revival associated with the Ayatollah Khomeini. The Islamic fundamentalism, which he stands for, is really a grass roots reaction to the failures of various regimes in the Middle East and it reflects the great uncertainty which has troubled the Moslem world for so long. In times of basic ambivalence people easily fall in with populist demagogues as they turn to the fundamental values of their political and social culture, although they may be gravely mistaken in assessing them. The Islamic revival may be anti-American in some of its manifestations, but it is socially regressive and rejects Marxism as an atheistic Western doctrine. A statement, attributed to Khomeini in 1942, and emblazoned on the banners draped around the occupied American embassy in Teheran in 1979 during the hostage crisis, made the position clear: "The US is worse than Britain, Britain is worse than the U.S., the USSR is worse than both. Each is filthier than the others." Yet the Soviets have somewhat pathetically tried to coopt even this movement. For example, the Soviet Middle East expert M. Mchedlov wrote after the overthrow of the Shah that it was "no rarity for members of the clergy or broad masses of believers to speak out against capitalism" and he stressed the "necessity of joint activity by working people—atheists and believers—aimed at the revolutionary renovation of the old world."[42] Even Brezhnev tried to climb on the Ayatollah's bandwagon when he told the XXVI Congress of the Soviet Communist Party that "the liberation struggle can unfold under the banner of Islam."[43] This, of course, is exactly what is happening in Afghanistan, except that there the struggle is directed against the Soviet Union.

Afghanistan

The motives for the Soviet decision to invade Afghanistan in force in December 1979 have naturally been a matter of much speculation. Basically, there are two schools of thought. The first holds that the Soviet intervention was little more than a possibly ill-judged effort to clear up a difficult situation in a neighboring country where a so-called Marxist-Leninist regime had been installed. The other argues that the invasion of Afghanistan merely represents the first step on the road to the Persian Gulf. There is no hard evidence to point to either conclusion, but it is a geopolitical fact that if the USSR ever wanted to push towards the Straits of Hormuz, military control over Afghanistan would be a very useful asset. Purely ideological consideration of revolutionary doctrine seem to have played a minor role in the Afghanistan decision. The Brezhnev Doctrine rather than the tenets of Leninism would appear to have been the more appropriate guide for action, if one was required.

By establishing itself as the paramount power in Afghanistan, the USSR has today succeeded where Imperial Russia had failed repeatedly. No doubt, the end of the British Raj in the Indian subcontinent facilitated this process. Even under King Zahir Shah, Soviet influence in Afghanistan had increased considerably, particularly as the dispute over Pushtoonistan between Kabul and Pakistan made the Afghans willing customers for Soviet arms because of Pakistan's alignment with the United States. The coup in 1973, which deposed Zahir Shah and led to the establishment of a republic under his cousin, Mohammed Daud, was followed by increased Soviet aid. The USSR was willing to pay for its position in Afghanistan. Since 1956, 95 percent of Afghan military equipment has come from the Soviet bloc, and Afghanistan has been one of the major recipients of Soviet economic aid, receiving $1,263 billion between 1954 and 1975.[44] Daud did not prove to be a very reliable ally. He tried to find alternative sources of economic aid, such as the Shah of Iran, and criticized Soviet efforts to transform the nonaligned bloc into an instrument of Soviet policy. He survived for a time, because the opposition on the left was divided into two "Communist" factions—the more radical and revolutionary Khalq party under Taraki and Hafizullah Amin and the Parcham faction under Babrak Karmal, who were prepared to work for change within the system established by Daud. Daud's fall became inevitable when the two Communist groups decided to act jointly in 1978. The Marxist regime under Taraki which then took power moved Afghanistan closer to the USSR, and Soviet shipments of aid and military assistance were accordingly increased. But Taraki's radical attempts to reform the social structure and the system of land tenure in Afghanistan aroused violent opposition in the country. This soon adopted religious overtones as the rebels claimed to be fighting for the Islamic way of life against a godless Marxist regime inspired by the Soviet Union. Taraki's efforts to moderate some of the regime's policies, presumably approved by Moscow, only led to his overthrow and death at the hands of Amin in September 1979. Amin intensified the radical policies which had led to the tribal revolt in the first place. The resulting surge of support for the rebels created the real possibility that a self-styled Marxist regime on the south-western border of the Soviet Union might be overthrown by an Islamic insurgency. In December 1979, when the U.S. was fully occupied with the Iranian hostage crisis, the Soviets invaded Afghanistan with 50,000 troops and installed Babrak Karmal at the head of a more compliant Afghan government. Amin was killed during the Soviet invasion.

Since 1979, the Soviet Union had to fight against a widespread guerrilla movement, and Soviet troop levels in Afghanistan increased to over 100,000. The cost of paramountcy in Afghanistan was high: large amounts of military and economic aid preceded the present withdrawal; the USSR conducted an unexpectedly prolonged and tough military campaign; and the invasion of a Third World country had the expected repercussions in turning some opinion in Africa, the Middle East and Asia against the Soviet Union. Because U.S. aid to the mujaheddin was increased to include weapons which enabled them to fight off the Soviet helicopter gunships, the Russians lost the upper hand on the battlefield. Though the Soviets have agreed to withdraw militarily, their investment in Afghanistan is very high and likely will be protected in some fashion.[45]

Asia

Asia ranks rather low in the order of revolutionary priorities adopted in Moscow. Lenin was certainly preoccupied with the possible impact of revolutionary changes in India and China, but in his day there was little the Soviet Union could actually do to promote revolution. The Comintern's early China policy concentrated on strengthening the "nationalist bourgeois" revolution represented by the Kuomintang, a policy continued by Stalin until 1945. The success of the Chinese Communists under Mao in achieving their revolution after years of fighting in defiance of Soviet advice,[46] and without much Soviet help except at the very end of the struggle has left its mark on Sino-Soviet relations. Although Mao's success vindicated Lenin's revolutionary precepts, the Chinese Communists created an alternative model of revolution, a dichotomy which the Sino-Soviet split has merely served to underline and emphasize. As Thomas W. Robinson has noted,[47] Soviet policy in Asia is faced with problems which are not encountered in other Third World areas. The physical magnitude of the continent makes the pursuit of an "Asian" policy virtually impossible and many of the countries of Asia represent large, relatively powerful and generally economically viable units, making poor candidates for adoption as Soviet clients. Furthermore, they possess homogenous political cultures of long standing which tend to channel political developments along independent lines, while remaining intensely nationalistic. The Soviet Union is "reduced to the military/conspiratorial tool—the only one in which the USSR excels."[48] The correlation of forces in Asia is also unfavorable to the USSR. It cannot match the economic influence of Japan, its relationship with India is bedevilled by the Indo-Pakistani quarrel and the Sino-Soviet split, which helped to move Communist China so close to the United States, dominates Soviet policy in a negative manner.

The USSR's commanding position in India, dating from the Indo-Soviet treaty of 1971, has created a state of affairs the British tried to prevent for more than a century. Pakistan's dependence on U.S. support, and later its friendship with China, inevitably made India amenable to Soviet influence. The border dispute with China, which flared up dangerously in the 1950s and led to open fighting in 1962, remains unresolved. It strengthened India's ties with the USSR, especially since the Sino-Soviet split has virtually become a permanent feature of the international landscape. It has also affected the Indian Communists, who are divided into the Communist Party of India, which generally follows the Soviet line, and the Communist Party of India-Marxist, which is more sympathetic to the Chinese side. The "Marxist" party is much more successful electorally. At times it cooperates with the other Communists (as in Kerala in 1980) and it certainly represents a powerful challenge to Congress. In the 1980 national elections it gained almost 12 million votes and a few months later it won control in West Bengal. India is therefore one of the few Third World countries with a large and well-organized Communist movement, but even the Communist

Party of India-Marxist is a long way from being able to challenge the traditional parties—Congress and Janata—nationally. The Soviet Union prefers to leave ideological considerations aside and to concentrate on maintaining its influence in New Delhi. It has been India's main supplier of weapons since 1965, although the country is large enough to have diversified its sources of arms. The policy of supporting India against Pakistan and emphasizing the close ties between Moscow and New Delhi has continued under Gorbachev, who singled out Rajiv Ghandi for a specially warm welcome when he came to Moscow for Chernenko's funeral. Ghandi paid a further visit to Moscow in May 1985. The Soviet commitment to India obviously has made it virtually impossible for the USSR to establish its influence in Pakistan. Relations between the two countries have also suffered as a result of the Soviet invasion of Afghanistan and Soviet objections to Pakistani support for some of the Afghan rebels.

Vietnam continues to be the USSR's closest ally in Asia, but it cannot be regarded as a mere client. Ho Chi Minh fashioned the Vietnamese Communist movement as an instrument of nationalist revolution, directed first against the French, then the Americans and now the Chinese. The Soviets supported the Vietnamese Communists throughout the Vietnam War, and in fact made it possible for them to keep the war going. This was not just a revolutionary duty, but a most expedient policy which tied down large numbers of U.S. troops without the expenditure of a single Soviet soldier.[49] Vietnam continues to draw on Soviet assistance, which is readily given because of Hanoi's differences with China. Soviet behavior with regard to India and Vietnam is a perfectly logical application of the correlation of forces theory. It really amounts to old-fashioned, balance of power politics, with revolutionary doctrine left far behind, unless one believes that what is good for the USSR must ultimately also be good for the cause of world revolution.

In Indonesia, however, both Soviet power politics and Communist-led revolutionary activities have failed. Sukarno, who could be regarded as a typical "national-bourgeois" leader, was staunchly anti-Western, if only because of the dispute with the Netherlands over West Irian. But as one of the founders of the nonaligned bloc he opposed attempts to align it with Soviet policy, and he was more sympathetic to China than the USSR after the Sino-Soviet split. The same was basically true of the large Communist Party of Indonesia. The fatally abortive Communist insurrection of 1965 destroyed the Party and the right-wing generals, who followed Sukarno in power, have certainly given no indication of wishing to seek a closer relationship with the USSR.

In the Philippines a Communist insurrection is indeed taking place, but it has little to do with the Soviet Union. The oppressive and corrupt Marcos regime, which the revolutionaries had been trying to overthrow, was in fact honored by the USSR in August, 1985, when President Marcos ceremoniously received a Soviet decoration for bravery in World War II from the Soviet ambassador in Manila. The revolutionary situation in the Philippines stems from by no means untypical indigenous causes, but the Soviet Union's chosen instrument—the Philippine Communist Party—plays no part in it. It has been sliding towards ineffective oblivion ever since Ramon Magsaysay put an end to the Huk insurrection of 1946–54. The decision of the Party's leaders to accept the amnesty, which terminated the Huk revolt, spelt the end of its political life. A group of young nationalist-revolutionary radicals, claiming to be inspired by Mao's cultural revolution, formed the Communist Party of the Philippines, but their Maoist allegiance did not bring them much support from the Chinese People's Republic, which maintained relations with the Marcos regime. However, the lack of legitimate channels of opposition, underlined by the murder of Benigno Aquino in August 1983, created a revolutionary momentum, which the Communist Party of the Philippines exploits. It has succeeded in uniting some opposition forces in the National Democratic Front, which it dominates. Its 15,000 guerrillas do not pose a military threat to the Philippine armed forces for the time being, but their tactics have created a large number of insurrectionary flash points throughout the archipelago and have proved to be more effective than those adopted by the Huks, who concentrated their operations on Central Luzon. The insurrection led by the Communist Party of the Philippines would have given much comfort to Lenin and Mao and it forced Marcos into positions critical of the United States as he tried to avoid being outflanked by the nationalist left. A segment of Corizon Aquino's support is provided by this same nationalist left. It therefore represents a threat to American strategic interests. Its leaders act independently of Moscow, but if they were to succeed, the USSR would be the principal beneficiary at very little cost to itself.

In Asia, more than in Africa or Latin America, Soviet policy has had to be content with playing power politics in the traditional way. Military strength counts for more than revolutionary doctrine. In some ways, the Sino-Soviet split has served to nullify the revolutionary dynamic of Asian Communism and this state of affairs could only be reversed if the Sino-Soviet alliance were to be restored. Gorbachev seems to be aware of this. The Chinese Vice-Premier Li Peng was the only foreign leader to be accorded an especially warm welcome, apart from Rajiv Ghandi, at the meetings held on the occasion of the Chernenko funeral. In his speech to the Soviet Communist Party's Central Committee immediately after his appointment as General Secretary, Gorbachev said: "We would like a serious improvement of relations with the Chinese People's Republic and believe that, given reciprocity, this is quite possible,"[50] but there are no signs of this actually happening.

Conclusion And Summary

"The world outlook and class aims of socialism and capitalism are opposite and irreconcilable."[51] This is, and always has been the official doctrinal foundation of Soviet Communism. The entire system of ideas and concepts which, it is claimed, determines the Soviet Union's international behavior is based on the premise that there can only be one outcome to this confrontation. Yet the ideological structure by means of which the USSR had hoped to achieve this purpose has shown itself to be fallible and defective. The evolution of capitalist societies has practically deprived Marxist concepts of revolution of their relevance as far as industrialized communities are concerned. Even Lenin's hope that the struggle for national liberation in colonial territories would encourage revolutionary movements in the metropolitan countries has materialized only in the case of underdeveloped Portugal, where the pressures and costs of colonial warfare brought about the fall of the Caetano regime in 1974. The Soviet Union's revolutionary endeavors have had to be concentrated in the Third World, where the prospects appeared to be reasonably favorable because of its political instability and the perceived and real need for systemic change. But even in the developing countries Marxism-Leninism has not proved to be especially relevant, except perhaps as a means for soliciting Soviet support for totalitarian regimes of doubtful ideological constancy. The USSR realized in the 1950s that the Communist revolutions in Africa which, it hoped, would provide opportunities for establishing its influence, would not occur. Instead, Khrushchev had to back all anticolonial movements as long as they were "anti-imperialist" and thus the USSR acquired some very capricious allies. But even though the Soviet Union had to make do with "liberal-bourgeois" regimes like, for example, India, the ideologues in Moscow clung to their Leninist clichés. Thus Konstantin Zarodov:

A revolutionary majority for the Third World does not result from the creation of representative and elected organs, but is created in the course of direct revolutionary action by the masses, through their independent political activity which goes beyond the bourgeois norms of peaceful conduct. . . . to believe that the results of an election are capable of expressing the will of the majority is opportunistic and reflects the degeneration of 'revolutionary democrats' into parliamentary cretinism.[52]

Zarodov's critique of parliamentary democracy must certainly meet with the approval of many Third World regimes—perhaps the only aspect of Leninist doctrine they can subscribe to with any degree of sincerity.

Otherwise Leninism has been an unreliable guide for revolutionary action, perhaps because the working class in the Third World is characterized by "numerical weakness, low cultural levels and petty-bourgeois, tribal and religious prejudices" and is also "underdeveloped, disorganized and politically immature."[53]

In Asia in general the USSR has been compelled to fall back on traditional methods of power politics. In the Middle East, the Islamic revival has thrown up unforeseen and unresolved problems. Only in Central America have revolutions conformed to some of the variables in Lenin's blueprint, but even there orthodox Marxism has been outflanked by more militant and radical doctrines. Where so-called vanguard regimes have come to power, they have to rely completely on Soviet support for survival and thus represent a further drain on the Soviet Union's economic resources. The Soviets themselves admit that it "must be stated clearly that the national liberation movements could not emerge victorious, if the Soviet Union did not exist."[54]

The use of surrogates, such as the Cubans in Africa or East German security specialists, has been tried with some success, as they are frequently more acceptable locally and as they are often quite keen to play this role in order to enhance their international standing and add to their bargaining power in relation to the USSR. But although, for example, the Cubans may be motivated by a genuine desire to share their revolution with others, this does not solve the basic Soviet problem of ideological wastage and bankruptcy. An essentially static and conservative society, such as the Soviet Union has become, cannot really be expected to export revolution on a worldwide basis—power is the only commodity it has to offer.

While the Soviet Union can afford the present subsidies it pays to its allies and clients in the Third World, the state of the Soviet economy does not permit any expansion of economic aid. Moscow has to peddle arms to regimes which need them for use against their own subjects and at times against neighboring countries. Military power is the Soviet Union's principal asset, which it is prepared to use to compensate for its economic and ideological weakness. The USSR's capability in this respect, however, is prodigious.

During the 1970s the Soviet Union greatly improved its capacity to transport arms over long distances by developing long-range cargo aircraft and by expanding its maritime capabilities. In the previous decade Moscow's ability to aid Lumumba in the Congolese civil war was limited. No such logistical problems hampered the impressive capability of the Soviet Union to bring Cubans to Angola and Ethiopia or to support them with sea and airlift operations, ferrying thousands of tons of arms and military supplies.[55]

In short, the USSR has been reduced to the role of an old-fashioned imperialist power, using its military strength and reinforcement capability to influence the correlation of forces, to terrorize its opponents and support its clients.

There is a twofold danger in this situation. First, the West has failed to develop a credible means of countering this military threat and has devised no method capable of influencing Soviet behavior patterns in the Third World. Secondly, the men in the Kremlin survey a scene where the growth of military power represents by far the most successful aspect of Soviet development. The temptation to use it to achieve their goals instead of relying on the threadbare appeal of ideological doctrine, or the lame-duck performance of the Soviet economy, or the dubious attractions of the Soviet model of society, must be great.

Does all this mean that ideology is dead? Certainly not, because the leaders of the Soviet Union cannot escape from the constraints placed on their thinking by the political training they have received. Ideology provides them with the only tool of analysis they possess, for in the Soviet Union there are no alternatives to Marxism-Leninism. It is a prism, which often distorts their view of the world, but it is the only one they have. Marxism provides the only political language they know, and thus it must exert great influence upon the formation of their policies and the making of their decisions. Any assessment of any aspect of Soviet policy must take ideology and doctrine into account, for at the very least it provides the Soviet leaders with a tool for rationalizing their policies even when they consciously put national interest above the cause of world revolution.

It is perhaps not very useful to spend too much time on trying to analyze whether specific Soviet actions are dictated by power politics or by the dictates of revolutionary ideology. The Soviet leaders are probably as confused as the Western commentators who try to solve this particular puzzle. It is more than likely that the concepts of Soviet national interest and Communist world revolution have become so intertwined in the minds of Soviet decision makers that they no longer recognize the difference.

There is, of course, a simple explanation of Soviet policies in the Third World which is not much affected by ideological considerations. The USSR is a world power, and as such it sees itself pursuing a global range of interests. To concede an absence of Soviet interests in any part of the world would be an admission of diminished status. As a world superpower, the USSR is convinced that it must have policies for all contingencies in all parts of the world and its ideology maintains that it must obtain advantages wherever and whenever it can. Opportunities presented by Western mistakes and failures must be seized—it would be ideologically and practically inadmissible to ignore them. Of course, errors are committed and miscalculations occur in the pursuit of these self-fulfilling goals, but that, too, is part of the game which great powers play. Beneath the elaborate superstructure of ideological motivation and great power interests, Soviet policy in the Third World may, after all, be just an exercise in role-playing.[56]

Notes

The author is indebted to Margot Light, of the University of Surrey, for helpful comment.

1. Gian Carlo Pajetta: *La Lunga dell' Internazionalismo* (Rome: Riuniti, 1978) p. 164.
2. *Pravda*, 30 May, 1985.
3. *Pravda*, 25 July, 1985.
4. *Novoye Vremya*, July 1975.
5. Quoted in Stuart R. Schram: *The Political Thought of Mao Tse-tung*. (New York: Praeger, 1963) p. 163.
6. V. I. Lenin: "Address to the Second All-Russian Congress of Communist Organizations of Peoples of the East, 22 November, 1919.", *Selected Works*, Vol. 3, pp. 304–305.
7. V. I. Lenin: "Report on the Commission on the National and Colonial Question, 26 July, 1920". *Selected Works*, Vol. 3, p. 468.
8. *Ibid.* p. 466.
9. Lenin: "Address to the Second All-Russian Congress," .p. 307.
10. TASS, 23 April, 1985.
11. TASS, 11 March, 1985.
12. B. Pockney: "Soviet Trade with the Third World" in E. J. Feuchtwanger and Peter Nailor, eds.: *The Soviet Union and the Third World* (London: Macmillan, 1981) p. 68.
13. Stephen T. Hosmer and Thomas W. Wolfe: *Soviet Policy and Practice toward Third World Conflicts* (Lexington, MA: Lexington Books, 1983) p. 70.
14. *Handbook of Economic Statistics* (Washington, DC: U.S. Government Printing Office, 1980) pp 72–107.
15. Emilio Gasparini: "East-South Economic Relations" in *NATO Review*, April 1985, pp. 24–32.
16. For a full discussion of this trend see Elizabeth Kridl Valkenier: "The USSR, the Third World and the Global Economy", *Problems of Communism*, July/August 1979, pp. 17–33.
17. Gasparini, pp. 29–30. According to an OECD report issued in July 1985, in

1984 aid from CMEA countries fell to 0.16% of their GDP; OECD remained at 0.36%.

18. In 1983, Syria, Iraq, Libya and Algeria received 59% of Warsaw Pact arms deliveries.

19. For an excellent appraisal of the military factor in Soviet third world policy, see Jonathan Alford: "The New Military Instrument" in Feuchtwanger and Nailor, pp. 12–29.

20. See S. G. Gorshkov: *Morskaya Moshch Gosudarstva* (Moscow: Voeyenizdat, 1976)

21. *Time*, 17 June, 1985.

22. See also Carla Anne Robbins: *The Cuban Threat* (New York: McGraw Hill, 198 Pedro Ramet and Fernando Lopez-Alves: "Moscow and the Revolutionary Left in Latin America," *Orbis*, Summer 1984, pp. 341–363; Augusto Varas: Ideology and Politics in Latin American-USSR Relations", *Problems of Communism*, January/February 1984, pp. 35–47.

23. The Cuban revolution has not been cheap. The Soviet premium for Cuban sugar went up by approximately half a billion dollars between 1982 and 1983. In 1982 it was $2.6 billion; in 1983 $3.1 billion, even though Soviet imports of sugar went down that year. (Gasparini, p. 29) On the other hand, the oil subsidy has declined as the CMEA average oil price has gone up.

24. Robbins, p. 39, quoted by Ramet and Lopez-Alves, p. 345.

25. *Pravda*, 20 November 1968.

26. E.g., Johan Galtung: "A Structural Theory of Imperialism", *Journal of Peace Research*, 8:2 (1971).

27. Ramet and Lopez-Alves, pp. 347–349, deal with this process in some detail.

28. Ramet and Lopez-Alves, pp 349–350.

29. E.g. V. Y. Chirkin and Y. A. Yudin: *A Socialist-Orientated State—Instrument of Change*, (Moscow: Progress, 1978) and K. Brutens: the "liberated countries are and for a long time will remain an undampened hotbed of anti-imperialist actions and sentiments." (*Komunist*, No. 3/1985.)

30. Quoted in Ramet and Lopez-Alves, p. 352. The summary of developments in Nicaragua in this paper has relied to some extent on the material presented by Ramet and Lopez-Alves. For details of Soviet aid to the Sandinista regime, see pp 353–356.

31. See Patrick Moore: The Soviet Threat to Western Interests in Central America", Radio Free Europe Research, Munich. RAD Background Report 163.

32. *Grenada Documents: an Overview and Selection.* (Department of State and Department of Defense: Washington DC, September 1984).

33. Idem p. 3.

34. The Tunney amendment, passed by the Senate in December 1975, preventing any further allocation of funds for covert action in Angola, was certainly interpreted by the USSR and its Cuban allies as proof of American disinterest in Angola and generally as a sign of loss of will in consequence of Vietnam to oppose Soviet actions in the Third World.

35. In February 1979, the Soviet Union concluded a $36 million aid agreement with the PDRY.
36. Quoted in D. E. Albright: *Communism in Africa* (Bloomington Ind.: Indiana University Press, 1980) p. 125.
37. In an interview with James Reston, New York Times, 10 October, 1957. Quoted in Karen Dawisha: "The Soviet Union in the MiddleEast" in Feuchtwanger and Nailor, p. 119.
38. Arnold Hottinger: "Arab Communism at Low Ebb", *Problems of Communism*, July/August 1981, p. 30.
39. E.g., *Pravda*, 6 May, 1983.
40. See Z. Khalilzdad: "Islamic Iran: Soviet Dilemma", *Problems of Communism*, January/February 1984, pp 1–20.
41. Hottinger gives an excellent account of the decline of Arab Communism.
42. *Pravda*, 16 November, 1979.
43. *Pravda*, 24 February, 1981.
44. Shirin Tahir-Kheli: "The Soviet Union in Afghanistan" in Robert H. Donaldson, ed.: *The Soviet Union in the Third World* (Boulder CO: Westview, 1981) pp. 219–220. Tahir-Kheli presents an excellent summary of the Soviet involvement in the murky politics of Afghanistan, on which this section of the paper has gratefully drawn.
45. Since Dr. Pick wrote this chapter, the United States has sent antitank weapons to the Afghan guerrillas that have raised the price of the war to the Soviet Union significantly. It is no longer clear that the Soviet Union will remain there indefinitely. (M. A. K. 1986).
46. Sino-Soviet relations are dealt with in another paper at this conference and have therefore been generally excluded from this paper.
47. Thomas W. Robinson: "On Soviet Asian Policy: A Commentary" in Donaldson, pp. 294–302.
48. Robinson, *op. cit.* p. 299.
49. See Douglas Pike, in Donaldson, pp. 251–265.
50. TASS 11 March, 1985.
51. L. I. Brezhnev: *Following Lenin's Course* (Moscow: Progress, 1975) pp. 94–95.
52. *Pravda*, 8 August 1975, quoted in Alexander R. Alexiev: The New Soviet Strategy in the Third World (RAND, No. N-1995-AF, Prepared for the U.S. Air Force: Santa Monica, CA, June 1983), p. 14.
53. Vadim Zagladin, quoted in Alexiev, p. 15.
54. Boris Ponomaryov, quoted in Alexiev, p. 15.
55. Andrew J. Pierre: *The Global Policy of Arms Sales* (Princeton NJ: Princeton University Press, 1982) p. 77.
56. Otto Pick: "Political and Ideological Aspects", in Fuechtwanger and Nailor, pp. 10–11. The most frequently quoted statement in this context is Gromyko's remark at the XXIV CPSU Congress: "Today there is no question of any significance which can be decided without the Soviet Union, or in opposition to it." (Pravda, 4 April 1971).

4

Russo-Chinese Relations: Historical Background and Prospects for a Future Settlement

PETER S. H. TANG

Historical Background: The Sources of Conflict

The history of Russo-Chinese relations is permeated by conflicts and hostilities. The "catalogue" of the issues making for conflicts is practically endless. They can be classified as territorial, political, economic and ideological. Russia has steadily encroached on Chinese land since the mid-seventeenth century. Russia has gotten 93,000 sq.mi. (238,000 sq.km.) by the Treaty of Nerchinsk (1689), 40,000 sq.mi. (102,000 sq.km.) by the Treaty of Kiakhta (1727), 185,000 sq.mi. (473,000 sq.km.) by the Treaty of Aigun (1858) and 133,000 sq.mi. (340,000 sq.km.) in Manchuria and Central Asia by the Treaty of Peking (1860).[1] Politically, Russia's continuous manipulation of China has been from time to time accompanied by military expeditions. Economically, Russian exploitation has sometimes been perpetrated by outright plunder. Ideologically, Russian offensive maneuvers have been keenly felt by China ever since the establishment of Communist rule in Russia.

The present state of Russo-Chinese relations remains tense and abnormal, distinctly contradictory to what both powers advertised earlier as a new type of international relations between "fraternal" socialist states dedicated to Communism. Thus, although both giant neighbors operate under a professed Communist system, the traditionally divisive territorial, political and economic issues not only persist but are greatly amplified by intense ideological disagreements.

In the present nuclear and technological age, the genuine national interests of both Russia and China would best be served by the settling of their long-standing disagreements and conflicts. This would contribute to their respective stability and progress at home as well as to international peace and security, which would be in the best interests of the progressive development of both these nations. The much-mentioned five principles of peaceful coexistence may be used as the basis for such a reasonable and peaceful settlement of disputes between them. It remains to be seen whether Russia and China can resolve their problems under the present Communist regimes. On the whole, this is not very likely, for in Communist systems regime interests usually take precedence over national interests. It would be therefore much more realistic to associate the real possibilities for a Russo-Chinese settlement with political changes in both countries that would end the present Communist regimes and establish as their successors nationally minded, popular governments.

Russian Expansion into China

Russian expansion into China (particularly since the nineteenth, but beginning in the seventeenth century) is unique in history in the sense of the methods used, the size of the territories acquired, and the length of time these acquired territories have been held. The dramatic historical record of Russia acquiring over 1.5 million square kilometers of Chinese territory was achieved through deceptive Russian diplomatic maneuvers and veiled military threats during the times when China suffered from either internal or external distress or both. The tactics of persistent Russian pressure, coupled with China's determination to avoid a major war with Russia while the country was in turmoil, made Russia's use of military force to achieve her goals in China practically unnecessary.

Indeed, although both countries have been involved in foreign wars on numerous occasions,[2] the remarkable feature of Russo-Chinese relations has been the absence of a full-scale war between them. China has always gone to great lengths to avoid a major war with Russia in every instance of a crisis in their relations. For example, China tolerated Russian incursions on her territory in the seventeenth century, the Russian occupation of the Ili region in the mid-nineteenth century[3] and of Manchuria following the 1900 Boxer Rebellion. The Russo-Japanese War of 1904–05 was fought on Chinese soil, in Manchuria, without China getting involved in the war on either side. Similarly the Soviet military occupation of Outer Mongolia since 1921, the 1929 Soviet military expedition into Manchuria, and the illegal Soviet annexation of Tannu Tuva (Urianghai) in 1944 did not provoke a military response on the part of China either. China has also learned to live with the Russian occupation of Sixty-Four Settlements to the east of the Amur River (Heilongjiang) in Manchuria, and of the Pamirs in Sinkiang, which continues unabated under the Soviet regime despite the latter's disclaiming the heritage of the Tsarist imperial expansion.[4]

In 1969, the Soviet Union and China, although both were under Communist rule, and thus supposedly fraternal states, surprised the world by engaging in bloody border clashes at Chenpao (or Damansky) Island, on the Ussuri (Wusuli) River and the Pacha Islands on the Amur River.[5] These skirmishes, although not constituting major wars, unmistakably manifested a disastrous disregard of the Communist claim for proletarian internationalism, particularly the unbreakable solidarity between the two giant Communist Party-states who were once coleaders of the "socialist" camp.

Russian Exploitation of China

In the lengthy history of Russo-Chinese relations, while China was cooperative, Russia was exploitative. Yet numerous cases of such exploitation were misrepresented by the Russians as "cooperation." Such misrepresentations attended a series of bilateral agreements, from the first Russo-Chinese treaty concluded in Nerchinsk in 1689 to the particularly unequal 1858 Aigun and 1860 Pekin treaties. Ironically, the largest Chinese territorial concessions to Russia have been the result of these supposedly cooperative treaties. The same should be said of the 1896, 1924, 1945, and 1950 treaties, as well. All of them, under the facade of cooperation, masked Russia's political, economic and military exploitation of China.

The first Russo-Chinese treaty, signed in Nerchinsk on August 27, 1689, delineated the Russo-Chinese frontier between eastern Siberia and Manchuria, along the line from the Ud Bay at the Sea of Okhotsk to the Stanovoi (Dzhugdzhur) Range and Yablonoi (Yablonovoi) Mountains to the Argun River. While putting an end to 40 years of incursions into the Amur region by the Lo-Ch'a or Russian Cossacks, this treaty marked a substantial "legal" concession of Chinese territory to Russia. The subsequent 170 years of Russo-Chinese peaceful coexistence were due to Russia's respect for China's power during the zenith of the Ch'ing (or Manchu) dynasty (1644–1911).

In 1846, however, Tsar Nicholas I of Russia violated the 1689 Treaty of

Nerchinsk, when he authorized the exploration of the then Chinese inland river of Amur. In 1854, 1855, and 1856, Count Nicholas Muraviev, governor-general of eastern Siberia, led military expeditions into China, forcing a passage along the Amur, which elicited strong Chinese protests. At that time, the Manchu dynasty was preoccupied with the internal T'ai-P'ing (1850–1854) and Nien-Fei (1853–1868) rebellions, as well as with English and French external aggression, and was thus unable to prevent *de facto* Russian military occupation along the Amur. Later, China was forced to sign the May 28/16, 1858, Aigun treaty, ceding to Russia the left bank of the Amur to the Ussuri River, and both banks of the Amur below that point.[6]

In 1860, Russia again exploited Chinese distress, during the Anglo-French occupation of Peking, by forcing her to cede the Trans-Ussuri territory which included the warm-water port of Vladivostok. This was presented as payment for the use of Russian "good offices" in mediating the conclusion of the Anglo-French War against China by the November 14/2, 1860, Treaty of Peking. Surprisingly, territorial gains assigned by the 1860 Peking treaty to Russia far exceeded the combined gains of both the victorious belligerents, Britain and France. Davidov described the relations between Russia and China in the period before the Russo-Japanese War of 1904–05 as "becoming a confusion of a peace-loving southern neighbor with the aggressive activities of the north."[7]

In 1858–1860, when concluding the 1858 Aigun and the 1860 Peking treaties, the Chinese made a double concession to the Tsarist drive conducted under the disguise of Russia's "cooperation" with China: first by tolerating Russian violations of the 1689 treaty, and then by being forced to make enormous new territorial concessions to Russia. These concessions, however, only whetted the Russian appetite for more Chinese lands. Following the Moslem rebellion of June 1864 in northwest China, Russia occupied the Ili region in Sinkiang. In negotiating and renegotiating the return of this strategic region, China had to dismiss, imprison, and sentence to decapitation her Envoy Plenipotentiary, Ch'ung-hou, who was duped by the Russians into signing the Treaty of Livadia. This 1879 unratified treaty nominally restored Ili to China, but ceded to Russia seven tenths of the strategic area, including the military pass that controlled communications with southern Sinkiang. Russia accused Peking of "bad faith" in denouncing the Treaty of Livadia and staged a 23-ship fleet "naval demonstration" under Admiral S.S. Lesovskii. The denounced treaty was soon replaced by the 1881 Treaty of St. Petersburg in which China paid a larger sum of indemnity in order to cede a smaller piece of territory around Ili.[8]

Despite these Chinese sacrifices Russia did not hesitate to occupy Manchuria during the 1900 Boxer Rebellion. At this juncture, the Russian

troops literally drove all the Manchu inhabitants in the Sixty-four Settlements to the east of Amur (Chiang-Tung-Lu-Shih-Szu-T'un, located across
the Zeiia or Chinch'ili River to the south of Blagoveshchensk and across
the Amur to the east of Aigun). The Chinese merchants in Blagoveshchensk, more than 7,000 in all, were pushed into the Amur River. The
Russians bayonetted those who did not drown. In the course of difficult
negotiations about the evacuation of Russian troops from Manchuria, Russia exacted from China additional territorial concessions. Still dissatisfied,
Russia simply ignored certain stipulations of the Russo-Chinese Agreement
of April 4, 1902, concerning the evacuation of Russian troops from Manchuria, which foreshadowed the 1904–05 Russo-Japanese War.[9]

Despite their revolutionary rhetoric, the Soviets in their relations with
China continued the deceptive diplomatic maneuvers and exploitative policies of their Tsarist predecessors.

On July 25, 1919, Leo Karakhan, Soviet deputy people's commissar for
foreign affairs, issued a declaration addressed to "the Chinese people and
governments of North and South China," which in part reads:

> The government of workers and peasants has then (since October 1917) de-
> clared null and void all the secret treaties concluded with Japan, China and
> the ex-Allies, the treaties which were to enable the Russian government of
> the Tsar and his Allies to enslave the people of the East and principally the
> people of China. . . . The Soviet Government return to the Chinese people
> without demanding any kind of compensation, the Chinese Eastern Railway,
> as well as all the mining concessions, forestry, gold mines, and all the other
> things which were seized from them by the government of the Tsars. . . . The
> Soviet Government gives up the indemnities payable by China for the insur-
> rection of Boxers in 1900. . . .[10]

Because at that time Siberia was not yet under Soviet control, the Karakhan Declaration did not reach China until March 26, 1920, when the
Soviet representative at Irkutsk, Janson, telegraphed it to the Peking government. Upon publication, the declaration evoked an enthusiastic response from the Chinese intelligentsia and the people at large for mainly
symbolic reasons. China wished to abrogate all the unequal treaties with
the imperialist powers, and hoped that the Russian move would serve as
a persuasive example and convincing argument to sway the imperial powers
in the direction desired by the Chinese.[11] This sentiment was reinforced
by the fact that the other imperial powers were reluctant to give up their
privileges in China. This was demonstrated by the Versailles treaty of June
28, 1919, which assigned former German interests in China's Shantung
Province to Japan. Upon publication, the declaration did not particularly

SKETCH MAP OF CHINESE TERRITORIES DETACHED

•••—••—• The boundary prescribed by the 1689 Sino-Russian Treaty of Nerchinsk.
— — — — The Boundary prescribed by the 1727 Sino-Russian Treaty of Kiakhta.
▬▬▬▬▬ The Chinese Boundary prior to 1860.
—••—••—•• The 1884 Sino-Russian Kashgar Boundary Agreement for Further Demar
cation prescribed starting from Wuzibielishankou. The Russian Boundary
turned Southwestward and the Chinese Boundary turned Southward.
•••••••• The line of Tsarist military occupation at the end of the 19th century.

Upper Tunguska River

Land originally under
the jurisdiction of
Cheşektu Khanate.

Land originally under
the jurisdiction of the
Dzhugdzhur Khanat tribe.

USSR

Angara River

Ob River

Irtysh River

Yenisey River

More than 440,000 sq. kilometers
of the Chinese Territory detached
and incorporated by Tsarist Russia
through the 1860 Sino-Russian
Treaty of Peking and the 1864 Sino-
Russian Agreement for Demarcation
of the Northwestern Boundary.

Lake Ubsa

Lake Höbsögöl

Lake Balkhash

Lake Kirgis

Selenga River

Hovd

Lake
Hara
Usa

Uliastay
(Javhlant)

Lake Ata

Tacheng

Lake Hara

TASHKENT

Chu River

Alma Ata

Ili River

DZUNGARIA

More than 70,000 sq. kilometers
of Chinese Territory detached and
incorporated by Tsarist Russia
through the 1881 Sino-Russian
Treaty of Ili and the subsequent
five boundary demarcation
agreements.

Lake Issyk

TIEN SHAN

MON

Narin River

Andizhan

Ürümqi

KUNLUN MTS

Hami

Lake Bagrach

PAMIRS

Yarkant River

Lake Gashun

CHINA

Hotan River

Tarim River

AFGANISTAN

Lake Lop

Shule River

PAKISTAN

Quarqan River

Indus River

Yingchuan

KASHMIR   Source: Chinese Historical Museum, Chinese History for Junior High School, Vol. III
(First ed.; June 1984, Shanghai; Geographical Map Publishing House and Xinhua Shudin
Islamabad   Publisher) (The Chinese Boundary on this map is based on the Chinese People's Republic in
★   1980).

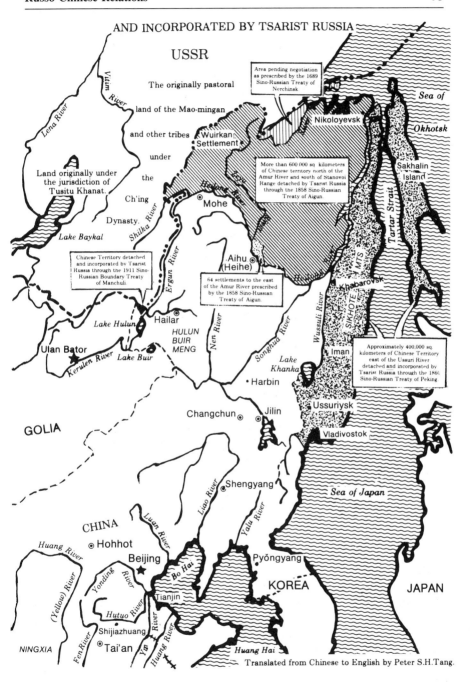

Translated from Chinese to English by Peter S.H.Tang.

impress the Peking government. Since Russia was defeated by Germany in World War I as evidenced in the February 28, 1918, Treaty of Brest-Litovsk, China had recovered control over the Chinese Eastern Railway and cancelled Outer Mongolia's autonomy. In addition, other Russian privileges, such as consular jurisdiction and customs supervision, had also been recovered and the payment to the Russian portion of the Boxer indemnity had been stopped. However, the Peking government welcomed the opportunity for a dialogue, such as the Yourin mission to Peking and General Chang Shih-lin's reciprocal mission to Moscow in 1920.[12]

The Second Karakhan Declaration, dated September 27, 1920, was handed by Karakhan to General Chang Shih-lin in Moscow. As expected, this declaration pressed for normalization of relations between the two countries by expressing regret for Chinese procrastination in responding to Soviet offers. Among its proposed seven points was the following sweeping statement that the Soviet Government declares:

> Null and void all the treaties concluded with China by the former Government of Russia, renounces all seizures of Chinese territory and all Russian concessions in China, and (restores) to China, without any compensation and for ever, all that had been predatorily seized from her by the Tsar's Government and the Russian bourgeoisie."

Surprisingly, however, the 1920 Karakhan Declaration quickly dismissed the promise given in the 1919 Karakhan Declaration with regard to the Chinese Eastern Railway. Point 7 of this declaration proposed that: "China and Russia were to enter into formal diplomatic relations, and sign a special treaty on the way of working the Chinese Eastern Railway, with due regard to the needs of the Russian Socialist Federal Soviet Republic. . . ."[13]

Even more outrageously, on November 5, 1921, Soviet Russia concluded a secret treaty with Outer Mongolia under which "the Soviet Government recognized the People's Government of Mongolia as the sole legal authority of Mongolia." Worse still, Alexander Paikes, head of a subsequent Soviet mission to China, denied the existence of the secret Soviet-Mongolian treaty. His denial came upon his arrival in Peking on December 21, 1921, as the Washington Conference was in the midst of its proceedings. By doing so, he tried to compete with the latter for the attention of the Chinese government in discussing the matters concerning the Chinese Eastern Railway and the restoration of diplomatic relations between China and Russia. Paikes even attributed China's apprehension of Soviet ambition in Outer Mongolia to a mere misunderstanding. He, however, became tongue-tied after the secret Soviet-Mongolian treaty was published. On May 1, 1922, China's Ministry of Foreign Affairs sent Paikes a strong protest:

The Soviet Government has repeatedly declared to the Chinese Government that all previous treaties made between the Russian Government and China shall be null and void, that the Soviet Government renounces all encroachments on Chinese territory and all concessions within China, and that the Soviet Government will unconditionally and for ever return what has been forcibly seized from China by the former Imperial Russian Government and the bourgeoisie. Now the Soviet Government has suddenly gone back on its own words and secretly and without any right concluded a treaty with [Outer] Mongolia. Such action on the part of the Soviet Government is similar to the policy which the former Imperial Russian Government assumed toward China.[14]

As this repudiation tolled the death knell for Paikes' mission, Adolf Joffe, another Soviet deputy people's commissar for foreign affairs, was authorized to settle all outstanding issues with China, including the questions of the Chinese Eastern Railway and Outer Mongolia. On September 2, 1922, Joffe proposed formal negotiations to the Chinese Foreign Ministry on the basis of the Karakhan declarations of 1919 and 1920. But Foreign Minister Wellington Koo demanded the withdrawal of Soviet troops from Outer Mongolia as a prerequisite. He also requested the Soviet government to reaffirm the Karakhan Declaration of 1919 quoted above: "The Soviet Government returns to the Chinese people without demanding any kind of compensation, the Chinese Eastern Railway, as well as all the mining concessions, forestry. . . ."[15]

Evidently, Soviet Russia's improved international situation after the conclusion of the Allied Intervention, e.g., the Japanese evacuation from Siberia, and the absorption of the Far Eastern Republic into Soviet Russia, helped uncover the earlier motivation behind the Karakhan declarations. Ironically, when the Chinese government insisted on negotiations specifically based on the Karakhan declarations, Joffe now retorted, untruthfully, that the passage concerning the Chinese Eastern Railway, as quoted by Dr. Koo, was not contained in the 1919 declaration. He also referred to the altered provision about the Chinese Eastern Railway in the 1920 declaration. He further contended that the Soviet move was contingent upon a stipulation in the same declaration that the Chinese refrain from aiding Russian counterrevolutionary activities in the Chinese territory. Apparently, the Soviet government was unwilling to evacuate Outer Mongolia and caused its "envoy to be bent on modifying and qualifying the Karakhan Declarations and disavowing their most important clauses."[16]

Astonishingly, in his note of November 6, 1922, to the Chinese Foreign Ministry, Joffe openly denied any obligation to implement the Karakhan declarations, saying that "while still regarding the declarations of 1919 and

1920 as the basis of her policy, Russia repudiated any inference that all her interests in China had been thereby renounced."[17] In his note of December 8, 1922, to the Chinese Foreign Ministry, Joffe stressed that the 1919 Soviet declaration to abandon the Chinese Eastern Railway did not mean its "unconditional return to China." He even warned that the Karakhan declarations "could not be regarded as valid forever."[18] Matters were complicated when the Chinese refused to negotiate until the Russians withdrew from Outer Mongolia. At the same time, the Soviets remained adamant that alleged aid by the Chinese to White Russian counterrevolutionaries be ended."

After five months of futile negotiations, Joffe left Peking for Shanghai en route to Japan "for reasons of health." While in Shanghai, he conferred with Dr. Sun Yat-sen and, as a result, a joint declaration was issued on January 26, 1923. While sharing Dr. Sun's view that "the Communist order or even the Soviet system cannot actually be introduced into China," Joffe assured Dr. Sun of Russian support for the national unification and full independence of China. The Sun-Joffe joint declaration[19] served as the basis for cooperation between the Kuomintang and Soviet Russia up to 1927. It also touched on the questions of the Chinese Eastern Railway and Outer Mongolia but left them for further Sino-Soviet renegotiations. Joffe officially clarified and reiterated to Dr. Sun, at the latter's request, that the "Russian Government is prepared and willing to renew Sino-Russian negotiations on the basis of Russian renouncement of the Russo-Chinese treaties concluded during the Tsarist era (including Contracts on the Chinese Eastern Railway and others)."[20]

Joffe's departure was followed shortly by the arrival in China of Leo Karakhan, author of the 1919 and 1920 declarations. He received a warm, official, as well as popular welcome when he arrived in Peking on September 2, 1923. But far from coming to implement his two declarations in letter and spirit, Karakhan, as already noted, immediately pressed for the revival of Soviet Russian exploitation of the Chinese Eastern Railway and tried to secure diplomatic recognition from China for the Soviet Union. Consequently, like Joffe, Karakhan went first to Harbin in Manchuria and spent some time there, trying to reach a prior agreement on the Chinese Eastern Railway with Marshal Chang Tso-lin, military governor of Manchuria. In this, however, he failed. Then, during an official call, Karakhan notified Chinese Foreign Minister Koo that the "Soviet Government desired China's recognition as a preliminary condition for formal negotiations." Karakhan also tried to present his credentials directly to the newly inaugurated President of China, Ts'ao K'un, even though, in the absence of bilateral diplomatic relations, he did not enjoy the status of an accredited regular envoy.

Karakhan likewise raised the issue of China's recognition of the Soviet government in the very first conversation with Dr. C. T. Wang, the newly appointed director of the Sino-Soviet Negotiation Commission. He even warned that "the Soviet people had the right to demand a proof of sincerity and friendliness on the part of China," because the Chinese Government "had participated in the Allied Intervention against Soviet Russia with the purpose of overthrowing the Soviet Government," and "had also supported the White Guards, who had a similar purpose." Karakhan's demand for immediate and unconditional diplomatic recognition was not only a diplomatic blunder, but also a calculated strategy to weaken the Chinese position in the negotiations.

While this self-created issue of diplomatic recognition as a precondition for formal negotiations caused an impasse, Karakhan did a further injustice to himself and his mission by promoting the publishing of the "authorized versions" of the 1919 and 1920 declarations in the English newspapers in Peking. These versions contained very serious modifications of the original ones. The supposedly "authorized" version of the 1919 declaration specifically omitted the clause relative to the Soviet surrender of the Chinese Eastern Railway, without compensation, as well as the clause providing for reciprocal responsibility to suppress the activities of organizations whose purpose was to jeopardize the security of the two governments.

Thus, serious discrepancies surfaced between the "authorized versions" and the original French version of the 1919 declaration received by the Chinese Foreign Ministry from the Soviet representative at Irkutsk which also literally corresponded with the Russian version published in Harbin and in the Soviet Far East. This unexpected deception tainted the Chinese public's favorable opinion of the USSR.

After this episode, Karakhan was bold enough to send a lengthy note to Dr. Wang, reemphasizing that China had to recognize the Soviet government before formal negotiations could start. Karakhan would have China believe that after recognition was granted, the Soviet government would consent to settle all questions with full regard to China's interests and still adhere to the declarations of 1919 and 1920. Ironically, the so-called "authorized" copies of the 1919 and 1920 declarations were attached to this lengthy note as a "negotiations guide."

Dr. Wang's reply to Karakhan, dated January 9, 1924, pointed out that in the light of discrepancies which had arisen between the original declarations and the subsequent altered ones, the version received by the Chinese Foreign Ministry should be regarded as authoritative. As to Karakhan's persistent demand for recognition of the Soviet government, Dr. Wang reaffirmed his previous position that recognition should be discussed together with other questions.

On March 14, 1924, after protracted exchanges between them, Wang and Karakhan reached an agreement consisting of 15 articles that provided for the following: joint administration of the Chinese Eastern Railway, immediate establishment of diplomatic and consular relations, Soviet evacuation of Outer Mongolia as soon as the conditions for such evacuation were agreed upon, Soviet nullification of all Tsarist treaties affecting China's sovereign rights, China's nullification of her treaties affecting Soviet sovereign rights, and return by China of former Russian church property to the Soviet government.

After Wang initialed the preliminary text of the agreement along with Karakhan, he submitted it to the Chinese cabinet for consideration. The cabinet refused to approve the agreement primarily because of the following considerations: (1) the agreement ignored those treaties between Soviet Russia and Outer Mongolia that virtually treated Outer Mongolia as an independent state and thus violated China's sovereignty over it; (2) the agreement attached "conditions" to Soviet evacuation of Outer Mongolia, whereas such evacuation should have been effected unconditionally; (3) The transfer to the Soviet government of the property of Russian churches would have set a precedent that might have been utilized by other countries.

Karakhan flew into a rage when he learned of the cabinet's rejection of the agreement. On March 16, 1924, he sent a note to Dr. Wang, setting a three-day limit for the confirmation of the agreement by the Chinese government, and declared that "upon the expiration of this time limit, the agreement would be no longer binding and the Chinese Government would be held responsible for the consequences." The Chinese government, however, "deemed it improper for the Soviet envoy to set a three-day limit."

Three days later, on March 19, 1924, Karakhan addressed a strong note to Foreign Minister Koo, stressing that "the Soviet Government warns the Chinese Government against committing an irretrievable mistake" that "after the time limit previously set had expired, the Soviet Government would not be bound by the agreement signed on March 14" and that "in such eventuality the Chinese Government would not be able to resume negotiations until it had first of all unconditionally recognized the Soviet Government."

On the same day, in a much longer note to Wang, Karakhan refuted the view of the Chinese government that the negotiations had not been completed and charged that the Chinese government had no sincere wish for friendship with the Soviet Union. He even suggested that the undeniable cause of the disavowal by the Chinese government of the signed agreement with Russia was pressure from foreign powers. In his reply to that statement, Dr. Koo, on March 22, wrote to Karakhan that "Dr. Wang had no authority to sign the agreement." He also expressed surprise about the time limit set by Karakhan and rejected his charge that China's foreign affairs were subject to foreign influence. Dr. Koo notified Karakhan of his willingness to continue the negotiations, but Karakhan absolutely declined to carry on any further talks unless they were preceded by immediate resumption of normal official relations between the two countries.

On May 31, 1924, as a result of a last-minute compromise following the British and Italian recognition of the Soviet government, the Sino-Soviet Agreement on General Principles, an Agreement for the Provisional Management of the Chinese Eastern Railway, seven accompanying declarations and an exchange of notes were nonetheless signed. Thereby the Soviet Union recognized Outer Mongolia as an integral part of China, and pledged to withdraw Soviet troops from Outer Mongolia "as soon as the questions for the withdrawal were agreed upon at the stipulated conference."[21]

In the final analysis, the Soviet Union became the sole beneficiary of the Sino-Soviet agreement of 1924. It not only granted at once to the Soviet Union its much sought diplomatic recognition from China, but also enabled the USSR to inherit Tsarist Russian property rights, including, most importantly, the Chinese Eastern Railway, then supposedly under joint Sino-Soviet ownership and management. On the other hand, the Chinese gained nothing save the unredeemed Soviet assurance of readiness to negotiate the outstanding issues. However, even this pledge did not fully materialize as the Soviets intentionally delayed the convening of the proposed conference for 15 months, until August 26, 1925, although they had previously agreed to hold it within one month. Instead of resolving the outstanding issues within six months as stipulated in the 1924 agreement, the session was aborted when Karakhan, under pretext, departed to Moscow before any substantive issue could be debated and resolved.

Having thus deceptively inherited certain Tsarist privileges, the Soviets did not, however, honor the obligations under the 1924 agreement either. They reduced it to a mere instrument of exploitation. Violating the cardinal principle of joint ownership and management of the Chinese Eastern Railway, they utilized the railway to promote Communist activities. The Soviet general manager of the railway continually abused his power at China's expense, and the Chinese Eastern Railway itself was ultimately sold, unilaterally and illegally, by the Soviets to Japan through the latter's puppet state of Manchoukuo. Disgracefully, the Soviets indirectly, through the Allies, compelled China to reconcede the joint ownership and management of the railway under the August 1945 Sino-Soviet treaty that was supposed to implement the then already obsolete and superfluous February 11, 1945 Yalta Agreement Concerning China.

Unequal Russian Treaties with China: the Deceptive "Alliances"

Going beyond usual exploitative practice, Russia, under the facade of cooperation, but actually through deception, further promoted opportune alliances to bind China with unequal treaties. The three exploitative alliances of 1896, 1945, and 1950 epitomize the 300-year history of relations between Russia and China. These questionable alliances were born of biased treaties which victimized the Chinese. Russia capitalized on the inequitable nature of each alliance in order to acquire concessions and privileges. The first alliance of 1896 was concluded by Tsarist Russia with the weakened Chinese Ch'ing dynasty. The second alliance of 1945 was signed by the Soviet Union with Nationalist China. (This marked the first unequal treaty since the abrogation in 1943 by China's wartime allies of such agreements imposed on the late Ch'ing dynasty.) Surprisingly, the third alliance, though signed by the two Communist regimes in 1950, was as inequitable in character as those of 1896 and 1945.

The first "alliance" was initiated by Count Witte, the leading minister of Tsar Nicholas II, following the humiliating and disastrous Chinese defeat in the Sino-Japanese War. Witte offered a full-fledged alliance with China, allegedly to counter further Japanese expansion. The primary aim of this ploy was to bait China into making strategic railway concessions across Manchuria to facilitate Russian military movement if and when China required her assistance. This concession, under the guise of international commercial investment, resulted in the Russian imperial scheme of creating a state within a state in Manchuria, and making that region of China a battleground between the two imperialist powers of Tsarist Russia and Japan. Following Russian defeat in the Russo-Japanese War of 1904–05, China was ultimately forced to recognize the transfer of the leased ports of Port Arthur and Dairen, and of the southern branch of the Chinese Eastern Railway, from Russian to Japanese control.

The second "alliance" resulted from the 1945 Sino-Soviet treaty. Both the Yalta Agreement Concerning China and the ensuing Sino-Soviet treaty of 1945 were Soviet ploys to exact greater concessions from the Allies who desired Soviet entry into the war against Japan. President Chiang Kai-shek frankly admitted: "It would be unrealistic to deny the influence which the American policies toward Soviet Russia and China had exerted on Sino-Soviet negotiations in the Spring of 1945."[22] However, the August 6, 1945, Hiroshima, and the August 9, 1945, Nagasaki bombings precipitated the Soviet and Mongolian march into Manchuria, without waiting for the implementation of the Yalta agreement via a Sino-Soviet treaty. Since the 1945 Sino-Soviet treaty was concluded after Soviet entry into the war against Japan, the very purpose of this treaty had already been overtaken by events.

Ironically, after two rounds of tough negotiations that took place before and after the Anglo-American-Soviet Summit Conference in Potsdam, the treaty was finally signed on the morning of August 15, 1945, the day of the Chinese delegation's departure from Moscow. Incredibly, the treaty was predated to give the appearance that it served its original purpose of ensuring Russian participation in the war against Japan. Regardless of who initiated the predating of that treaty, the Soviets perpetrated a similar deception when they announced its signing in their media two hours before the announcement of the Japanese surrender on the afternoon of August 14, 1945 (Moscow time). This broadcast was heard repeatedly by this writer while in Moscow at the time. In fact, President Chiang Kai-shek wrote to the same effect: "When the war with Japan ended, the Chinese government signed a Treaty of Friendship and Alliance with Soviet Russia."[23] Despite this, the thus updated treaty opens with the following completely misleading statement: "The High Contracting Parties undertake . . . to wage war against Japan until final victory is won . . . (and) to render one another all necessary military and other assistance and support in this war." (Art. 1).

It is indeed regrettable that this treaty, which was already pointless by the time of its signing, was nevertheless imposed on China. President Truman representing the leading ally working with China could have relieved China of this awesome sacrificial burden as soon as the Soviets greedily and instinctively rushed into the war against Japan in its waning hours for their obvious self-aggrandizement. The Soviets obviously did not consider the Sino-Soviet treaty a prerequisite to their entry. At that time negotiations could have been aborted or carried out for a more equitable outcome. The Chinese Nationalist government, too, could have independently resisted and further procrastinated. In retrospect, presence and consultation of both United States ambassador to the USSR, Averell Harriman, and the Chinese delegation, headed by Premier T. V. Soong, in Moscow, could have reversed this course. Even after this dubious treaty was signed, the Chinese Nationalist government could have followed the recent Iranian example of refusing to ratify the treaty. With the treaty ratified, however, the Soviet Union was left with a free hand to reap its bountiful harvest.

There is no doubt that it would have been better for the Western Allies, China and Japan if the Pacific theater of World War II had concluded without the participation of the Soviet Union altogether. The entry of Soviet and Mongolian forces into Manchuria during the last six days of the war had contributed nothing to the Allied solidarity in victoriously ending the war. It was motivated solely by Soviet desires to establish the USSR as *de facto* overlord and arbiter in that region, and served exclusively the Soviet interests of self-aggrandizement. The treaty of 1945 served only to provide the Soviets with a legal basis for freely pursuing these selfish interests. However, in their aggressive pursuits the Soviets did not stop at grossly violating even that same treaty, whenever they found it opportune to do so.

American diplomatic notes on the Open Door policy in Manchuria, compatible with the Chinese Nationalist government's economic policies, could not stop Soviet Russia from plundering Manchuria of its industries and pillaging its economic resources. According to the report by Edwin Pauley, American representative on the Inter-Allied Reparations Commission, published by the U.S. Department of State on December 15, 1946, the loss of industries in Manchuria, that was due to the dismantling and shipping of industrial equipment to the USSR during the Soviet occupation there, was valued at $2 billion.[24]

The Soviet military presence was like a plague upon Manchuria. The Soviets not only stripped Manchuria of its material resources, but also terrorized the populace. The female population had to shave their heads like Buddhist nuns in order to avoid being raped by the undisciplined Soviet Red Army soldiers. Yet this was still considered less pressing than many other Soviet violations of the 1945 Alliance Treaty with China.

The Nationalist government of China continually refused to sign this treaty without a prior, unequivocal pledge from the Soviets to withdraw all support from the Chinese Communists and dissociate themselves from Chinese Communist attempts to topple the Nationalist government with a view to taking power in China exclusively for themselves. After some hesitation—since at that time it was opportune for the Soviets to have the treaty signed regardless of its content—the Soviet side had agreed to refrain from dealing with the Chinese Communists and to channel all aid exclusively to the Chinese Nationalist government. It was only on the basis of this pledge that the Chinese Nationalist government had agreed to put its signature to the 1945 Sino-Soviet Alliance Treaty. In a further exchange of notes on Sinkiang, Manchuria and aid to China—an Agreement Related to the Sino-Soviet Treaty of August 14, 1945—Soviet Foreign Minister Molotov wrote to Chinese Foreign Minister Wang Shih-chieh: "The government of the USSR agrees to render to China moral support and aid in military supplies and other material resources. Such support and aid are to be entirely given to the National Government as the Central Government of China."[25]

In reality, however, the Soviets not only shielded the Chinese Communists, but also supplied them with arms. While occupying Manchuria at the end of World War II, the Soviets did not permit the landing of the Chinese Nationalist forces at Manchurian ports, including Dairen, acknowledged to be under Chinese administration. Chinese troops were also deterred from landing at the naval base of Port Arthur, agreed to be under joint Sino-Soviet control.

The Soviets further violated the agreement by supplying the Chinese Communists with all the surrendered Japanese arms, a quantity more than adequate to equip over one million men. Upon marching into Manchuria after their declaration of war against Japan on August 9, 1945, the Soviets sent the Outer Mongolian forces to invade Charhar and Jehol in Inner Mongolia. Outer Mongolia, though still recognized by the Soviets as an integral part of China rather than an independent state in the community of nations, ostensibly declared war against Japan on August 11, 1945. On August 23, under the cover provided by the Soviet and Mongol forces, Chinese Communist troops entered Kalgan. In the name of their Outer Mongolian puppets, Soviet troops sent arms and ammunition to "Inner Mongolia," and dispatched the so-called "Soviet-Mongolian Military Mission" to Kalgan to train and equip the Chinese Communist forces there.

Far from rendering the aid to the Chinese Nationalist government stipulated in the 1945 treaty, the Soviets consistently prevented the Chinese Nationalist government from assuming full authority over the recovered territory then under Soviet occupation. Moreover, despite repeated protests from the Chinese Nationalists, the Soviets continuously sent Mongolian forces to the Paitaishan area, on the Mongolian-Sinkiang border, to invade Sinkiang. At the same time, Moscow accused the Chinese of invading Outer Mongolia. These activities of Soviet and Outer Mongolian forces in the Chinese border regions, particularly in Manchuria, were not simply contrary to their obligations under the 1945 Alliance Treaty—they aided the Chinese Communists to create an invincible base for Mao's subsequent conquest of the mainland.

It is henceforth an undeniable fact that Stalin, in blatant disregard of all his official pledges to the Nationalist government of China, directly instigated the Chinese Communists to rise against that government and who, by providing them from 1945 onwards with all the necessary help, played the decisive role in the Nationalist government's loss of the Chinese mainland to the Communists.

Thus, the 1945 alliance serves as another vivid illustration of the Soviet Union's misuse of offers of cooperation and alliances as bargaining chips, which are ignored as soon as immediate Soviet objectives associated with their conclusion are realized.

Following the adoption by the UN General Assembly on February 1, 1952, of the Chinese resolution condemning the Soviet Union of treaty violations[26] the Nationalist government of the Republic of China on Taiwan, on February 25, 1953, issued a proclamation abrogating the 1945 Sino-Soviet Treaty of Friendship and Alliance and Related Agreements

while retaining the right to demand compensation for all the losses suffered.
The third alliance concluded in 1950 closely followed the Chinese Communist takeover of the mainland. During the "golden decade of relations," 1949–1958, the Soviet Union enjoyed a period of intimate friendship and collaboration with the Chinese Communists. However, this collaboration was still at the expense of the Chinese partner. The close alliance was unprecedented in the diplomatic history of these two nations. The unflinching Chinese support for an absolute compliance with the treaty amazed the world. The Chinese Communists were aware of the fact that "Stalin never had any confidence in Mao"; Stalin consistently regarded Mao "as a peasant revolutionary leader who received only a little indoctrination in Communism and who was therefore not a 'genuine Marxist [-Leninist]', i.e., Stalinist." Furthermore, "Stalin's disdain for Eastern culture . . . , prolonged support for [the former CPC General Secretary] Wang Ming, etc. . . . ," all deeply troubled Mao.[27] Nevertheless, the Moscow-Peking axis forged by Stalin and Mao in 1950 was based on Mao's and his Party-state's complete allegiance to Stalin and the Soviet Party-state, as evidenced by Mao's animated call for his entire nation to learn from the Soviet Union.

Mao's blind loyalty and his unrestrained effort to sway China one-sidedly toward the Soviet Union was appalling. Mao placed his allegiance to Stalin and the Soviet Union ahead of China's interests. For example, Mao completely ignored the Chinese patriotic sentiments regarding the age-old Chinese irredenta—the recovery of lost territories—still aggressively retained by the Soviet Union: the Sixty-Four Settlements to the east of the Amur River in Manchuria, five out of six Pamirs in Sinkiang, and the moral and legal issue of Tannu Tuva, or Urianghai, originally an integral part of Outer Mongolia and China, which was secretly annexed by the Soviet Union in 1944. Under Mao, Communist China's submission to the USSR went to such an extent that it simply adopted the Soviet position in regard to Sino-Soviet boundaries, as recorded in maps and atlases of both countries and refrained from the public discussion of any territorial issues.[28]

Another illustration of this trend can be found in Mao's economic policy toward the Soviet Union, which once again flagrantly defied Chinese national interest. In order to promote the "socialist international market," China deliberately diverted about 75 percent of its foreign trade to the Soviet Union and the Soviet bloc. Mao's display of comradeship was again taken advantage of by his Soviet partner: China willingly purchased Soviet commodities at a price normally higher than that of the international market. In addition to this obvious sacrifice, China was repeatedly saddled with defective Soviet equipment.

Mao persisted in the above-mentioned territorial and economic relations with the Soviet Union, even though, as mentioned above, Stalin did not trust Mao and did not consider him a full-fledged Communist. Stalin continually discriminated against Mao and his Party, often depicting Mao as an agrarian reformer and not yet an authentic Communist. Mao once admitted that China went to war in Korea in order to convince Stalin that China was not a second Yugoslavia.[29] In spite of such humiliations, Mao always regarded Stalin as his mentor, and was happy to allow China to serve as a *de facto* Soviet satellite and proxy. In doing so, Mao was motivated by his dedication to Communism which he sought to serve through Stalin. Mao shouldered the Soviets' burden of fighting in Korea since he was anxious to spare Stalin's reputation.

The Chinese Communist regime paid a high price for its alliance with the Soviet Union. The partnership involved China in two foreign wars against the world's strongest power, the United States. One openly for nearly three years in Korea, and, afterwards, for an even longer period in Vietnam, though this was conducted by China secretly and, consequently, in a less bloody manner. The Korean War alone cost China about one million casualties.[30]

Chinese national interest suffered gravely under Mao, especially in the Sino-Soviet-Mongolian triangular relationship. Previously, the Soviet Union, while occupying Outer Mongolia since 1921, had officially recognized this occupied territory as an integral part of China and thus as being under Chinese sovereignty. This attitude was in accordance with the May 31, 1924, Sino-Soviet agreement and the numerous, solemn, though ostensible, reaffirmations of that position by Soviet authorities, including statements to this effect by the Soviet People's Commissar for Foreign Affairs, Maksim Litvinov. Under the 1945 Sino-Soviet treaty, China, as the sovereign over Outer Mongolia, granted its independence on the condition that a national plebiscite be held in 1946 to affirm this end. This, however, only nominally took place. Soviet Russia had, in fact, invaded Outer Mongolia and has established there two of her earliest, but separate, satellites of Outer Mongolia and Tannu Tuva, in 1921, called since 1924 the Mongolian and Tuvanian "People's Republics." The USSR has continued to hold on to the Mongolian and Tuvanian satellites ever since, even annexing Tannu Tuva in 1944, despite any agreements and treaties with China. Mao, in this respect, went far beyond the positions officially enunciated in the Sino-Soviet agreements of 1924 and 1945 by "honoring" the Soviet military occupation of 1921 as the date of Outer Mongolia's "independence."

Similarly, Chinese interests were compromised allowing the Soviets to circumscribe the commencement and extent of Sino-Mongolian relations. The Chinese Communists also suffered considerable economic losses by extending generous economic and technological assistance to Outer Mongolia between 1952 and 1960, far exceeding Soviet aid to the same. The Soviets had almost entirely neglected this region during their decades-long military occupation, which did not preclude Stalin from ruthlessly exploiting Mongolia's raw materials and human resources during World War II.

Mao's earlier unqualified pro-Soviet policies and his subsequent reversal of those policies emanated from his dedication to Communism and the Communist cause. He was utterly disappointed with Khrushchev's "modernizing revisionism" which became manifest in 1956 with the renunciation of Stalin's "personality cult," and Soviet adherence to unconditional "peaceful coexistence" with capitalism. For Mao this meant the Soviet Union's abandonment of the cause of the world proletarian revolution. Soviet revisionism, in Mao's view, from that time on had to be relentlessly combatted and unmasked alongside with the imperialist U.S.

Since revolutionary dedication based on common ideology was the catalyst and reciprocal prerequisite of Mao's earlier, unqualified loyalty to the Soviet Union, Khrushchev's revisionist adventure dismantled this foremost binding consideration. As a result, the Sino-Soviet contradictions on such long-suppressed issues as economic exploitation, territorial disputes, and leadership of the world Communist movement have been revived with the intention of proving that, ideologically, the revisionist Soviet Union is continuing the imperialist policies of Tsarist Russia. Conflicts that could have easily been ignored in relations between fraternal Communist states became insuperable in the newly evolved relationship between a genuinely revolutionary state and its revisionist counterpart. Khrushchev's high-handed response to Mao's criticism only poured more oil on the flame and pushed Mao, then totally desperate, to reverse drastically his earlier policies toward the USSR—from unconditionally pro-Soviet to bitterly anti-Soviet.

Among the various unbearable pressures Khrushchev exerted on Mao were the Soviet rejection of sharing the technology for producing the atom bomb, the Soviet noncooperation with and disapproval of the 1958 Chinese Communist offshore venture at Quemoy and Matsu, the Soviet demand to integrate the Chinese Communist navy into the Soviet Pacific Fleet, flatly rejected by China, the Soviet support for India in the Sino-Indian dispute, the Soviet insistence on the immediate payment for the heretofore unrequested cost of supplies for the Chinese Communist combat forces in the Korean War, in addition to an earlier $1 billion as the much inflated charge for the supposedly Soviet-built fortifications of Port Arthur before its return to China in 1955.

Incidentally, the merciless Soviet demand for repayment was instantly complied with by Mao's regime at the cost of the starvation to death of untold millions throughout China in what was commonly called "the Communist Wind." That happened because of bad harvest in China and the subsequent necessity to deliver even the seed grain for shipping to the Soviet Union in payment of the "debt." In doing so, Mao was evidently motivated by his desire for keeping high China's self-respect and her sense of superiority as a truly revolutionary power over the USSR.

Following the Moscow-Peking schism, further suffering of a psychological nature was inflicted on the Chinese when the First Secretary of the Mongolian People's Revolutionary Communist Party, Yudzhmagiyn Tsedenbal, fabricated lies concerning Chinese aggressive designs against Outer Mongolia. Similarly, the 10,000-man Chinese construction corps was abused by the Mongols and eventually expelled following the Sino-Soviet rift. Chinese nationals abroad who passed through Mongolia to reach China suffered similar mistreatment.[31]

The once monolithic Stalin-Mao Treaty of Friendship, Alliance and Mutual Assistance and Related Agreements lapsed in 1980. This 30-year treaty produced an intimate 10-year axis and then, like the short-lived alliances of 1896 and 1945, was essentially disregarded. What distinguished the 1950 alliance from its earlier counterparts was the signatories' proclaimed affiliation and dedication to Communism, which was supposed to extend their cooperation far beyond their respective national interests.

The failure of the 1950 alliance vividly reflects the fact that today Communism is not sufficient to provide for a long-term cohesion between the Communist Party-states. The endings of each of the three historical Sino-Russian alliances provides the policy-makers of both Russia and China with useful, though painful lessons.

Unequal Partnership and Schism: Consequences of Soviet-exported Communist Ideology

The Soviet ideological conquest of China must be regarded as the most successful export of Communist revolution on record. Despite Stalin's slighting and shortchanging of Mao, Mao's devotion to Stalin as mentor and teacher of the Chinese people made China a willing, subservient partner of the Soviet Union in a formidable axis that lasted from 1949 to 1959. Khrushchev's revisionist innovation, articulated through his de-Stalinization campaign, alienated Mao and led him to challenge the ideological purity of Stalin's successors. Peking's persistent antirevisionist struggle, up to 1977 supported by the Party of Labor of Albania and by Marxist-Leninist dissidents from other Communist and workers' parties, fragmented the international Communist movement. The post-Mao pragmatism, under the Deng Xiaoping-Hu Yaobang-Zhao Zhiyang leadership, negated the Proletarian Cultural Revolution of 1966–1976 and soft-pedaled earlier anti-revisionist struggle. Consequently, this pragmatism discounted the earlier antirevisionist polemics, particularly the noted 1963–1964 Nine Comments of the Communist Party of China on the July 14, 1963 Open Letter of the Central Committee of the Communist Party of the Soviet Union. In the light of the past, the role of Communist ideology in normalizing and improving relations between Russia and China is doubtful, to say the least.

Until recently, Sino-Soviet ideological contradictions, already systematized and institutionalized by the late 1970s, have been sharp and persistent.[32] In their protracted (and unreserved) polemics, Soviet attacks on China were primarily a desperate retaliation against the formidable and comprehensive ideological challenge on the part of the Chinese Communists.[33]

Favored themes of Soviet polemics include the cult of Mao's personality, the sinicization of Marxism, anti-Sovietism or anti-Communism, as well as chauvinism, hegemonism, and militarism. Characterizing Mao Tse-tung thought as a "metaphysical" and "idealistic replacement for genuine Marxism," the Soviets also accused Mao of vulgarizing and falsifying Marxism for the sake of systematic promotion of his personality cult. In fact, Suslov criticized the hegemonic ambition inherent in Mao's personality cult: "Like Stalin in his day, (he) sit(s) aloft like a god above all the Marxist-Leninist Parties and settle(s) arbitrarily all matters of their policy and work."[34]

Soviet and Chinese attacks on each other's "monstrous fabrications" and "slanders" in their protracted ideological polemics thoroughly debased Communism and tarnished the image of the international Communist movement. Different interpretations of the restrictive Communist ideology had shattered in toto the solidarity between the two giant Communist Party-states.

Since Mao's death, the differences between Peking and Moscow in ideological concepts and domestic politics have diminished. Their influence on the developments of Sino-Soviet relations have declined. Similar examples can be found in the improvement of relations between China and Yugoslavia, the East European satellites, and the Eurocommunist parties. The result of these pragmatic considerations has been the relaxation of their ideological strife by both Russia and Communist China. The less ideologically zealous, the more pragmatically and nationally oriented the Communist countries become, the easier appears to be the settlement of differences and conflicts between them.

Prospects for Future Settlement
Between Russia and China

The historical difficulties as well as relatively new ideological issues between Russia and China still exist and can multiply and intensify. Since no nation in the contemporary world can afford strictly to isolate itself from its neighbors, or, even less, enter into a state of war with them, something must be done. Russo-Chinese relations have never been characterized by either extreme. Yet, in order for Russia and China to enjoy peaceful coexistence through normalization of relations, existing disputes between them require equitable settlement. What are then the prospects for such a future settlement?

Necessity for Settlement Between Russia and China

Normally, for political, economic and strategic reasons, Russia would seek a peaceful environment that would ensure her domestic stability and a strong international position. The primary step towards improving Russia's relations with China would involve the relaxation of tension and mutual reduction of forces along their 4,000-mile border which China has frequently requested in the past. According to one estimate, "the Soviet Union has nearly a third of its entire 3.7 million-man army positioned on or near the Russian-Chinese border. These Soviet troops are armed with the latest weapons and nuclear missiles."

China also has concentrated a considerable portion of her "4.2 million-man People's Liberation Army . . . near the sensitive border with the Soviet Union." As some military analysts suggest, "the military preparations on the Sino-Soviet border represent the biggest arms buildup the world has ever seen." China is said to have "missiles capable of hitting Moscow, Leningrad and other major centers in European Russia." China's nuclear program has "grown out of its atomic diapers," with a considerable capacity for nuclear retaliation. Many diplomatic observers today "virtually dismiss the possibility of a Russian preemptive strike against China" which was still feasible over a decade ago. The increased Chinese military potential naturally makes peaceful coexistence with China more attractive.

Incidentally, many foreign diplomats in the USSR sense that "the Russians are obsessed with a fear of the East." The Russian "demographic fear of China is indelibly ingrained in the Russian consciousness." On the other hand, Russia's Sinophobia is reciprocated by China's Russophobia. Alarmingly, "the heated battle of words continues, (between them) with varying intensity." If hostilities were to occur between them, "the Chinese have publicly vowed to fight a 100-year war, if necessary, to achieve victory in any Sino-Soviet conflict that might erupt." According to recent observations made by Western military experts, "if Russia went into China, she may never come out." Aleksandr Solzhenitsyn in his "Letter to the Soviet Leaders" suggested that "a war against China would last 10 to 15 years and would cost Russia at least 60 million dead." Thus, it is generally agreed that "the risks of a Soviet strike against China are clearly prohibitive. Such a war would be futile and counterproductive for all concerned."[35]

Nonetheless, according to Premier Zhao Zhiyang, "the Soviet Union is still the most significant threat to (China's) national security," although China's overall strategic position vis-à-vis the USSR has improved, not only in nuclear and conventional forces, but also in terms of long-range economic strength. This potential has been particularly enhanced by China's technological, economic, and political cooperation with the West, especially the United States and Japan.[36] China's improved strategic potential will certainly place pressure on the leaders of Russia, whatever their intentions, for peaceful cooperation.

Moreover, Soviet strategists are afraid of being engaged in a two-front war with Europe and China. The nature and degree of the Sino-Soviet conflict within the Asian and Pacific region remains unchanged despite some continuing relaxation outside that region. China still insists on three prerequisites before the normalization of Sino-Soviet relations could be realized; namely, the removal of Soviet forces from Afghanistan, the retraction of Soviet support from Vietnamese hegemony in Laos and Cambodia, and the reduction of Soviet troops on the Sino-Soviet frontier. A subsequent requirement is that the Soviets reduce the number of intermediate-range missiles in the Far East. Thus, China continues to utilize all of her political and military might to break through Soviet strategic encirclement. Kremlin planners would do almost anything to prevent the dire prospect of worsening relations with China and the resultant negative impact it would have on Russia's eastern flank.

Of even greater significance to Russia will be the adjustment and expansion of her role in the triangular strategic relationship among herself, the United States and China. Presently, relations between Washington and Moscow are much more tense than those between Washington and Peking. For the superpowers, the "China factor," at least in the Asian and Pacific theater, has assumed unprecedented importance, while at the same time becoming more dynamic. Thus, Russian authorities may find it necessary to strike a political deal with China through accommodation and reconciliation. Indeed, despite a quarter of a century of mutual inflammatory accusations, the Sino-Soviet dispute is not necessarily "fixed in concrete." Both sides are aware of the enormous mutual benefit afforded by recent cooperation. For example, Sino-Soviet trade totalled more than $1 billion in 1984. They should also be aware that even greater advantages can be enjoyed under full reconciliation.

Though presently Sino-Soviet political confrontation continues, economic and cultural relations have made further progress. China's "economic reform and open door" policy, now in progress, has deepened the interdependence of the Chinese economy and the world market. During the past two years, foreign trade has constituted approximately 15 percent of China's gross national product, with possibilities of further expansion.[37] Russia could also benefit from China's desire for foreign capital, technology, and management techniques. These ostensibly could promote the reconciliation of their respective political and strategic interests as well.

Conditions for Settlement Between Russia and China

Many Western Kremlinologists and China-watchers presently maintain that the Soviet Union and China are "privately interested in a cautious normalization of relations over the long term."[38] But both sides realize that certain changes must be made before their relations can be improved. Hu Yaobang, the former General Secretary to the Communist Party of China (CPC), in his report to the XII National Congress of the CPC in September 1982, commented that the CPC "has suffered from the attempt of a self-elevated paternal party to keep [it] under control." For normalization of Sino-Soviet relations based on equality Hu recalled the five principles of peaceful coexistence that were initially advanced and elaborated by China and India, with the cooperation of Burma, at the 1954 Bandung Conference in Indonesia. They establish necessary guidelines for peaceful coexistence, and include the following: mutual respect for territorial integrity, political independence and national sovereignty; mutual noninterference in internal affairs; mutual nonaggression; mutual benefit; and generally peaceful relations.

In order to have peaceful relations, Russia and China both need to meet these prerequisites of peaceful coexistence. Soviet leaders have made repeated references to peaceful coexistence, initially enunciated by Lenin. In practice, however, the USSR has not considered the five principles of peaceful coexistence as a requisite to normal relations with other countries. Lenin's thesis on the inevitability of war has not been openly denied by his successors, despite Khrushchev's efforts to the contrary. Propaganda and psychological warfare bear the theme of "detente," which in reality, merely suggests a limited relaxation of tension between nations.

The Chinese Communists have consistently emphasized the five principles as quintessential to the realization of peaceful coexistence. Nearly all of the bilateral treaties which China has entered into over the past three decades have incorporated these operational principles of peaceful coexistence. They are now regarded as the central axiom of Chinese foreign policy.

It remains to be seen for how long the Chinese Communists will continue to recognize that "axiom" in practice. If, in the end, their commitment to Communist ideology prevails over the present drive for economic reform and normalization of relations with the West, they will be found, sooner or later, to resume their belligerent stance toward both the "U.S.-dominated capitalist imperialism" and "Soviet revisionist hegemonism." If, however, China unreservedly follows its present path of development, the country will inevitably be transformed from a Communist to a normal nation-state, minding its genuine national interests and trying to preserve a peaceful environment that would be most conducive to the effective pursuit of these interests.

The Soviet Party-state, on the other hand, is today also experiencing a crisis of its Communist identity. In 1921, Lenin embarked on the New Economic Policy, and invited Dr. Armand Hammer to be the first foreigner to take concessions from the Soviet government; Lenin frankly admitted to Hammer that he was doing so because "Communism is not working."[39] These words of Lenin are more true today than ever before. According to the analysis of a number of authoritative students of Soviet politics, the Soviet system finds itself at present on its last legs. Therefore one could expect, in the not too distant future, its demise and the emergence of a new Russia.[40] As Alexander Shtromas has suggested, the first post-Soviet government of new Russia will hardly be democratic; it will nevertheless have to be a popular government committed to a rational and radical solution to Russia's outstanding grave domestic and international problems. Among other tasks, this government will have to put an end to Russia's artificial, ideologically motivated, confrontation with the outside world. By any rational standards, it is unnecessary and nationally damaging. As Shtromas concludes, new Russia, whatever the form of her government, will seek to cultivate genuine cooperation with the West and all her numerous neighbors, including China.[41]

New Russia cannot conceivably foster any illusions of the benevolence of its neighbor, Communist China. Due to Russia's own long Communist experience, she will be bound to consider Communist China as a hostile force and a potential threat. The same would also apply to new China's attitude toward Russia, if indeed Russia were to remain Communist after the transformation in China. It seems therefore that a harmonious relationship between Russia and China only could develop when both these nations firmly relegate Communism to their past history and evolve a new order adequately reflecting their true national characters. In other words, one should not expect much improvement in the relations between the Soviet and Chinese Communist party-states, but one should be quite sure of the potential for relations between new Russia and new China gradually becoming harmonious.

Under these new conditions however, the path for Russo-Chinese reconciliation and cooperation will not be entirely smooth and straightforward. The traditional, mutual mistrust is not so easy to overcome. Russian Sinophobia, particularly Russia's fear of "yellow alliance" through the merger of Japanese technological proficiency and Chinese manpower, will, no doubt, remain an obstacle to truly good relations for some time to come. Russia's self-perceived mission of keeping out the "yellow peril" is also a snag. So is the Russophobia of the Chinese and their long-standing mistrust of Russia. However, since the survival of Russia and China requires their collaboration, they will have to overcome such stumbling blocks through a mutually enlightened approach to one another's interests.

Striving for respect, territorial integrity, national sovereignty and political independence, new China would expect new Russia genuinely to acknowledge her national sovereignty and territorial integrity. China would also anticipate Russia's demonstration of sincerity and willingness to negotiate protracted territorial issues. Such negotiations would inevitably have to include Chinese irredenta, related to the territories incorporated into Russia throughout the duration of history without the sanction of any treaties. China would naturally not make claims against Russian sovereignty over territories ceded under old unequal treaties. She would expect, however, a candid and sensible acknowledgment by Russia of her past territorial acquisitions made at China's expense.

Russia's good faith could also be demonstrated by the recognition and remedy of past exploitative economic practices which have victimized China, including the wanton removal of assets from Manchuria. China would also expect a new spirit of equality and friendship to be the hallmark of Sino-Russian relations. Both countries must realize that imperial expansionism and exploitation belong to the past, and that colonialism has given way to economic and technological assistance. So far in this shift of paradigms, the Soviet Union has not been an equal partner. Since the end of World War II, the United States has donated $160 billion in foreign aid to its former enemies, to its allies, and to Third World countries. During the same period, the Soviet Union has loaned only $20 billion, with four percent interest. Hopefully, new Russia will adopt the orientation of the former colonial powers, who presently have a net inflow of assets into the developing Third World.

Hu Yaobang, the former General Secretary of the CPC, listed three major obstacles that first must be removed by the Soviets before relations can be normalized: 1) The massive stationing of Soviet troops along the Outer Mongolian border, 2) Soviet support for the Vietnamese invasion of Cambodia, and, 3) The Soviet occupation of Afghanistan. Deng Xiaoping, pursuing a pragmatic approach and not withstanding his protege's earlier statement, told 60 American commercial leaders and reporters in October 1985 the following: "We realize that removing all these obstacles at the same time 'might' be difficult. [So now we say] one at a time."[42]

On the Soviet side, Gorbachev, in his first major speech after becoming CPSU General Secretary, expressed a desire to see "a serious improvement in relations with China." In a statement he made in 1986, Gorbachev pointed out the following: "We view as very important the fact that the two Asian nuclear powers, the USSR and the PRC, have both undertaken not to be the first to use nuclear weapons."[43]

Presently, while political differences continue to beset the two Communist giants, relations in the diplomatic, economic and cultural spheres have advanced. They improved in 1985, though the persisting tripartite issues of the border troops, and the Afghan and Vietnamese situations continued to cast their towering shadows. On June 21, 1985, the USSR and China agreed to reopen their respective consulates in Shanghai and Leningrad. In addition, a five-year trade agreement and an economic co-operation accord were signed in Moscow on July 10, 1985. Exchanges of visits have become more frequent and varied. In 1985, the first exchange of parliamentary delegations since the mid-1960s occurred. On November 18, 1985, a group of Mainland China writers visited Moscow. Sino-Soviet sports exchange protocol were also signed for 1986.[44]

Russia can maximize the mutual benefits of its foreign relations by responsibly acknowledging her past exploitation and correcting her past mistakes to China. By these concessions, Russia would be able to win Chinese understanding and friendship.

Possible Benefits of Future Settlement Between Russia and China

Once existing negative issues between Russia and China are settled, the door for possible cooperation will be open. Notably, economic, cultural and scientific exchanges would benefit both countries. The amelioration of relations between Russia and China would not only enhance their own national interests, but international peace and prosperity as well.

Common characteristics of both Russia and China include their large size, multiple nationalities, and relatively low standard of living. The Soviet Union has experienced a lower standard of living than several of her East European satellites, including East Germany, Hungary, and Czechoslovakia. In a similar comparison, China's standard of living ranks lower than that of Albania. Being less developed nations, Russia and China may be more inclined to cooperate with the rich and privileged states. However, a feasible remedy to their problems of chronic shortages and economic backwardness might be the sharing of their available means for mutual assistance.

Since the advent of new technology serves as a catalyst for further joint economic development projects, a new international environment portends rising expectations in the Russo-Chinese equation. Painful lessons drawn from earlier episodes of mutual contacts can prevent a repetition of previous unfortunate consequences. The new spirit of mutual benefit will enable the two countries to extend the scope and variety of cooperative projects. The joint enterprises, however, must only be embarked upon on a truly reciprocal basis. For instance, Russia and China might examine the possibility of the once proposed joint exploration of natural resources and navigation of inland waterways along the border regions of the two countries.

If centered around equitable mutuality, cooperation will develop positively between Russia and China and genuine friendship will be fostered. Progress has already been made: Peking has made it known that it does not demand the return of the 1.5 million sq. km. of Chinese territory. Furthermore, it is willing to readjust 33,500 sq. km. of disputed territory and to conclude a new treaty. In addition, as an apparent gesture of good will, Peking has rescheduled construction of the 240 km.-long Urumchi-Usu section of the trans-Sinkiang Railroad (which was interrupted in 1960 because of fear of Soviet aggression) during the Seventh Five-Year Plan. This railway will be connected to the Soviet Turksib Railway via the Friendship Railway at the border city of Aktagay in 1988.[45] Then no further episodes of encroachment and resistance will follow, but the frontier belt will possibly be viewed as a common "backyard" for both countries, similar to the free passage across the U.S.-Canadian border.

Cooperation can likewise be realized in social and cultural spheres by exchanging personnel in a variety of official and nonofficial capacities and by the reciprocal visits of representatives of various public bodies, including churches and trade unions. Culturally, academic institutions and research organizations can also participate in various exchange programs which potentially may serve as the basis for better understanding between the two peoples. Even now, after the end of the Chinese Cultural Revolution, the exchange of students and academics has been reinstituted. Further expansion of these exchange programs, without political and ideological restrictions, would benefit Russia and China in facilitating their peaceful cooperation.

Thus, if a sensible and reliable settlement between Russia and China were achieved, a higher degree of interdependence could develop between the two countries. Naturally, geographic, demographic, economic, scientific, and technological factors could largely contribute to the upgrading of the degree of mutual understanding and possible cooperation between them. However, in order to successfully build a future harmonious relationship between Russia and China, a careful scrutiny of the history of that relationship should first be undertaken by both sides. For only through such a scrutiny could the grievances be redressed, the mistakes averted, and the proper lessons learned.

Notes

1. Immanuel C.V. Hsu, *The Ili Crisis: A Study of Sino-Russian Diplomacy: 1871–1881*, (Oxford: The Clarendon Press, 1965), p. 2; cf. W.A. Douglas Jackson, *The Russo-Chinese Borderlands*, (Princeton, 1962), pp. 112, 113, 116.
2. Russia has been involved in significant wars with virtually all her neighbors including Sweden, Poland, Lithuania, Romania, Turkey, Persia (Iran), and Afghanistan. She suffered disastrous defeats during the Crimean War, 1856–58, and the Russo-Japanese War, 1904–05. China, under the pressure of the imperialist powers, was forced to fight a series of major foreign wars: the Opium War of 1840–42, the Anglo-French War of 1857–58, the Sino-Japanese War of 1894–95, and the Chinese War of Resistance against Japan, 1937–45.
3. According to the unratified 1879 Treaty of Livadia, China would have lost to Russia vast territory around Ili if the renegotiated 1881 Treaty of St. Petersburg had not restored some of this territory in exchange for additional indemnities. This modest accommodation was probably agreed by Russia because of her already achieved unparalleled expanse into Chinese territory.
4. For more details, see: Peter S.H. Tang, *Russian and Soviet Policy in Manchuria and Outer Mongolia 1911–1931*, (Durham, N.C.: Duke University Press, 1959), pp. 3–35, 208–241, 371–398, 400–425; Peter S.H. Tang, *Russian Expansion Into the Maritime Province: The Contemporary Soviet and Chinese Communist Views*, (Washington, D.C.: Research Institute on the Sino-Soviet Bloc, 1962), pp. 1–50; Peter S.H. Tang, "Sino-Soviet Border Regions: Their Changing Character," in Kurt London (ed.), *Unity and Contradiction: Major Aspects of Sino-Soviet Relations*, (New York: Praeger, 1962), pp. 265–270, 273–277, 281–283, 289–291; Peter S.H. Tang, "Sino-Soviet Territorial Disputes: Past and Present", in *The Russian Review*, Vol. 28, No. 4, October 1969, pp. 404–407.

5. For further details, see: Peter S.H. Tang, "Sino-Soviet Territorial Disputes . . . ," pp. 410–411, 413.

6. For Russian accounts of Russia's expansion into China, see: Russia. Imperial Academy of Sciences, *Atlas Russicus*, No. 17, p. 19; "Kitai vo vtoroi polovine 17 v." ("China in the Second Half of the 17th Century"), in *Bol'shaia Sovetskaia Entsiklopediia* (*Great Soviet Encyclopedia*), (2d ed.; Moscow: Gosdarstvennoe nauchnoe izdatelstvo, 1953), Vol. XXI, p. 209 (map) and reprinted in *Kitai* (*China*), (Moscow: Gosudarstvennoe nauchnoe izdatelstvo Bol'shaia Sovetskaia Entsiklopediia, 1954), pp. 124–125; D.A. Davidov, *Kolonizatsiia Man'chzhurii i S.-V. Mongolii* (*Colonization of Manchuria and Northeastern Mongolia*), (Vladivostok: Izd. Vost. Ins., 1911), pp. 11–14; D. Romanov, "Prisoedinenie Amura k Rossii: Period I: Otkrytie i zavoevanie reki Amura, 1636–1689" ("The Annexation of the Amur to Russia: Period I: The Opening and Conquest of the Amur River, 1636–1689"), in *Russkoe Slovo* (*The Russian Word*), Part I, April 1859, p. 200; Ivan P. Barsukov, *Graf Nikolai Nikolaevich Murav'ev Amurskii po ego pis'mam, dokumentam, rasskazam sovremennikov i pechat-nym istochnikam* (*Count Muraviev Amurskii: According to His Letters, Documents, Tales of Contemporaries, and Printed Sources*), (Moscow: Sinodal'naia Tipografia, 1891), Vol. I, pp. 170–171 and 477–478.

For the author's more detailed accounts and extended comments on Russia's expansion in China, see Peter S.H. Tang, *Russian and Soviet Policy in Manchuria and Outer Mongolia 1911–1931*, pp. 26–33; Peter S.H. Tang, "Sino-Soviet Border Regions", in K. London, *op.cit.*, p. 268.

See also, Aitchen K. Wu, *China and the Soviet Union*, (London: Methuen and Co. Ltd, 1950), pp. 64–67.

7. Davidov, *op.cit.*, p. 16; quoted in Tang, *Russian and Soviet Policy in Manchuria and Outer Mongolia 1911–1931*, pp. 34–35.

8. For more details, see Hsu, *op.cit.*, pp. 2, 191–195.

9. See: William L. Langer, *An Encyclopedia of World History*, (Boston: Houghton Mifflin Company, 1958), p. 883; Tang, *Russian and Soviet Policy in Manchuria and Outer Mongolia 1911–1931*, pp. 4–5; Tang, "Sino-Soviet Border Regions: Their Changing Character," in K. London, *op.cit.*, pp. 268–269.

10. The Russian text is in V.P. Savvin, *Vzaimotnosheniia Tsarskoi Rossii i SSSR s Kitaem* (*Relations of Tsarist Russia and the USSR with China*), (Moscow: Politizdat, 1930), p. 97. For its English translation, see: L.T. Dennis, *The Foreign Policies of Soviet Russia*, (New York: Dutton, 1924), p. 316.

11. Tang, *Russian and Soviet Policy in Manchuria and Outer Mongolia 1911–1931*, pp. 138–139; cf. Allen S. Whiting, "The Soviet Offer to China of 1919," in *Far Eastern Quarterly*, August 1951, pp. 356–357, 362–364.

12. For more details, see V.P. Savvin, *op. cit.*, Tang, "Russian and Soviet Policy in Manchuria and Outer Mongolia."

13. For the Russian text of the 1920 Declaration, see Savvin, *op.cit.*, Appendix, p. 128; the official Chinese translation is in *Chung-O Hui-Tsien-kao Wen-chien* (Sino-Russian Conference Reference Documents) (referred to herein

after as *C.O.H.T.W.*), Peking, 1923, Vol. II, sh. 4–6; English translation in *China Year Book* (Peking and Tientsin, 1924) (referred to herein after as *C.Y.B.*), pp. 870–872.

14. *C.Y.B.*, 1924, p. 872.
15. Quoted in Wei, China and Soviet Russia, *op.cit.*, p. 25.
16. *C.Y.B.*, 1924, p. 860.
17. A. Joffe, "Russia's Policy in China," in *Living Age*, January 13, 1923, p. 73; *C.O.H.T.W.*, Vol. II, sh. 83; cf. *North China Herald*, November 18, 1922.
18. *C.O.H.T.W.*, Vol. II, sh. 93–95; cf. *C.Y.B.*, 1924, p. 861.
19. Text in *C.Y.B.*, 1924. p. 863; a Russian summary in *Izvestiia*, February 1, 1923; cf. Tang, *Russian and Soviet Policy in Manchuria and Outer Mongolia 1911–1931*, pp. 145–146.
20. *C.Y.B.*, 1924, p. 866; cf. V. Villenskii (Sibiriakov), "Sovetskoe Imushchestvo na Kitaiskoy zemle" ("The Soviet Property on Chinese Soil"), *Izvestiia*, September 13, 1923, p. 1.
21. On facts and circumstances related to the conclusion of the 1924 Sino-Soviet agreement, see: Wei, *op.cit.*, pp. 30–38; Tang, *Russian and Soviet Policy in Manchuria and Outer Mongolia 1911–1931*, pp. 148–156. Quotations are from these two sources and also from *C.Y.B.*, 1924, pp. 879–883, and *China Weekly Review*, March 22, 1924, p. 126.
22. Chiang Chung-Cheng (Chiang Kai-Chek), *Su-O tsai Chung-Kuo; Chung-Kuo yu O-Kung Sen-shih-nien Ching-li Chi-yao* (*A Synopsis of China's Thirty Year Experience with Soviet Communists*), (Taipei: Chung-Yang Weng-wu Kung-ying she, 1957) (referred to herein after as Chiang, *Su-O*), p. 139. The English version of this book is entitled, *Soviet Russia in China: A Summing-Up at Seventy*, (New York: Farrar, Straus and Cudahy, 1957) (referred to herein after as Chiang, *Soviet Russia*), p. 135.
23. Chiang, *Su-O*, p. 95; Chiang, *Soviet Russia*, p. 191.
24. Referred to in Chiang, *Su-O*, p. 175; Chiang, *Soviet Russia*, pp. 170–171.
25. For the complete text of this "Exchange of Notes on Sinkiang, Manchuria and Aid to China," see Wei, *op.cit.*, p. 336.
26. Because of the flagrant Soviet violation of the 1945 Sino-Soviet Alliance Treaty, particularly its Articles 5 and 6, concerning sovereign rights and economic aid, as well as Article 2(4) of the United Nations Charter concerning territorial integrity and political independence, the Chinese Nationalist government submitted a resolution of indictment (condemnation) to the Fourth, the Fifth and the Sixth Sessions of the United Nations General Assembly in 1949, 1950, and 1951 respectively. In both 1949 and 1950, the Chinese Nationalist resolution was not discussed at the Assembly sessions but was referred to the "Little Assembly" for study, a likely result of the then prevailing international situation and alignment. However, the Sixth Session of the UN General Assembly finally adopted the Chinese Nationalist resolution of February 1, 1952, 24 against 9, 25 abstentions. Among the charges were the Soviet purposeful procrastination of evacuation from Manchuria, not within three weeks up to three months as provided, but until May 1946; the Soviet plunder

through removal of US $2 billion-worth of equipment; and the Soviet prohibition (rejection) of the Chinese Nationalist landing in Dairen, Yingkou, and Hulutao to restore sovereign rights, while facilitating the Chinese Communist takeover of the latter ports through interference.

27. Li Meng, "Chung-Su Guan-hsi ti Tsung-chien-yueh: (Shang)" ("A General Review of Sino-Soviet Relations: Part I") in Lu K'eng (Chief Editor), *Hsin Tu-li P'ing-lun* (*New Independent Review Weekly*), No. 59, February 18, 1985; *Hua-yu K'uai-pao* (*Sino Daily Express*), February 18, 1985, p. 2. According to the editor of the *New Independent Review Weekly*, Mr. Li Meng is a visiting scholar from Mainland China and a specialist in matters concerning international relations and comparative politics. He is a visiting senior research associate of the American Atlantic Commission. He has done penetrating research in Sino-Soviet and U.S.-Chinese relations.

28. The maps and atlases published in Communist China follow exactly their Soviet counterparts in regard to the boundary lines between China and the USSR. They have utterly disregarded the sensitive irredenta shown on the end-paper maps of this writer's *Communist China Today: Domestic and Foreign Policies*, 1st ed. (New York: Praeger, 1957) and 2nd enlarged ed. (Washington, D.C.: Research Institute on the Sino-Soviet Bloc, 1961) that are consistent with maps and atlases published in Taiwan, Republic of China. The present writer enquired in 1981 about the discrepancy concerning the Chinese irredenta with Ambassador Chan Zemin of the People's Republic of China in Washington, D.C. The writer raised the same question in 1982 with academicians of the Chinese Academy of Social Sciences and particularly with those in the Xinjiang (Sinkiang), Heilongjiang (Heilungkiang), Jilin (Kirin) and Liaoning Academies of Social Sciences during a tour of the mainland as a participant in the United States' "Distinguished Scholar Exchange Program with the People's Republic of China." On both occasions, no relevant responses were forthcoming.

29. Li Meng, in *Hua-yu K'uai-pao* (*Sino Daily Express*), February 18, 1985, p. 2.

30. The Chinese Communist active participation in the Vietnam War against the United States was first mentioned to this writer in 1982, on a Yangtze voyage from Shanghai to Wuhan, by a high-ranking Chinese Communist general who considered China's tacit, *de facto* belligerent involvement a well-known fact, and therefore did not care to ask that the subject be kept confidential.

31. For example, a Chinese national holding a Romanian passport as well as his accompanying Romanian wife and mixed-blood children were insulted in Ulan Bator during their journey to Peking.

32. For the evolution of major Sino-Soviet contradictions, see Peter S.H. Tang, "Stalin's Role in the Communist Victory in China," in *American Slavic and East European Review*, Vol. XIII, No. 3, October 1954, pp. 375–388; Tang, "Soviet Plan for Peking," in *Current History*, Vol. 37, No. 219, November 1959, pp. 284–290; Tang, "The Sino-Soviet Bloc: An Appraisal of Its Strengths and Weaknesses," in Yuan-li Wu (ed.), *Realities of Communist*

China, (Milwaukee, Wisconsin: Marquette University Press, 1960), pp. 41–57; Tang, "Moscow and Peking: The Question of War and Peace," in *Orbis*, Vol. V, No. 1, Spring 1961, pp. 15–30; Tang, *The Twenty-Second Congress of the Communist Party of the Soviet Union and Moscow-Tirana-Peking Relations*, (Washington, D.C.: Research Institute on the Sino-Soviet Bloc, 1962), pp. 1–141; Tang, "Sino-Soviet Tensions," in *Current History*, Vol. 45, No. 266, October 1963, pp. 223–229; Tang, *The Chinese Communist Struggle Against Modern Revisionism: Theory and Practice*, (Chestnut Hill, Mass.: Research Institute on the Sino-Soviet Bloc, 1964), pp. 1–50; Tang, "Mao Tsetung Thought and the Soviet Union: Ideological Conflict," in *Asian Thought and Society*, Vol. II, No. 2, September 1977, pp. 185–195; Tang, "The Soviet, Chinese and Albanian Constitutions: Ideological Divergence and Institutionalized Confrontation?", in *Studies in Soviet Thought*, Vol. XXI, No. 1, March 1980, pp. 39–58. For the Chinese Communist ideological challenge and the Soviet retaliation, see also: Tang, "A Soviet Defense Mechanism," in *Studies in Soviet Thought*, Vol. XIV, No. 4, December 1972, pp. 391–400; Tang, "A Soviet Self-Reflection," in *Studies in Soviet Thought*, Vol. XIV, Nos. 1–2, March–June 1974, pp. 77–87; Tang, "The Soviet Onslaught of Mao Tsetung Thought: The Rumyantsev School," in *Studies in Soviet Thought*, Vol. XV, No. 3, September 1975, pp. 197–217; Tang, "Peking vs. Moscow on Détente: A Credibility Issue," in *Asian Thought and Society*, Vol. I, No. 2, September 1976, pp. 205–214; Tang, "Soviet Distortion of Mao Tsetung Thought in the *Filosofskaya Entsiklopediya*," in *Studies in Soviet Thought*, Vol. XVII, No. 1, March 1977, pp. 81–89; Tang, "China's International Image in the Soviet Mirror," in *Studies in Soviet Thought*, Vol. XIX, No. 3, January 1979, pp. 317–329; Tang, "Soviet Polemics Against Mao Zedong Thought: Themes and Motivations," in *Asian Thought and Society*, Vol. V, No. 12, December 1979, pp. 81–85.

For Russian-language sources including publications attacking Chinese anti-Sovietism, see D.B. Borisov and B.T. Koloskov, *Sovetsko-Kitaiskie Otnosheniia 1945–1970 (Soviet-Chinese Relations 1945–1970)*, (Moscow: Izdatel'stvo "Mysl," 1972), pp. 197–472; A.M. Rumyantsev, *Istoki i evoliutsiia idei Mao Tsze-duna (The Origin and Evolution of the Thought of Mao Zedong)*, (Moscow: Izdatel'stvo "Nauka," 1972), pp. 8–379; G. Girginov (ed.), *Reaktsionnaia sushchnost ideologii i politiki Maoizma (Reactionary Essence of the Ideology and Politics of Maoism)*, (Moscow: Izdatel'stvo "Mysl," 1974), pp. 58–333.

33. The open polemics between Moscow and Peking started with the Letter of the Central Committee of the CPSU to the Central Committee of the CPC, March 30, 1963. It was followed by the Chinese Proposal Concerning the General Line of the International Communist Movement, June 14, 1963. The Open Letter of the Central Committee of the Communist Party of the Soviet Union to All Party Organizations, to All Communists of the Soviet Union, dated July 14, 1963, intensified ideological disputes into polemics, in the form of the Chinese response of Nine Comments on the Open Letter, September

1963–July 1964, which, in part, led to Khrushchev's downfall, October 14, 1964.

For an essential collection of official polemic documents, see *The Polemic on the General Line of the International Communist Movement*, (Peking: Foreign Language Press, 1965), pp. 1–586. A number of these documents also appear in William E. Griffith, *The Sino-Soviet Rift*, (Cambridge, Mass.: The M.I.T. Press, 1964), pp. 239–490.

For documentary extracts concerning Sino-Soviet ideological disputes, see John Gittings, *Survey of the Sino-Soviet Dispute: A Commentary and Extracts from the Recent Polemics 1963–1967*, (New York: Oxford University Press, 1968), pp. 1–402.

34. M.A. Suslov, "On the Struggle of the CPSU for the Solidarity of the International Communist Movement" (Report on February 14, 1964 at Plenary Sessions of the CPSU Central Committee), *Pravda*, April 3, 1964, quoted in Peter S.H. Tang, *Chinese Communist Struggle Against Modern Revisionism: Theory and Practice* (Chestnut Hill, Mass: Research Institute on the Sino-Soviet Bloc, 1964), p. 49.

35. Li Meng, in *Hua-yu K'uai-pao* (*Sino Daily Express*), February 18, 1985, p. 2.

36. Li Meng, "Chung-Su Guan-hsi ti Tsung-Chien-yueh: (Hsia)" ("A General Review of Sino-Soviet Relations: Part II"), in Lu K'eng (Chief Editor), *Hsin Tu-li P'ing-lun* (*New Independent Review Weekly*), No. 60, *Hua-yu K'uai-pao* (*Sino Daily Express*), February 25, 1985, p. 2.

37. Li Meng, in *Hua-yu K'uai-pao* (*Sino Daily Express*), February 25, 1985, p. 2.

38. *Ibid.*

39. Dr. Hammer went to Russia initially to establish a field hospital to fight the spread of typhoid fever in 1921. While there he was struck by the extent of the famine, so he personally donated one million bushels of grain purchased from the U.S. at his own expense for one million dollars. This act of generosity caught Lenin's attention. Hammer was granted concessions to engage in business activities. He sold his business after nine years due to brutality and cruelty committed by Stalin whom he called a "despot". He is a unique foreigner who has had contact with Soviet authorities for some 64 years. As late as January 1985, he talked to the late President Konstantin Chernenko shortly before his death. Dr. Hammer relayed his above-quoted conversation with Lenin to Dr. Robert Schuller and his huge (thousands strong) congregation for Christian worship in Garden Grove, California, aired nationwide on ABC as "Dr. Robert Schuller's Hour of Power" program on Sunday, March 24, 1985, 7.30–8.30 a.m., Channel 5, WCVB, Boston. Also aired the same day on the educational channel, Channel 38, WSBK, Boston, as "Dr. Robert Schuller," 8.30–9.30 a.m.

Possony points out Lenin's rationale for the NEP. "Capitalism had to be reintroduced to preserve the political system of Communism." (S.T. Possony, *Lenin, The Compulsive Revolutionary*, [Chicago: Henry Regnery Company,

1964], p. 326.) According to Richard Löwenthal, the Communists had to "correct (and reformulate) their doctrine in order to maintain their power". (R. Löwenthal, *World Communism: The Disintegration of a Secular Faith*, [New York: Oxford University Press, 1964], p. XVIII.) He further emphasized: "The history of the Communist world movement has become a critique of its ideology." (*Ibid.*, p. XIX).

40. See, for example, M.K. Dziewanowski, "The Future of Soviet Russia in Western Sovietology," in *Coexistence*, Vol. 19, No. 1, April 1982, esp. the references to M. Fainsod's article, "Roads to the Future", on p. 97; A. Shtromas, *Political Change and Social Development: The Case of the Soviet Union*, (Frankfurt a/M. and Bern: Verlag Peter Lang, 1981). A penetrating analysis of the state of the Soviet system leading to the conclusion about the imminent fall of that system is given by a Soviet scholar writing under the pen-name F. Znakov. He is extensively quoted by Shtromas in English, but for a full text of his *Pamyatnaya zapiska* (Memorandum) in the original Russian, see Radio Liberty, *Arkhiv samizdata*, No. 374, 1966.

41. A. Shtromas, *op. cit.*, esp. pp. 132 and 138.

42. Wen-Hui Bao, Oct. 30, 1985, pp. 1–2; Yin Ch'ing-yao, "Peking-Moscow Relations; An Analysis," *Issues and Studies*, Vol. 22, No. 3 (March, 1986), p. 39.

43. "Statement by Mikhail Gorbachev, General Secretary of the CPSU Central Committee," International Affairs, No. 3 (March, 1968), p. 9.

44. *Issues and Studies*, Vol. 22, No. 2 (February, 1986), p. 61.

45. Wen-Hui Bao, Aug. 28, 1985, p. 3; Yin, *op. cit.*, pp. 47–48.

5

Prospects for Sino-Soviet Reconciliation: A Commentary on Chapter 4

HSI-SHENG CH'I

Professor Tang's essay tackles Sino-Soviet relations on three different levels. The descriptive level gives us a historical overview of Sino-Russian relations of the last 300 years; the analytical level highlights a clear pattern of relations and identifies its contributing factors; the prescriptive level stipulates the conditions that must exist to develop good relations.

The descriptive task is ably accomplished. From the Treaty of Nerchinsk (1689) to the Sino-Soviet Treaty of Friendship and Alliance (1950), Professor Tang's essay shows how the Russians have exploited China. Particularly fascinating is his detailed account of the twists and turns of the Karakhan Declaration.

On the analytical level, Professor Tang's major thesis is that Russia has consistently employed a cooperative facade to cloak an exploitative policy toward China, whereas China basically and naively pursued a policy of genuine cooperation toward the Russians. Professor Tang certainly has no trouble arousing our indignation over Russian acts of treachery and bad faith, but the effectiveness of his analysis is somewhat undercut by an exclusive focus on Russian deviousness without mentioning other relevant factors.

One serious omission is the impact of China's internal conditions or government policies on the outcome of Sino-Russian negotiations. For instance, it would be inadequate to attribute the Soviet gains from China in the 1920s to the cunningness of Soviet diplomats when we remember that the Soviet government itself had only recently been established, that it was also the victim of international intervention, that it was eager to win China's diplomatic recognition, and that it certainly was in no position to employ force against China.

A far more important factor is the inability of the Chinese diplomats to defend their own national interest. As a deeply divided nation at this time, China had neither institutional nor policy continuity in foreign relations. Factional masters had no concern for foreign affairs unless their own interests were affected. Viewed against a broader negotiating context, it becomes clear that China's own weakness and incompetence contributed at least as much to the outcome as Russian slyness. This also explains why China was not only victimized by imperialistic countries (e.g., Japan) but by her professed friends (e.g., the U.S. at Versailles) as well.

In contrast to the narrow-minded, self-serving, anachronistic warlord regimes, the Nationalist government under Chiang Kai-shek acquired power on the strength of its nationalistic appeal. In the 1930s, this government went to war against Japan to uphold China's national sovereignty, and subsequently applied vigorous pressure upon her allies to renounce their unequal treaties with China. Yet, barely two years after winning back China's lost rights from the Western Allies, she signed a new, unequal treaty with the Soviet Union which not only restored Soviet rights in Manchuria, but granted independence to Outer Mongolia.

Nobody would dispute that the Soviet behavior was reprehensible, but why did China accept the treaty? In spite of the substantial disparity of power between the two countries in 1945, the Nationalist government could have rejected the treaty and let the chips fall wherever they might. Had the Nationalist government done so, it probably would not have lost more rights than it actually did through the instrument of the treaty, but could conceivably have improved its bargaining position by exerting strong diplomatic pressure on both the United States and Soviet Union to compromise.

There was, however, one critical difference: without the treaty, the Soviet Union would not promise to withhold all assistance from the Chinese Communist Party and treat the Nationalist government as the sole legitimate government of China. Again, China's internal division played into the Russian hands. No matter how reluctantly, the Nationalist negotiators agreed to sign the 1945 treaty in exchange for a Soviet pledge to give the Nationalist government a free hand in settling its internal squabble against the Communists.

In view of Stalin's long involvement in China, it is not surprising that he reneged on his promise. But Professor Tang gives the Soviet Union undeserved credit by stating that her assistance was the main reason for the CCP's success. The Soviet arms and extended occupation surely gave the CCP the time and the means to consolidate their control over Manchuria. On the other hand, the Kuomintang government had been the sole beneficiary of foreign (including Soviet) military and economic aid to China for eight years. But Nationalist leaders let numerous opportunities to upgrade their armed forces slip through their fingers while allowing the Communist forces to expand to a position of parity with their own loyal troops.

The critical factor explaining the downfall of the Nationalist regime is not the Soviet intervention in the civil war, but the strategic blunders and political incompetence of the Chiang Kai-shek government. Chiang's decision to gamble with his best troops to crush the Communists in Manchuria, his refusal to broaden the political base of his government, and his inability to restrain the greed of his political allies and family members all contributed to his own demise.

The Soviet aid in 1945–46 certainly gave the Communist armed revolution a much-welcomed headstart, but there is little evidence of continued Soviet aid to the CCP. On the contrary, Soviet designs on China were so cautious that Stalin actually tried to persuade the Chinese Communists to halt their advance in central China and enter into a coalition government with the Nationalists.[1] Of course, Mao politely ignored Stalin's counsel and proceeded to drive Chiang out of the mainland. There is little evidence to show that the CCP leaders ever needed the direct instigation of Stalin to start the civil war, or that the Soviet Union provided the CCP "from 1945 onwards with all the necessary help," or "played the decisive role" in the CCP's eventual victory over the Nationalists as Professor Tang contends. All this is not meant to absolve the Soviet Union from her abominable schemes on China, but merely to point out that the latter's own internal weakness and incessant factional strife presented temptations of intervention that very few foreign governments could easily resist, regardless of their political ideologies.

While the Soviet exploitation of China in 1924 and 1945 was facilitated by China's internal division, the 1950 treaty was concluded at a time when China's national power was at its highest in over 200 years. The revolutionary zeal and confidence of the CCP leaders was overflowing, the popular support for the new regime was enthusiastic, and the military power under the unified command of the new government was enormous. At no point since China came into contact with the West was she in a better position to wipe the diplomatic slate clean and inaugurate a new era of equal treaties with all foreign powers. While this was precisely what Mao promised to do in March 1949 when he announced that the new China would exercise the right to recognize, abrogate, revise or renegotiate all her existing treaties with other foreign powers,[2] the PRC nonetheless chose to honor the 1945 treaty with the Soviet Union by incorporating its key unequal features into the new 1950 Treaty of Friendship and Alliance.

What accounts for the Chinese Communists' behavior? Professor Tang's answer is that Mao "placed his allegiance to Stalin and the Soviet Union ahead of China's interests." One can speculate that other factors may also have played a role. One obvious factor was a genuinely felt sense of ideological affinity and solidarity by the Chinese toward all socialist regimes. By the late 1940s, Chinese leaders had uncritically accepted the "two camps" thesis, and believed that they should side unflinchingly with the forces of revolution.[3] The prolonged isolation of the Communist guerrilla bases from the vortex of world affairs during the Sino-Japanese war also exacted a heavy toll by depriving their leaders of the opportunity to become acquainted with the intricacies of international politics. Possibly this naivete and ignorance blinded Mao and the entire CCP leadership to the potential of developing a more versatile, flexible, and equidistant approach toward all foreign powers. Instead, they foreclosed their diplomatic options by a premature announcement (July 1949) of the policy of "leaning to one side" and sealed their destiny with the Soviet Union.[4]

As Professor Tang correctly points out, the Chinese Communists paid an exceedingly high price for their alliance with the Soviet Union as attested by the trade terms, the Korean War cost, and China's diplomatic isolation. The worst miscalculation of the CCP leaders was their assumption of the existence of strong common interests within the world Communist bloc, and their conviction that Chinese interests would be better served by the spirit of internationalism. However, once they realized this assumption to be false, they quickly abandoned internationalism in favor of nationalism and pushed Sino-Soviet relations toward a breaking point.

Professor Tang's essay cites Communist China's position with respect to Sino-Soviet boundaries as evidence of the PRC's subservience to the Soviet Union. However, we need to remember that Mao first raised the issue of the status of Outer Mongolia with the Russians in 1954 when both countries still had very good relations.[5] The Chinese began to press the Soviets for renegotiation of the borders in August–September 1960, and by the early spring of 1963 reverted to the pre-Communist Chinese official position of regarding the Sino-Russian borders as the product of "unequal treaties" and demanding their renegotiation.[6] From this point on, border disputes became the most reliable barometer of Sino-Soviet tension and culminated in the Chengpao Island clash of 1969, marking the very first instance in two centuries that a unified national government of China resorted to arms to settle her border dispute with the Russians.

This brief historical review cautions us that the causes of unhealthy Sino-Soviet relations go far beyond Soviet deviousness or Mao's subservience to Stalin. Ideological differences were certainly important but there were other dimensions of the split as well. More than a manifestation of Mao's undying loyalty to Stalin, Chinese reaction over de-Stalinization was also a function of the clash between two very large egos (Mao and Khrushchev), as well as an expression of Chinese anxiety at the potentially damaging impact the Soviet action might have on Mao's own position in China. Indeed, Mao and the entire CCP quickly came under stinging attack by China's dissidents during the Hundred Flower Campaign, silenced only by a ruthless antirightist campaign.

If the Russians had been more circumspect and shown greater sensitivity to Chinese national pride and interests, the ideological differences of the mid-1950s might have remained well contained. Once the Chinese leaders concluded that they always seemed to get the short end in dealing with the Soviets, then all other repressed grievances burst into the open. In this sense, the course of Sino-Soviet estrangement signifies the triumph of Chinese nationalism over ideological solidarity. As Mao himself remarked in 1936, the Chinese would not seek emancipation from Western imperialism only to fall under the domination of the Soviet Union.[7]

In the history of the world Communist movement, its member-states have constantly felt the pull of two opposite forces: nationalism and internationalism. While many Communist East European countries have harbored a strong dislike for the domineering Soviet Union, only two of them (Hungary and Czechoslovakia) ever dared open defiance against the latter, and both paid dearly for their audacity. The Chinese began asserting their national independence in the mid-1950s and have stood their ground ever since. This contrast in styles can be quite helpful to our evaluation of the third dimension of Professor Tang's essay.

Professor Tang's prescription for better Sino-Soviet relations raises two highly provocative issues: first, whether the Communist systems in both Russia and China will pass away, and second, whether the new non-Communist Chinese and Russian states will be capable of peaceful coexistence. On the first question, the empirical evidence seems to be overwhelmingly against the possibility that either Communist system will be replaced in the foreseeable future. However economically incompetent and politically oppressive Communist systems may be, they have developed highly sophisticated techniques of insuring regime survival. If a smooth and constructive Sino-Russian relationship must be predicated on both countries becoming non-Communistic, then the future will look bleak indeed. On the second question, the history of the last 300 years as presented by Professor Tang amply demonstrates that a pattern of exploitation has persisted in spite of numerous changes of regimes and ideologies in both countries.

To put it differently, Professor Tang may be unduly pessimistic about the ability of communist China and Russia to develop harmonious and friendly relations, and overly optimistic about the ability of non-Communist "new China" and "new Russia" to strive for respect, territorial integrity, national sovereignty and political independence. One may wonder whether even a Westernized, democratic Russian government will be able to admit "her past territorial acquisitions made at China's expense" and make amends. How could "new Russia" be sure that China would not make excessive demands on her that in turn may trigger the latent nationalistic or separatist sentiments existing in other parts of today's Russian political community? If democratic Great Britain refuses to give up Gibraltar and the Falkland Islands, and if democratic India believes in the sanctity of the boundaries she inherited from the British Empire, what reason is there to believe that a new Russia will be more accommodating?

However, we may not need to despair about the future of Sino-Soviet relations even if both countries' internal political systems remain unchanged. There are both external and internal factors indicating a reasonable expectation for improved relations in the years to come.

Externally, China's stated position on improved Sino-Soviet relations is contingent upon the removal of three obstacles: the withdrawal of Soviet military backing of the Vietnamese invasion of Cambodia, the termination of Soviet military occupation of Afghanistan, and the reduction of Soviet troops along Sino-Soviet borders.[8] It should be noted that ideological reconciliation is not a precondition. By 1990, it is likely the Soviet military role in either Afghanistan or Vietnam will have become superfluous, and even heavy Soviet troop deployment in the Far East may become less important once the new trans-Siberian BAM (Baikal-Amur Mainline) is capable of expeditiously transporting large troop reinforcements into troubled spots.[9] The removal of these irritants will foster a more propitious environment for both countries to normalize their relations.

Internally, both countries have been quite anxious to bring their economies on track. China's four modernization programs will keep her occupied at least until the year 2000. In the short run, both countries may find it wise to reduce that part of their military spending directed against each other. During 1985–86, China demobilized one million soldiers from the PLA, giving the Soviets a reassuring signal to reduce their force deployment in the Far East accordingly. In the long run, China's new programs may put her in a more favorable power position vis-à-vis the Russians than at any time since the initial Manchu-Russian encounter.

With the passage of time, the once vehement Sino-Soviet dispute has lost much of its steam. Analytically, there were three major areas of Sino-Soviet conflict in the 1950s and 1960s: the personality clash between Mao and Khrushchev; the ideological dispute over revolutionary strategies and tactics; and the conflict of national interests over trade relations, terms of nuclear cooperation, and the settlement of borders. In the last decade the first two have lost their relevance, and the third one has changed its complexion enormously. The Chinese have made substantial criticism of Mao's legacy and disowned many of his policies. Today's China is pursuing domestic and international policies that are far more "revisionistic" than anything Khrushchev ever dared to contemplate. Bilateral trade and technological cooperation are no longer critical to either country. Both countries are less encumbered by their old quarrels and are in a better position to develop a new relationship on the basis of national interest.

If a lesson is to be extracted from the history of Sino-Russian relations to prevent its replay, it would contain at least two major points. First, China must avoid internal division and factional strife so as not to tempt the Russians. Second, Chinese leaders must avoid the kind of gross miscalculations they made in the early 1950s. Given the nature of the contemporary international system, "benevolence" and "neighborly love" have been, and will remain, scarce commodities. China's leaders must learn to protect their national interests with their own strength, rather than hope to live among angels.

Notes

1. Milovan Djilas, *Conversations with Stalin* (New York: 1962), pp. 182–83; Dedijer, *Tito Speaks* (London: 1953), p. 331.
2. *Mao Tse-tung hsuan chi* (Peking, 1961), pp. 1435–36; David Floyd, *Mao Against Krushchev: A Short History of the Sino-Soviet Conflict* (New York: 1963), pp. 388–90.
3. Liu Shao-ch'i, "Internationalism and Nationalism" (Peking: 1949).
4. *Mao Tse-tung hsuan chi*, pp. 1477–78.
5. William E. Griffith, *Sino-Soviet Relations, 1964–1965* (Cambridge, Mass.: 1969), p. 28.
6. *People's Daily*, March 8, 1963.
7. Stuart Schram, *The Political Thought of Mao Tse-tung* (New York: 1963), p. 286.
8. *Beijing Review*, 29 (July 19, 1982), p. 3.
9. Allen S. Whiting, *Siberian Development and East Asia: Threat or Promise* (Stanford, Calif.: 1981), pp. 81, 93–4, 99–107, 212.

6

The Continuing Threat of the Soviet Union to the West

WILLIAM R. KINTNER

It is difficult, if not impossible, for the majority of Western intellectuals to comprehend the deep, sustained determination of Soviet leaders ever since the 1917 revolution to destroy all societies rooted in freedom, pluralism and genuine democracy. The source of this determination is Vladimir Lenin. Every Soviet leader claims to be an embodiment of the principles and beliefs uttered by Lenin, even those that are both paranoid and ridiculous. Shortly after he seized power, Lenin's perceptions of the United States, for example, were set forth in his "Letter to American Workingmen from the Soviet Socialist Republic of Russia," written in August 1918. In this document, the United States was seen as a house divided between a few greedy plutocrats on the one hand, and the mass of destitute workers on the other. Lenin said, "America has become characteristic for the depth of the abyss which divides a handful of brutal millionaires who are stagnating in mires of luxury, and millions of laboring, starving men and women who are always staring want in the face." It was only a question of time, in Lenin's view, until the revolution would come to America. On August 30, 1918, the day he was shot and seriously wounded, Lenin gave a speech in Moscow in which he once again revealed his view of the United States: "A handful not of millionaires but of billionaires takes over everything, and the entire population remains in slavery and subjection."[1]

Lenin's distorted image of the U.S. still shapes Soviet domestic propaganda concerning American society.

Many scholars have attempted to analyze this unusual man whose misanthropic political views have inflicted massive misery on hundreds of millions of people. Vaclav Havel, who spent five years in Czech jails, compressed Lenin's fantasies into the following capsule:

> To this day, we cannot understand how a great, civilized nation or at least a considerable part of it could, in the twentieth century, succumb to its fascination with a ridiculous, complex-ridden, petit-bourgeois man, could fall for his pseudo-scientific theories and in their name exterminate nations, conquer continents, and commit unbelievable cruelties.[2]

The Soviets, however, still speak of Lenin as an earthly Messiah. A notable example is V.G. Afanasyev's work, *The Fundamentals of Scientific Communism*.[3] Afanasyev credits Lenin with originating the theory of "scientific communism."[4] Afanasyev describes the theory as:

> . . . the science of the ways and means of overthrowing capitalism, of the ways and laws of building the new, communist society and the economic, social, and cultural conditions for the all-round development of Man; it is the science of communist society as a complex social organism; and it is the science of the deliberate, purposeful, control of social processes in the interests of Man.[5]

Needless to say, Mikhail S. Gorbachev is a dedicated disciple of Lenin. Toward the end of 1985, he arranged to have published in the United States a collection of statements he had made between March and October 1985 since his election as General Secretary of the Communist Party Central Committee. The title chosen for this salubrious collection was "A Time for Peace."[6]

Also included in this collection was a speech given by Gorbachev at the 113th anniversary of Lenin's birth on April 22, 1983. This speech was entitled "Leninism: A Living and Creative Science. A Faithful Guide to Action." In this speech Gorbachev asserted.

> . . . reactionary trend has triumphed within the U.S. ruling circles and, in Lenin's words, a "war party" which "says to itself: force must be used immediately, irrespective of possible consequences," has taken the upper hand. The most aggressive circles of imperialism and above all, the U.S. imperialism are trying to clamber out of the crisis, to find the answer to the historic challenge of socialism by continuing the arms race and by building up the threat of war.[7]

In short, one can not comprehend the hostility of the Soviet Union toward all Western values without grasping the immense, cruel megalomania of its founder.

When Lenin and his Bolsheviks captured power in Russia they inherited the geographical environment that had faced the Tsars. They discarded the Pan-Slavic vision which had inspired their predecessors and replaced it with the more universal creed of Marxism. They added the conspiratorial tactics of Lenin to the Byzantine diplomacy practiced by the Tsars. Lenin's work *Imperialism: The Highest Stage of Capitalism*, provided the ideological rationale for an endless campaign to destroy the Western democratic industrial system. Only in recent years would the comprehensive tasks first outlined in Lenin's *Imperialism* be undertaken by the Soviet Union. Soviet expansionism is thus a blend of old Russian security concerns and geographical drives and the aggressiveness inherent in Marxist-Leninist ideology.

Many Western observers tend to downplay the role of ideology in Soviet strategy and operations, contending that the Soviet masses are either indifferent or hostile to its claims and authority. Yet, while the Soviet intelligentsia indeed is cynical about Soviet ideology, Marxism-Leninism does provide a plausible rationale for the Soviet leaders to marshal their efforts to make the Soviet Union the paramount world power. Mikhail Suslov, long chief Soviet ideologist, addressed the important All-Union Society for Knowledge as follows:

> It should be stressed, comrades, that in all our ideological work, the slightest slackening of the struggle against reactionary bourgeois ideology is impermissible. Since the futility of attempts at military, political and economic pressure on the Soviet Union and the socialist community as a whole is becoming increasingly obvious as the situation in the world arena changes in socialism's favor, it is precisely the struggle in the ideological sphere the sphere where peaceful coexistence between capitalism and socialism does not and cannot exist that is assuming particular urgency.[8]

Characteristically, the Soviet leaders assert that regardless of improved relations between capitalist and socialist states, ideological peace and hence genuine cooperation is impossible. The Bolsheviks, conceiving themselves as the self-chosen agents for moving mankind from capitalism to Communism, believe they must destroy the old society by any means in order to establish the new. When their potential victims resist this process, the Communists accuse them of aggression. As Leonid Brezhnev expressed it:

> The more restricted imperialism's possibilities of dominating other countries and people become, the more fiercely do its representatives react to this.[9]

Ideologically inspired antagonism between Moscow and the non-Communist world will continue as long as the Soviet Union hews to Marxism-Leninism as its informing philosophy. Milovan Djilas, perhaps the most defiant and knowledgeable former confidant of both Stalin and Tito, holds that "communism is ideologically and structurally incapable of transforming itself into a democratic, parliamentary, pluralistic polity...."[10]

When the Soviet Union was relatively weak, the necessity for cooperation with its capitalist adversaries was obvious. According to a resolution of the 1928 Sixth World Congress of the Communist International, "The peace policy of the proletarian state does not imply that the Soviet State has become reconciled with capitalism. It is merely a more advantageous form of fighting capitalism, a form which the USSR had consistently employed since the October revolution."[11]

Peace offensives and detente continue to be important aspects of Soviet strategy. While Soviet strategy and tactics vary as the correlation of forces between the superpowers changes, the ideological commitment to eliminate all political systems not based on the Moscow brand of Marxism-Leninism remains. The Soviet leadership devotes vast resources to propogating their archaic ideology which bestows the harsh Soviet system with some legitimacy. A *Pravda* editorial of June 9, 1979, stressed "the strength of ideological conviction" the "conviction of the rightness of our cause, of our Marxism-Leninist ideology."

Most Western analysts who have studied the Soviet Union agree that there is no evidence that the Kremlin shares an interest with the Western democracies in the mutual development of a peaceful and cooperative world community. Nor is there evidence that the ultimate objective of Soviet foreign policy has ever been to establish a worldwide Soviet-American condominium which merely required that they bring down American power and influence to their level. They saw detente, which flowered in the aftermath of the 1972 SALT agreement, not as a step toward the Soviet-American condominium, but as an opportunity to gain strategic advantage over their American adversary. The erosion of detente began when the Soviets, following the defeat imposed upon the United States by the capture of Saigon in 1975, started to pursue a more activist policy. The first manifestation of this activist policy was the 1975 Soviet-Cuban intrusion into Angola. The Soviet invasion of Afghanistan in December 1979 will not be the last Soviet foray into the world beyond their frontiers.

With the fading of detente, the Soviet global position has become much stronger than it had ever been. The Soviets operate on the fundamental principle of the irreversibility of the socialist revolution. (This explains why the U.S. invasion of Grenada was so hard for them to swallow.) A Soviet strategy probes Western weaknesses and, taking advantage of Western vulnerabilities, exploits sociopolitical conflicts in unstable countries in order to bring about further changes in the global correlation of forces in their favor. The Soviet objective appears to have become some form of Soviet hegemony in which the Soviet Union will be clearly recognized as the preeminent global power. The Soviet performance record over the past ten years supports this conclusion.

Brent Scowcroft, former national security advisor to President Ford, has critically assessed the U.S. response to the Soviet challenge. After stating that the Soviets "comprehend far better than we the political value of military power," he concluded:

> On the basis of the historical evidence of our behavior, the Soviets have reason to believe that time favors them and that ultimately their policies will be successful. Thus far, each burst of American energy has been only a temporary phenomenon, following which we have lapsed again into complacency and left the U.S.S.R. free to resume its careful but persistent tactics of encroachment.[12]

The Soviet Record: From Stalin to Gorbachev:

> Although it is almost incomprehensible to Western peoples, the totalitarian leaders of the Soviet Union belie and act as if they are constantly at war with us. As Stalin put it in his Problems of Leninism, the Bolshevik seizure of power "jeopardized the very existence of world capitalism as a whole.[13]

Scowcroft also stated that the task of overthrowing "the national bourgeoisie of Russia had been replaced by the new task of overthrowing the international bourgeoisie." Yet the initial weakness of the newly born Soviet Union initially imposed on the Kremlin a policy of gaining time by peaceful coexistence, not in order to acquiesce in the status quo, but to enhance the cause of Communism.

The University of Miami analysis, "Soviet Strategy for the Seventies: From Cold War to Peaceful Coexistence," asserted that the Soviets think of peaceful coexistence as a struggle with unlimited objectives in which no holds are barred, at least on the Soviet side, short of antagonists' attempts to shoot each other down. This vital point is emphasized by Soviet writers. Typical is a statement in the authoritative treatise, "Leninism Today":

> Peaceful coexistence does not extinguish or cancel out class struggle; it is a new form of class struggle employed by the working class and the socialist countries in the world arena. It "cancels" only one type of struggle war as a means of settling international issues.[14]

There have been four main waves of Soviet expansion. Following the 1917 Bolshevik revolution, the Soviet Union under Lenin spread its power first in Eurasia.

Between 1917 and 1921, the Soviet Union expanded its borders to include the Ukraine, Byelorussia, Kazakhstan, Azerbeijan, Armenia and Georgia. Outer Mongolia was colonized and subsequently became a Soviet satellite. After taking power, Stalin first focused on developing socialism in one country, the USSR, and on building up its military industry and the Red Army. Stalin represented the logical outcome of the doctrines of Marx as modified by Lenin. Stalin perfected the political-military machine which Lenin designed.

After 1939, the second wave of Soviet expansion took place, beginning with the annexation of eastern Poland, eastern Rumania and northeast Prussia. The three Baltic states were absorbed in 1940. In 1944, the USSR seized more territory from Poland, and then, in violation of the Yalta agreement, imposed Marxist-Leninist regimes on not only Poland but also Bulgaria, Rumania, Hungary, Albania and East Germany. Stalin attempted unsuccessfully to engineer revolutions in southern and Southeast Asia, culminating in his biggest mistake: launching the North Korean attack on South Korea in June 1950, which resulted in the remobilization of the United States.

Following Stalin's death in 1953, two men, Khrushchev and Brezhnev, dominated the Kremlin. It took almost three years for Khrushchev to become the fully acknowledged leader of the Soviet Union. Khrushchev moved the Soviet Union out of its Stalinist shell and into the modern world. In Asia he plowed the ground for the development of a Soviet alliance with India and paved the way for the eventual Soviet-backed Vietnamese victory in Indochina. The foundation for both the Soviet naval development and the growth of the Soviet strategic nuclear forces were also laid during Khrushchev's years in the Kremlin.

The third wave of Soviet expansionism began under Khrushchev. Within a year of the Soviet invasion of Hungary, the launching of Sputnik in September 1957 initiated a worldwide Soviet offensive that reached its culmination in the Cuban missile crisis of 1962. Soviet leaders often articulated with unusual candor both their rationale for the conflict and their strategy for its conduct.

The militancy and braggadocio of the Soviet leadership in those days was exemplified by Nikita Khrushchev's challenge to the United States: "I have told Americans: you have missiles that can send up oranges. We have missiles that can send up tons. Imagine the kind of bombs that could be contained in our missiles compared with . . . yours."[15] Later in the same year, Khrushchev expanded on this theme in still more ominous terms:

Let those people abroad learn that I am not hiding anything. In one year the factory we visited made 250 hydrogen rockets on the production line. That is many millions of tons, if we figure in terms of ordinary explosives. You can see that if such a deadly weapon were to be exploded over a country, there would not be anything left there at all.

Premier Khrushchev, on January 6, 1961, delivered a chilling programmatic statement of the strategy the Soviet Union would pursue in the 1960s. He informed his audience, composed of party members from the Higher Party School, the Academy of Social Sciences, and the Central Committee's Institute of Marxism-Leninism, that:

> In recent years, the initiative in the international arena has been in the hands of the Soviet Union, the socialist countries, while the imperialist states and their governments defend themselves with their backs to the wall; their prestige and foreign political stock have never been so low.

He continued:

> The slogan of the struggle for peace does not contradict the slogan of the struggle for communism. Those two slogans harmonize with each other . . . the slogan of the struggle for peace appears as a satellite of the slogan of the struggle for communism.

During the Khrushchev years the Soviets established themselves in the Middle East (Egypt, Syria, Iraq) and Indonesia, linked up with India, acquired a base in Cuba, and built the Berlin Wall. Khrushchev was thrown out of power by his political colleagues after the failure of his scheme to deploy Soviet missiles in Cuba.

When the initial Brezhnev-Kosygin-Podgorny team came into power in 1964, a colorful, flamboyant Soviet leader was replaced by a seemingly stodgy and uninspiring trio. For many years, there was no clear indication as to which of these men was preeminent, but Brezhnev eventually emerged as the dominating figure in the Soviet system. Much of the tremendous growth in Soviet power and influence which has taken place in the past 20 years can be attributed to Leonid Brezhnev's regime. Brezhnev brought the work of his predecessors to fruition and presided over a major shift in the world balance of power. With the marriage of concept and means, and the integration of Leninist operational principles and nuclear doctrine, the dynamics of Soviet global strategy became more visible.

Following the 1975 U.S. defeat in Vietnam, the Soviets embarked on their fourth wave of expansion into Angola, Mozambique, Nicaragua and many areas of the Indian Ocean. Some of the salient features of this wave included expansion into the Horn of Africa under a policy aimed at creating a strong position in the Gulf of Aden and the Indian Ocean. In November 1967, Soviet activities in southern Arabia shifted to the National Liberation Front government in Aden, in order to acquire naval facilities in the People's Democratic Republic of Yemen (PDRY). In return for Soviet aid, the USSR was granted use of port facilities at Aden and they also maintained forces and facilities in the nearby island of Socotra.

The 1969 coup in Mogadishu, which replaced the government of the Western-oriented Egal with the regime of General Mohammed Siad Barre, was welcomed by the Soviet Union and increased involvement in Somalia was undertaken.

With the Numeiri revolution of May 1969, Soviet influence in the Sudan was greatly enhanced. The Soviets encouraged Numeiri's pursuit of socialist policies. However, in July 1976, an allegedly Soviet-backed attempt to overthrow Numeiri's regime led to a major change in the Sudan's foreign policy. Numeiri soon became the Soviet Union's most outspoken adversary in Africa. He was deposed in 1985 and the Sudan is again veering toward the Soviet Union.

In Ethiopia in March 1975, the imperial Ethiopian regime was deposed. In February 1977, an internal power struggle was followed by Ethiopia's launching on a radical course of "socialization." Moscow also indicated support for this move, and began maneuvering for an alliance with Ethiopia without breaking its ties with Somalia, which claimed some of Ethiopia's territory. This maneuver failed.

In November 1977, Mogadishu ordered all Soviet advisors to leave Somalia within one week; ended Soviet use of strategic naval and air facilities on the Indian Ocean; abrogated the 1974 Treaty of Friendship and Cooperation; and broke diplomatic relations with Cuba. In response, the Soviets took steps to guarantee that its Ethiopian client would win the war against Somalia.

A solid foothold in Ethiopia has provided Moscow with a base for operations in central Africa, as well as for naval and air operations in the Red Sea and the Indian Ocean.

On the western shore of the Persian Gulf are located the oil-rich countries of Iraq, Kuwait, the Arab Emirates, Saudi Arabia and Oman. The turmoil in the region created by the Iranian revolution and the Iraq-Iran war will lead to far-reaching changes in the political alignments of the region. The presence of hundreds of thousands of Palestinians in the Persian Gulf states is a favorable factor for the Soviet Union.

Moscow has had on-and-off relations with Iraq. Relations improved steadily between 1963 and 1972, culminating in the 1972 Soviet-Iraqi Treaty of Friendship and Cooperation. The Soviet role in the Gulf war has not been clear. Libya, Syria and North Korea, all linked to the Soviet Union, have sent arms to Iran. The outcome of the Iraq-Iran war will present a unique opportunity for the USSR. The Soviet Union, with contacts in both camps, sought the role of peacemaker so that it might be the final arbiter in the Persian Gulf area, but the United Nations-negotiated cease fire precluded this. The Soviets also hope to come out on top in Iran after Khomeni dies.

Moscow's relations with Afghanistan illustrate the marriage of strategic considerations and ideology in Soviet policy. In 1978 and 1979 several bloody coups elevated Amin to power in Afghanistan, and the Soviet Union indicated support for this change. However, on December 27, 1979, Amin was ousted from power and executed in a coup supported by Soviet troops. The Soviets as of 1985 were still engaged in crushing Afghan resistance to their puppet regime.

The Soviet Union has won a position of strength in the Middle East. In 1980, after Iraq launched its attack against Iran, the USSR and Syria signed a treaty of peace. In 1983 the Soviets moved troops into Syria to man the advanced SAM weapons deployed there. These are under Moscow's direct command. Soviet-Libyan relations opened in 1969 when Col. Qadaffi came to power. The Soviets would like to eliminate the United States' influence in the Mediterranean and maintain a large enough presence there to counter the U.S. Sixth Fleet.

Soviet policy in the north central sector of the Indian Ocean region has been largely India-oriented. India is the largest and strongest regional power, and solid ties with New Delhi add to Moscow's prestige and influence in southern Asia and in the Third World in general. Moreover, India's arch-foe, Pakistan, was tied to the West. In 1971 India entered into the Indo-Soviet Treaty of Friendship and Cooperation as a form of insurance in case of war between India and Pakistan over Bangladesh.

China has always been and will remain the central focus of the Soviet Union's policy towards Asia. In the aftermath of Hanoi's victory in Indochina, the struggle between China and the Soviet Union has become more bitter.

Indochina has become a primary battleground in the struggle between the Soviet Union and the People's Republic of China. With the Soviet-Vietnamese alliance, the Soviet Union has gained a new Soviet base, altering the strategic equation in Asia. This alliance has grave implications for peace and stability in Southeast Asia, as the Communist Party of Vietnam regards itself entitled to rule over all of Indochina. The Soviets have also expanded into the area by permanently establishing a South China Sea squadron. In 1981, they began the construction of base facilities at Kompong Som, Cambodia, which will provide the USSR's navy with a deep bay, major submarine base as well as an excellent fleet anchorage. Vietnam provides the USSR with a formidable ally in a region in which the Soviet Union had never before been an actor. Now that they have a major presence in this vital area they can more easily attempt to encircle China and challenge the U.S. position in the western Pacific.

Due to careful preparation, the transfer of power from Leonid Brezhnev to Yuri Andropov went smoothly. In his brief reign, Andropov sought to move the Soviet Union along the path set by Lenin and his successors.

In the speech Andropov gave at Brezhnev's funeral on December 15, 1982, he presented the standard Soviet appraisal of the East-West equilibrium:

> In the complicated international situation when the forces of imperialism are trying to push the peoples onto the road of hostility and military confrontation, the party and the state will firmly uphold the vital interests of our homeland, and maintain great vigilance and readiness to give a crushing rebuff to any attempt at aggression.

It was fitting that a man who headed the dreaded KGB for 15 years become the top man of the Soviet secret police state.

Andropov died in February 1984 and was succeeded by the 72-year-old, Konstantin U. Chernenko. Chernenko was a protégé of Brezhnev who came up in the party ranks as a master of agitprop, but without managerial experience. Chernenko died a year later.

The ascent of Mikhail Gorbachev to power in the Kremlin in March 1985 brought a young, adroit, talented man to the Soviet helm. For all his facile charm and cosmopolitan airs, Gorbachev was cast in the same iron mould as his predecessors. Nothing Gorbachev has done before or after becoming General Secretary of the CPUSSR suggests any deviation from the Soviet pursuit of global hegemony. Gorbachev's performance at the November summit meeting with President Reagan was a masterpiece of disingenuousness. He sought to convey his willingness to walk with President Reagan toward common goals on the one hand while masterminding the Soviet strategy aimed at undermining the West. Our goals are not the same nor can they be as long as the Soviets try to extend their oppressive system over all the earth. Once the summit euphoria is dissipated, the first Reagan-Gorbachev summit will be seen as another stage in a long, tough struggle.

Gorbachev is aware that many opinion makers in the West believe that superpower arms control provides the surest way toward global peace and security. He will appeal to such people by volunteering radical cuts in offensive nuclear weapons provided the U.S. abandons its SDI program;

the comparable Soviet missile program will of course continue. The campaign to scuttle Reagan's SDI will be relentless and will involve well-orchestrated peace campaigns in Europe, the United States and Japan.

In the introduction to his book *A Time for Peace*, Gorbachev asserted:

Peace, peaceful coexistence, equality, and mutually beneficial cooperation are the basic principles of our foreign policy. The Soviet Union seeks neither foreign territory nor foreign resources. We have enough of everything. Besides, the Soviet people know the horrors of war and its tragic aftermath only too well from their own bitter experience. The vital need for peace and ways of achieving it are a major theme of this book.

The stressing of peace to mask Soviet expansionism will be the key feature of Gorbachev's strategy in the next several years.

Soviet Strategy for Tomorrow

The actual strategy Gorbachev will pursue is embodied in a new party program that was unveiled in *Pravda* on October 26, 1985. This program, with minor modifications, will be adopted by the Communist Party Congress to be held in February 1986. Some of the salient features of this program will reveal its basic contradiction.

The CPSU'S approach to foreign-policy problems combines the firm defense of the interests of the Soviet people and resolute opposition to the aggressive policy of imperialism with a readiness for dialogue and the constructive resolution of international questions through negotiations.

"*The general crisis of capitalism is deepening*, the sphere of its domination is shrinking inescapably, and its historical doom is becoming increasingly obvious.

US imperialism is the citadel of international reaction. The threat of war emanates from it, above all, in laying claim to world domination; it arbitrarily declares whole continents zones of its "vital interests." The US's policy of diktat, imposing unequal relations on other states, supporting repressive antipopular regimes and discriminating against countries that are disagreeable to the US, is disorganizing international economic and political relations and impeding their normal development.

The bloody war against Vietnam, the many years' blockade of Cuba, the trampling of the Palestinian people's legitimate rights, the intervention in Lebanon, the armed seizure of defenseless Grenada, the aggressive actions against Nicaragua these are just some of the countless crimes that will remain forever among the most shameful pages of imperialism's history.

Peaceful coexistence corresponds to the interests of all countries and all peoples. (See the forthright definition of coexistence in the previously cited *Leninism Today*.) Never before has such an ominous danger hung over mankind. But never before have there been such real possibilities of preserving and consolidating peace. By pooling their efforts, the people can and must avert the threat of nuclear annihilation.

The Communist Party of the Soviet Union program as cited is only the fourth in the entire history of the Bolshevik party. Consequently, Gorbachev's strategy is contained within the program bearing his imprimatur. The overall strategy to bury the West, preferably without war, has three major components. The first is to achieve scientific-technological supremacy. The second is to gain military superiority, so as to deter the United States from launching a desperation nuclear strike against the Soviet Union. The third is to detach more and more countries from the U.S.-led, Western coalition so as to deny the industrialized democracies access to essential resources and markets.

The Communist Party of the Soviet Union has promoted science and technology as the primary means of overcoming stagnation in the Soviet economy and achieving military superiority over the West.

The Soviet science technology program has four components: (1) a major increase in the allocation of resources in the Soviet science budget, (2) the allocation of much greater effort towards scientific education, (3) a major effort in military RDT&E so that its total share of the military budget is increasing at a very rapid rate, (4) massive campaign of espionage and concealed purchase to steal or buy advanced technology from the West.

Concerning domination of the nuclear escalation, the Soviet margin of strategic superiority is made up of (1) strategic nuclear offensive weapons and defensive systems including all-purpose space programs, particularly antisatellite measures, (2) nuclear/conventional combined arms theater forces, (3) a large naval maritime fleet and sizeable force projection capabilities, and (4) very large, trained military manpower reserves.

Victory in the peaceful coexistence strategy, achieved without major war, could be defined as political dominance by the Soviet Union over the Eurasian landmass, the Middle East, the Mediterranean, and Africa, plus naval domination over the rimlands of the three oceans bordering on the Eurasian landmass and Africa. An isolated United States, confronted with Soviet strategic nuclear superiority and Soviet mastery in space, would most likely become a frustrated "Fortress America."

There are serious obstacles, however, in the path of Soviet strategy.

Under Gorbachev, the Soviet Union in the future will face growing domestic problems. Although most of these have existed since the founding of the USSR, they will become more acute during the 1980s and 1990s.

Internally, the disastrous performance of Soviet agriculture must be addressed. In addition, the unsolved nationality question will continue to grow more vexing as the Russian birthrate continues to decrease while the Asian Moslem rates soar.

Though not as vulnerable as some Western analysts predict, the Soviet economy requires overhaul. The commitment to military projects retards Soviet economic growth. A shortage of modern equipment and advanced technology, high rates of alcoholism and absenteeism, and a lack of a genuine work ethic also contribute to the economic ills.

As serious as these problems are, it can be expected that they will either be corrected or endured. The major focus of the new CPSU program is addressed toward developing industry and agriculture up to the year 2000. The Soviet Union has faced challenges before, including fighting and winning the most devastating war in history and building a massive military industrial base to produce the world's largest military machine. Consequently, Soviet internal troubles will have little impact on its foreign policy and strategies.

Erosion of the West will be a key component of Soviet strategy. The Soviets have long waged a peace campaign against the United States and its allies designed to disarm the West, while at the same time the Soviets have immunized themselves from peace campaigns within their own borders. The widespread opposition to the deployment of U.S. intermediate range missiles in Europe and the dynamic growth of the nuclear freeze movement in the U.S. testify to a growing unwillingness on the part of Western peoples to rely on the U.S. deterrence to maintain the peace. While the Soviets have not been the initiators of these campaigns, they have certainly found those launched by others to be very effective and have facilitated them whenever possible. Under the banner of peaceful coexistence, the Soviets hope to win a kind of global hegemony without the risk of war.

For the next several years Gorbachev's

> . . . obvious strategy is to cast President Reagan as the main impediment to arms agreements and, with a show of reducing tensions, to gain credibility and acceptance for his case in the West. "Geneva will give relaxation to public opinion," said Genrikh Borovik, a veteran Soviet journalist, explaining the Soviet scenario. 'And quite a big shift in public opinion will follow.'

Soviet psychological strategy has two components: insulation of its own people from outside influence by coercion and by indoctrination, and manipulation of Western public opinion by propaganda barrages, misinformation and deception.

The process by which the Soviet people acquire their distorted perceptions about the United States was succinctly described by Serge Schmemann. According to him:

> Feelings toward America and Americans have ebbed and flowed with the tides of Soviet-American relations. Yet even in the low times, the longing for American culture has thrived. Not surprisingly, one of the frequent questions in Moscow about the impending Soviet-American summit meetings is whether it might produce a new cultural agreement and renew the trickle of officially sponsored American cultural visits to the Soviet Union.
>
> Yet when one discusses with Russians their impressions of America, it soon becomes evident that something is missing. None list Abraham Lincoln, the Constitution, human rights, freedom, or any other term that might reflect an appreciation of the American political system, of the values that Americans feel must distinguish them from the Russians.

Schmemann attempts to explain the darker side of Soviet attitudes about America and its intentions toward the USSR which is

> . . . evident in the extraordinary security in which the Soviet Union wraps itself, in the instinctive action against the Korean jetliner, in the obsession with espionage, in the control and surveillance of foreigners, in the stringent restrictions on all foreign sources of information. . . . contact with foreigners and the outside world still remains a carefully and stingily rationed privilege, and unsanctioned dealings are risky. Foreigners in Moscow remain segregated in carefully guarded compounds under intensive surveillance, barred from vast swatches of Soviet territory. The press and television regularly carry horror stories about perfidious foreigners who are provocateurs, spies or worse, and Soviet ideologues inveigh against rock music, Western fashions and current fads as "diversions" concocted by "Western special services.

A collective sense of insecurity about the outside world characterizes most of the Soviet people from the top to the bottom. The presumably suave Gorbachev was visibly irritated when asked about human rights by French reporters on his 1985 visit to Paris.

> The issue, he said, was being "artifically played up by Western propaganda and exploited to poison relations between nations and states.

The aggression the Soviet Union is carrying out in many troubled areas of the globe has been more exposed than its frequently malevolent nature. In an editorial, "Soviet Toys of Death," *The New York Times* commented on a report to the United Nations Commission on Human Rights concerning Soviet atrocities in Afghanistan:

The types of booby-trap toys encountered include those resembling pens, harmonicas, radios, matchboxes, and little bombs shaped like a bird. This type of bomb, consisting of two wings, one flexible and the other rigid, in the shape and color of a bird, explodes when the flexible wing is touched. The Special Rapporteur was also able to obtain a number of photographs, especially those of children between 8 and 15 years of age, with hands or legs blown off, either by handling booby-trap toys or during the explosion of mines. To the generalized horror of war that has claimed 500,000 lives since 1979, there is thus added the special horror of toys of death.

Paradoxically, because of the naivete of many Westerners, the vast Soviet propaganda machine has been rather successful in projecting the image of a peace-loving country that wants nothing more than to live and let live. The Soviets take the propaganda struggle against bourgeois ideology most seriously. It actively propagandizes the Soviet way of life, and discloses:

> . . . in an aggressive and well-reasoned way, the antipopular, inhuman nature of imperialism and its exploitative essence. It will instill in Soviet people a high level of political consciousness and the ability to evaluate social phenomena from clear-cut class positions and to uphold the ideals and spiritual values of socialist society.
>
> The role of the mass information and propaganda media in the life of society is increasing. The CPSU will strive to have the media thoroughly analyze domestic and international life and economic and social phenomena, actively support everything new and advanced, raise urgent questions that trouble people, and suggest ways of resolving them. The press, television and radio are called upon to persuade people though the political clarity and purposefulness, the depth of content, the timeliness, the completeness of information, the vividness and the intelligibility of their reports. The Party will continue to give active support and assistance to the press and to all mass information and propaganda media.

But again, the fundamental line the Soviet Union will be taking is that the United States is the chief menace to humanity and the lives of every person on earth. They will portray the United States as an aggressive, imperialistic power whose plans for a strategic defense against Soviet ICBM's could lead to the end of civilization. This ploy was artfully developed by a Soviet scholar, long known by this author, G. Trofimenko, in an article which came from the Soviet embassy in Washington:

> Mutually acceptable solutions can be found as far as offensive weapons are concerned. Everything depends on the U.S. stand: Will it agree to abstain from starting a new round of the strategic arms race or not? What does the U.S. Strategic Defense Initiative (SDI) represent? It is actually a challenge

inviting the Soviet Union to start a new round of the arms race, this time in space . . .

Some Americans claim that the Soviet Union fears the arms race in space because it will be defeated. If we are forced to, we will give an effective and original answer to the SDI. But to waste a trillion dollars and rubles in order to reach, in a quarter of a century, the same parity between the Soviet Union and the United States in the best case, or to vanish as world civilizations in the worst case, is sheer madness.

Why then launch another arms race in space when we can prevent it by scrapping—by mutual accord—the weapons that a "space shield" is designed to beat off? This is a pivotal issue that cannot be brushed aside.

The Soviet game is quite obvious. They seek to portray a possible nuclear war as the sole evil confronting humanity. A former Soviet intellectual, who is now a professor of psychology at Stanford University, tackles the real pivotal issue head-on:

"The truth of the matter is that a great number of people have already accepted the primacy of physical survival over traditional values, over human rights and dignity. And that is exactly what the Soviets were counting on when they launched their massive campaign of "struggle for peace" in 1980 under the slogan: "The people have the power to preserve peace—their prime right." Confronted with the absolute value of the survival of mankind, people have been required to sacrifice their other rights and have been willing to do so, particularly when they have been skillfully reminded of the potential holocaust caused by artificially created international "tension."

Unfortunately, the governments of the free world have not been much wiser than some of their citizens. Instead of calling the Soviet bluff, they have bowed to the pressures of the "peace" movement and engaged in negotiations on security and cooperation without regard to human rights, thereby rendering the process senseless.

Once again we are stuck in a vicious circle: How can we control the arms race without verification, and how can we conduct verification without mutual trust? For that matter, how can anyone trust a government that doesn't allow its people to know the truth and discuss it, and that deliberately pumps hostility and hatred toward other nations into the minds of its population? How can we build trust with a nation whose citizens are not allowed to have a sincere dialogue with foreigners, under threat of imprisonment?"

Only one of these Soviet-trained scholars can be right. Trofimenko is a likeable human being who has chosen to defend the system under which he lives. But until and when the Trofimenkos within the Soviet Union are willing to stand beside the Bukovskys, who have fled its harsh tyranny, there can be no real peace between the Soviet Union and Western democracies.

In sum it will be a long time before we see light at the other end of the tunnel.

Notes

1. Lenin, quoted in George F. Kennan, "The Decision to Intervene" (Princeton: Princeton University Press, 1958), p. 462.
2. From "Thriller", by Vaclav Havel, in the June/July issue of the "Idler", a new magazine published in Toronto. Havel, a playwright and essayist, spent five years in Czech jails for his political activities.
3. Progress Publishers, first edition 1967, second edition 1977, Moscow.
4. *Op. cit.*, p. 41.
5. *Op. cit.*, p. 12.
6. Copyright © by Mikhail Gorbachev. Introduction Copyright © by Mikhail Gorbachev. All rights reserved. For permission write to Richardson & Steinman, 246 Fifth Avenue, New York, N.Y. 10001.
7. *Ibid.*, p. 24.
8. Moscow, *Tass International Service* June 20, 1972.
9. Speech at meeting with voters, February 22, 1980, Novosti Press Agency Publishing House.
10. George Urban, "A Conversation with Milovan Djilas," *Encounter*, December 1979, p. 13.
11. *The Struggle Against Imperialist War and the Tasks of the Communist*, 2nd ed., New York: Workers Library Publishers, July 1934, p. 22.
12. "Soviet Dynamics—Political, Economic, Military," A report of the World Affairs Council of Pittsburgh 1978. *Rapporteur's* Summary by Lt. General Brent Scowcroft, USAF (ret.).
13. Stalin, Joseph, *Problems of Communism*, Foreign Languages Publishing House, Moscow, 1940, p. 20.
14. Foy D. Kohler, Mose L. Harvey, Leon Gouré and Richard S. Soll, *Soviet Strategy for the Seventies: From Cold War to Peaceful Coexistence* Washington: Center for Advanced International Studies, University of Miami, Monograph in International Affairs, 1973), p. 8.
15. M. Sidorov, "Lenin on the Irreconcilability of Socialism and Bourgeois Ideologies," in *Leninism Today* (Moscow: Novosti Press Agency Publishing House, 1970), p. 28 quoted in Kohler, et al. *op. cit.*, p. 3.

7

The Fate of Ideology
Under Developed Socialism

DAVID GRESS

When his Father Confessor asked Narvaez on his deathbed, "General, have
you forgiven your enemies?" the General answered: "I have no enemies. I
had them all shot."

The question of ideology in the Soviet Union and its empire can be discussed under a variety of aspects. Not being either a professional Sovie-
tologist or political scientist, but a historian of modern Europe with an
interest in political philosophy, I make no claim to theoretical sophistication
in what follows. My purpose is simply to present a series of remarks and
arguments concerning the matter of Soviet ideology, and to draw out their
implications for Western interests and policies.

The last phrase may seem to some like giving the game away. It would
be futile, and in my view also unnecessary, to pretend that one can pursue
the study of the Soviet Union, its institutions, actions, and policies, without
reference to one's own interests as a citizen of the West. For such study
to be of interest, it must have some bearing on what we, as Westerners,
should be doing to preserve our own institutions and liberties. The Soviet
Union is not just one of a set of remote political cultures, like the Roman
Empire or that of the Habsburgs in early modern Europe, which have a
claim on the historian's attention per se, but do not involve his judgments
of existential interest. It is a powerful and highly organized state whose

rulers conceive of their interests in terms that are at best different from, and arguably incompatible with, those of the democratic societies of Western Europe and North America. This fact is unavoidable, and it is therefore better that the historian's own judgments, based on experience and understanding, be made explicit rather than having to be deduced indirectly. Even the most ingenuous policy analysis of Soviet institutions and practices includes latent judgments about the significance of those institutions and practices for the analyst's own life and society, and about that society itself. To take an example, Professor Jerry Hough has made it clear, in public pronouncements, that he does not think that the Soviet Union is a threat to the West, and that a more accommodating attitude on the part of the United States would contribute to a relaxation of tensions between the two superpowers. This view is just as clearly related to his well-known theory of the "institutional pluralism" of the Soviet system,[1] and its subsidiary thesis of a gradual liberalization of the system with its inevitable consequences for Soviet conduct in international relations. Other Sovietologists are equally explicit about the relationship between their views of the Soviet Union and their preferences in regard to Western actions and policies. This raises the additional question, which I cannot go into here, of priority; in other words, whether views of the Soviet Union are dependent on personal politics or whether the latter are rather influenced, over time, by what one discovers, or thinks one is discovering, about the Soviet Union. Both processes undoubtedly occur; in my own case I can only say that what views I have of Soviet institutions and actions have been influenced, but not decisively, by my preferences for Western policy, and that the latter are likewise influenced, also not decisively, by what I find in the Soviet Union.

The aspects under which I shall present my remarks on Soviet ideology are its content, its influence, its political function, its relation to reality, its nature and condition at the present time, and its operation in Soviet foreign policy.

The Content and Function of Soviet Ideology

The ideology propounded by Soviet rulers in the period that they themselves have defined as that of "developed socialism"[2] is no longer composed exclusively, or even mainly, of Marxist-Leninist elements. In the words of Leszek Kolakowski, it is:

> a polluted, disorderly hodgepodge . . . a diffused shapeless, collection of adages
> of varied origins: a few remnants of Marxist vocabulary, seemingly ambiguous

yet well-understood hints of nationalism and racism, vague humanist gener-
alities, obvious lies, useless truisms, and meaningless absurdities all in confusion and with almost no semantic bearing to social reality but related to it
by the intermediary of effective instruments of coercion.[3]

Each of these elements has a function within the overall purpose of Soviet
ideology. To get a better idea of its content, it will be useful to recall the
main stages of its development from the time of Lenin to the era of "developed socialism." The question of the status of this term itself—ideological phrase or description of reality—can be left aside for the moment.

Soviet ideology, defined as the principles by which Soviet rulers judge
their interests in the world and the rhetoric they use to describe it, has
never borne more than a tenuous resemblance to the principles and premises of democratic socialism as it evolved and was practised in Western
Europe. Nevertheless, Leninism is recognizably descended from Marxism,
even more than National Socialism was recognizably derived from the
nationalist and anti-Semitic ideologies of late nineteenth century Central
Europe. As Kolakowski has pointed out, it was no accident that the Bolsheviks read Marx and used Marxist ideas as a basis for their doctrines
and their practice, just as it was no accident that the Nazis used certain
ideas of Nietzsche. Whether this use was unjustified or represented a de-
basement of an originally valuable and beneficial body of thought is a less
interesting and less important question than what that use was.[4] Much has
been written arguing either that Lenin was a faithful follower of Marx (and
further, that this is either a good or a bad thing), or that he was not. I am
saying here that the issue is essentially trivial, because it can never be
decided, or rather, that it can only be decided according to the preferences
of the author. If Marx was a great humanist and progressive, the use of
his ideas to justify totalitarian rule is obviously an embarrassment. If, on
the other hand, the rule of the Soviets was and is itself humanitarian and
progressive, the proof of Marxian descent is valuable. Fortunately, the real
world is more complicated than such simplicities.

The original ideology of Marxism is inseparable in form and content
from the historical and political context of Western Europe, which was
that of industrialization and political liberalism.[5] It is this Western origin
of Marxism that was continued in social democracy, but drastically modified
in Leninism. The latter seized on the eschatological and moralistic elements
of Marxist doctrine, those that predicted the inevitable overthrow of the
reactionary status quo and the political ascendence of true humanity following the revolution. Since the preparations for this final overthrow necessarily demanded fanatical discipline and commitment, however, the
Soviet ideal of socialism was focused on control, order, and power. The

Western ideal of socialism, by contrast, was fundamentally emancipatory, concerned with individual freedom, even though the socialist understanding of freedom may seem perverse to a liberal or a conservative. That Western socialists in recent decades have taken on a more collectivist tinge and have, in many cases, abandoned freedom as a goal is, of course, not due in the first instance to Soviet influence, but rather to institutional and political changes within Western societies themselves. This development in Western social democracy from humanitarian individualism to ideological collectivism is outside our focus here, though it is not without significance for the degree of vigilance, or lack thereof, displayed in Western societies vis-à-vis the Soviet Union and its policies. It is also a type of "convergence" between West and East, although not what is usually implied when that term is used.

The emancipatory, progressive purpose of Western socialism was emphasized in the definition given by the Catholic social philosopher Gustav Gundlach. In Gundlach's words, socialism is:

> an all-encompassing project, belonging intimately, in its values and means, to the capitalist era, and directed toward bringing about and permanently securing the liberty and happiness of all in this world by their unrestricted and full inclusion in the material benefits and institutions of a human society shaped by instrumental reason and devoid of any traces of rule or arbitrary authority.[6]

It is one of my points in this paper that the current social and political order of the Soviet Union, defined by its rulers as developed socialism, is the diametrical opposite of the social order envisaged by socialism as defined by Gundlach. Soviet developed socialism does not belong intimately to the capitalist era. It is certainly not directed toward liberty and individual happiness, it does not aim at including all its subjects in the benefits of a human society shaped by reason. And last but not least it is anything but free of rule and arbitrary authority. Another point is that this opposition between the aims, if not the results, of Western social democracy and the concrete order of Soviet developed socialism is not a matter of accident. The rulers of the Soviet Union have not adopted the ideology and practice of developed socialism *faute de mieux*, or in the hope of adjusting it to the aspirations of social democracy when this becomes materially possible. On the contrary, their purposes and policies are precisely and exactly manifested in developed socialism. The latter is not a product of errors and misjudgments, but the well-tended consequence of almost seven decades of "universal bureaucratic ideocracy."[7]

The origins of this universal bureaucratic ideocracy must be sought in the encounter of revolutionary Marxism, in a form largely devoid of the democratic, emancipatory elements of the doctrine, with the political and social collapse of the Russian Empire in World War I. The Bolshevik revolution was in itself the symbol of failure of the central claim of Marxism in its Western form, namely, the assumption of the rise to power of the working class as an inevitable consequence of the bourgeois and industrial revolutions. In Russia, Marxism became the state ideology of a gigantic country on the threshold of modernity and was thus the premise, not the consequence, of its industrialization.[8] This event determined the subsequent fate of the doctrine as well as that of the empire it came to rule. While adopting some of the rhetorical and propagandistic trappings of technical progress and modernization ("Communism is Soviet power plus electrification of the whole country"), Soviet ideology revealed itself in practice as the absolute enemy of civilizational progress and modernity, which are characterized by pluralism and the toleration of pluralism, social differentiation, and the rule of law.[9]

The manner of the Bolshevik seizure of power and the character of the cadres and rulers who emerged from it further determined the content and function of the ideology from that day to this. The classic exposition of this development is that of Kostas Papaioannou.[10] He first shows that the novelty of Marxist regimes is not state control of the economy, the destruction of free thought, forced industrialization, expropriation of the peasantry, the crushing of independent workers' organizations, draconian factory discipline, imperialism, terror, or the presence of a dominant class of service bureaucrats, since all of these phenomena are found singly or together in other types of regime, but two additional and overarching characteristics: (1) "The extraordinary rapidity with which all these traditional and even archaic elements of power were instituted and perfected, after a century of 'progress' and the triumph of a double revolution that had promised socialism in the cities and had established a free peasant economy," and (2) "The integral concentration of traditionally separate political, ideological, and economic powers and the theoretically absolute centralization of total power."[11] The second of these two characteristics was institutionalized in the Bolshevik party and heralded by the claims of Lenin as they were articulated after the seizure of power. The first was put into practice in the two aspects of Stalin's "Third Revolution" of 1929–39, the collectivization (i.e., the destruction) of agriculture, and the Great Terror. Even under Lenin and in the 1920s, however, the fateful changes in ideology were taking place that, in Papaioannou's phrase, turned Marxism into an orthodoxy from which no dissent was tolerated.

The key to understanding this development is Lenin's notion of the professional revolutionary, member of a "minority of ex-bourgeois intellectuals, strongly centralized and subject to an iron discipline."[12] As long as the Bolsheviks were still a secret party, imagination and independence were qualities in demand, and the despotic and conformist potential of the notion of the ideological cadre were not yet manifest. After Lenin took power, characteristics that were formerly required for survival became dangerous. The persecution of deviant thought and expression began immediately, as Gorky so vividly described it in his articles.[13] The regime of Lenin thus already displayed two crucial features of Stalinism: the cult of personality, not so much of Lenin himself as of Stalin, Trotsky, and others, and incipient dogmatism. However, after Lenin's death, there ensued the remarkable interlude of the mid-to-late 1920s, when the Red Terror was in abeyance and considerable freedom was allowed to science, art, and even the discussion of social questions.[14] The adherents and upholders of the ruling ideology were still capable of listening to criticism and consequently of responding to it. The principle of free discussion was still understood, although it was increasingly endangered.

With Stalin's defeat of his rivals, the total control in the ideological sphere of the dogmatists and "monopolizers of truth" was likewise guaranteed, and despite the modifications of style and temper that have later occurred. The most dramatic such modification of style was the so-called *glasnost* installed by the new CPSU general secretary, Mikhail Gorbachov, in 1985. The word *glasnost* does not mean openness, as many Westerners think, but rather "loudness, outspokenness", and describes a situation where people dare speak aloud what they always knew, but formerly only dared to say in whispers. In my view, *glasnost* and the associated program of *perestroika* or "restructuring" of the Soviet economy, has two purposes. One is domestic: to convince the subjects of communist rule that Gorbachov is their best chance of a better life and thereby to mobilize human resources to strengthen the state. The other is international: to convince the West that Gorbachov is a liberal reformer who deserves aid. The second purpose may well succeed even if the former fails.[15]

Gorbachov's most significant contribution to ideology has been to pretend that it is unimportant. As part of that contribution he has permitted an openness and looseness of language that, as far as it goes, is genuinely unique in Soviet history. Much of what follows, therefore, is only conditionally valid for the post-1985 period. Until that time, Soviet political language was frozen like a fly in amber and, with the passing decades, became ever more removed from reality. This discrepancy, however, did not prevent the ideology from shaping reality to its purposes. In fact, one can argue that it is the very fact that the ideology does not describe reality that makes it so apt an instrument of power. Seen in this light, the dogmatization of orthodoxy in the early years of Stalin was no error nor a sign of decadence, but rather the expression of the true nature and strength of the regime. The utility of Soviet ideology as a political instrument of combat is directly proportionate to its freedom from the constraints of reality. The denunciations of enemies and the redefinitions of basic principles of international relations are not expressions of objective judgment concerning the matters in question, but of the coercive power of the ideology.

> It is the very essence of the ideology which is manifest behind these pseudo-dialectical acrobatics: its function consists precisely in removing reality from the purchase of reflective thought, in increasing to a maximum the latent discrepancy between words and their objects, and in transforming reality into a fathomless 'mystery' beyond the grasp of reason. It is this line of thought we need to follow if we want to understand the decay of Marxism under the rule of orthodoxy.[16]

The shift from genuine debate within the limits of a Marxism that was still seen as a tool to understand social reality and not merely to control it to dogmatic orthodoxy appeared first in the growing tendency, as the regime established itself in the 1920s, to use quotes out of context instead of arguments to deal with opponents. By the early 1930s, serious argument had disappeared and was replaced by ideological struggle as it is still understood today. This notion of ideological struggle has very little, if anything, to do with the rational competition of ideas and a great deal to do with the power to silence adversaries or, alternatively, to compel them to adopt the right ideological language ("self-criticism"). In the show trials of 1936–39, the two functions were combined: hundreds of thousands of real or imagined adversaries were successfully induced to denounce themselves in the appropriate terms and were then killed for good measure. Since the death of Stalin, the two methods have been generally kept separate, at least in the Soviet Union and its satellites (the Chinese continued to apply them jointly until after the death of Mao). In the Cold War of the 1940s and after in Europe, the ideological struggle as waged by the Soviet Union is at bottom an attempt to induce Western elites to begin using the language of Soviet ideology, specifically its definitions of peace, war, and reasonable behavior. Once this has been achieved, the military and political consequences inevitably follow.

The freezing of the ideology as orthodoxy was as essential an aspect of the "Third Revolution" as collectivization, the purge of the Party, and the Great Terror. Its sociological correlate was, as has been mentioned, the rise to power and influence in the system of persons of a specific type, one very different from the type needed by the Bolsheviks before the seizure of power. The rise of this type of person was ensured by Stalin by the means just mentioned. Collectivization physically destroyed the most independent and productive elements of the peasantry and drove other millions to the cities. Here many of them found their chance of social mobility in the purges that emptied the ranks of Party and state institutions. Their sheer survival depended on absolute loyalty to the *Vozhd* and was ensured by an ingenious combination of pressures: the threat of expulsion, loss of career, or death in the camps on the one hand, and the fact that the survival of the millions of new urban dwellers depended on the forced levy of grain from the wreckage of Russian agriculture and hence on the permanence of collectivization. The victims of collectivization were thus made dependent on the very system that had destroyed their culture. Appropriation of the orthodoxy as laid down by the "Great Leader" was the price paid by millions for membership in the new *Nomenklatura*. Sincere belief, however, was not required and was even a liability for the very same reasons that had caused rational argument to be replaced by logomachy as the method of ideological struggle.

The consequence of the "Third Revolution" was thus social change of vast dimensions, but social change of a peculiar and unique kind, unknown to Western experience: it had few, if any, decisive effects on the political system that upheld the ideology and was in turn upheld by it. The most obvious such effect was the change, after Stalin's death, from execution to relegation as the primary method of dealing with defeated adversaries within the system. In a more general sense, however, this great process of social change triggered by Stalin and his *apparat* is the clue to the character and endurance of the Soviet Union. As the founder of the modern study of society pointed out, the key question to ask of any social formation is what kind of person it promotes and why:

> Without exception, any and all order of social relations must, if one is to *judge* it, be examined with respect to the question of *what human type* it gives the best chances of rising to power and what sorts of motivations are objectively and subjectively rewarded within it. No empirical investigation is exhaustive without that question, nor is there an adequate factual basis for any evaluation claiming either subjective or objective validity.[17]

The type of character elicited and rewarded by the Soviet system and its ideology since the time of Stalin is the "homo sovieticus" described by Alexander Zinoviev. Without making explicit judgments in Weber's sense on the resulting nature of the system, the mere fact that the homo sovieticus is obviously different from his counterparts in Western elites should give the latter food for thought.[18]

The rise of the Stalinist and post-Stalinist elite of "illiterate educators" and the extraordinary stability of the *apparat* marked the final turning away of Soviet Russia from the Western orientation that had been intermittently tried under the Tsars from Peter the Great to Nicholas II. In this sense, as in others, the major effect of Stalin's social revolution was to arrest and reverse the slow and painful steps that Russia had previously taken in the direction of Western modernity. From being a model, as it still was to some extent for Lenin, the West now became not only an enemy, but the source of all pernicious and corrupting influences.

> In the name of the fabulous 'principles' [of Marxism-Leninism], the innu-
> merable links that tied Russia to Europe were broken. The orthodoxy had
> no trouble subordinating the Marxist myth of a 'class truth' to the messianic
> imagery of the providential nation. To recognize any merit in Western culture
> was, after the promulgation of the *ukazes* of Zhdanov, to commit the grave
> sin of 'bourgeois cosmopolitanism' and of 'slavish kow-towing to the West'.[19]

The demonization of the West in Stalin's later years—the *ukazes* of Zhdanov date from 1947–48—was tempered under Khrushchev, but revived under Brezhnev, Andropov, and Gorbachev under the guise of the "struggle for peace against the imperialists" whose "blood-dripping hands" will be raised against the "camp of peace and socialism" unless vigilance is perpetually maintained and strengthened. It is, in essence, but an example and a logical development of the basic purpose of the ideology referred to above, namely its prevention of thought about reality. The transformation of reality into a "fathomless mystery" leads directly to the schizophrenic vision of history that is so immediately recognizable as a feature of the ideology. On the one hand, there is the "march of peoples towards the radiant future"; on the other, the monstrous machinations of the imperialists, deviationists, saboteurs, and other enemies whose actions and even existence are logically inexplicable and irrational. Papaioannou makes the interesting point that this underside of history, this demonic imagery and the associated show trials, purges, and witch-hunts fulfills another essential function of the ideology, namely as a release of unconscious self-criticism: "The monstrous confessions, then, have the purpose of allowing the masters of orthodoxy to externalize their deepest thought, their *basic distrust* not only of this or that aspect of the regime, but of the *human type* itself that the regime has produced."[20] We are thus brought back to Weber's question and to its application to the Soviet Union. Behind that question lies another, which we shall touch on before going on to the fate of Soviet ideology under developed socialism and its significance in international relations. This is, quite simply, the question of *why* this particular regime was able to consolidate itself, *why* its promotion of the specific type of character associated with it was possible and successful, and what the answers to the two parts of that question imply for the rest of us.

The first part of the question, namely why the regime won the struggle for power in 1917–20, should, I believe, be answered along the lines drawn by Martin Malia, whose masterly work has the additional merit of summarizing the other possible answers. He points to three basic circumstances. First, the peculiar denouement of the revolution of 1905, which was potentially a political revolution of the classic (nineteenth century) European type and which, had it succeeded, would have meant the decisive movement of Russia into the mainstream of Western political and social development. Despite the establishment of the Duma and other measures, however, the "liberal breakthrough" failed in Russia. Even so, Russia might still have joined the Western mainstream if the reaction of the authorities had taken the form of an "intelligent conservative solution on the Prussian model," that is, social reform from above as practised by Bismarck. This did not happen.[21]

Second, a consequence of the first and of World War I, the absence of an adversary capable of subduing the Bolsheviks in 1917.

> It was not so much because the revolutionaries had a real grip on the country, but rather because of the political power vacuum that they were able to control the situation. The dramatic events of 1917 allowed this small group of blanquist conspirators and *carbonari* to seize the locales of power in Petersburg. Even more important than the political power vacuum was the absence of social structures capable of resisting the seizure of power by this blanquist group. The impact of World War I, the first "democratic" war in history . . . on an old regime with a weak civil society could only be disastrous. In fact, during 1917, Russian civil society came apart, but this phenomenon was wholly independent of the will of the Bolsheviks. . . . By "civil society" we understand all those elements of society capable of organizing themselves independently of the state.[22]

The third circumstance was that the Bolsheviks, once they had seized the power that was lying in the street, reconstituted civil society in their own image, a process the decisive stages of which were executed in 1919–20 and which was "a case of substitution unique in . . . world history: the preceding, defunct civil society was replaced by a Party-state, a universal ideocratic bureaucracy."[23] On this view, the NEP and the relaxation of the 1920s was a temporary retreat, an example of "Bolshevik realism." Stalin's "Third Revolution" completed the process of installing socialism, a phenomenon that in practice turned out to be nothing other than "a system of universal slavery."[24] Since it was impossible to admit this in public, the ideology—and here we rejoin Papaioannou's analysis—was made to cover up the discrepancy between the ideal and the real by mystifying the latter.

The second part of the question, namely why the regime's promotion of its specific character type was possible and successful, has generally been answered in terms of an alleged predisposition of the Russian character (or, in more contemporary terms, of Russian social psychology or political culture) toward the meek acceptance of despotic rule. In writing his *Oriental Despotism*, Karl Wittfogel, a former Communist, was indirectly arguing, from the evidence of the Ancient Near East and China, that vast territorial states such as Russia could only achieve unity and political order under despotic regimes, and that this condition was clearly not going to change merely because the government of such a state was overthrown by a revolutionary party promising a "march toward the radiant future."[25] Wittfogel's argument was sociological and geographical: the natural environment is political destiny, or at least a great part of it. Some such idea underlies much of the loose speculation on the relation between Russian history and Soviet rule.

A somewhat different line of argument, and one that has recently received some interesting, if tentative, confirmation, was adumbrated by Bertram Wolfe in the first chapter of *Three Who Made a Revolution*, where he speaks of the patriarchalism of the " 'undivided family' and the communal village *mir*," two institutions that

> set their unmistakable patriarchal, communal stamp on much of Russian life. . . . To them is attributable the corporateness of Russian rural life, the comparative speed with which the village could be collectivized into the *kolkhoz*, the readiness with which bolshevism was transformed from a program of rule from below into rule by a small élite and then into a personal dictatorship, once more of a "Father of the People". Perhaps, too, these forces help to explain such practices as the taking of hostages and the holding of an entire family legally responsible for the acts of any one of its members.[26]

What is merely a passing thought in Wolfe, namely the link between the Russian family type and the political system of Communist rule, has been raised into a general hypothesis on the relation between family types and political structures by Emmanuel Todd. According to Todd, the Russian "undivided family" is an example of the type known as the "communitarian exogamous family," whose basic characteristics are the equality of male offspring with respect to inheritance and succession, the tendency for married sons to bring their families to live with their parents, and absence of marriage between the children of brothers (that is, cousins of male descent).

Todd formulates his hypothesis of the political consequences of communitarian exogamy as follows:

Communism is the transfer to the Party-state of the moral characteristics and regulatory mechanisms of the communitarian exogamous family. When threatened with disintegration by urbanization, literacy, industrialization, in a word, by modernity, the communitarian exogamous family bequeathed its authoritarian and egalitarian values to the new society. Individual members, though equal in rights, are just as crushed by the political apparatus as they were formerly overwhelmed by the extended family when it was still the dominant institution of a traditional society.[27]

The objection that the Bolsheviks sought precisely to destroy the family is, for Todd, additional confirmation of the pervasiveness of the psychological and sociological legacy of the Russian family type: "The anthropological individualism of Communist regimes is evident: they proclaim the end of paternal power and the autonomy of the married couple. Only the communitarian exogamous family elicits such feelings of hatred, such a determined drive to sociological murder."[28] Todd sees the prime reason for this hatred and its explosive force in the male rivalry within the undivided family, a rivalry that was especially pronounced in Russia, where (as evidence shows), there was a pronounced tendency for younger men to marry slightly older women. Frequent cohabitation of men of 40–45 years with the wives of sons aged about 20–25 led to dramatic conflicts, known to Russian folklore and poetry and noted by Engels in his *Origins of the Family*. Adding some Freudian insights concerning the impulse of younger men in the undivided family to kill their fathers, and by extension to kill, or replace, the *rodnoi otets* or "own dear father," a popular name for the ruler of the country, Todd concludes:

To liberate man, it is not enough to dissolve the communitarian exogamous family and destroy its habits of discipline and internal egalitarianism. The destruction of a family type does not touch the value system that underlies it. No sooner is freedom won than it is seen as anarchy, as a source of anxiety rather than pleasure. The development of Communist systems permitted the reinstatement of individuals in a familiar, authoritarian and egalitarian framework. The Party replaced the family. Its cells artificially reproduced the former, dense, intolerable, and occasionally murderous fraternal relations. Its hierarchy replaced paternal power on all levels. At the base, the cell secretaries intervene in the family life of Soviet couples. At the top, the fathers succeed one another: a dynamic, loquacious, and violent father in the case of Lenin; a sadistic father in the case of Stalin; an aged father in the case of Brezhnev, who carried the Russian politico-familial metaphor to its ultimate point. The senility of Soviet rulers is the destiny of all patriarchs.[29]

Combined with the sociological and political analyses of Malia, Heller and Nekrich, and others, and with an understanding of the content and operation of the ideology such as that provided by Papaioannou, it seems to me that Todd's approach, however tentative in its present form, might yield a considerable advance in the direction of answering Weber's question regarding the Soviet Union.

The Fate of Ideology under Developed Socialism

In 1971, at the XXIV Congress of the Party, Brezhnev introduced the doctrine of developed socialism, replacing the doctrine of the Third Party Program of 1961, which was that the Soviet Union was moving rapidly through the phase of socialism and would enter the final stage of Communism by 1980. The XXVII Congress of 1986, the first presided over by Gorbachev, did not in the event produce the long-expected Fourth Program, but rather a series of guidelines of programmatic status. In these guidelines, the Party, reflecting Gorbachev's desires, confirmed that the road to completed socialism was long and hard, and that the Soviet Union and the socialist camp would indeed remain for the foreseeable future at the level of "developed socialism". However, Gorbachev has surprised some observers by repeating not infrequently that the ultimate goal remains full communism for the entire world, presumably in the paradisical form defined by Khrushchev in 1961. When asked to put a date on the achievement, Gorbachev has indicated about a hundred years as the time needed to complete the transition. Western liberals might take note that Gorbachev has never, anywhere, renounced world communism as the goal of his efforts; in fact, he has gone to some pains to confirm it.

Because Soviet ideology is not meant to describe or interpret reality but to obfuscate it in the interests of Soviet power, the question to ask regarding the doctrine of developed socialism is how it serves those interests. The answer is simple and we need not waste much space on it. The doctrine has two main strategic functions, one external and one internal. For external consumption, the doctrine tends to promote the idea that the Soviet Union has abandoned extremism, including mass terror and genocide, in the pursuit of its goals; indeed, it implies that those goals themselves no longer include global hegemony, but simply a defensive maintenance of the status quo. Domestically, within the "camp of peace and socialism" and more specifically in the Soviet Union, the doctrine of developed socialism means that the system and methods of rule as enforced under Brezhnev are going to continue for the indefinite future. There will neither be mass terror as under Stalin nor feeble movement in the direction of liberalization as under Khrushchev. Gorbachev's *glasnost* and *perestroika* must not be confused with genuine liberalization. As I stated above, I believe that the purpose of both strategies is to centralize power and win Western support. An astute observer, John Dunlop, has accurately argued that Gorbachev is another Peter the Great, committed to streamlining and modernizing his economy and administrative system. The liberals of the eighteenth-century Enlightenment in Western Europe admired Peter. They ignored the most important fact about the Russia he built: that it was militaristic, aggressive, and successfully expansionist. It was Peter who first introduced Russian military and political power into Central Europe, whence it has never since receded.

The social control of the regime has become routinized, but so has the formulation and use of the ideology, and, in accordance with its nature, the routinization of ideology is tantamount to its final and irrevocable consolidation. Because the ideology is a mystification and, as an "orthodoxy erected as public truth,"[30] the expression of the complete alienation of reality from language, it finds its natural finality and perfect stage, not as the apocalyptic imagery of total revolutionary change and the achievement of utopia, but as "a technique of conditioning of the human spirit, of the transformation of man into Soviet man. . . . The ideology regulates the behavior of Soviet subjects and, thanks to a system of precise procedures, arouses in them the emotions and the reflexes that the Party needs at any given moment. Soviet subjects need not believe. They must only repeat the slogans dictated to them."[31] We differ from Papaioannou in not seeing the fate of ideology under developed socialism as a decay, but rather as its inevitable completion as an instrument of power. The double imagery of a "march toward the radiant future" on the one hand and the machinations of monstrous enemies of the other that characterized the ideological vision of the world from the start has become routinized in its two surviving principal elements, namely that the Party is always right, for it leads the way to the radiant future, and that the hatred of the enemy is an inseparable part of Soviet man.[32]

Ideology and International Relations

The Soviet rulers use ideology to wage the Cold War with their main enemy, the United States, in accordance with the two strategic functions, domestic and international, listed above. Domestically, the United States now occupies, along with Israel, the position formerly held by the deviationists, saboteurs, rightists, "Hitlerite fascists," and imperialist agents of Stalin's day, that is, the position of chief actor in the apocalyptic drama we have come to associate with the underside of the ideological vision of history. The language of Soviet life is (once again) full of words and phrases like "Victory!", "We Will Defend Peace," and "The USSR is the Bulwark of Peace." Internationally, the purpose of ideology has changed somewhat, if not in essence, since the early days. Then, the purpose was to convince the West that the Soviet Union was something other than it really was, in order to obtain diplomatic recognition, trade, and other forms of aid that could be used to bolster the system. This purpose is still relevant and has indeed been achieved to a considerable degree, as can be gathered from the perusal of academic and official political arguments claiming that the Soviet Union has become a power primarily interested in defending its interests (which are basically those of Russian nationalism), and above all from the West's formal acceptance, in the Helsinki Accords of 1975, of the Soviet Union as a legitimate European power and a presumptive upholder of the peaceful status quo. Moreover, beginning in the 1920s, "the capitalists have demonstrated an unshakable determination to assist communist states who have never concealed the fact that their goal is to annihilate capitalism."[33] However, since the mid-1970s the Soviet rulers have tended to modify this, as it were, pure ideology of détente with direct or indirect threats of force. Soviet military power has become a factor of influence in its own right, tending to induce in Western elites what Hans-Peter Schwarz calls "a desire, in view of the decline of American power, to come to terms with the new lord and master."[34] The effect of this combination of threats and peace talk has been to create a schizophrenic confusion in the attitude of many Westerners toward the Soviet Union, a confusion analogous to the split between reality and language in the ideology itself. This confusion tends in turn to generate an ideology of its own, the Western ideology of détente, characterized, just as the Soviet ideology is, by the simultaneous presence in the minds of its victims of two logically incompatible elements, in this case an unhealthy fear of Soviet power and overt insistence on the peaceful, reasonable, and respectable intentions and policies of Soviet rulers.

The irony is that there is no reason at all for the existence of such a Western ideology of detente, other than the domestic neuroses of Western leaders incapable of dealing rationally with the fact that the richest nations on earth are not willing to pay for their own defense. Soviet leaders have never tried to hide the meaning of detente and by extension of their foreign policy. According to the *Short Political Dictionary*, detente is "a defeat of the imperialist forces" and the result of "the constant strengthening of the positions of the socialist camp." It moreover "creates a favorable situation for the gradual spread of communist ideology and of the values of socialism, and promotes an offensive ideological struggle under the conditions of the peaceful coexistence of states with differing social systems."[35] Brezhnev himself, at the XXV Congress of the Party in 1976, stressed that "detente in no way puts an end to, nor can it modify, the laws of the class struggle. . . . We do not hide the fact that we see in detente the means of creating conditions more favorable to the peaceful construction of socialism and communism."[36] In other words, the West was forced to its present "reasonable view" of international relations by the growth of Soviet power, and by nothing else. The corollary is that the further growth of Soviet power, necessary and inevitable in any case, will further the fulfilment of "the revolutionary strategy of popular liberation from class oppression," inasmuch as "the interests of mankind coincide with the class interest of the international working class and of socialism," that is, of the Soviet Union.[37]

Soviet ideology on international relations does not tell us how those relations really stand in the Cold War between Western democracies and Soviet power, for that is not its purpose. It does, however, provide us with a message that, partaking of the nature of the ideology itself, is both intentional and indirect. The message is simply that Soviet power will grow until its very weight compels the reordering of the world in the Soviet interest. The international function of the ideology rejoins its domestic function as outlined by Kolakowski: "The socialist class of exploiters is not eager to retain and extend its power because it professes a false doctrine . . . rather, they adhere to this doctrine as a tool to retain and extent their power. . . . Its purpose is to demonstrate who is in power."[38] Ultimately, the core principle of Soviet ideology in the era of developed socialism remains the same as it was under Stalin, namely "beat, beat, and, once again, beat."[39] The difference is that the beatings are now administered primarily in regions remote from the limited imaginations of postimperial Westerners (for example, in Afghanistan, Indochina, and Nicaragua), remaining elsewhere as a barely veiled threat that, as shown above, is being taken seriously by many of the same people who profess not to believe that the Soviet Union aims at global hegemony.

Conclusion

The fate of ideology under developed socialism is to have achieved its natural role and purpose as a false "public truth" designed not to describe reality but to demonstrate who is in power. In international relations, the

Soviet rulers "still believe sufficiently in the myth of the proletariat and of the Marxist-Leninist party to make it impossible for them to agree to a peace of the classical type within a homogeneous state system."[40] Nevertheless, as the same author notes, the makers of Soviet foreign policy in the mold of Gromyko—a mold likely to endure for decades yet—see their chances of victory more in the ideological struggle than in open conflict with the United States. "For such diplomats, who think and act with a view to the long term, it would be unreasonable to take the risk of a general, nuclear war, if their objectives can be attained by the weight of force alone, supported by the ordinary methods of propaganda and terrorism."[41] As we have seen, this approach is explicitly accepted by Soviet rulers and planners. In addition to the statements quoted, we may add the view of Leonid Zamyatin, the head of the International Information Department of the Central Committee of the Party, as expressed to the British historian John Ericsson: "The nineteenth century belonged to Europe. The twentieth century belongs to America. The twenty-first century will belong to the Soviet Union."

We are here at the point where ideology intersects the reality it is so often used to obscure. The ideology has it that the Soviet Union that is bound to extend its vision of world order across the globe will be a Communist Soviet Union, a utopia free of the rule of man by man. The reality is that the Soviet Union is in fact engaged in trying to extend its world order system, and the real nature of that system is incompatible with essential Western interests shared as much by Western socialists as by liberals and conservatives. This is why the study of Soviet ideology, actions, and practices must inevitably be part of a judgment in two senses: an evaluation of the system in accordance with Weber's question, and an evaluation of the past, present, and potential future effects of the system on us.

Notes

1. Jerry Hough and Merle Fainsod, *How the Soviet Union is Governed* (Cambridge, Mass.: Harvard University Press, 1979). The very use of the word "governed," replacing Fainsod's "ruled," begs the essential question of the nature of the regime by assuming that it is engaged in the civilized activity of "governing."
2. The most thorough survey of the history and use of the notion of developed socialism by Soviet rulers is Alfred B. Evans, Jr., "Developed Socialism and the New Program of the CPSU," unpublished paper presented at the Con-

ference on Ideology and Soviet Politics, London, May 1985. See also Ronald Tiersky, *Ordinary Stalinism* (London: George Allen & Unwin, 1985).

3. Leszek Kolakowski, "Ideology in Eastern Europe," in Milorad Drachkovitch, ed., *East Central Europe* (Stanford: Hoover Institution Press, 1982), pp. 50–51.

4. Leszek Kolakowski, *Main Currents of Marxism* (Oxford: Oxford University Press, 1978), vol. 1, preface.

5. Ernst Nolte is the contemporary scholar who has most intensively studied and presented this perspective on Marxism; see his *Marxismus und industrielle Revolution* (Stuttgart: Klett-Cotta, 1983).

6. *eine nach Wertideen und Mitteln dem kapitalistischen Zeitalter innerlich zugehorige allumfassende Lebensbewegung zur Herbeifuhrung und dauernden Sicherung der Freiheit und des diesseitigen Glücks aller durch ihre uneingeschränkte Einführung in die Einrichtungen der von höchster Sachvernunft geformten und jedes Herrschaftscharakters entkleideten menschlichen Gesellschaft.* Gustav Gundlach, S.J., *Die Ordnung der menschlichen Gesellschaft* (Cologne: Bachem, 1964), 2:122, quoted in Johannes Schwarte, *Gustav Gundlach, S.J.* (Paderborn: Schöningh, 1975), p. 421.

7. For the phrase, see Martin Malia, *Comprendre la revolution russe* (Paris: Seuil, 1980), pp. 211, 220. See also Carl A. Linden, *The Soviet Party-State: The Politics of Ideocratic Despotism* (New York: Praeger, 1983).

8. Nolte, *Marxismus*, p. 19.

9. The notion that Soviet ideology, and by extension the Soviet Union itself, essentially antimodern and the chief example of what Karl Dietrich Bracher calls "Brechungen des Fortschrittsgedankens," has been touched on by many scholars. See, for example, Kenneth Minogue, *Alien Powers: The Pure Theory of Ideology* (London: Weidenfeld & Nicolson, 1985), p. 224 ("ideology is essentially hostile to modernity"); Karl Dietrich Bracher, *Zeit der Ideologien* (Stuttgart: Deutsche Verlags-Anstalt, 1982), pp. 11–18 (on the ambiguity of notions of "progress" in ideology); Malia, *Comprendre la revolution russe*, pp. 213–23 (the regime based on destruction of civil society which, in Russia as elsewhere, was the social basis of modernization); Ernst Nolte, *Deutschland und der Kalte Krieg*, 2d ed. (Stuttgart: Klett-Cotta, 1985), pp. 571–78 (modernity of Western socialism opposed to premodern socialism of USSR); and Papaioannou (see next note). Cf. also the image of an "ice age" as an appropriate symbol of Communist rule, as in Hugh Seton-Watson, "Europe's New Political Ice Age," in Drachkovitch, *East Central Europe*, pp. 175–83.

10. Kostas Papaioannou, *L'ideologie froide* (Paris: Pauvert, 1967).

11. *Ibid.*, pp. 15–17.

12. *Ibid.*, p. 42.

13. Eloquent excerpts are quoted in Bertram D. Wolfe, *The Bridge and the Abyss: The Troubled Friendship of Maxim Gorky and V.I. Lenin* (New York: Praeger, 1967), pp. 66–72.

14. Papaioannou, *L'ideologie froide*, pp. 62–69.

15. Gorbachov's popularity, and the West's never-ending belief that the Soviet

Union is about to turn into a liberal society, has spawned a vast literature, most of which is valueless. The newspaper and magazine contributions by Adam Ulam and Alain Besançon, however, are always worth reading, and one hopes either or both of these scholars will soon produce the definitive interpretation of the Gorbachov era.

16. *Ibid.*, p. 133.

17. Max Weber, *Gesammelte Aufsätze zur Wissenschaftslehre*, ed. J. Winckelmann, 4th ed. (Tübingen: Mohr, 1973), pp. 517–18 (Weber's italics). I have not used the standard English translation of this passage, which expresses Weber's basic interest, because it trivializes the point and is generally misleading; see Wilhelm Hennis, "Max Webers Fragestellung," *Zeitschrift für Politik* 29 (1982), pp. 279–80.

18. The point that Soviet and Western political cultures are radically different has been made frequently by Robert Conquest; see especially his *We and They* (London: Temple Smith, 1979).

19. Papaioannou, *L'ideologie froide*, p. 86.

20. *Ibid.*, p. 145 (Papaioannou's italics).

21. Malia, *Comprendre la revolution russe*, pp. 86–87. To understand more generally why the social and political forces present in 1905 failed to achieve one of these two solutions, one may refer to another work that is in many ways a necessary "companion volume" to Malia, namely Marc Raeff, *Comprendre l'ancien regime russe* (Paris: Seuil, 1982). Since both these works, though written and published in French, are by Americans—students of Michael Karpovich at Harvard—one may hope that English editions are forthcoming.

22. Malia, *Comprendre la revolution russe*, p. 213.

23. *Ibid.*, p. 214.

24. *Ibid.*, p. 218.

25. Karl A. Wittfogel, *Oriental Despotism*, preface to the reprint ed. (New York: Vintage, 1982). Originally published New Haven: Yale University Press, 1957.

26. Bertram D. Wolfe, *Three Who Made a Revolution*, 4th ed. (New York: Dial Press, 1964), p. 28.

27. Emmanuel Todd, *La troisième planète: structures familiales et systèmes ideologiques* (Paris: Seuil, 1983), p. 43.

28. *Ibid.*, p. 44.

29. *Ibid.*, p. 50. Cf. Michel Heller and Aleksandr Nekrich, *L'utopie au pouvoir* (Paris: Calmann-Levy, 1982), p. 546: "The ideology fulfils an essential function in Soviet society: the infantilization of the population."

30. Raymond Aron, *Les dernières années du siècle* (Paris: Commentaire Julliard, 1984), p. 126.

31. Heller and Nekrich, *L'utopie au pouvoir*, pp. 545–46.

32. *Ibid.*

33. *Ibid.*, p. 529. The Soviets in general put great faith, amply justified by history, in the ability and willingness of banks and some business circles to restrain the anti-Soviet tendencies of "organized monopoly capitalism" and its political leaders, e.g., Ronald Reagan. For an authoritative exposition of this faith,

see Andrei Gromyko, *Vneshnyaya ekspansiya kapitala* (1982), summarized in Heinz Brahm, "Zur politischen Philosophie A. Gromykos," Bundesinstitut fur ostwissenschaftliche und internationale Studien, *Aktuelle Analysen*, No. 31/1984.

34. Hans-Peter Schwarz, "Die Alternative zum Kalten Krieg? Bilanz der bisherigen Entspannung," in Hans-Peter Schwarz and Boris Meissner, eds., *Entspannungspolitik in Ost und West* (Cologne: Heymanns, 1979), p. 302.
35. Quoted in Heller and Nekrich, *L'utopie au pouvoir*, p. 522–23.
36. Quoted *ibid.*, p. 542.
37. Quoted *ibid.*, p. 541.
38. Kolakowski, "Ideology in Eastern Europe," pp. 45, 49.
39. Stalin's words to an investigating judge as reported by Khrushchev in the "Secret Report"; see Bertram D. Wolfe, *Khrushchev and Stalin's Ghost* (New York: Praeger, 1957), p. 204. Wolfe's text and commentary is the most useful edition of the "Secret Report."
40. Aron, *Dernières anneees*, p. 145.
41. *Ibid.*, pp. 147–48.

Soviet Military Policy and Post-Soviet Russia

PETER VIGOR

The chief tasks of the Soviet armed forces may be said to be the following: (i) At the grand strategic level, to deter war. The USSR does *not* want a major war against a powerful and well-equipped enemy (e.g., NATO). So all potential aggressors must be deterred. This deterrence is to be achieved by Soviet armed forces being both sufficiently numerous and also sufficiently well equipped to make it plain to any potential aggressor that, if he were to start a war against the Soviet Union, he could not hope to win it. The Soviet armed forces, therefore, must not only be strong in reality, and in all branches of warfare (nuclear, conventional, chemical and all the rest of it), but they must also be *seen* to be strong by the outside world. Deterrence is achieved not only by physical, but also by psychological means, by affecting the *minds* of potential enemies and getting them to believe (what indeed is true) that the Soviet armed forces are extremely powerful, and therefore not to be trifled with.

(ii) If, however, deterrence should fail, and some country or group of countries should attack the USSR, then the Soviet armed forces must be fully capable of fighting the resulting war, whether nuclear or conventional, and fighting it successfully; though what will be meant by the word "successfully" will of course depend on the nature of the war in question. In the case of the war in Afghanistan for instance, its successful conclusion, as seen by the Kremlin, can only be the smashing of Afghan resistance and the ensuring to Babrak Karmal and his successors of unquestioned authority over the Afghan people. In the case of a war against NATO, on the other hand, its successful conclusion might only mean the repulse of that infamous "imperialist attack," the imminence of which is regularly proclaimed in the speeches of the Soviet leaders. Alternatively, it might mean the advance westwards of the Soviet armed forces to a predetermined boundary, whether the Rhine or the Channel, and the retention in Soviet hands of the area which would thus have been occupied. Whichever it would be, the Soviet armed forces, in order to attain their success, would have had to have been equipped and trained and organized to fight the war with nuclear weapons, with chemical weapons, with conventional weapons, or with any conceivable mixture of these three.

(iii) Another major task of the Soviet armed forces is said in Soviet official pronouncements to be "to defend the gains of October." This means more than just defending the Soviet Union against attack by an external enemy, though of course it means that too; but it also means ensuring the continuance of the Soviet regime in Russia and of Soviet control of the "satellites," both by suppressing, when necessary, civil disturbances inside Soviet territory and also by performing a similar function in the countries of Eastern Europe and in Mongolia. It is not only for the purpose of containing NATO or facing down Communist China that large contingents of Soviet troops are stationed near the frontiers of these countries; it is also for that of preventing rebellion among Russia's reluctant allies. Of course the Soviet leaders seldom mention this latter possibility, and instead prefer to harp on NATO's "aggressive intentions," but the prevention of serious revolt in the "satellite" countries is not the least of the functions of the Soviet forces stationed in that part of the world. Furthermore, the invasion of Czechoslovakia in 1968 proves how effectively they fulfil that function when the Kremlin requires them to do so.

(iv) Another function of the Soviet armed forces is to give whatever support is deemed expedient to Soviet foreign policy. Under this heading have come such operations as the mounting of the Guinea patrol by units of the Soviet navy during the late 1960s and the early 1970s in order to prevent that country's Marxist government being ousted by non-Marxist opponents shipped in by sea from anti-Marxist neighbors; and also the putting on full alert in 1967 of a number of its airborne units in order to induce the U.S. to put pressure upon the Israeli government to refrain from exploiting its successes over the Egyptians by destroying the Egyptian Third Army and marching upon Cairo.

(v) Yet another function of the Soviet armed forces is to support the "National Liberation Movement" in every part of the world. This the Soviet armed forces have done with very considerable success. There would be no Marxist government in Ethiopia if it had not been for Soviet military assistance, nor would there be one in Angola or Mozambique. This is not to say that these Marxist revolutions took place because of Soviet armies being transported to these countries in their hundreds of thousands and driving out the anti-Marxist forces in full-scale conventional campaigns. The bulk of the manpower necessary was supplied by the indigenous revolutionaries. The Soviet Union's role was confined to supplying the arms and ammunition in the necessary quantities and also (and most importantly) the crews for the aircraft fulfilling the most vital functions and for much of the key armor.

(vi) The sixth main task of the Soviet armed forces is to act as a "school for Communist youth," and thus assist the Party in its struggle to see to it that the rising generations of Soviet citizens should accept the principles of Marxism-Leninism, accept the role of the Communist Party as the leading, guiding and controlling element in every aspect of Soviet life, and should show themselves willing to adopt the values which the Party sets out to inculcate. In seeking to perform this task, the Soviet armed forces concentrate their attention upon the conscripts. These, during the term of their obligatory military service (two years for the army and air force, three years for the navy), spend quite a lot of time attending classes run by the political officers, whose job it is to inculcate in their audiences (or, to put it more accurately, to do their best to reinculcate) the principles, attitudes and values which have just been mentioned above. That the Party regards this job as of great importance is evident from the fact that a large amount of valuable military training time is appropriated to this kind of indoctrination. This view is confirmed by a glance at a celebrated article in *Kommunist* written by General A.A. Yepishev, at that time the head of the Chief Political Directorate of the Soviet armed forces, which gives the impression that at least in the eyes of the general (and therefore presumably of the Party) the political indoctrination of the conscripts was at least as important as the implanting in them of the basic military skills.

The above are the six main tasks of the Soviet armed forces and, while one ponders their implications, it may be thought appropriate to note that the USSR has really got only two enemies (or, perhaps I should say, potential enemies) with any real power to harm her. These are the United States of America, with or without her NATO allies, and China. The nuclear forces of Britain and France are capable of a damaging retaliatory strike; but they are not able to do such damage as to endanger the existence of the Soviet regime, if acting independently of the U.S. In view of all this, the question then arises whether these countries would still be the enemies of Russia if a non-Soviet regime were established there, and also whether such a regime would attract new, quite different enemies.

The answer to this question must inevitably depend upon what sort of post-Soviet regime is to come to power in Russia. In terms of economics, is it to be capitalist, or is it to adopt one or another of the myriad varieties of socialism; or is it to have some kind of economic setup which is at present quite unknown to us? In terms of politics, is it to be a dictatorship of one form or another, or perhaps an oligarchy, or is a Western-type liberal democracy to be installed in it? The permutations are virtually endless; and if each one had to be examined in detail, this little paper would become a weighty tome. On the other hand, it is reasonable to suppose that the post-Soviet regime will not be Marxist-Leninist nor even Marxist. Otherwise, why make a change? I therefore base my analysis on the assumption that a post-Soviet regime would be, broadly speaking, democratic; and that it would proceed to operate an economic system which would be very largely capitalist. Given all this, who would be its enemies and what would therefore be its military policy?

As far as relations with the West are concerned, the removal from Russia of the Soviet Communist Party and the Marxist-Leninist element would presumably also remove a great deal, if not all, of the ideological element which at present bedevils relations between East and West. There would be no need for a post-Soviet Russia to proclaim as not only inevitable, but also supremely desirable, the destruction of what the USSR today likes to describe as "imperialism," a word defined in standard Soviet reference books as a form of society characterized in its economic aspect by a highly developed capitalist system, and by some form or other of parliamentary democracy in its political aspect—in other words, the Western way of life. By the same token, the United States would no longer feel a moral compulsion to plan "crusades" against Russia.

As a consequence of this, it is not wholly impossible that something of vital importance for the whole of mankind might materialize. If neither side is continually proclaiming its longing to see the destruction of the other's form of society, the likelihood of their resorting to nuclear war would very considerably diminish. For the nuclear weapon, as all agree, is the ultimate. It will therefore only be used when the *ultimate* interests of either, or both, protagonists are involved. It was, after all, with great misgivings, and even then only to save the lives of the enormous numbers of their own forces, own prisoners-of-war in Japanese hands, and Japanese civilians whom the Western Allies expected to be killed if the conquest of Japan were to be undertaken by conventional means only, that President Truman finally agreed to the use of the atomic weapon, a weapon which must be reckoned to be almost innocuous by comparison with those of today.

A decision to resort to nuclear war can surely be undertaken only when one's whole existence is at stake, a principle enunciated by Clausewitz when discussing the ultimate in war; though for him the ultimate was less horrific than our own ultimate, because he naturally had no notion of nuclear weapons. Nevertheless he was right in what he said: one only resorts to the ultimate when one's own ultimate interests are at stake; and the history of nuclear weapons up until now confirms that principle's validity.

But if neither Russia nor the U.S. were threatening the other's existence, the ultimate interests of neither country could possibly be in jeopardy; neither side would have any motive for seeking to destroy the other's political and economic system. That contrasts very sharply with the present situation, where the USSR is continually saying that the Western way of life (or, as the Soviets describe it, imperialism) is doomed by the laws of history to total destruction and, in addition, deserves to be. In consequence of this, the Soviets hold it is the duty of all "progressive humanity" to take what action they appropriately can to hasten imperialism's downfall. Similar menaces to the continued existence of the present regime in the USSR are regularly uttered in Washington, though not so regularly as the Soviet menaces nor based on such a determinist view of history.

Nevertheless, each side's menaces alarm and enrage the other; and an end to these, which must surely result from the coming to power of a post-Soviet regime in Russia for the reasons already given, are bound to lead to a dramatic reduction in tension, and to a sharp abatement of the fear and suspicion with which each side regards the other. Such an improvement in East-West relations must surely be highly conducive to the signing and faithful observance of a whole series of arms control treaties relating to nuclear weapons, which are, after all, the most important of all arms control treaties, and the ones which the world is most longing to see effected.

On the other hand, it would seem to be most unlikely that the mere replacement of a Soviet regime with some sort of quasi-capitalist, liberal, parliamentary democratic one would put an end to conflicts of *national* interest (national, as distinct from ideological). The United States has a large Polish community, to say nothing of Czech, Hungarian and other elements. A change of regime in Russia would surely seem to whomever might be the U.S. President at that moment, the opportunity to restore to Poland and these other countries that full independence and sovereignty which the Communists forcibly took from them, and which the United States has pledged itself to return to them.

From the point of view of the Americans, this would be simply an act of natural justice to which no one could object. Can we be so sure, however, that the Russians, even the post-Soviet, presumably liberal Russians, would view it similarly?

In the first place, much of Poland was part of the Russian Empire for roughly 200 years. There was a very brief interregnum between the two world wars when Poland regained her independence; but then in 1939 she was recolonised. The Russians mostly dislike the Poles intensely (a sentiment heartily reciprocated), and have the feeling that Poland is by nature a country of second-rate citizens. They are not very fond of Hungarians or Romanians either.

Such sentiments by themselves, of course, might well not be sufficiently powerful to prevent the post-Soviet regime in Russia from restoring to the Poles their freedom, and to the Hungarians and Romanians also. A far greater obstacle to their doing so is posed by the problem of Germany.

It would probably not be NATO as such which would trouble the members of the new government in the Kremlin.[1] If they were intelligent men, as one would expect them to be, and people moreover who knew at least a little of what went on in the world outside, they would quickly realize that it is really quite impossible for NATO to attack their country. The Americans, going it alone, might just conceivably have done it, if they had felt it necessary to start a preventive war; but that would have been in the days of their nuclear monopoly, because they would have had to have done it by nuclear means, as they had (and have) no other with which to do so with any hope of success. No man embarks upon nuclear war lightly. With a bit of luck, no man will embark on it at all.[2]

NATO as such would therefore quite likely be regarded by the new regime in Russia with comparative, if not total, equanimity. The same, however, would not be true of Germany. Neither of the Germanies, as they exist at present, is capable on its own of attacking Russia, with conventional means only, with any chance of success. A reunited Germany, however, might be another matter. Furthermore, the post-Soviet regime in Russia would be sure to remember that it has not only been ideological differences which over the years have impelled the Germans to attack their country. In 1914–18, for instance, it was purely Great Power differences which motivated the Germans' move to war and led to their advance eastward; and in 1941 the desire for territorial expansion was at least as strong a motive for "Barbarossa" as Hitler's hatred of Communism. Consequently, post-Soviet Russia must be expected to be as little inclined as its predecessor to see the reappearance of a united Germany.

But then the post-Soviet regime in Russia would be faced with the difficult problem of how to prevent this happening. One way might be, at least in theory, to come to an agreement with the Western powers (and with the United States in particular, of course) by virtue of which all the NATO allies of West Germany on the one hand and the post-Soviet regime in Russia on the other would combine to forbid the two Germanies from ever reuniting. This may be fine in theory; it would be difficult to achieve in practice.

The reasons for this are twofold. First, it is really very unlikely that the Western powers would agree to such an arrangement. No democracy could surely contemplate preventing, by force if necessary, an ally which is also a fellow democracy from linking up with kith and kin if it wanted to and thereby rescuing the kith and kin from servitude. This would be absurd. Second, with the economy of post-Soviet Russia being essentially capitalist in nature, the economic links between the two Germanies would grow very quickly indeed. On the basis of these economic links there would soon be forged political links; and these would grow, smoothly and uninterruptedly, until reunification of the two Germanies would have taken place *de facto*, even though no actual official declaration by the two German governments on the subject of reunification would ever have been made. It is hard to see how anyone can dispute this. It must surely be conceded that the growth of strong economic links between the Germanies, which even today are on a considerable scale, must be reckoned to be inevitable in a world in which there was a liberal-democratic, quasi-capitalist Russia, unless something were done to prevent it. Unless it were prevented, it would give birth to strong political links, and hence to reunification. A post-Soviet Russia would no more want this reunification of Germany than does her predecessor; and that the only sure way she would have of preventing this happening would be to retain East Germany under strict Russian control. But it would be impossible to do this without at the same time retaining the other countries of Eastern Europe in something like their present status. Poland, Czechoslovakia and Hungary, for instance, could hardly be given back their freedom and sovereign independence while East Germany remained a Russian colony. The riots and other disturbances which this would provoke in *both* the Germanies would be on such a scale as to threaten the peace of the world. If East Germany has to be retained in its colonial status (and we have just seen that for Russia there would really be no alternative), then the other present 'satellites' must too.

The result would be the continuation of the present division of Europe, and therefore the need for post-Soviet Russia to continue with the Communists' present policy of stationing in Central and Eastern Europe considerable numbers of troops. These troops would be there, above all, to prevent rebellion in the "satellite" countries, and also to prevent the Western powers from coming to the "satellites' " help. Soviet military policy in the area would thus perforce be perpetuated by the present regime's successors.

Let us now turn to China which, we agreed earlier, is the only other dangerous potential enemy of the USSR. At the present time, the enmity between them is fueled both by nationalistic differences and also by ideological ones. China may be a Marxist-Leninist country, but her brand of Marxism-Leninism is not the same as the Soviet one. Furthermore, it was

not the same in the days of the cult of Maoism; and even today when
Maoism in all its pristine glory and self-centred righteousness is no longer
fashionable in the Chinese People's Republic, its place has not been taken
by the Soviet version of Leninism and certainly not by the Soviet version
of Leninism now current in the USSR.

Of course, we all know that ideological schism breeds enmity of at least
as vicious a kind as that engendered by outright ideological opposition.
Insofar as the enmity between China and present-day Russia is due then
to ideological differences, it is likely to be less in the event of a liberal
democratic, quasi-capitalist government coming to power in Russia than
it is now, when both countries' governments are nominally of the same
persuasion.

But the differences due to national self-interest are a different matter
altogether. The present Soviet government has been making quite stren-
uous efforts to reconcile itself with Peking, but with little success so far.
The Chinese have long had certain demands which they insist must be met
by the Russians, if the talks in progress are going to come to fruition. Of
these the most important are the settlement of various territorial disputes
and a big reduction in the Soviet forces massed along the Chinese frontier.
To what extent could these demands be met by a new, non-Soviet, Russian
government?

The answer surely must be "very little." This is because disputes like
these arise from clashes of interest which are national, not ideological, in
character, and which therefore will not be eradicated by the substitution
of a democratic government for a Soviet government in Moscow. In view
of all this, it is a reasonable assumption that the military policy towards
China of the post-Soviet regime in Russia would almost certainly be much
the same as its predecessor's.

We must now turn our attention to another area of current Soviet military
policy, which is "aid to the national liberation movement." The "national
liberation struggle" is an important part of the Marxist-Leninist *Weltan-
schauung*; and it exerts a considerable influence upon Soviet foreign policy
as well as military policy. The concept may be summarized as follows: One
way of destroying imperialism is for proletarian revolutions to break out
and be successful in the imperialist countries (but this is thought to be not
very likely at present). Another way is to weaken imperialism by depriving
it of its access to sources of important raw materials, particularly those
which it has traditionally obtained cheaply from its colonies or former
colonies, or from those territories which are so much under imperialist
economic domination that they effectively count as colonies. In those cases
where they are still actual colonies, such territories must first of all win
independence from the colonial power. But they will still remain exploit-

able, and indeed will be exploited, by the imperialist countries until such time as they manage to accomplish the second stage of their national liberation revolution. This consists of removing their bourgeois or petit-bourgeois (albeit indigenous) governments, and putting Marxist-Leninist ones in their place. Once a Marxist-Leninist government is securely installed in a Third World country, then, so Leninism teaches, the "world correlation of forces" will be tilted still more in favor of the camp of socialism; and this is highly desirable from the Soviet viewpoint.

The importance attached over the years by the Soviet leaders to helping to bring these revolutions about can be seen very clearly by reading, for instance, the speeches uttered at successive party congresses. A party congress is a major occasion for the Party "boss" (i.e., the General Secretary) to review the past and set out the tasks for the future. At party congress after party congress since the end of the Second World War, the man in charge has made it plain that one of the most important tasks for the future is "aid to the national liberation movement." The outcome of the XXVII Party Congress, which is due to be held in the early part of 1986 is not yet known; but it is a fair bet that Gorbachev, at the first congress which he will have attended as leader of the Party, will proclaim "aid to the national liberation movement" to be a major Party commitment for the future.

These sentiments, uttered by the most powerful men in the country, are bound to affect the Soviet Union's military policy. The winning of power, in the view of Marxist-Leninists, is generally speaking dependent on the use of force, while the winning of power in the less politically mature countries is *very heavily* dependent on it. Consequently, if the Kremlin is seriously trying to see Marxist parties installed in power in the sort of country we are talking about, it will have to provide at least some of the force that is necessary.

So long as the sort of country in question was within marching distance of the USSR, the provision of the requisite amount of force was not a difficult matter. As time went on, however, countries fulfilling this condition either became ruled by Marxist-Leninists with due help from the Soviet Union (Mongolia for instance) or else they were left alone by the Kremlin for reasons we can only guess at (Iran for instance and also, until 1979, Afghanistan).

But if the whole of the Third World was ever to be incorporated within the "Socialist Commonwealth," the USSR would have to acquire the ability to provide military help for countries overseas. The Western defense community therefore grew very worried when during the 1960s and 1970s the USSR built up a formidable oceangoing navy, formed a marine corps, constructed landing craft, and produced new bombers and transport aircraft with ranges very much greater than they had ever had before. It was consequently not unreasonable to suppose that what the Russians were striving for was an ability to mount large-scale amphibious operations at great distances from the Soviet Motherland, and hence to be able to ensure the success of coups d'état led by Marxist-Leninists in countries in far-off continents.

By the middle 1980s, the evidence accumulated since the 1960s and 1970s makes it patently obvious that this analysis by Western defense experts was wrong. The fact that the Soviet corps of naval infantry has not gone on expanding and that neither has, to any meaningful extent, the fleet of Soviet landing craft, must surely be conclusive evidence that the Kremlin's aim, whatever else it might have been, was not to enable the Soviet armed forces to mount big campaigns of the traditional sort for the military conquest of Africa or Latin America. A much more probable hypothesis is that all the above improvements to the Soviet inventory were chiefly designed to render the Kremlin more capable of responding effectively to the kind of threat it saw as emanating from NATO and the United States.

Certainly, long-range aircraft were an important factor in permitting the Russians to provide their client Marxists in Angola with what was necessary for them to seize power and hold it (to the extent, of course, that they *do* hold it); and it was an equally important factor in the cases of Ethiopia and Mozambique. Also very important was the existence of a large Soviet merchant fleet to carry the bulk of the requisite supplies to these countries, and also of a modern Soviet navy to afford whatever protection might be considered necessary.

But the benefits the Kremlin derived from these ships and aircraft must surely be reckoned windfalls. It was not for the purpose of securing the latter that the long-range aircraft, the merchantmen and the oceangoing navy were built. On the contrary, they were built for other purposes. Nevertheless, having once been built and in consequence being available, they were naturally used, when use of them seemed likely to be profitable, to gain additional advantages for the Soviet Union, over and above the ones they had been intended to provide.

If this analysis is accepted, the men and equipment detached from the Soviet armed forces to provide "aid to the national liberation movements" must be seen as carrying out what for them is a rather ancillary function. Soviet military policy certainly includes the giving of the aid in question; but it has to give it with the types of unit and kinds of weapons and equipment designed for other purposes (in other words, for confronting NATO and the Americans and for holding back the Chinese).

Consequently, although at first sight it would seem to be a reasonable conclusion that the coming to power of a new regime in Russia would at least do away with this particular commitment of Soviet military policy, further reflection suggests that this may very well *not* be so. Big and powerful countries, whatever their form of government, traditionally strive to maintain their existing influence in the various parts of the world which are of interest to them and furthermore, when possible, to increase it. It is idle to suppose that Russia would be different, whatever the nature of the regime which supplanted the Communists'.

One might reasonably hope that, with a new regime (particularly if of a democratic and capitalist nature), the ideological bitterness which has attended this struggle for influence between the USSR and the Western countries would be completely eliminated. However, great-power rivalry engenders bitterness, albeit not necessarily of an ideological character, and bitterness of whatever nature bedevils international relations. So although one may hope that in a post-Soviet world the degree of bitterness would be markedly lessened, one must still expect it to persist and one must still therefore expect international relations to be somewhat short of the ideal.

That being so, post-Soviet Russia will surely maintain roughly the same sort of capacity for intervening militarily at a distance from its shores as has its predecessor. It will assuredly preserve approximately the same number of posts for military advisers to Third World countries, if only because their presence is of very great help to those advisers' governments when it comes to securing arms contracts in the countries in question. Arms contracts in the modern world are very attractive to the supplier state, first because they are very profitable, and second because they confer influence. At the present time, the USSR is one of the two largest suppliers of arms to other countries. It is hardly to be expected that the post-Soviet regime would be willing (or even able) to forego the profits and influence which the policies of its predecessor have made available to it.

We may therefore sum up this section by saying that, to a very considerable extent, present Soviet military policies would be likely to be continued by any successor regime; though the present level of bitterness in international relations, due largely to ideological differences, might reasonably be hoped to be lowered somewhat.

But all this recondite discussion of the most likely military policies of a post-Soviet regime in Russia is only of any value if such a regime manifests itself. The task of the present (Communist) regime's armed forces is to see that it does not. In view of this, what chance is there of a successor regime in the Soviet Union?

In the opinion of most commentators, virtually none. Of course, in the very long term the regime will change, if only because the history of the world has demonstrated that all regimes eventually do. But we are not, presumably, concerned with the distant future; it is the foreseeable future of not more than 25 years ahead which is of concern. It is hard to believe that during that time the Soviet regime will collapse. On the other hand, beliefs are one thing, realities often another. This paper therefore ought at least to examine the possibility of the regime's collapse; but since it is focussed on the Soviet military, it will be Soviet military policy and its attendant consequences with which we shall be dealing. Will that policy and its consequences be such as to cause the regime's downfall; or will they, on the contrary, serve to preserve it?

We will begin by examining the economic aspects of our question. The view is widely held in the West that the burden of Soviet military expenditure is already so great as to endanger the regime. If this is true, any significant increase, such as might be incurred by attempts to keep up with the new American technology, will actually bankrupt the Soviet economy, and set the stage for the downfall of the CPSU.

The maintenance of large and powerful armed forces is a very expensive business for any country. As far as the USSR is concerned, however, it is pertinent to remark that, year after year since the mid-1950s, the value of Soviet industrial production has regularly increased. In the recent past, the rise admittedly has been rather small in percentage terms; but in absolute terms, it is a formidable amount of money. 4.2 percent is not a very big percentage; but 4.2 percent of 727 billion roubles is 30.5 billion roubles. With that sort of sum you can buy yourself an impressive quantity of armaments.[3] Of course, in reality part of that money has got to be spent on things other than armament. Soviet industry, for instance, is screaming for more investment; while the annual pay rise to the Soviet worker, itself very small in percentage terms, nevertheless accounts, in absolute terms, for a significant slice of that annual moderate increase in the Soviet net national product. Inflation swallows up a bit more.

All this is true. The fact remains, however, that it is this large annual increase in absolute terms which has made it possible for the Kremlin to continue to fund the Soviet armed forces in the manner to which they are accustomed. The question that then arises, obviously, is whether they will be able to continue this.

One characteristic of the Soviet economy will assuredly help it to do so. This is that Soviet weapons procurement is more economical than ours. Their main weapons systems (aircraft, tanks and submarines) cost only about half or two thirds the sum which their equivalents cost in the West. Furthermore, the Soviet Ministry of Defence appears to be good at keeping such costs down.

On the other hand, weapons are getting increasingly expensive, in the East as well as in the West. This means that, for instance, the cost of Soviet shells is rising steadily. The Soviet authorities are therefore faced with the dilemma of whether to spend approximately the same amount on defense (and thus buy fewer shells per annum), or whether to buy as many shells as previously and thereby increase their defence costs.

The above still leaves unanswered the basic question of whether the Kremlin will continue to be able to fund the Soviet armed forces in the manner to which they have been accustomed. The answer is probably "yes."

We may begin by agreeing that it is indisputable that it has done so up to now. Strains may have been placed upon other parts of the USSR's economy; and indeed the budget of the Soviet armed forces may itself have been unable to accommodate the various (and presumably growing) demands which the service chiefs would presumably have liked to place upon it. Nevertheless, the war-fighting ability of the USSR is said by its leaders to have grown over the years to a point where it has attained an approximate strategic parity with that of the U.S. Of course, that assessment is taken from open Soviet sources.[4] It might well be argued that these in essence are purely propagandistic pieces. On the other hand, Western governmental sources agree in saying that the USSR has either approximate strategic parity or else, more likely, clear strategic superiority. If we omit the frightening possibility (many would say, the probability) that these Western statements are just as propagandistic as those of the Soviet Union, we are bound to conclude that despite the apparent difficulties the Soviet economy has continued to fund the Soviet armed forces in a manner acceptable to its leaders.

One reason for this may very well be that the Soviet accounting system is in many ways very different from the capitalist. To take one obvious but very important example, a Soviet factory calculates its costs by a method which is not acceptable to capitalist factories; the prices it charges its customers are arrived at differently too. If we knew the details of the ways in which the Soviet military-industrial complex assesses its costs and fixes the prices of its weapons systems, we might very well find that, by Soviet reckoning, it is less of a burden on the Soviet economy than many Western commentators are given to thinking. This is not to say that it is not a burden, but it is to say that it may not be, by Soviet reckoning, such an *inescapably crushing* burden as is often supposed in the West.

To take just one example to support this view, the introduction of new and sophisticated weapons systems is obviously a very expensive matter for any country, whether capitalist or Communist; but in either case much of the expense is incurred in the research and development. In the capitalist world the remuneration given to the firms engaged in the supply of arms is made up of agreed development costs plus a margin for contingencies plus an agreed proportion of profit for the firms concerned. Since one cannot foretell at all accurately what future development costs are going to be, it is not too difficult to get government officials, who have nothing personal to lose anyway, to agree to a sum for contingencies. In the event these contingencies do not materialize, the suppliers still keep the money and are thus furnished with additional, and very substantial, sources of income. Those interested in these matters in the context of the U.S. may like to consult the regular reports of the General Accounting Office (GAO). These give chapter and verse of huge disbursements of the Defense Department for goods and services which it could have acquired a very great deal more cheaply, if it had ever really wanted to do so.

If we turn from the U.S. to the USSR, we are surely not being naive if we assert that this waste of governmental money is not likely to occur in the latter country. This is not to say the Soviet government's money is never wasted. Far from it! It is wasted, however, in ways which are often different from those in the West.

Moreover, it should not be forgotten that in Western countries a large proportion of the defense budget is taken up with the pay and allowances of those serving in the armed forces. In the USSR on the other hand, the lowest ranks of the three services are conscripts; these are paid virtually nothing. Nor are they given marriage allowances or provided (if married) with married quarters; their rations are far more Spartan than would be acceptable in the West's armed forces; and their barracks are more primitively furnished. The cost of maintaining the personnel of the Soviet armed forces is therefore, per man, considerably less than that, for instance, of maintaining the personnel of the Bundeswehr.

What we are saying, therefore, is that the United States' repeated boast that, by increasing its own armaments and thereby compelling the Russians to follow suit, it could "spend the Soviet Union into the ground," has *not* so far proved itself in practice. We must therefore conclude that, as things are going at present, the Soviet Union's expenditure on its armed forces is probably higher than the Politburo would like, but is not so high, nor anywhere near being high enough, to put the Soviet regime in danger.

There is intense debate among Western scholars about what exactly the Russians spend on their armaments; and there is a big difference between the CIA estimates and those put out, for example, by Steven Rosefielde.[5]

Of course, the American SDI program may prove to be the instrument which will compel the Soviet Union to spend on defence the gigantic sums which will bring about its bankruptcy. As against this, there are two points to be noted: first, we do not as yet know to what extent the SDI will succeed. It may well be that it will make some progress, but would then turn out to be unviable. If that were to happen, the pressure upon the

USSR to spend even greater amounts of money in order to counter the American threat would at once be sharply reduced. Second, it is by no means certain that, even if SDI were to achieve the success which its sponsors are clearly hoping for it, we should therefore conclude that the Soviet response would be to try and construct a replica of it.

Indeed, what little the Soviet leaders have said on this subject does seem to indicate that their response, measured in financial terms, will be comparatively modest as compared with the American. Thus Mr Gorbachev has recently stated that the USSR "is not developing attack space weapons or a large antiballistic missile system."[6] These are among the most expensive options among possible Soviet responses to SDI; so we must surely take this as further evidence that whatever response may ultimately be chosen, it will not be such as to bankrupt the USSR.

When speaking of what the Soviet Union *may well do*, as distinct from what it will *not*, the Kremlin has, as we would expect, been very guarded. It seems to have confined itself to hinting darkly at "developing offensive weapons."[7] Such a phrase, of course, can mean almost anything; but there are two possible interpretations of it which are relevant to our present purpose. The first is that it is the USSR's intention to improve still further, and perhaps enlarge, its arsenal of ICBM's. The claim that SDI will turn out to be that "leakproof umbrella" of which President Reagan has spoken, protecting everyone and everything within the confines of U.S. territory, now seems to have been abandoned, even by Reagan himself. If SDI does manage to be successful, its success will almost certainly consist in doing no more than providing "point" defence for selected areas. These areas are likely to consist of important command-and-control centers and ICBM sites; the rest of America can go hang. That being so, it provides the Soviet Union with a good opportunity to use its own missiles in an effective way by increasing its capability to devastate the unprotected areas of the U.S. That would be good deterrence, while if war were to come it would be a good way of fighting it. Also it would be relatively cheap.

An additional, or possibly alternative, option for the Russians would be to develop their offensive capability in the realm of antisatellite weapons. It should not be impossible for them to be able to destroy those American SDI systems which are to be deployed in space above Soviet territory. These installations, in Soviet eyes, would be hostile, and would also be situated in what could be claimed was an extension of Soviet airspace. The USSR could not unreasonably say that, because they were so very much more than just "national technical means of verification," the Soviet Union had every right to get rid of them. If the Americans wished to prevent this happening, they would have to go to war in order to do so.

If this option were to be implemented successfully, it would confer two very considerable benefits upon the Russians. It would hamstring SDI, and it would achieve this object at a comparatively low cost. Accordingly SDI could not be a factor that would imperil the Soviet regime—unless, of course, the destruction of the U.S. installations brought about a war between East and West in which the Soviet Union was totally and utterly defeated.

Another circumstance making it unlikely that economic pressures will bring about the downfall of the Soviet regime is the rise to power of Mr Gorbachev. If his proposed reforms were to prove to be wholly successful, the economic power of the USSR would be improved considerably, thus enabling the burden of military expenditure to be borne a great deal more easily.

But even if his reforms do not turn out to be as successful as he obviously wants them to be, the Soviet economy under Gorbachev's leadership is still going to be more efficient than it has been during the last decade or more. Therefore, whatever happens, the Soviet economy, although it may not positively flourish, is bound to improve to some extent. This too makes it seem unlikely that the Soviet regime will collapse under economic pressures.

Let us suppose, however, that my analysis is wrong. We will assume that Gorbachev, in practice, proves to be even less capable of revivifying the Soviet economy than Brezhnev, Andropov or Chernenko. We will also assume that SDI elicits a much more expensive response from the Kremlin than I have postulated. This would still not mean that economic ruin would necessarily engulf the Communists.

The seizure of power by Communists in a country where hitherto the regime has been bourgeois or feudal, is, as we know, an important policy objective for Marxist-Leninists. An even more important objective, however, is to maintain a Communist government in power, when once it has managed to seize it. Lenin's policies after the revolution were aimed at this above all things. During the 1970s, the outcry in Moscow over the downfall of President Allende of Chile was inspired by this. The Soviet invasion of Czechoslovakia in 1968 was aimed at preventing the reins of power in that country being snatched from the hands of the Czech Communists as a result of Dubcek's promised free elections. We must therefore suppose that if things went as badly for the Soviet economy as I have postulated in the preceding paragraph, the Kremlin would take the measures necessary to keep things, if not under control, at least not sufficiently unstable to imperil the Soviet regime.

This could be done quite easily. Aid to the national liberation movements eats up enormous quantities of Soviet resources; so does aid to Cuba. The Soviet leaders would obviously be very reluctant to abandon long-standing and valuable clients and allies; but if the only foreseeable alternative was to be loss of power for themselves, they would surely take the realistic attitude which Lenin adopted, and which his various successors have regularly praised him for doing.

But might they not instead decide to cut back on military expenditure? Not, I think, if the result of the cuts were to render the Soviet armed forces unable to perform those tasks which we listed earlier. If, for instance, they were to find themselves incapable of protecting their "Socialist Motherland" from imperialist attack, then, according to Leninist reckoning, the Soviet grip on power in Russia would be at very great risk. We have just agreed that such a situation would be totally unacceptable to the Politburo. Serious cuts in the Soviet armed forces would therefore be ruled out— which is not to say that Soviet generals and admirals are always given everything they want, still less that they always will be.

We may therefore sum up by saying that, so far as one can see, Soviet defense spending will never become, and indeed will never be allowed to become, so serious a burden on the economy as to threaten the Communists' grip on power in Russia.

Even if SDI materializes in the way in which its apologists today are prophesying, that does not mean that the USSR will feel bound to spend more than it can possibly afford in order to match the Americans. It may feel obliged to spend more than it would really *like* to spend on its defense budget; but that does not mean incurring such astronomical expenditures as would bust the Soviet bank.

We must conclude, therefore, that if indeed the Soviet regime in Russia is to be got rid of, whether in this century or the next, the economic consequences for the USSR of Soviet military policy are not likely to have much to do with the getting rid of it.

Having analyzed the economic consequences of Soviet military policy in this context, we now turn to look at the political ones. The question to be examined is whether (and if so, to what extent) Soviet military policy as at present practiced has, or is likely to have, consequences which will upset the sociopolitical structure of the USSR, as distinct from its economic structure, to a degree that could endanger the stability of the Soviet regime.

We need to begin by reminding ourselves of the obvious. The preservation of the Soviet system is a prime duty of the Soviet armed forces. In pursuit of this aim they are required, when necessary, to suppress internal dissent. Of course, this is a role which all armed forces in all countries are expected to perform; and the Soviet armed forces' historical record shows that they have performed it well. In other words, the Politburo has very good cause for believing that the armed forces, in an emergency, will *not* seek to overthrow the rule of the Soviet Communist Party, but instead will help to preserve it.

No emergency could be greater than that which confronted Stalin and his henchmen in the early days of the Nazi invasion of Russia. The Party's grip on the levers of power was very severely weakened; yet the armed forces made no attempt to stage a coup to replace the Party as the government of Russia with a military or any other government. They might, of course, have *liked* to do this, but in any event they did not. Ever since the October revolution, the Soviet Communist Party has always realized that, apart from a successful bourgeois military invasion of the country, the only real threat to its hold on power was some sort of military coup. Over the years it has therefore spent a very great deal of money and effort in preventing such a coup from materializing. Its chief tools for accomplishing this task have always been, and still are, the political officers of the armed forces together with the KGB and the MVD (Ministry of the Interior) troops. The latter, whose total establishment is about 350,000, play an important role which not everyone in the West is aware of. There is, for instance, a division of them permanently stationed in Moscow and at least a regiment in all other major cities. It is they, not the regular Soviet army, who carry out internal security duties in these places. In order to be able to do so, they are trained and equipped as infantry, and given some light armour. They are not a force to be trifled with, and any potential conspirator must reckon with that fact.

As for the KGB guard force, which numbers about 50,000, it guards such key installations as the Kremlin, Party HQs and the Strategic Nuclear Forces.

A further role of the KGB in maintaining Party control of the Soviet military consists of its network of informers to be found in all units of the armed forces (as well as, of course, in all civilian organizations). These report to the KGB officers attached to the forces for surveillance purposes; no one, however senior, escapes their scrutiny.

This control mechanism, consisting of the political officers, the KGB and the MVD troops, is clearly very effective. It might just be possible to devise some sort of scenario, in which the officers and men of the Soviet armed forces play the role in bringing about the downfall of the existing government in Russia which was played by some parts of the Tsarist forces in 1917; but it is not possible to devise a convincing one. It may be correct that in the not so distant future the Soviet regime will be replaced, hopefully by a much nicer one. We can be perfectly sure though that the Soviet armed forces will not have conspired to bring that change about. Therefore, in this respect too the Soviet military will not have contributed to the emergence of a post-Soviet Russia. However, another possibility remains to be examined.

The principal way in which the Soviet armed forces impinge on the life of the ordinary Soviet citizen is conscription. All Soviet officers are volunteers, of course, but in percentage terms Soviet officers form only a small fraction of the population. It is obligatory service as conscripts which brings into firsthand contact with the Soviet armed forces the overwhelming bulk of young Soviet males. A few of these naturally gain exemption, usually on medical grounds, but by far the great majority are obliged to serve. The life is hard, comforts are few and the training is exacting. Consequently it might be thought that those who had been subjected to it would be very resentful of the armed forces; and that some sort of a "protest movement," aimed against the military and the defence budget, would be emerging in Russia by now.

Apart from the virtual impossibility in the USSR of organising an effective protest movement against any institution or organisation which is favored by the Party, there are several reasons why no such movement has materialized. First, Western research has established that although the young conscript left to himself would probably never join the forces, yet, when the time comes for him to serve, he puts a remarkably good face upon it. Of course he is glad when his time is up and he can return to his home and family; but while he is serving he does his best and on the whole makes the best of it. Some do more. Some find that, for whatever reason, life in the armed forces has sufficient attractions to get them to sign on voluntarily for a further term of service, once their conscript service has expired. In view of all this, it is impossible to conclude that the effect of conscription on Soviet youth is to instill into them a profound aversion to the USSR's armed forces. The proportion of those who as a result of their service have learnt actually to *love* the military must no doubt be reckoned small. But those who have learnt to *hate* the military seems to be not much bigger. Individual circumstances, of course, will naturally make a difference. A conscript who does his service in Afghanistan may well be more disaffected towards the services than one whose time has been spent in the USSR. Even so, it cannot be said that conscription has instilled into Soviet youth such a profound loathing of the armed forces that the latter's ability to do its job has been at all seriously impaired.

Indeed, the Soviet authorities' view is almost the exact opposite. In their eyes, one of the great advantages of universal conscription is that it provides them with a first-rate opportunity for reindoctrinating their 18-to-20-year-olds with Marxist-Leninist values. By the time that they reach the age of call-up, Soviet youths, especially those who are city dwellers, are likely to have shaken off to some extent (and in many cases to a considerable extent) those attitudes and values which the Communist Party worked so hard to instill into them during their schooldays. Their two-year stint in the army or the air force (three years, if in the navy) provides the Party with a tremendous opportunity to rectify this unsatisfactory state of affairs. Indeed General A. A. Yepishev, former head of the Chief Political Directorate of the Soviet Army and Navy, has stated on a number of occasions that conscript service is a wonderful "school for Communism."[8]

The Party devotes very considerable resources to making it as effective a school as possible. One clear indicator of this is the large proportion of total training time which is allotted to political education. On top of this, the Soviet conscript is compelled to spend some of his very limited free time in listening to talks by Party activists. The funds involved in the printing of the endless pamphlets, the upkeep of the "Lenin corners" in every unit must be enormous, to say nothing of the cost of the political officers themselves. So the Party must obviously think that the cost is worth it.

One would be very foolish to deduce from this that every Soviet conscript, having completed his term of service, conforms exactly to the standards set by the Party for Soviet citizens. Obviously this is not so. No system of education (or, if you prefer it, indoctrination) has ever proved to be effective in every instance. Luckily, however, we are not concerned with trying to assess the extent to which the time spent by the conscript in political education periods results in him conforming more closely to the Communist ideal. For our present purposes it is sufficient to note that we have no evidence to indicate that the Soviet conscripts return to their homes, having finished their term of service, any *less* in sympathy with Soviet values than they were when they first embarked on it.

And that is the key point. In order for the Soviet military to play an important role in the downfall of the Soviet regime, either those in uniform have got to be disaffected towards it, and be able to translate their disaffection into revolutionary practice (or, as a Marxist-Leninist would put it in these circumstances, into "counterrevolutionary practice"), or else it will be the former conscripts, fired by their experience of service life with a burning hatred of all things Soviet, who will break the Party's grip on power, and lead long-suffering Russia into the post-Soviet era.

Presently, neither of these things seems likely. The serving soldiers, sailors and airmen are *not* going to revolt. There may be occasional small-scale mutinies such as the recent one in the Soviet navy, but they are not going to be on a scale even remotely sufficient to affect the cohesion and effectiveness of the Soviet armed forces as a whole. The latter, then, will *not* conspire to overthrow the present regime, and they *will* continue to suppress, when necessary, any internal dissent in the USSR.

As for the former conscripts, those who are now in their twenties or thirties or forties, the men one meets at every step as one walks through the streets of any Soviet city, these may be apathetic about the ideology of Marxism-Leninism, they may find plenty to grumble at in the course of their daily lives, but they are not going to combine together to bring down the Soviet regime. Rather the exact opposite! They are, in fact, the bulwark of that regime, the buttress of its existence, the support without which it would long ago have vanished. Of course, that support has been secured by endless indoctrination and by police coercion, as well as by genuine pride in Russia and by empathy with the Soviet cause. Admittedly (and very importantly) it has also been secured by keeping these men, together with their female counterparts, in virtually total ignorance of what goes on elsewhere in the world, and indeed, to a very large extent, of what goes on in Russia. Nevertheless, the fact remains that their support *has* been secured, and can be relied upon. In this respect, the Soviet military can be said to have played some part in *strengthening* the Soviet regime; they have certainly not weakened it.

There is, however, one area where Soviet military policy might play a part, and a big part, in endangering the Soviet Communist Party's grip on power in Russia; and it is to that area that we must turn our attention now.

Assuming that the Soviet Communist Party continues to be able to keep its armed forces under tight control (and there seems no reason to doubt it), the only thing which could seriously endanger its existence, and therefore that of the Soviet regime, would be war with a powerful enemy (e.g., NATO). Obviously, if the war were brilliantly successful and the USSR won quickly, the Soviet regime would survive—indeed, would be greatly strengthened. If the war were a failure, however, and the Soviet armed forces were defeated, the present regime's downfall would be a distinct possibility.

Of course, the defeat would have to be a major one; a comparatively minor setback would not be enough. A halt at the Rhine when the Russians' original objective had been the English Channel could fairly be described as a defeat for them; but it would not be one of sufficient proportions to bring down the Soviet regime.

A defeat sufficiently serious to bring that event to pass could only occur in the form of a successful invasion of the Soviet Union by NATO forces; and by "successful" is meant an advance by NATO at least to the far side of the Urals. Only when the whole of European Russia was in non-Communist hands could the vital work of dismantling the Communist Party apparatus at *oblast'* and *raio:* levels be carried out effectively. Of course the destruction of the central apparatus, the Politburo and the Secretariat, would be a great step forward towards restoring freedom to Russia. So long as the Party apparatus at local levels remained comparatively intact though, the Party would retain considerable power in Russia, with good chances of effecting a total comeback at some suitable later date. To guard against that, the Party must be totally eradicated, and that can be done only as the result of a Western military conquest of the country and subsequent occupation of it.

We are not concerned here with trying to assess the likelihood of such a thing coming about. The likelihood is probably small. It is not, however, *wholly* inconceivable if the USSR were to attack NATO and its troops were to be thoroughly defeated. The NATO armies then having smashed the Soviet offensive, would themselves go over to the counteroffensive, and might, if victorious, then decide to invade the USSR. And under such conditions, with the Soviet armed forces routed, they might be more successful than either Napoleon or Hitler.

But, as has just been said, the likelihood or otherwise of such things coming to pass is not our concern, fortunately. Here we are concerned with one aspect only of this matter. That aspect is the fact that the above scenario is the only form of military defeat which could bring down the Soviet regime.

It is not, however, the only way in which military activity could do so. All-out nuclear war, for instance, might so shatter the whole fabric of life in Russia that the Soviet regime would collapse. This view has been forcefully argued by a number of Western strategists, who think that, with careful targeting by the West of Party offices and local Soviets, the nuclear exchange could literally blast into nothingness the Communists' grip on power. Personally, I do not think so. It is impossible to say how many Russians would survive that apocalyptic experience; but it is not unreasonable to postulate that, whatever the actual numbers might be, there would be approximately the same proportion among them of Party members to ordinary citizens as there is today in peacetime. If anything a higher proportion of Party members might be expected to survive because Party members in key positions would have better protective facilities.

That being so, Communist rule would continue. The Party members among the survivors would have a much better idea of what needed to be done, and how to do it, than their non-Party fellow citizens. They would also have the advantage of having access to whatever means of communication throughout Russia were still functioning after the nuclear strikes had hit it. The ordinary people of Russia who had survived them would simply have to go on obeying the Communists, because there would really be no alternative. Not only would years of obeying Communists have conditioned them into doing so again, but in the poststrike hell it would be plain to all that some sort of organized response would be necessary if all were not to perish in the aftermath. The Communists alone would have the background knowledge and the facilities necessary to allow such a response to be effected.

The above though is only an opinion, which might very well prove to be wrong. For the sake of our present argument, let us assume that it would. That is to say, we will now assume that all-out nuclear war between the superpowers would indeed destroy the Soviet regime. It is a point of view which is popular in many circles in the West; and one gets the impression that the Soviet leadership also shares it sufficiently to make it regard with added horror the prospect of nuclear war. That is a very important point, to which we shall return later.

Moreover it is a tenet of Marxism-Leninism that war imposes tremendous strains upon those countries which engage in it, and the bigger the war the greater naturally are the strains which it imposes. As Karl Marx put it, "War puts nations to the test. Just as mummies fall to pieces, the moment that they are exposed to the air, so war pronounces its sentence of death on the social institutions which have become ossified."[9]

A war between the Warsaw Pact and NATO would clearly be the biggest war imaginable; so the strains it would impose would be colossal. This would be true whether it was Western or Soviet society. Of course, the Soviet propaganda machine would seek to persuade both themselves and us that it is only "class" societies to which Marx's dictum applies; but the Politburo in their heart of hearts cannot possibly believe this. For one thing they know as a matter of fact that Soviet society in the Second World War was exposed to the most tremendous strain, and that the reason that it held together and won was due principally to the barbaric behavior of the Nazis. In a Third World War in which the Russians were not speedily victorious, tremendous strains would again be imposed upon the citizens of the Soviet Union, and there presumably would be no bestial Nazis to enforce cohesion. Under these circumstances and in a prolonged struggle, would the Soviet people's morale resemble that of their fathers and grandfathers in the Great Patriotic War, or rather that of their Tsarist ancestors in 1916–17? National pride would impel the Politburo to back the former alternative. Marxist logic (and they are all Marxists) would indicate the latter. It may be that Marxist logic would turn out to be the loser; but it is powerful logic, backed by historical experience, and not likely to be readily discarded by the Politburo.

The result will be to reinforce the message put out by our two previous scenarios: "It is war against a major enemy, and that alone, which can endanger the Soviet regime. Avoid such a war, and the Communist Party is safe." In view of this, it is pertinent to note that the Soviet leaders for very many years now have made a point of avoiding such a war.

Of course there have been confrontations with the West, some of them very serious. The Berlin Airlift and the Cuban Missile Crisis are obvious examples of these. Nevertheless, no war resulted from them; and the Soviet leadership can be seen, with hindsight, to have taken pains to ensure that no war should. Brezhnev was even more cautious, and none of his successors, so far at least, has shown any urge to be otherwise. Nor is there any reason why they should. Indeed, if our analysis is correct, they have every reason for avoiding a major war. We must therefore conclude that if after all a war between the Warsaw Pact and NATO should materialize, it must either be because NATO has started it, or it has broken out by accident. Neither possibility is credible. We must therefore suppose that, so long as the international scene continues to be much as it is today, and no one makes a breakthrough in military technology and acquires a "secret weapon," NATO and the Warsaw Pact will not engage in direct fighting.

This, therefore, leads us to our final conclusion, which is that Soviet military policy will do nothing to assist a changeover to a post-Soviet form of society in Russia. On the contrary, it is likely to militate very strongly against any such change occurring.

It will, however, no doubt be objected that this is a rather superficial view. Other contributors to the symposium have suggested circumstances in which the Soviet military might *not* support the Party and the existing regime in the unswerving fashion which I have depicted in the preceding paragraphs. There is something to that. I will therefore end my paper by considering the five most important sets of circumstances concerned with the military destroying the Party which other contributors have mentioned. They are: (i) a repetition of the army-Party disagreements which we saw in the Khrushchev era and which led to the sacking of Zhukov; (ii) mutinies in the Soviet armed forces succeeding to the point where they topple the regime and introduce another; (iii) the Soviet armed forces playing a role similar to that played in Spain in 1975 by the Spanish armed forces (what Dr. Shtromas calls "the Spanish model"); (iv) the Soviet armed forces playing a role similar to that played in Chile in 1973 by the Chilean armed forces (what Dr. Shtromas calls "the Chilean model"); and (v) the Soviet armed forces playing a role similar to that played in Portugal in 1974 by the Portuguese armed forces (what Dr. Shtromas calls "the Portuguese model").

My comments on these five sets of circumstances are as follows: (i) *The Zhukov Affair.* To my mind, there are three things about the Zhukov affair which prevent it from serving in any way as a useful pointer to the future. First, it happened a long time ago, and nothing remotely resembling it has occurred since. Second, the military's grievances were really quite substantial. Not only was a lot of training time being used by the Party for *agitprop* instead of what a senior officer would regard as proper military training, but Khrushchev's policy of drastically reducing the size of the Soviet ground forces was not only what the generals believed to be a militarily unsound policy, but it was also causing considerable personal hardship to those thousands of Soviet captains and majors who were dismissed from the service and without more ado returned to civilian life. When the British army engaged in something comparable, it went about it in a much more civilized fashion. Those who were to leave the service were given training for civilian life and also considerable sums in compensation. This was the famous "golden bowler" (a bowler hat in those days being obligatory wear for a gentleman working in London), and it proved very popular with many. But no such "golden bowler" was issued to Soviet officers. They were simply let loose in civilian life to fare as best they could. Many of them fared very badly and ended up by getting jobs as laborers in factories, where the contrast between their new pay and conditions and what they had enjoyed previously was extremely marked. It much alarmed their former colleagues still serving in the forces who feared, not without reason, that it might be their turn next to experience something similar. No such serious grievances have since been felt by the officers of the Soviet armed forces, at least so far as we know. Presumably the Party has learnt its lesson and has taken steps to see that they never should. The third reason, in my opinion, why the Zhukov affair cannot be used to indicate a possible successful uprising of the military against the Party is that in the Zhukov affair no such thing occurred. It is a plain matter of historical fact that there was no military revolt against the Party. Yet if there was no revolt in those circumstances, when could there possibly be one? Zhukov, it will be remembered, was the darling of the Soviet people as a whole and of the armed forces in particular. During the Great Patriotic War, he had been commander of the reserve, the Leningrad and Western Fronts, then first deputy commander-in-chief, USSR armed forces, in which capacity he had coordinated the *fronts* operating at Stalingrad, and had gone on from there to take Berlin and to be the officer appointed by Stalin to receive the German surrender. At the time of his dismissal, he was actually a member of the Presidium, as the Politburo was then called, as well as being minister of defence. Yet overnight he was summarily dismissed. Nor was it Stalin who did this thing, Stalin the almighty, Stalin who at least had been commander-in-chief of the Soviet armed forces throughout the whole of the war and had presided over the winning of it. No, it was Khrushchev; and Khrushchev in wartime had risen no higher than to be the political member of the military councils of a number of fronts—admittedly a powerful position, but not, one would have thought, comparable in the esteem of the armed forces with that of Marshal of the Soviet Union

Zhukov, the conqueror at Berlin and Stalingrad. Yet Zhukov was sacked by Nikita Khrushchev at a time when the Soviet armed forces were suffering from considerable grievances; and the Soviet armed forces never so much as stirred.

(ii) The second set of circumstances which some contributors believe could lead to the toppling of the present regime in Russia by the Soviet armed forces consists of a mutiny succeeding so well that, presumably after sparking off other mutinies, it would break the Party's grip on power and replace it by some other form of government. It is an undoubted fact that a number of mutinies have taken place in the Soviet armed forces in the course of the last decade or so, and probably as many in preceding decades, if only we had got to know about them. Some of these, moreover, have been serious. None, however, have been sufficiently serious to have enjoyed anything more than brief, local successes; and all have been put down with little trouble. There may, or may not, have been more mutinies in the Soviet armed forces than there have been in the armies of the NATO countries; but, even if so, they have not achieved anything. Nothing in the history of the mutinies among the Soviet military gives any grounds for expecting that they will ever succeed in putting an end to Communist rule in Russia.

(iii) The first of Dr. Shtromas's three "models of change" is the "*Spanish model.*" It is not really relevant to the present discussion because, as Dr. Shtromas agrees, the changes in Spain which occurred after the death of Franco were not introduced by the Spanish military, but by King Juan Carlos and his civilian ministers. Indeed the attitude of the armed forces towards these liberal, democratic reforms was to oppose them. It was previously stated that the attitude of the armed forces in the USSR would be to support the Party in resisting the introduction of liberal reforms into Russia. Dr. Shtromas's "Spanish model" does little to support his view that the Soviet armed forces are a potential instrument for introducing change to Russia, but much to support the thesis of this paper, which is that they are not.

(iv) The next two models, however, are very different. Both in Portugal and Chile it was indeed the armed forces who swept away dictatorial governments (a left-wing dictatorship in the case of Chile, a right-wing one in Portugal); so it might be thought that these two models have real, practical relevance to the USSR.

We will start with Chile; it is slightly misleading to speak of a left-wing dictatorship in Chile. In actual fact, at the time of the coup there was no dictatorship in Chile. Allende and his left-wing colleagues were undoubtedly working towards one; and it was the introduction in 1973 of a package of very left-wing measures, some of which violated the constitution and seemed clearly intended to lead to a dictatorship (a dictatorship not of one man, but of the proletariat), which provoked the armed forces to rise. Nevertheless, at the actual time of the coup there was no dictatorship; and if there had been, the coup might well have failed. These points must be borne in mind while considering what Dr. Shtromas calls the "*Chilean model.*"

In this model, as he describes it, success depends upon the armed forces being brought into a country's government in a period of crisis, or else in being, in Dr. Shtromas's words, that government's "exclusive support." He actually envisages the Communist Party of the Soviet Union "in the pursuit of its expansionist policies becom[ing] entirely dependent on the Army or . . . , in a situation of crisis and ensuing anarchy and disarray, try[ing] to call on the Army to assume greater powers (by joining the government or otherwise) in order to help the Party to restore order."

It is hard to envisage anything less likely. Of course, in a crisis the Party would expect the army to help it to restore order; but it would take care *not* to become "entirely dependent on the Army," and indeed it has created the MPA, the KGB and also the MVD troops precisely in order to avoid this. For the Party "to call on the Army to assume greater powers (by joining the government or otherwise)" is a form of that Bonapartism which Lenin condemned and which all agree to be total anathema to the Kremlin. In support of that view, it may be noted that Stalin did not take either course in the summer and autumn of 1941; and it would be hard to imagine a greater crisis than the Party was experiencing then. To return to Chile, in 1973 the Chilean armed forces undoubtedly removed a left-wing civilian government which was bent on introducing social, political and economic changes that would have brought about a Marxist dictatorship. At first sight, therefore, we seem to have an example which the Soviet armed forces might follow. There were, however, two reasons why the military coup in Chile was successful. The first was that senior officers were participating in Allende's government; and one of them, General Pinochet, like General Prats before him, held the key post of minister of the interior as well as being commander-in-chief. The second was that in Chile there was no equivalent of the KGB to spy upon the Chilean armed forces, whose officers consequently had virtually total freedom to plot and plan as they liked. Neither situation is to be found in the Soviet Union, and neither is ever likely to; and I therefore find the "*Chilean model*" inapplicable to the USSR.

(v) Last to be considered is Dr. Shtromas's "*Portuguese model of change.*" In Portugal, as in Chile, it was indeed the military who put an end to dictatorship; though in Portugal it was a right-wing dictatorship, while in Chile it would have been one of the left. The Portuguese military did *not* form part of the government when they staged their successful coup, nor had they ever done so. They therefore destroyed the government entirely *from without*. As a consequence, they might be imagined to offer a useful model to the Soviet military, who, if they are to destroy the rule of the Soviet Communist Party, would have to do so *from without*. Further investigation, however, reveals that the Portuguese model is really wholly inapplicable to the Soviet Union.

The reason for this is very simple. Although the two Portuguese dictators, Salazar and Caetano, both operated a very efficient and ruthless "secret police," neither Salazar's PIDE (Policia Internacionale de Defesa do Estado) nor Caetano's DGS (Direccao Geral de Securanca) were allowed to concern themselves with the Portuguese armed forces. Surveillance over the officer corps was therefore left to commanding officers and general officers commanding, whose usual method of dealing with dissenters was either to post them somewhere else or transfer them to the reserve. In neither case was the officer corps' ability to plan a coup d'etat very much affected.

In addition, had it come to a shoot-out, the secret police would have been no match for the armed forces. They had only old-fashioned rifles— no artillery or armor,[10] no aircraft—and were trained to operate in small groups and not at battalion or brigade levels. In other words, they were designed to hold down the civilian population, not to confront the military. The Soviet armed forces are not blessed with such lax controls as these.

This concludes the discussion of the five sets of circumstances which might, it has been suggested earlier, allow the Soviet armed forces to effect a change in the present regime in Russia (assuming, of course, that they felt the wish to do so). Upon examination, it appears that none of the five would be such as to permit this. We therefore return to the view which I expressed earlier. Change may sometime take place in Russia. (Change indeed is *bound* to take place in Russia sooner or later because sooner or later change takes place with everything, even among dinosaurs.) But it will not have been the Soviet armed forces who will have taken the lead in promoting it—unless and until, that is, the Communist Party sees fit to dismantle that formidable apparatus of control over the Soviet military which has so far made it impossible for the latter to confront the former with any chance of success; or unless and until the personnel of the various "control apparati" themselves experience a wish to destroy the Party. But when will that be?

Notes

1. I say "in the Kremlin" because I think it is most unlikely that any post-Soviet regime of whatever complexion would think of reappointing St. Petersburg to be the Russian capital. For one thing, modern governments need much larger staffs and much more elaborate infrastructures than were needed by those of the nineteenth and early twentieth centuries. Moscow today is equipped to fulfil these requirements; Leningrad is not. Furthermore, for very many Russians, St. Petersburg was essentially a "foreign," non-Russian city; and the same attitude towards Leningrad seems to be quite prevalent today. Of course, if it should happen that the post-Soviet regime turned out to be a monarchy, St. Petersburg would be the obvious choice; but I think it must be agreed that such a thing is really very improbable.

2. There has never yet been nuclear war on our planet. Whatever one thinks of Hiroshima and Nagasaki, they were not nuclear *war*. This is because war, by definition, involves the active participation of two sides (at a minimum), and in 1945 Japan did not possess any atomic weapons. If she had and in addition had possessed the means of delivering them against U.S. territory, Nagasaki and Hiroshima might well have not had any atom bombs dropped on them.

3. These calculations are taken from the 1983 figures for the Soviet economy, as given in *Narodoe Khozynistvo SSSR v 1983g.* (Moskva: "Finansy i Statistika." 1984, pp. 43 and 44).

4. See, for example *Red Star*, June 22, 1985 or Boris Ponomarev's speech in Madrid (*Pravda*, June 19, 1984).

5. Compare the CIA's "Soviet and US Defence Activities 1970–79. A Dollar Cost Comparison" (SR80-10005, January. 1980) with, for instance, Rosefielde's latest piece on the subject in *Problems of Communism*, March–April 1985, pp. 126–9.

6. *Pravda*, July 6, 1985.

7. See, for instance, Gorbachev's speech at Warsaw (Pravda, April 27, 1985).

8. For an English-language expression of this view see General of the Army A. A. Yepishev, "Some Aspects of Party Political Work in the Soviet Armed Forces" (Progress Publishers, Moscow, 1975), p. 277.

9. Marx-Engels, *Sochineniya.* 1st Russian edition (Moscow, 1953), Vol. 10, p. 535.

10. The DGS did have some so-called 'protected vehicles'; but these were designed for no more than giving some degree of protection to their crews while the latter were engaged in hurling smoke bombs at crowds or firing tear gas. In no sense were they tanks.

9

What are the Implications of Soviet Military Policy? A Commentary on Chapter 8

WILLIAM R. VAN CLEAVE

Peter Vigor, as always, has included a large number of thoughtful, cogent, and provocative points in a relatively short paper. All of his major points and conjectures are reasonable, and most I find quite agreeable. I would like to single out for brief discussion only a few having to do with relative U.S./Soviet military efforts and programs, the purposes and threats of burgeoning Soviet military capabilities, and the so-called U.S. Strategic Defense "Initiative."

First, I agree that the Soviet military receives and will continue to receive the highest possible priority in the Soviet Union; that this priority is reflected in the enormous sums (probably understated in official Western estimates) that Soviet leaders have devoted to an unremitting Soviet military buildup; and that any foreseeable problems or developments in the Soviet economy are most unlikely to change that situation.

For 50 years, optimistic Western pundits have expected Soviet economic problems to reduce the Soviet military effort and to make Soviet leaders more amenable to significant arms control agreements reducing that effort. It has not happened, and it is not happening today, even though—by our own standards—the Soviets are spending an economically dangerous amount on defense. It is certainly symbolic of a fundamentally different way of thinking, and a fundamentally different order of military priority, that Republican as well as Democratic political leaders in the United States today criticize Reagan defense spending as "too much" when it is barely 6% of GNP; while, at the same time, we officially estimate Soviet military spending at 15–17 percent of GNP and rising.[1]

In contrast to some expectations, or even reports, of a downturn in Soviet military spending and arms procurement in recent years, the facts are to the contrary. The Department of Defense currently describes Soviet arms programs as "increasingly ambitious." It reports that "there is clear evidence of an *upturn* in Soviet weapons procurement," and that Soviet military spending now shows "a significant increase at a rate faster than overall economic growth."[2]

The Central Intelligence Agency, which has traditionally been conservative, supports these estimates. In the area of strategic nuclear forces, offensive and defensive, the CIA, in a recent official report to Congress, states that the "Soviets are *increasing* their resource commitments to their already formidable strategic forces" at a rate between five and ten percent per year.[3]

In view of history and political reality, Peter Vigor's reference to an alleged U.S. "repeated boast that, by increasing its own armaments and thereby compelling the Russians to follow suit, it could 'spend the Soviet Union into the ground,' " is humorous and fanciful. His point that this has not proved so in practice is certainly true, but in fact (a) there has been no such policy or boast, and (b) Soviet arms programs follow their own doctrine and dictates, and lead our own far more than ours lead theirs. (What Vigor refers to was a hypothetical suggestion—i.e., that economically and industrially the U.S. *could* do so if determined—made by Ronald Reagan well before he was President of the United States, and not by the U.S. government officially.)

Over the past decade, including the years of the Reagan defense increases, it is officially estimated that the Soviets have outspent the United States on military capability by some *$500 billion*, and over the past years by nearly *$700 billion*; and as Vigor points out the lion's share of U.S. defense spending goes to people costs, while most of Soviet spending goes to arms. The Reagan administration, despite media-inspired impressions to the contrary, has not much changed this situation. Given the past disparity in spending, and given the levels to which our military capabilities had fallen by 1981, the Reagan program, as the prestigious Committee on the Present Danger has concluded, has been inadequate *in the first place*.[4] Given the administration's own cuts in previously announced defense budgets, and given those subsequently imposed by Congress, Reagan administration expenditures (outlays) for the first five years have been actually *under* those proposed by Jimmy Carter for the same period. Reagan's FY (Fiscal Year) 1986 defense budget is about $75 billion less than initially proposed by the administration, and $20 billion less than Carter's for the same year.

What all of this leads to are a couple of points that perhaps supplement more than contradict Mr. Vigor's points: (a) The Soviets are well beyond the United States in military effort and in most military capabilities (in nuclear strength, for example, which the Soviets hold to be the "high ground" of military capability, there is now not a single general comparative advantage held by the United States in either theater or intercontinental nuclear forces—not weapons systems, not delivery vehicles, not megatonnage or equivalent megatonnage, not counterforce capability, not defensive capability, not even numbers of warheads). (b) That the Soviets are doing what they are doing for their own purposes, because they expect to reap strategically significant military and political advantage, which we should recognize as more ominous and threatening to our security than Mr. Vigor seems to imply. (c) That in the area of strategic nuclear programs, the Soviets are proceeding *regardless* of the U.S. Strategic Defense Initiative (SDI).

Point (a) needs no further elaboration here. The reader may consult the documents already footnoted for more than ample data. Let me turn to point (c) and then finish with a brief comment on (b).

Each of the programs, or "reactions," Mr. Vigor postulates as possible responses to the U.S. SDI are in fact *already* strong Soviet programs, well in advance of any U.S. SDI progress, and well in advance of any comparable U.S. programs; and in each case the Soviets plan to pursue these programs whatever happens to the U.S. SDI.

In strategic nuclear offensive forces, the Soviets are already developing—and deploying—a plethora of new generation weapons systems: ICBM's, fixed and mobile; SLBM's, MIRVed and intercontinental range; bomber aircraft; cruise missiles—and in each category the Soviets are quantitatively and qualitatively ahead of the United States. For details, again, the reader may consult the aforementioned documents. But the point is that none of these programs is a "reaction" to the U.S. SDI, which has barely begun and only as a studies or research program, not a weapons program.

In strategic defense forces, the situation is at least equally stark in contrast. In fact, to be accurate, the U.S. strategic defense program should have been labelled the U.S. Strategic Defense *Response* to the Soviet Strategic Defense *Initiative*.[5]

The awesome sums that the Soviets have spent on strategic offensive forces, and the awesome capabilities that have been developed and deployed as a result, have been noted. What I have not mentioned is that during this same period of time the Soviets have been spending an *equal* amount of resources and effort on a multilayered strategic defensive capability, and are years ahead of the United States in essentially every category. Compare the following categories:

(1) *Existing ABM defenses.* The Soviets have an operational ABM system—the only one in the world—which is now being upgraded with brand new radars and interceptor missiles, for which the Soviets have open production lines. The Soviets also have a rich "air defense" system of some 12,000 launchers and 6,000 radars which is acknowledged to have significant and growing ABM capability. The deployment of the SA–10 and SA–12 missiles blurs any distinction between air defense and antiballistic missile defense. The United States has no such systems or capabilities.

(2) *Modernization Programs for Existing ABM.* The Soviets, as just mentioned, have an extensive modernization program that the President has told Congress is probably designed to provide the basis for a rapidly deployable nationwide ABM defense. Aspects of these programs have been officially certified by the President of the United States as violations of the SALT I ABM treaty. The United States, having no existing ABM systems, obviously has no modernization programs for them.

(3) *Research & Development for Advanced ABM Systems.* This is the one category into which the U.S. Strategic Defense Response fits, but the emphasis remains merely on research and not on systems development. The administration has truthfully emphasized over and over again that the U.S. program "is a research program, not a program to deploy weapons."[6] And as Henry Kissinger has observed: "Even its most tough-sounding statements [about SDI] are limited to continuing research."[7] Administration officials have acknowledged that the United States is ten years behind the Soviet Union in R&D on advanced systems. In fact, the Soviet Union has prototype laser systems with ABM potential already deployed at Sary Shagan and is working on laser and particle beam concepts that the United States has not yet begun to work seriously on.[8]

(4) *Military Space and Antisatellite Programs.* Suffice it to say that the Soviets have a doctrine for the military importance and control of space, while the United States does not; that the Soviets conduct five to six times as many space launches per year as the United States; and that of those 80–90 percent are clearly military in application, compared to about 30 percent or less for the United States. Also, that the Soviet Union still has the world's only operational ASAT systems, while the United States ended its own ASAT testing years ago and only recently resumed testing. Soviet ASAT is not limited to the (unwisely) maligned co-orbital ASAT system, but includes "direct ascent" weapons, and the two Sary Shagan lasers, which are capable of ASAT missions.

(5) *Civil Defense, Leadership Protection, Transition from Peace to War.* Clearly this is another area of defense against ballistic missiles and nuclear

weapons in which the United States has essentially no program, while the Soviets have an extensive one. The Soviets have long believed in passive ballistic missile defense, and as long ago as 1972 elevated the director of civil defense to deputy defense minister level.

In sum, it is ridiculous to suggest that the U.S. SDI is forcing the Soviets into anything.

A short word on the U.S. program, which I believe needs no "apologists" (Vigor's term)—unless the administration should apologize for the flimsiness of the program and the fact that it has *no* neartime defensive goals. The President's ultimate goals for the SDI are certainly praiseworthy, but there is too much focus on only those goals and only those purposes of ballistic missile defense. The SDI, however, has not yet been defined in terms of concrete goals, and there are several ones that are accomplishable to one degree or another that would be strategically significant and advantageous to the defense of the West: Defense of vulnerable deterrent forces, such as the ICBM force and critical communications; theater or tactical ABM for Europe (against the massive Soviet theater nuclear strike capability); point or semi-area defense of selected national assets and resources; and defense of broad areas of the nation.

It is not necessary to have a "leakproof" defense in order to bolster deterrence or to meaningfully limit damage in the event that deterrence fails. A defense of our retaliatory forces could impose attack demands and uncertainties on Soviet leaders contemplating an attack that would reduce incentives very substantially; and a broader defense would do the same. Consider (whatever targets are being hypothetically attacked): If each layer of a four-layer defense had only 50 percent effectiveness (the design goal is 80 percent), it would take some 50,000 Soviet warheads for the 3,000 necessary to a successful attack against U.S. land-based deterrence forces to get through; if only two layers each had 80 percent effectiveness, it would take nearly 30,000 Soviet attacking warheads for 1,000 to get through. *That* is *deterrence*. It is also virtual arms control: Facing such a situation the Soviets would surely be more amenable to true reductions in offensive weapons than they have been to date.

A final, too-brief word on the Soviet military threat in general. It seems to me that Mr. Vigor depicts the Soviet military capability in somewhat too defensive terms, although he does cite enforcement of the Brezhnev Doctrine and support of national "liberation" movements as tasks of the Soviet armed forces. (Indeed, if one just thought through the implications of those tasks, and compared today's global political map with that of ten to twelve years ago, the aggressive character of Soviet military efforts should be rather clear.)

The Soviets see military force as the key to the "correlation of forces," which determines world events and the international "progress" of Soviet socialism; and they view military superiority as coercive and intimidating. The military capabilities that have been developed by the Soviets are not necessary to protect the Soviet Union from real, imagined, or fabricated threats, but are intended to weaken the West's will to oppose Soviet expansionism. Moreover and unfortunately, whatever one *believes* about the likelihood of the overt use of those forces against the West—in a limited geographic region, against Western Europe, on the United States itself— the Soviets prepare their military forces precisely to wage war at any level, including nuclear, and work very hard to develop surprise attack capabilities against the major deterrent forces of the West. One cannot prudently ignore those objectives and capabilities. That the Soviets may wish (reasonably) to accomplish their (unreasonable) objectives without going to war does not necessarily mean that the Soviets will forego their objectives in order to avoid war. *That* depends largely on the relative military strength of the United States and the West, which should under all circumstances be capable of making the resort to war highly unattractive and disadvantageous to the Soviets. Unfortunately, I do not believe that we have maintained such capabilities, and I do believe, therefore, whatever incentives the Soviets might have to use their military forces, they are increasing.

To end on an even more somber note, The Soviets have been working very determinedly to develop the forces most threatening to the United States and NATO: surprise nuclear attack forces. Zbigniew Brzezinski has written of the greater vulnerability of the West to this threat, and of Soviet capabilities to execute it, and he concludes: "gradually the military attractiveness of this option is again increasing."[9] I am afraid he is right; therefore, we *must* do much more than we are to decrease it. Among other things, the SDI carries such a promise.

Notes

1. Department of Defense, *Soviet Military Power, 1985*, Washington, D.C., U.S. GPO, April 1985, p. 10.
2. *SMP, 1985*, Preface and p. 10 (emphasis added).
3. Central Intelligence Agency, *Soviet Strategic Force Developments*, Testimony, Joint Session Armed Services and Appropriations Committees, U.S. Senate, June 26, 1985 (emphasis added).
4. *Can America Catch Up? The U.S.-Soviet Military Balance*, Committee on the Present Danger, Washington, D.C., December 1984.
5. For an analysis, discussion, and detailed comparison of the two, see my

Fortress USSR: The Soviet Strategic Defense Initiative and the U.S. Strategic Defense Response, forthcoming from The Hoover Institution Press.

6. *The President's Strategic Defense Initiative*, The White House, January 1985, p. 7.

7. "Talking Down Arms," *Los Angeles Times*, September 8, 1985, IV-1.

8. See Paul H. Nitze, *SDI: The Soviet Program*, U.S. Department of State, Current Policy No. 717, July 1985.

9. "From Arms Control to Controlled Security," *The Wall Street Journal*, July 10, 1984.

10

American Policy in the Event of a Soviet Crisis

MORTON A. KAPLAN

The considerations outlined in this paper are not intended as prescriptions for American policy should a crisis break out within the Soviet system. The particular details of that crisis might contraindicate many, and perhaps most, of the recommendations that I will make. Reality more often than not outstrips our imagination. However, even in that case, the content of my analysis could be useful as a benchmark against which alternative states of the world could be taken into account during an actual crisis in the Soviet system.

The problem of how to deal with a possible crisis in the Soviet system is complex. It might seem to be obvious to some that the United States should do everything it can to stimulate, to provoke, and even to exacerbate the development of a system or regime crisis in the Soviet Union. Indeed, Georgi Arbatov of the Institute of the USA and Canada has proclaimed that such is the policy of the Reagan administration. He argues that Reagan intends to spend the Soviet Union into a crisis that will wreck it. The premise that this is the objective of the Reagan administration is dubious. And even if the Reagan administration had such an objective, the obvious Russian counter—since it knows that NATO will not start either a war or a war crisis—is to not allow itself to be provoked into escalatory military spending. I doubt very much that the Soviet Union really has such fears, although its internal relations with its own military may make it difficult to reduce military expenses. Its military spending is driven additionally by the desire to hold a threat over NATO. However, bilateral reductions in military spending that do not threaten the relative military advantages of the Soviet Union may indeed be desired by the regime. And it may be annoyed that Reagan has not played this game. In any event, it is less than clear to me that a Soviet crisis, as opposed to evolutionary change, is consonant with American interests.

I do not deny that the transformation of the Soviet dictatorship into a democratic system would be good for the peoples of the Soviet Union, the world, and the United States. However, crisis-driven conditions of transformation might be internationally explosive and such a transformation conceivably could produce a resulting regime that is even worse than the existing Soviet one in terms of security and in terms of the values that most Westerners hold dear. Furthermore, even if these potential debits should be discounted, it is not entirely unlikely that American, or even Western European, attempts to influence the process could be highly counterproductive.

First, let us briefly consider the character of the Soviet Union and inquire into if or why it might be dangerous to American interests in its current state. In the first place, in view of the failure of its collectivist type of economy, Marxian socialism is relevant to the regime only externally. By that, I mean that the declaratory ideology of the Soviet Union constrains it in terms of its natural allies abroad. Although these allies temporarily can include so-called bourgeois nationalist elements, on the whole the Soviet Union is restricted to allies who will attempt to change the domestic economies of their nations into state-operated systems that are socialistic in a declaratory sense. Other parties from the Soviet standpoint are the natural allies of the United States at worst or uncommitted at best, because their elites would be threatened by the Communist embrace, particularly if they are geographically close to the Soviet Union. Afghanistan is a case in point.

Internally, regimes such as the Soviet one produce a form of state capitalism with a very rigid class structure that operates through an ossified bureaucratic apparatus. Normally, regimes of this type would be extremely conservative, highly wary of taking risks, and unlikely to precipitate crises. However, in the actual Soviet system, this bureaucratic apparatus is symbiotically attached to a powerful military machine which, though dominated by the Party apparatus, is useful in succession struggles. For this reason, the Soviet military establishment gains considerable leverage within the system in terms of access to funding and other perquisites. The system thus depicted fits Joseph S. Schumpeter's model of an imperialist system much better than did his actual examples of the Egyptian or Assyrian empires.

This type of regime would not create difficulties for the West except for the fact that the Soviet system lacks a substantial basis for legitimacy other than its external success. The Politburo obviously is not appointed by God or put in office by the free choice of the peoples of the Soviet Union. The legitimacy it might have gained as the authoritative interpreter of true Marxist doctrine has been forfeited by the failure of the Soviet collectivist economy.

The Soviet regime does have legitimacy but only because the Soviet Union is one of the two strongest military powers on earth. The average Russian worker or peasant takes pride not in his conditions of life, which are meager, but in the sweep of power manifested by the Soviet armed forces and in the deference paid to that power by other nations. This is a fragile type of authority that cannot withstand disillusionment in the one remaining source of Soviet legitimacy: external success.

Although it is true that the average Russian desperately wants peace, that average Russian is also a very strong nationalist and also very suspicious of foreigners, a characteristic that draws deeply upon Russian historical memories. Conquests by the Tatars and the Mongols, invasions by the Swedes, by Napoleon, and by Hitler have created an essentially defensive mentality that is satisfied best by complete control of the milieu in which the Soviet Union finds itself. The average Russian applauds the success of the Soviet leadership in producing this result. I do not deny that there are ambivalences and that many Russians resent foreign expenditures. But, on balance, I believe that external success does help to legitimate the Soviet regime.

Furthermore, the Russian, leader and led alike, views anarchy as a threat and weakness with contempt. Weakness leads to anarchy and demands Russian control. These "natural" Russian traits are combined with training in Marxist dialectics, as contrasted with doctrine, at least among the educated that inclines them to see the world as a total correlation of forces in which potentially hostile states unceasingly subject each other to test. Only then can control be maintained and anarchy fought off.

The world is seen as threatening by Russian leaders and they believe that it is imperative to anticipate disorder and actively to control it. Thus, each American president is confronted with a Russian military probe when he enters office. The greater the Western failure to respond in peripheral areas, the more likely it is that military probes will accompany the political probes that are unceasingly directed at more central areas.

Although the Russians feel extremely strong militarily, they also feel extremely weak because of the threats they perceive. They fear the Chinese masses on their border despite the grave comparative weakness of the actual Chinese state. They fear their internal minorities, particularly the

Moslems, whose Sufi sects eventually may confront them with a genuinely serious problem.

Thus, the strength that the Soviet Union has is perceived as a fragile strength that may collapse. Hence, its unwillingness to make what an impartial observer might regard as modest pragmatic compromises with the Chinese on the border issue or with the Japanese on the issue of the northern Kuril Islands. Despite its long history of recognizing the value of strategic retreat in war, Soviet peacetime policies do not appear to be able to contemplate such strategies. It sees such retreats as portending further demands and retreats rather than as consolidating strengths, eliminating unnecessary quarrels, and restoring good relations with neighbors. Moreover, such retreats may be seen internally as weakness that threatens anarchy and, thus, may diminish political legitimacy. The Soviet leadership fails to perceive that its quest for greater security may threaten the security of its neighbors.

The struggle for the Russian soul is a complex one. The contrasting strains within Russian society are now fought out inside the Communist Party. There are forces in the Party that wish to rationalize the economy and even perhaps to liberalize society. There are forces that would like to extend Russian imperial domination as far as possible. There are forces that feel so threatened by demographic changes inside the Soviet Union that they would like to get rid of all the Asian and colored peoples and retreat to a "small Russia" policy. They would increase strength and fight anarchy by allying with Europe and with other white nations. Secretary Brezhnev once said to President Nixon that a war between the United States and the Soviet Union would be a terrible thing because the world would be taken over by the black and the yellow peoples.

Which of these forces would be dominant if the Soviet regime was transformed? And how would American or Western European intervention influence the process? Is there any reason to believe that democratic development would naturally occur in Russia? Or would the lack of experience of the Russian people with democracy produce an authoritarian regime that might be reactionary, anti-Semitic, anti-Black, and altogether intolerable to a multiracial United States?

In addition, we must remember that a large part of the privileged classes in the Soviet Union would have no respectable place in a transformed regime. Scientists, teachers, and some other professional types might be able to play normal roles. But much of the *Nomenklatura* and Party bureaucracy would have its privileged position destroyed and would possibly even be subjected to heavy criminal penalties.

If a regime crisis threatens, the Soviet leadership will search for any international activity that might be presented as a threat and that could be used to rally the masses and disaffected parts of the regime to it. It might even initiate a crisis or even a small military venture, not intending to start a general war—but perhaps miscalculating—to change the balance of forces during a regime crisis. With the low value that it places upon human life, it might even stage an internal disaster that could be blamed upon the West if our complicity could be made to look plausible.

I am not arguing that there are no circumstances under which we could give direct assistance to forces striving for democratic change in the Soviet Union or to nationalities seeking their independence. But potential costs are more likely than opportunities for desirable intervention. Furthermore, even apart from the possibility of explosive war that intervention might portend, miscalculated American attempts to influence the process might only give rise to a xenophobic Russian nationalism that, under some circumstances, could be even worse than the current Soviet regime. (Pamyats, that is memory, is an organization that includes such elements. M.A.K., 1989) In any event, the likelihood that the United States would be able to intervene intelligently and effectively, even if in principle this would be possible, is small and the likelihood that the Soviet regime could use such attempts to its advantage is comparatively high.

Furthermore, we must remember that quite apart from the dangers or advantages of influencing transformations in the Soviet regime, there is the possibility that no radical transformation of the Soviet regime may occur and that excessive preoccupation with the prospect could be counterproductive with respect to cooperative activities with the Soviet Union designed to make the world a safer place. When I say this, I am not implying that destabilizing Soviet tactics, as in the case of Central America, should not forcibly be countered by the United States, but rather that detente is both desirable and necessary in the central theater of Europe. That is the area of greatest strategic interest for the United States, of greatest cultural and political concern, and where an explosion could blow up the world, or at least the United States and the Soviet Union.

Therefore, any line of policy that convinced the Soviet leadership that the United States was engaged, not in a military contest at the peripheries, which would be quite understandable to a Soviet leadership which directs such policies against us, but in a direct thrust at the jugular of the Soviet Union could threaten a range of activities that are not only highly desirable in terms of their direct consequences but also necessary in terms of maintaining the alliances with Western Europe and Japan that are essential to the containment of the most serious Soviet threat to the West. The United States may be at a disadvantage in the political war with the Soviet Union in contending that its defense of its sea lanes is essential to Western interests, but it would be a mistake to exacerbate that disadvantage, which is compensated for by other strengths, by appearing so hostile to the Soviet Union that the European publics see *our* policies as war threatening. This would weaken NATO's cohesion.

Much of the Soviet propaganda about the presumed hostility of President Reagan can be accounted for as an attempt to influence the doves of Western Europe and the United States, and as a useful notion during a transition period in the Soviet leadership, in which a consensus on policy was absent. But at least some of the Soviet rhetoric probably represented the paranoid fears of an imperial class that feels even more threatened by internal than by external forces. Although I think it would be a distinct mistake to accept unequal arms control treaties or to fail to protect our interests in an effort to reduce such Russian fears—indeed, this would only give them an incentive to inflame their rhetoric—prudence should lead us to place change within the Soviet Union toward the low end of the spectrum of American objectives.

I am aware that this may seem cruel not only to refugees from the Soviet Union but especially to the conquered nationalities inside the Soviet Union and to the Eastern Europeans who feel imprisoned by Soviet imperialism. But there is a limit to the price that the United States can be expected to pay to right the wrongs of the world. This becomes even more the case when not mere selfishness but prudent evaluation of the potential disasters that could lie in wait are taken into account.

Thus, although no actual policy can be formulated in the absence of the concrete conditions of particular cases, there are likely to be few cases in which direct intervention in the internal Soviet struggle is likely to look very good in cost-benefit terms. Even if there are direct requests for intervention, some of which may be genuine and others the work of *agents provocateur*, the risks are likely to outweigh the potential gains.

Policies designed to reassure the internal contestants for power in the Soviet Union of American nonaggressive intentions are far more likely to convey credibility if they occur within the framework of a prior policy emphasizing such restraint. Thus, for instance, some variant of my proposal for mutual withdrawal of Soviet and American forces from the central theater of Europe and massive reductions in military strength in all nations of this central area might provide that kind of credibility. In the absence of such a radical program, at least modest reductions in military forces, including perhaps the placement of intermediate-range nuclear forces into the seas, and the implementation of advanced crisis management proposals that are now being negotiated, might play a useful role.

During a crisis itself, it would be advisable to coordinate with the West German government so that we can jointly announce that the territorial readjustments involving Germany and Poland that resulted from World War II will not be challenged. In addition, if it is possible to convince the

People's Republic of China of its utility, a statement by China that the disturbances inside the Soviet Union would not be the occasion for any agitation concerning the demarcation of the border between the Soviet Union and China would be desirable.

It may not be possible to maintain a completely hands-off attitude toward developments in Eastern Europe, where Soviet hegemony lacks any legitimacy and where American sympathies will be so readily aroused. However, it might be useful during a crisis to emphasize the much-maligned Yalta agreement. For instance, the United States could declare its support for that democratization within Poland called for by the Yalta accords while making it clear that under no foreseeable circumstances would Poland be drawn into the NATO alliance. Should revolts appear to be succeeding in Eastern Europe, it might be possible for the United States to exercise its influence to prevent harsh treatment for Communists, with the exception of those who are guilty of crimes under the civil law of the country affected. If most of Eastern Europe appears to be pulling out of the Warsaw treaty organization, we could announce that we are ready to negotiate the conditions for the dissolution of NATO and for massive arms reductions in Europe.

The Helsinki Accords to which the Soviet Union is party could also be used in similar fashion. The effort here would be to show both the legitimacy of our interest within the framework of agreements that the Soviet Union has signed and the moderation of the policies supported. Although, no doubt, attempts would be made by the most reactionary forces within the Soviet Union to portray this behavior in a hostile light, and perhaps to some extent successfully to do so, those attempts would be blunted, if not entirely forestalled, by a framework of behavior that may even be reassuring to other important elements in the Soviet Union.

Despite all these efforts there remains a danger that the turmoil in the Soviet Union might produce military adventurism on the part of leading cadres in the regime. Therefore, it is highly important that the prospects for such successful aggressive behavior be shown to be minimal. This means that the defenses of the NATO area must be exceptionally strong and not vulnerable to a tactical surprise attack. Because many of the measures that would be defensive would also be consistent with an offensive posture, it is extremely important that the previously mentioned crisis control measures be in operation.

It is, of course, possible that a regime crisis in the Soviet Union could occur without a simultaneous nationality crisis inside the system. In that case, the dispute might be between those trying to maintain the existing system, those attempting to rationalize it in terms of greater economic efficiency and modest internal liberalization, and those promoting political pluralism. The most threatening alternative for the United States would be the reestablishment of hegemony by the most reactionary forces in the Communist Party. This would sustain the continuing legitimacy problems of the Soviet Union, which can be solved primarily, and only temporarily, by external expansion. Even in this case, however, it is doubtful that the United States should exercise any initiative to affect the process.

Counterintuitively, the rationalization of the regime's economy might be the best result from the American standpoint. It likely would sufficiently solve problems of economic production to increase legitimacy, or at least to forfend excessive lack of legitimacy in a country that has no democratic tradition. Thus, a Soviet system with a rational economy and a liberated managerial class might have much less need to expand or to threaten areas vital to American interests. Its legitimacy might best be served by technology transfers and by improved relations with the capitalist powers. It probably would be forced into certain compromises with the military, but these need not be threatening to Western interests.

Although, superficially, political pluralism in the Soviet Union might seem the outcome most consonant with American values, it might also set off the most provocative tendencies in terms of the territorial integrity of what is now the Soviet Union. The Russian reaction to these nationality claims might be extremely cruel and xenophobic: producing relative pluralism only for the Russian areas but dictatorial domination for the rest. This could have unpredictable consequences. But it most likely would result in some new form of authoritarianism that would be extremely xenophobic in form and that would be supported by important military leaders.

It is possible that such a Russia might seek an alliance with the West against the Chinese and the colored races of the world. We must not forget that such an alliance would be contrary to American values and to the character of the United States as a multiracial country. Yet, such a new Russia would still possess nuclear weapons and it might strike out blindly at vulnerable targets on the border of the new Russia, although not at the United States.

Let us suppose for a moment that a crisis inside the Soviet Union is complicated by nationality uprisings. For the same reasons that we should not seek directly to influence the process inside the regime, we should not directly assist breakaway efforts by the various nationality groups. Such assistance would most likely dampen the conflicts within the regime or produce a victory by one of the contending factions, in combination with military leaders, that would then respond with military force in an attempt to maintain the Soviet empire.

The United States, however, should have a policy for such circumstances. This policy should be that whether the Soviet Union remains a single nation or breaks up into a number of nations is a matter that concerns the peoples of the Soviet Union and not the United States. Yet, within this constraint, we should recognize that the institutional arrangements that have built up within the Soviet empire over the period of the last 70 years probably create a web of common interests so great that an absolute dissolution of that system, as contrasted with a measured decentralization, might be contrary to the interests of the various nationalities. Therefore, our policy should be that, regardless of the relations between the Russian and the other national entities in the system that emerges after a crisis, whether continued union or some form of separation, the common interests of the parties may require some degree of institutionalization. These positions should not be announced in the form of authoritative or dogmatic proclamations. But, in one form or another, these policies should be communicated to the contending leaderships within the Soviet Union so that they can comprehend that our intention is not one of pouncing on that regime to dismember it.

If dismemberment comes without our assistance, so be it. That may or may not be in the American interest, depending upon circumstances. However, it cannot likely be in the American interest actively to support the dismemberment of the Soviet Union. If eventual dismemberment should occur, it will more likely occur in a benign fashion if it does so as the consequence of a long evolutionary process than as the outcome of individual revolts within the nationality areas. Furthermore, premature dismemberment may not last in the absence of a war by the West against the Soviet Union that could turn nuclear. That kind of radical dismemberment is more likely to produce reconquest by a Russia that rules the armed forces of the Soviet Union, even if a majority of the soldiers are from other-than-Slavic nationalities. A reduced threat of dismemberment is more likely to produce some degree of collegial decision making that produces greater autonomy and more evolutionary possibility.

Everything that I have said so far may be contraindicated by the actual circumstances of a particular regime crisis in the Soviet Union. Generalizations of this kind can do no more than provide a framework for thinking about the problem. Even if the likelihood of a crisis in the Soviet regime is not particularly high, neither is it so negligibly small that prudent statesmen can afford not to think about the situation. In the absence of such analysis, Western governments would be more likely to make precipitous decisions that involve a greater risk of untoward results than if prior thought has gone into the process. Thus, to think about possible crises in the Soviet system is not to display an innately hostile attitude toward the Soviet regime, no matter how much we disapprove of the Soviet regime in terms of our values. Such analysis represents instead an intellectual analysis that is necessary if we are to understand the world in which we live. Prudent American statesmen cannot afford not to consider how they would respond if the Soviet system goes into crisis.

11

U.S. Foreign Policy and Russian National Aspirations

A Commentary on Section 10

NICOLAI N. PETRO

In his paper "American Policy in the Event of a Soviet Crisis," Professor Kaplan raises the question of how the United States might respond to the emergence of a crisis situation in the Soviet Union. He deals with two aspects of this issue. The first is what steps the U.S. and its allies ought to take to reduce the risk of conflagration in the immediate event of a crisis. One can only agree with his recommendations for caution and prudence. The second is the broader issue of whether the United States should actively encourage those who seek changes, especially nationalist changes, within the Soviet system. Here his analysis and solutions become somewhat problematic, and more desirable options exist than the ones he suggests.

According to Kaplan, the Soviet regime is dangerous to the U.S. because it is expansionist. It is expansionist because its legitimacy stems largely from "external success" founded upon Russian militarism. The need for such "success" in foreign policy becomes more and more acute as the regime tries to direct attention away from its domestic economic failures. As Kaplan puts it, "the average Russian takes pride in the success of the Soviet leadership in producing and extending the sweep of its domination and influence."[1]

Kaplan concludes that Russian national aspirations have become firmly wedded to Soviet objectives. Both, he says, are inclined to view the outside world as threatening.[2] Hence, a regime change spawned under the aegis of nationalist forces would certainly not be an improvement, and "might produce a resulting regime that would be even worse than the existing Soviet one in terms of peace or of democratic values."[3] He therefore recommends pursuing policies that would reassure the present Soviet leadership that the United States does not intend to destabilize their regime. If we encourage the regime to rationalize its economic system, easing some of its domestic tensions, he believes that a "liberated managerial class" might arise that could see its interests best served by curtailing expansion and seeking improved relations with the West.[4]

An important assumption of Kaplan's argument is that "crisis" is readily distinguishable from "evolutionary change" and that by promoting the latter in the Soviet Union we can avoid the former. It has also been argued, however, that the two concepts are in reality linked—that a "crisis" is the most likely outcome of any serious attempt at "evolutionary change" within the Soviet system (hence, the hesitancy shown by Soviet leaders to embark upon serious economic reforms). If this were the case, then encouraging a "revolution of rising expectations" through a rationalization of the economic system, as Kaplan suggests, would only serve to make a future domestic crisis more likely, and our need to deal effectively with it all the more essential.

The idea that preserving the status quo within Communist systems better serves U.S. interests than encouraging the formation of more representative governments there is not new. As a matter of U.S. policy, the desirability of preserving the domestic status quo in Eastern Europe was elaborated during the 1970s by Helmut Sonnenfeldt, a member of Henry Kissinger's National Security Council staff. Kaplan now extends the "Sonnenfeldt doctrine" to the Soviet Union itself, arguing that reform-minded nationalist forces ought to be discouraged from setting off what he terms "provocative tendencies in terms of the territorial integrity of what is now the Soviet Union."[5] In particular Kaplan fears the resurgence of Russian nationalism which, owing to the "lack of experience of the Russian people with democracy," he feels might "produce an authoritarian regime that might be reactionary, anti-Semitic, anticolored, and altogether intolerable to a multiracial United States."[6]

At the center of Kaplan's opposition to encouraging radical change is the presumption that Russian nationalism is quintessentially xenophobic and aggressive, and that therefore enduring the Soviet regime may be the lesser of two evils for the United States. Like many Western observers, he fails to make any distinction between the jingoistic hostility toward the

West promoted by the Soviet regime, and simple Russian patriotism which, like patriotism elsewhere, stems from the love of one's country and people.[7] This patriotism shares none of the grandiose ambitions of Marxist-Leninist ideology, nor does it view the West or Western values with animosity. The Soviet regime would like to have the West believe that it has totally co-opted Russian nationalism in support of its foreign policy objectives, but there is much evidence to belie this contention.

Russian Nationalism and the Prospects for Change

The urgent need for domestic economic reform, Kaplan acknowledges, compels the regime to strive for a greater accommodation to popular aspirations. In foreign policy, he contends, the regime has already achieved such an accommodation by successfully merging Great Russian nationalism and Soviet patriotism. But a closer examination of the contemporary manifestations of Russian nationalism, which range from the tremendously popular writings of the so-called "village" or "rural" writers such as Belov, Rasputin, Mozhaev, Shukshin, Abramov, and Soloukhin to name a few, to the underground political/cultural critique of the regime given by Osipov, Ogurtsov, Shafarevich, Borodin, and Solzhenitsyn, shows that the bulk of today's Russian nationalist revival has arisen in opposition to the present regime and that it clearly disassociates itself not only from its oppressive practices at home but also, and in no less definite terms, from its expansionist ventures abroad. The growth of popular interest in prerevolutionary culture, literature, history, and religion has emerged in rejection of both the foreign and domestic pursuits of the regime.[8]

After examining the expressions of contemporary Russian nationalism, M. S. Bernstam and L. H. Gann, have reached conclusions opposite to those of Kaplan. They find that the majority of nationalists in the USSR are distinctly pro-Western in orientation and that all of them are profoundly opposed to the global orientation of the official ideology let alone its endeavours in sustaining and justifying economic and political centralization in the country itself. Bernstam and Gann also argue that recent manifestations of Russian nationalism are decidedly defensive in motivation. This in the above-writers' view, stems from a growing awareness among the Russians, as well as the other nationalities of the Soviet Union, that liberation from the system can only come about through their unity in opposition to that system. The defensive character of Russian nationalism has also been greatly reinforced, they say, by recent Soviet press revelations concerning chronic and widespread malnutrition and alcoholism and sharp increases in female infertility and infant mortality among the Great Russians.[9]

It is also far from certain that the majority of Soviet citizens accept the official propaganda's explanations for the Soviet Union's extensive global commitments, or view them as adequate recompense for deteriorating economic conditions at home. Soviet specialists like Alexander Shtromas, for example, have argued precisely the opposite:[10]

> The Russian public at large, however, senses the inconsistency of the official Soviet policy line. Accepting the commitment to peace totally and without reservation, it resents the other commitment to support the friendly governments and revolutionary movements acting in the outside world. First of all it resents this policy for purely economic reasons. The argument goes as follows—'we are hungry, almost naked and badly housed ourselves and here we spend millions of roubles every day helping strangers for some strange reasons about which we could not care less'.

"There is no doubt," Shtromas concludes, "that the Russians on the whole deeply resent everything to do with proletarian internationalism, foreign aid and Soviet global involvement in general. In this sense one could say that there is a fundamental disagreement between Soviet official policy and Russian mass public opinion."[11]

Many spokesmen of the Great Russian nationalist opposition have openly proclaimed that the Soviet government's involvement outside Russian ethnic boundaries is contrary to Russia's national interests. Some, like Solzhenitsyn and Osipov, have advocated a policy of Russia's isolation from the rest of the world after the end of the Communist regime—a period of "self-healing" and "self-repentance" during which Russia should concentrate on rebuilding her domestic economy and restoring normal domestic conditions.[12] There is nothing in their thought which smacks of militarism or external aggression.

The foreign policy of these nationalists tends to range from what one might call an "enlightened self-interest" to outright isolationism. But even so-called "enlightened self-interest" fully excludes for Russian nationalists Soviet support of national liberation movements and stationing of Russian troops abroad. Even the maintenance of Russian troops in Eastern Europe, which many Western analysts are inclined to view as a "natural" Russian interest, is justified by the nationalists only to the extent that their repatriation should not lead to chaos.

It is quite remarkable to find in the Russian nationalist opinion, so often fragmented on matters of ideology and domestic political arrangement, such a strong consensus on this one issue—it is not in the interests of the

Russian nation to continue with the Soviet regime's expansionist foreign policy stance, imposed by the Soviet rulers exclusively for their own ideological purposes that are totally alien to Russia as a nation.

The spectre of what Kaplan terms "xenophobic Russian nationalism" coming to power is thus without substance. Although there are minor strands of Russian nationalism which display such traits, they are no more characteristic of the Russian national character than the Ku Klux Klan is of American national character. A detailed examination of opposition thought contained in *samizdat* shows that the overwhelming majority of nationalists are well in the mainstream of the pluralistic and democratic tradition. There are surprisingly few among them who could be construed as "reactionary, anti-Semitic, anticolored." While some nationalists oppose importing Western political institutions wholesale to a post-Communist Russia and favor instead some form of autocracy, this need not be construed as hostility towards the West, or preclude good relations between a post-Communist Russia and the United States. Indeed, the United States has a long tradition of good relations, even alliances, with a number of authoritarian regimes. When one considers the unabashed hostility of the present Soviet regime toward the West, it is hard to imagine what policies a Russian nationalist government might pursue that would make it more dangerous to the United States than the present Soviet regime.

Should the United States Support Russian Nationalism?

There are no ideal solutions in foreign policy. We are reminded daily of how difficult it is to balance the imperatives of national security with those of prudent moral action. In this context, the question of whether a change of regime in the USSR might be desirable ought to be of paramount concern to policy-makers because it strikes at the heart of this conflict between morality and security. Yet, Kaplan's analysis and conclusions fail to satisfy because, among other things, his definitions of the American interest and of prudent diplomacy are too narrow.

Kaplan implies that the American interest in the Soviet Union is limited to avoiding a military confrontation between the superpowers. It is precisely his perception of the problem as primarily a military conflict between traditional powers that obscures from his view the conflict between Russian nationalists and the regime, and perpetuates an American policy toward the Soviet Union that looks only to preserving the status quo. We should question the wisdom of a policy that so quickly dismisses one of the most potent forces of the twentieth century—one that in recent years Americans have repeatedly failed to appreciate—nationalism. If it is true, as has been argued in this paper, that contemporary manifestations of Russian nationalism are in large measure reactions against the policies of the present regime, then policies aimed at preserving the status quo will probably result in antagonizing nationalist forces.

As we search for policies that combine realism with an affirmation of our ethical values, the avoidance of military confrontation between the superpowers remains a matter of paramount importance. Yet, it should not be used as an excuse to define away our other interests in the region. A realistic policy that is also true to ethical concerns cannot be indifferent to nationalist strivings in the Soviet Union, not only because we thus express our concern for the oppressed, but because only a truly representative Russian national government can alter the present regime's commitment to the global expansion of its ideology, and thus finally end the threat of nuclear and conventional conflict which that expansion poses.

While one can agree with Kaplan that it is not in the interests of the United States to encourage open revolt in the Soviet Union (which we could never effectively support), it is certainly in the interest of the West to be attuned to forces for change in the USSR and, within the boundaries set by the avoidance of direct confrontation, encourage those who will be friendly and discourage those who appear to be hostile.

One suggestion for our policy in the region is therefore to devote greater attention, and perhaps even appropriate and inconspicuous encouragement, when consonant with our own national interests, to broadly based nationalist elements seeking domestic change in the Soviet Union. Such nationalists exist at every level of Soviet society and form, perhaps, the most serious threat the regime faces internally. Far from being inconsistent with the ethical foundations of Western societies or our fundamental security concerns, such forces are, on the whole, motivated by values and concerns quite similar to our own. Certainly in the realm of foreign policy their attitudes are nonantagonistic to American interests for the simple reason that there is no real conflict between the genuine Russian national interests and American interests and that the present U.S.-Soviet confrontation is purely ideological in its nature.

It is furthermore desirable both from the perspective of humanitarian concerns and of our national security interests not to ease the burdens of the present regime. If the constraints on the present regime were loosened, the resources freed would almost certainly be used to reinforce its militaristic and ideologically aggressive posture. It can further scarcely be defined as prudent to focus our entire attention on preserving the present political status quo (which many, like Kaplan, view as inherently unstable) and to dismiss a priori those deeply rooted elements of society whose aspirations fundamentally contradict those of the regime. Given the sheer preponderance of numbers Russian nationalism is, potentially, the most significant of these.

Our inability (or unwillingness) to distinguish between varieties of nationalisms that are co-opted by the regime for its own self-preservation and others that are inspired by an alternate worldview obscures crucial divisions within the society and perhaps even within the Soviet elite itself. It undermines the flexibility of our policies in that region and weakens the case of those within the Soviet Union who seek alternatives to the present but fear that their efforts will not meet with understanding or approval in the West. It is too early to speculate about what specific effects Russian nationalism might have in shaping Soviet society or alternatives to it. Its domestic influence, however, is likely to grow in the future, and with it the opportunities as well as the challenges for U.S.-Soviet relations.

Notes

1. Morton A. Kaplan, "American Policy in the Event of Soviet Crisis," paper presented at the Second International Congress of Professors World Peace Academy, Geneva, Switzerland, August 13–18, 1985, p. 5.
2. *Ibid.*, p. 5–6.
3. *Ibid.*, p. 3.
4. *Ibid.*, p. 15–16.
5. *Ibid.*, p. 16.
6. *Ibid.*, p. 8.
7. It has long been common for people in the Soviet Union to distinguish between Soviet patriotism foisted upon them by the regime and authentic Russian patriotism. The Soviet regime's efforts to appeal to Russian nationalism during World War II—the resulting patriotic surge often mistaken in the West at the time as support for Stalin's regime—have been well documented. George Fischer in *Soviet Opposition to Stalin, A Case Study in World War II* (Harvard, 1952) and Alexander Dallin in *German Rule in Russia* (St. Martin's, 1957), have also documented some of the lesser known anti-Soviet manifestations of Russian patriotism which occurred during that period.

   Today the regime has tried to portray the war in Afghanistan as a patriotic cause, but apparently with limited success. In a speech before the Wilson Center (Washington, D.C.) in March 1984, writer Georgy Vladimov noted that Party officials had repeatedly offered any Soviet writer who would go to Afghanistan and write a patriotic novel about the war lucrative incentives. They were met, however, with only one acceptance.

   Outside the intelligentsia, a similar skepticism about the Party and its motives has been voiced. For example, in an open letter by an unskilled worker, O. Alifanov, reprinted in *Possev*, November 1985, p. 10. Alifanov writes:

What are young people giving up their lives for in Afghanistan? I think for world communist revolution, and for this goal nothing and no-one is too good for the communist party. True I don't know if, among the Soviet soldiers in Afghanistan, there are any children or grand-children of members of the Central Committee, of the military elite, or of other high ranking bureaucrats. . . . It is not concern for the security of the USSR (telling people that the Americans will place rockets there), but the necessity of creating by force, rather than by example, the world revolution, that is how I explain the occupation of Afghanistan by Soviet troops.

8. Revealing on this point is a recent interview in *Possev*, July, 1983, with Georgi Vladimov, popular Russian author and former head of Moscow section of Amnesty International. In it Vladimov discusses the origins and role in society of the cultural opposition dubbed "The Russian Party." Similar conclusions about the predominantly anti-Soviet nature of Russian nationalist opposition are drawn by John Dunlop in his *The Faces of Contemporary Russian Nationalism*, Princeton: Princeton U., 1983; and *The New Russian Nationalism*, New York: Praeger, 1985.
9. M. S. Bernstam and L. H. Gann, "Will the Soviet Union Stay Communist?" *The Intercollegiate Review*, Spring/Summer 1984, vol. 20, No. 1, pp. 19–20.
10. Alexander Shtromas, "The Soviet Union and the Politics of Peace," in Peter van Dungen, ed. *West European Pacifism and the Strategy for Peace*, London: Macmillan, 1985, p. 140.
11. *Ibid.*, p. 146.
12. See the author's "Morality and the Pursuit of Justice: Aleksandr Solzhenitsyn's Perception of International Affairs," *The Intercollegiate Review*, Fall 1983, vol. 19, #1, p. 19–30.

12

Concluding Chapter to Part I

MORTON A. KAPLAN,

ALAIN BESANÇON, JERRY F. HOUGH

As this volume neared completion, there was an interesting presentation of opposed views by Alain Besançon in Commentary and Jerry Hough in the New York Times about the foreign policy of Mikhail Gorbachev. Excerpts from their positions follow as the final chapter in Part I of this volume.

In April 1988, Commentary Magazine and The New York Times carried widely different views of Mikhail Gorbachev's foreign policy, authored by Alain Besançon and Jerry Hough respectively.

According to Hough, Gorbachev is a Europeanist who wants to make a reformed Soviet Union a partner in a peaceful Europe without barriers. According to Besançon, Gorbachev's foreign policy is a response to the economic debacle in the Soviet Union. He needs time, Besançon says, and economic assistance from the West which will be used eventually to Finlandize Europe as his clever new policy drives wedges between the NATO allies.

This is not the first time such a debate concerning Soviet policy has emerged. During the Brezhnev era, we learned that he told some Eastern European leaders not to worry about detente, that it was only a device to gain time. At that time there was a debate in Washington between those who believed that this revealed Brezhnev's true policies and those who believed that he was only reassuring the Eastern European leaders that the Soviet Union would not abandon them.

I used this debate in class to show my students why observers in Washington so frequently failed to understand world events. If there was nothing in the policy of detente to cause worry, Brezhnev would not have needed to reassure the Eastern European leaders. If his reassurance was implausible, it would serve no purpose. Consider the possibility, I continued, that Brezhnev's future policies would depend upon conditions and alternatives and that he could not be sure how they would evolve.

Policy makers like the kinds of views presented by Hough and Besançon precisely because they avoid indeterminicies and ambiguities. Those inclined to such views find in them elegant reinforcements of their beliefs. They seem to provide clear guidelines for choices from among policies. News commentators and reporters are able to understand and to repeat them easily. Their only fault is that the world only very seldom is like that.

The tendency to see policies as the product of fixed dichotomous alternatives, therefore, does pervade Washington. Consider the argument of the majority in Congress that the Reagan administration was opposed to negotiations with the Sandinistas and wished to overthrow them. Would it not have been appropriate for the administration to have a policy that could pursue either alternative under appropriate conditions and desirable to make the Sandinistas aware of this? Was it not a major blunder by the Johnson administration to assure the North Vietnamese that their home base was secure beyond question?

Let us start our analysis of the disagreement between Hough and Besançon with the points on which Besançon is strong. We know that Marxism is recognized as a failed doctrine in the Soviet Union regardless of how important it remains as a justification for Soviet rule. Soviet reports now reveal that the CIA overestimated the Soviet GNP by slightly over 100%. And even that may overestimate the economy because of the poor quality of so many of the products. Reports by emigres that the Soviet military budget exceeded 25% of Soviet GNP are now revealed as accurate. The estimates by the authors of papers in Volume II of this series that the Soviet economy was on a decline—the CIA was estimating modest increases—may have been too generous.

No one in the Soviet leadership doubts the need for reform. And all will support reform if it can be had at an acceptable price for the leadership, that is, if it preserves the power and persequites of the leadership. Perestroika and Glasnost, however, are most modest attempts to achieve reform without shaking the leadership. They are most unlikely to be effective in terms of solving the production problem and already have given rise to nationality problems, which remain essentially insoluble in the Soviet context. Somewhat more effective reform, which Gorbachev may indeed desire, would likely give rise to more serious internal problems.

Elements in the Soviet leadership are already building a case against

Gorbachev. If events worsen, as they well may, Gorbachev will be faced with three alternatives. He will be overthrown. He will lead the counter-reform efforts. Or, by far the least likely, he will find allies in the military who will help him overthrow the Soviet system. I find it difficult to believe that he would even consider this unless it were a realistic and the only alternative to his removal. It is most unlikely to be a realistic alternative.

There are other ways in which Gorbachev can reduce the immediate Soviet problem. Indeed I possibly pointed them out to him, for his Europeanism is a modification of a proposal of mine with which he is known to be familiar. No doubt this admission will increase the conviction of the La Rouchies that I am a KGB agent although they have not yet accused me of being involved in the international dope trade.

In 1983 I proposed an end to the division of Europe in which American forces would return to the continental U.S. while Soviet forces, except for modest frontier contingents, would retreat behind the Urals. The latter was necessary I argued because of reinforcement asymmetries, an argument Gorbachev noted in his modification. I also pointed out how large conventional reductions would enable the Soviets to postpone their economic crisis without reducing security. By 1985, I had got the Soviets to agree to send someone from Moscow to discuss my proposal in a public conference, although George Shultz refused to grant him a visa, and I had to use a Soviet expert who was already in the country.

Question. Is Gorbachev's Europeanism purely tactical and deceptive? I think this is unlikely, although in practice this is the most likely outcome. The economic problems of the Soviet Union have already produced the INF agreement, Soviet proposals for a troop drawdown in Europe, the shift in policy in Afghanistan, and reductions in assistance to Cuba and Nicaragua. The INF is a good agreement—except for political complications in Europe I would have been willing to pull these weapons out unilaterally—but I would be more wary of the START negotiations. Reductions of conventional forces in Europe, provided they do not increase Soviet advantages, also are desirable even if they ease some Soviet problems.

All these moves by the Soviet Union are consistent with tactical considerations. No doubt the Soviet Union will continue to exploit difficulties in the American position elsewhere in the world and attempt to produce disunity in NATO. Gorbachev, after all, is the leader of a system with institutional vested interests who leads because he can satisfy their minimal demands without threat to Nomenklatura personal concerns in a world that remains uncertain at best. He must keep open Soviet alternatives that do not shake these institutional interests and that permit them to be better satisfied if the correlation of forces should turn in the Soviet direction. If his own goals should lie in a somewhat different direction, he must keep these less than crystal clear if he is to survive politically. Prudence alone requires that he not jeopardize the system that has brought him to leadership until circumstances are highly favorable for major change.

If the Western alliance weakens, Gorbachev would have no political option except to pursue its demise even if he personally regretted this. Apart from institutional interests that would foreclose contrary policies, Russians fear anarchy in the international system almost as much as they fear it in the domestic system. They would seek to replace the failed Western system of order with their own.

With respect to the domestic system, as Gorbachev has himself stated, the Russian culture is not ready for democracy. Even if one disbelieves this, there are good reasons to believe that Gorbachev believes it. Although the Soviet leaders' fear of anarchy sometimes impels them toward unwise policies, the fear has a solid foundation with respect to reform. Past a certain point, reform of the Soviet system is likely to become unmanageable. The pressures for change will become powerful and the legitimacy and myth of omnipotence of the regime will have been undermined by the preliminary reforms.

I do not think that the protection afforded to Soviet Party mavericks, who do believe in democracy, by Andropov and Gorbachev were merely attempts to deceive the intelligentsia to gain their support, as Besançon believes, although there may be elements of truth in his belief. As tough as both men were, particularly Andropov, they manifested an (perhaps ambivalent) opening to the Soviet democrats. It would not surprise me if there was an element of truth in Hough's beliefs concerning Gorbachev's most cherished goals, although I believe that he already would be out of power if the rest of the Soviet leadership believed Hough's analysis. However, I doubt that Gorbachev thinks in the terms Hough and Besançon attribute to him. I think his beliefs are tied more concretely to unfolding events in terms of real alternatives and that, to the extent that he thinks of more ultimate goals, these are only loosely tied to policies. He could hardly survive politically otherwise.

Except for modest moves, with potentially contrary implications, I do not believe Gorbachev can move toward a European policy that recognizes the freedom and independence of all the parties except in a world in which there are no acceptable alternatives. That is very unlikely to be the case during his leadership and never will be the case if the foreign policy honchos in the Democratic Party—not that the Republicans stand for anything other than a more modest disaster in foreign policy—take over.

My advice would be to conclude agreements that are good because they are good, not because we will influence events inside the Soviet Union.

Giving hostages to Gorbachev, even assuming we really know enough about Soviet decision making to fine tune our policies to such considerations, may make it more rather than less difficult for him to pursue accommodationist policies. After all, he must be able to convince the Politburo that he got the best deal possible in terms of keeping all Soviet options open. Thus, we must be strong in defense of our geostrategic interests, although it should be clear that carefully considered agreements are possible. Our peaceniks, whom Lenin called useful idiots, might well be viewed as dangerous idiots by a Gorbachev who held the views Hough attributes to him.

We should have developed a European policy before Gorbachev took up a modification of my proposal. It was not for want of trying that this did not happen. However, Gorbachev has not yet, and cannot, firmly propose an end to the division of Europe. We still can take the lead in this, although it would be incumbent to consult fully with our allies before doing so to make sure that they do not interpret this as a rationalization for an effort to withdraw American protection from Europe. Deep down an end to the division of Europe is what Europeans, both East and West, want.

Although we should not oppose deep reductions of conventional forces from the Atlantic to the Urals, our challenge must be the removal of both the Russian and American hegemonies. Until this is accomplished, significant American ground forces and our strategic nuclear forces must remain dedicated to the defense of Europe. If we carry this through, the Soviet Union eventually will have to agree to end the division of Europe or become a third world country. Thus, the Soviet leaders will be faced with the risks of leading the internal Soviet changes themselves or of being swept away by internal opposition.

But even more important, we must pursue a policy tuned to the American vision of the world. That is why we should be pursuing a Global Democratic Community, with an International Court of Human and Political Rights, which, with the support of a police force, could assure the inhabitants of small nations, without a long tradition of democracy, that if they join voluntarily their individual rights are safe and the arrangements are consistent with their dignity. This will support our foreign policy. But it will also help to build a world that reflects the universal values imbedded in the Declaration of Independence and the American Constitution.

—Morton A. Kaplan

Gorbachev Without Illusions

Sheltered by distance, the perimeter of the Soviet Union is discreetly extricating itself from Moscow's grip while being careful to preserve the outward forms of Communist behavior; only an upheaval at the center is wanting before claims might even be pressed for independent existence. In the meantime, a civil society is slowly taking shape in these areas, and little by little integrating the party into its fabric.

The progressive weakening of the old levers of social command has entailed a similar and consequent weakening of the power of intimidation at home and of aggressiveness abroad. For a while it was possible for the government to say, in effect: let the productivity of the non-military sectors of the economy—the factories, the *sovhozes* (state farms), *kolkhozes* (collective farms)—lapse as it will into inefficiency and irremediable waste and fraud; let the standard of living fall below that of the underdeveloped countries of Latin America. None of this in itself would be a cause of concern to the government, for after all it never put wealth or popular well-being among its highest priorities. But this rotting away of the civilian sector of the economy threatens Soviet military strength in turn, and that is a matter of the deepest concern.

By concentrating on the military virtually all of its resources, all of its research-and-development efforts, the Soviet Union has succeeded in building an armed force that is competitive with that of its principal rival. But the huge arms build-up on which the Soviet Union embarked after 1964, and which still continues, has become technically unsustainable and politically risky. Technological and scientific resources no longer suffice to maintain a competition in which the necessary level of sophistication rises from year to year. In a land innocent of technological achievement (except in the military arena), without highways, without telephones, without the means of disseminating information, how is a modern army to be supported?

More: the "human factor" too is beginning to present problems. Decades of living under a regime of lies, and in unrelieved servitude, penury, and fear, have taken a profound toll. The ordinary Soviet citizen works little and badly, and his tendencies toward self-destruction are given abundant outlet in his addiction to alcohol and drugs. All his energies are directed toward procuring for himself the simplest material goods; the range of his concerns hardly extends beyond the narrow sphere of his own existence. With the progressive corruption and degradation of the Communist elites, he no longer even has models to look up to. The newspapers he reads all testify to the general rot. The postal system steadily worsens, the trains run ever more slowly, sanitary conditions deteriorate alarmingly. According to demographers, the Soviet Union is the only country in the world in which, because of poor nutrition and bad hygiene, average height is diminishing and life expectancy is shrinking. How is a decent army to be built out of soldiers who are ignorant, sickly, drunk, and thieving, and who refuse to show any initiative?

As passive as they were in domestic policy, however, so were Brezhnev and his successors extremely active, even bold, in foreign policy, where the prospects for success were anyway much greater.

Never since October 1917 have Soviet armed forces been adequate to the grandeur of Soviet military ambition, and periodic failure has also bedeviled Soviet intelligence and espionage activities. By contrast, in two areas Soviet policy has been an unmitigated success: in the conduct of diplomacy and in the manipulation of Western opinion. This is not due to the inferiority of Western diplomats or journalists, but to a simple built-in disadvantage from which they necessarily suffer, namely, the habits of traditional diplomacy and the habits of traditional journalism. Applying these habits of mind and action to so radically different a political phenomenon as the Soviet Union inevitably causes a kind of breakdown of the machinery.

From the moment Western diplomacy recognized the Soviet regime *de jure*, it conceded the premise that the Soviet Union was a state like any other, a state with which normal, peaceful relations could and should obtain. As the French President Francois Mitterrand declared to *Izvestia* just this past December, "The USSR is not our enemy, and not even our adversary." With such a state, diplomacy must tirelessly seek to define areas of common interest and locate grounds for political accommodation. By the same logic it is forbidden for others to adopt a global strategy aimed at destabilizing or undoing the Soviet regime—in other words, to adopt a strategy like the one the Soviet regime directs against the West.

As for the press, the moment it comes to deal with the Soviet Union it too accepts as a working assumption the proposition that West and East are symmetrical: that there exist in the Kremlin, as in London or Paris, or especially Washington, diverse currents of thought, "hawks" and "doves"; that everything in Soviet politics boils down to a question of individuals and of personality (for so it often does among us in the West); that something is always about to happen in the USSR, even when nothing is happening; that the country is going to change, is on the verge of changing, has already changed.

Under Brezhnev, and especially after 1975, the Soviet government undertook to educate itself more systematically about these spontaneous Western tendencies and rapidly became more adroit at exploiting them. Its efforts in this regard had two objectives.

First, to obtain Western subsidies. The "Great Grain Robbery" of 1972 demonstrated that it was more to the Soviet Union's advantage to buy American wheat with the money lent to it by American taxpayers than to invest pointlessly in Soviet agriculture. Within a few years the Soviet bloc had received more than $100 billion in credit, a sum nearly equivalent to the entire Marshall Plan. The legal and illegal procuring of Western technology has represented a boon of no lesser value. The sums involved are in neither case truly colossal, but they impart a decisive boost "at the margin." Insofar as the entire Soviet system is geared toward the military, the effect has been to enable Soviet armed forces to remain competitive.

Second, to extend the sphere of Communist domination. Within the space of a very few years in the 1970s Vietnam, Laos, Cambodia, Nicaragua, Ethiopia, South Yemen, Mozambique, and Angola fell under Communist rule. The use of Cuban troops for these purposes was a remarkably innovative tool. Afghanistan offered the Soviet military a proving ground for its weapons and tactics.

In all, the extension of Communist rule has been the excellent result of instilling despair in those already under the yoke, like the Czechs and the Cubans, while, at the same time, reinforcing at home the seventy-year-old alliance between Bolshevism and Russian nationalism. The average Russian feels proud to belong to such a great power. As the Marquis de Custine put it more than a century ago, "The slave on his knees dreams of world empire."

The balance-sheet of Brezhnev's foreign policy was therefore a brilliant one, and in *Perestroika* Gorbachev accords it a due measure of respect. Domestically, however, the rot continued, and it became increasingly clear as time went on that the political effects, though not yet openly manifest, could burst out at any moment. That is where things took when Gorbachev was elected General Secretary of the Communist party.

The columnist George Will has recently argued, in connection with the new round of arms-control treaties now being negotiated between the U.S. and the USSR, that either the Soviets have really renounced the Leninist intention of imposing their rule on the entire planet, in which case the treaties are not needed, or they have not, in which case the treaties must be viewed as but a tactic in their ongoing global strategy.

Actually all one need do is to open the pages of Gorbachev's book *Perestroika* to see that he has preserved intact the Leninist vision. According to this conception the world today remains divided, as it has always been, into two "camps," that of the "imperialists," which represents the past and that of "socialism," representing the future. The Third World is a disputed area between the two camps.

Gorbachev, who was born in 1931, has experienced only the international successes of the Soviet camp: the victory over Nazi Germany, the Sovietization of Eastern Europe, Communist triumphs in Asia, Africa, Central America. He has also seen the long-term weaknesses and confusion of the West and its inability (despite temporary aberrations, as under the early Reagan) to construct a coherent strategy. Gorbachev thus has no reason to disown the glorious heritage of Brezhnev, and he does not disown it. For three years now we have been able to observe his behavior in foreign policy: it is more activist, daring, and imaginative than that of his predecessor. The global strategy remains the same, but the tactics have been improved.

The strategy implies a designated principal enemy. The United States is, as ever, it. The strategic locale where victory will be decided is, as ever, Western Europe. The objectives are to decouple Germany from Europe, and Europe from America, and to impose a protectorate over Western Europe that will render it subservient to the Communist bloc. At the same time, however, Gorbachev has introduced important tactical changes which have led some in the West to believe—such indeed, was the intent—that he has altered the strategy.

Soviet military doctrine is now being deliberately oriented toward the non-nuclear. To many Soviet theorists, nuclear weapons since their inception have seemed a disagreeable infraction of the law of history. They upset the natural "correlation of forces," by enabling any country possessing them to resist destabilization and intimidation from without and to exercise a disproportionate influence in world affairs. Nuclear weaponry renders war uncertain and strategic calculation hazardous. By contrast, conventional warfare, particularly when it is conducted with modern, "smart" weapons, confirms the natural geostrategic advantages of the "socialist camp." Moreover, in conventional warfare of this kind one can better predict the flow of battle and calculate more precisely the relation of forces.

A number of military analyses appearing in 1986 and 1987 enable us to understand how the Soviet army views the next conflict. According to these studies, a third world war is a "probable" event, which could be sparked by almost any kind of local conflict. The "socialist camp" must prepare to enter hostilities under the best possible conditions. To this end it is necessary to relearn the lessons of the last world war, namely, the importance of the element of surprise, and the importance of preserving this element through a diplomacy that continuously stresses the themes of peace and the renunciation of violence. It is also necessary to remember the way in which, during the last war, the Soviet Union formed an "alliance with the capitalist nations" and with their aid was able to triumph over the common adversary. This means that in the coming war the USSR is contemplating the possibility of counting on the neutrality if not the technical and economic assistance of several European countries, whether the "little states" of Scandinavia and Benelux which it has been pushing toward neutralism or, indeed, Germany itself.

None of this means that Gorbachev has appointed the hour and is even now readying against Europe his version of Hitler's Operation Barbarossa. Certainly, however, the USSR is preparing for war—why else would it devote to this end most of its essential economic and technological resources, while being well aware that no one is thinking of attacking it? But ever faithful to Lenin, the Soviets view war as an extension of policy—a policy which cannot succeed unless the escalation to war seems always a plausible recourse.

Gorbachev understood from the beginning that the ceaseless accumulation of nuclear weapons was leading to an impasse. An arms race with the United States could not be won, at least so long as the latter was determined to keep up its end. To the contrary, such a race only served to expose the deepening technological and economic inferiority of the USSR. Making profitable use of his supreme diplomatic advantages, Gorbachev in effect opened a new front, translating into the military sphere the reasoning that had succeeded so well in the "Great Grain Robbery." Instead of investing heavily and fruitlessly in nuclear weaponry, why not try to disarm the adversary, or at least render problematic his continued reliance on the arms he already has? Gorbachev thus accepted the "zero option" the Americans had offered in 1981 as a sop to European opinion.

Once the INF treaty is ratified and the theater weapons are out of Europe, the next phase will consist of isolating the United Kingdom and France by rallying pacifist opinion in Western Europe against these countries' continued retention of nuclear arsenals. Then, once Europe has been rid of nuclear weapons, and once the American troops are gone—for without nuclear cover, how long would American public opinion abide their remaining?—it should be easy to brandish the Soviet strategic nuclear threat as a means of deterring the United States from even thinking of intervening in Europe in the event of conflict.

From that point forward, the only way to defend Europe will be with a conventional army capable of offsetting the hugely superior Warsaw Pact forces. Building such an army presupposes an unlikely degree of political will, all the more unlikely in view of the intense pacifist sentiments that will already have solidified behind the drive for nuclear disarmament, and the by now widely implanted belief in the peaceful intentions of the Soviet Union. At that point, and under conditions dictated by Moscow, Europe will find itself in the position of placing its economy and technology at the service of the long-range survival of the Soviet Union—which, as we have seen, is precisely the principal aim of Soviet foreign policy.

In preparation for this eventuality the Soviets have been deploying a number of stratagems, some of them predating Gorbachev.

One is the effort to endow the Soviet Union with an image that differs from reality. In fact the USSR has been disguising both its Leninist nature and its global aims since the New Economic Policy of 1921. In the 1920s it strove to create the impression of a maturing revolution, something along the lines of the normalization of France after Thermidor. In the 1930s it presented itself as a country bent principally on industrialization, modernization, and development. (Gorbachev has resurrected this particular image.) During the war, it emerged as Eternal Russia, defending an age-old identity and way of life which only happened to be encased for the moment in the skin of Communism.

In 1975, when Georgi Arbatov was sent to Washington to press the Soviet position on SALT II and the Helsinki accords, he portrayed a USSR that was now a superpower perfectly and symmetrically matched with the United States by reason of global responsibilities, spheres of influence, legitimate interests—and also by reason of an internal political life as variegated and diverse in its way as America's own. This new image was "sold" not to those who were once the officially designated Western consumers of the Soviet myth, the working classes and the intelligentsia, but to businessmen, diplomats, experts on Soviet affairs. It was in fact Western Sovietologists, especially the Americans among them, who marketed the new doctrine of political (not to say moral) equivalence in its most sophisticated and elegant form, and who in turn made it credible to Western politicians.

Thanks to its new image, which implied among other things a sound financial reliability, the USSR was able to participate actively in international capital markets. By now the actual debt incurred by the seven nations of the Eastern bloc has reached $127 billion, a jump of 55 percent in the last three years alone. To this may be added the secret credits that pass through Soviet financial institutions located in London and Paris. Agricultural surplus of the European Common Market is bought at a tenth what it costs the Europeans to produce, with the difference made up by the European taxpayer. The USSR is lobbying for membership in the International Monetary Fund and the World Bank. It is conducting "joint ventures" with German and Japanese investors, taking care to maintain control of the enterprises so created. Having nothing of its own to sell but weapons, gold, and oil, commodities not in overwhelming demand just now, the Soviet Union is endeavoring by political means to manipulate the terms by which international trade is conducted.

The Communist movement worldwide has been assigned its part in this grand design. The fact of this movement's existence, while not exactly denied, is hardly stressed these days, and its centralized direction is carefully dissembled. Still, the essential structure of the movement remains what it has always been, and in its new director, the former long-time Soviet ambassador to the U.S., Anatoly Dobrynin, it has found a man of considerable worldly experience.

In Western Europe, with the exception of Italy, the movement seems to have abandoned the effort to form mass-based parties; operating out of conspiratorial structures reminiscent of the early days of Bolshevism, it is content instead with small, tightly disciplined organizations that aim to seize control of a few key sectors (in France these include the electrical and railway workers, the ports, a number of municipalities). These narrowly based efforts can be counted on to engage the sympathies and the collusion of some within the more broadly structured social-democratic parties—such, for instance, has been the successful experience of the small Communist party in West Germany.

The grand design for Europe renders subordinate the other theaters of Soviet foreign policy. But those theaters have hardly been abandoned, even if, globally speaking, the USSR may be in need of a pause. In *Perestroika* Gorbachev declares his intention to be active in Asia, and the Soviet navy has for quite some time now been pushing methodically forward in the South Pacific. In Angola the annual offensives continue, striving to put an end once and for all to the rebellion led by Jonas Savimbi. Ethiopia, wrapped in its new constitution even as the Ethiopian people are wrapped in starvation, has won entry to the sacred rolls of "people's democracies." In Nicaragua, the Sandinistas with Soviet assistance are building an enormous offensive army. Soviet troops have not been withdrawn from Afghanistan, and will not be withdrawn until the political victory for which they were sent to fight has been secured.

In all this Gorbachev's only original contribution has been to persuade the West that the Soviet Union intervenes so far from its borders as a matter of self-defense; that he, Gorbachev, bitterly regrets these engagements; and that it is therefore incumbent upon the Western democracies, if they desire peace as intensely as he does, to help him achieve the undisturbed political dominion at home which will permit him to work for their mutual and common good. That he has indeed largely succeeded in thus persuading the West is testimony to the progress the USSR and the Communist movement have lately made in their understanding of, and hence their ability to manipulate, public opinion in the democracies. Where once upon a time they were hampered by Leninist ideology with its preordained "class analysis" of democratic institutions, today, no doubt owing in good part to the labors of specialized agencies like Arbatov's Institute of the USA and Canada, the Soviets have developed a much better feel for the internal workings of democratic politics. If one may put it this way, they have passed from Lenin to Tocqueville, and the realism thus gained has given them a handle on the intrinsic weaknesses of our way of life.

Foreign policy once again offered a compensatory avenue of hope. Several times over in the course of its history the Soviet regime has tottered on the edge of collapse; each time, Western aid has come to the rescue and provided a new lease on life. In large part the entire thrust of Soviet foreign policy today is aimed at securing those means of survival which the West has hitherto afforded periodically and as if by miracle but which henceforth, perhaps, it may be persuaded to provide permanently and as if by obligation. A race is thus on between the continuing and deepening process of internal decomposition, whose aggravating symptoms, although masked today, must sooner or later burst into the open, and the so-far successful policy of external diplomacy which may yet procure a lengthy reprieve, if not, indeed, eventual triumph.

—Alain Besançon

The Europeanization of Gorbachev

Since he came to power, Mikhail S. Gorbachev has been talking about Europe in extraordinarily warm terms, as well he might. He badly needs Europe to help pull off his political and economic reforms. Until Americans understand this, however, they run the danger of misreading Mr. Gorbachev's foreign policy actions and intentions, particularly in nuclear and conventional arms control.

Mr. Gorbachev has repeatedly referred to Europe as our "common home." In his book "Perestroika," he states, "Europe 'from the Atlantic to the Urals' is a cultural-historical entity united by the common heritage of the Renaissance and the Enlightenment, of the great philosophical and social teachings of the 19th and 20th century." Mr. Gorbachev has advocated "the end of the schism of Europe." Using biblical language, he has appealed to "deliver us from the thought that Europe is a theater of military operations." He calls for a reduction of 500,000 troops on each side in Europe and has pledged to remove any sense of military threat, "even an imagined one."

Many American analysts dismiss Mr. Gorbachev's words as propaganda that masks his real intention of breaking up the North Atlantic Treaty Organization and expelling the United States from Europe. Actually, the reverse is true. Far from propaganda, his words represent a historic departure that is destined to overturn many of the Soviet Union's domestic and foreign policies. And he certainly has no plans to divide NATO.

Mr. Gorbachev's approach to Europe is nothing less than a reversal of the traditional Bolshevik attitude toward Western civilization. Such core changes in party ideology are not taken lightly in the Soviet Union.

Marx had said that political institutions, ideas and culture are a "superstructure" that reflects the economic base of a society. If capitalism does inexorably follow feudalism, then Russia at the turn of the century would soon adopt not only Western European capitalism but also the evolving democratic, "bourgeois" superstructure that went with it.

The Mensheviks and other Russian socialists gladly accepted the prospect that Russia would Europeanize. Lenin, the great extremist of the Russian Revolution, could not. He was utterly contemptuous not only of capitalism but also of the "parliamentarism," the philosophies and values of the Western Europe of his time. He could not stand the Westernized elite—the Professors, businessmen, professionals, bureaucrats—that Peter the Great and his successors had created.

Thus, the essence of the Bolshevik Revolution was the construction of two iron curtains, one against Western ideas and culture, the other against Western market forces. Although Mr. Gorbachev cannot say it, he is reversing this basic policy, opening his country to Western ideas (the essence of glasnost) and market forces. As he does, Europe becomes crucial to him.

There are numerous reasons for this. For one, the United States is inclined to limit the flow of capital and technology to the Soviet Union, so Mr. Gorbachev has no recourse but to go to Europe and Japan to get them.

Moreover, to accomplish his economic restructuring, Mr. Gorbachev must divert money from defense to investment, and nuclear arms control saves little money. Only a reduction of conventional forces will achieve this, and that means focus on the central front in Europe. Reduction of the missile and conventional threat to Europe is also necessary to reassure Europeans that their investment in the Soviet Union would be safe.

Finally, Europe is quite useful in redefining Russia's relation to Western culture. Modern Western society has many attractive features and some very unattractive ones. Mr. Gorbachev needs to convince his countrymen that he is admitting only the attractive features, so he can say that Russia is reintegrating into the higher civilization of Europe, while avoiding the bourgeois crassness of America.

Of course, the opening to Europe could also undermine NATO. After all, NATO has been held together by the Soviet threat. So a reduction of the threat, let alone concessions to Germany (theoretically, up to and including neutralization and reunification), could fracture the alliance.

Many assume, mistakenly, that splitting NATO is Mr. Gorbachev's ultimate foreign policy aim. Yet, from a military standpoint the continuation of NATO under American leadership is in Moscow's best interests.

NATO provides the justification for Soviet troops in Eastern Europe, while keeping a lid on German military power. More important, the only military danger to the Soviet Union now comes over the North Pole; Soviet control of Western Europe would not reduce this danger. As a result, the Kremlin's major goals in Western Europe are, first, to prevent conflicts within the region that might draw America and the Soviet Union into war, and, second, to prevent nuclear proliferation to West Germany.

An independent Germany would eventually demand nuclear equality with France and Britain. Moreover, Japan, when confronted with a splintered NATO, might begin to rearm, mounting a costly challenge to Soviet power in the Far East. Thus, Moscow has the major stake in maintaining the military status quo.

Yet, Mr. Gorbachev cannot let the United States veto his internal reform; he must do what is necessary to break any American economic or technological blockade. And this is Mr. Gorbachev's great dilemma—his military interests lead in one direction, while his economic interests lead in another.

We need to think through our interests, too. Like the Soviets, we also must reduce conventional military expenditures to reduce our budget deficit and rebuild our national power. Moreover, a destabilization of Europe is no more in our interest than in the Soviet. If our intransigence in arms control negotiations, trade and other East-West issues drives Mr. Gorbachev to follow destabilizing policies in Europe, we will regret it as much as he does.

—Jerry F. Hough

PART

FROM CRISIS TO A POST-SOVIET REGIME

1

The Issue of German Unity in the Post-Soviet World

KLAUS HORNUNG

If more than mere speculations are to be offered on the issue of German unity in a post-Soviet world, then it seems essential to first recognize a few basic facts regarding the historical development of Russia's relationship with Europe in general and with Germany in particular. Even those who do not pay homage to a historical determinism, but instead are aware that history is always open towards the future, must, in the interest of any realistic and solid prediction, pay attention to the basic developments underlying history, and they must try to draw their conclusions from them. A second vital precondition for a prognosis is the politico-psychological, spiritual and social situation in Germany after World War II: because foreign policy and the history of a nation do not happen in a vacuum, but are most intensely connected to social, mental and collectively psychological facts and changes; that is, the former are based on the latter.

Outline of Russia's Relationship to Europe and Germany

It is important to recognize that Russia's influence on Europe and not the least on Central Europe, has consistently increased since the days of Tsar Peter the Great.[1] A simple look at the historical-political map will show this more clearly: In the middle of the eighteenth century, the western border of the Tsar's empire was still along the Duna and Dnieper rivers, just west of Smolensk und Kiev. Today, 200 years later, the Soviet-Russian military empire reaches to the gates of the city of Hamburg, to the Elbe River, and to the Thuringian Forest; it includes Bohemia, which Bismarck once called the "Citadel of Europe." This means that the western frontier of the Russian empire has been moved even several hundred miles farther westward of the line from Stettin to Trieste which anti-Tsarist journalist Karl Marx had predicted more than 100 years ago.

As a result of World War II, Russia today rules over half of Europe and half of Germany. The—still—remaining free part of the continent and of Germany stretches like a narrow strip, almost like a rug at the doorsteps of the Soviets' *de facto* western border. Without the United States' commitment in Europe since World War II, this relic-continent sooner or later after 1945 would have been subjected to full Soviet hegemony. If a connecting line between Moscow and Paris is drawn, then Russia's western border 200 years ago extended to the mark on this line tantamount to one fifth of the distance; today, it extends to the four-fifths mark on this line (at the crossing point of the line with the western border of East Germany— also called "Moscow's farthest western province") and the leaders of the Soviet Union have not ceased hoping to also bring the last fifth under their control. At that time a United States that has been pushed back to the western hemisphere, would no longer hold a globally relevant political position. Politically, geographically, militarily and strategically, the Soviet Union today at least is still at the peak of its position of power in Europe and in Germany—a position that is backed solidly by its position as a superpower.

How could all this happen? One first will have to concede that Hitler's imperialist policy vis-à-vis Russia substantially contributed to the collapse not only of the German position within Central Europe, but also of the European system of states as a whole. At the end of World War II Germany and Europe were a vacuum of political power which the main victor nation on the continent of course intended to make maximum use of—and succeeded in doing. Hitler's unleashing the war on September 1, 1939, however, would not have been possible without the non-aggression treaty with Stalin of August 23, 1939. This agreement was directed against the European settlement of 1919, the destruction of which both dictators intended to be the decisive breakthrough for each of their—naturally totally contrary—political-ideological goals. In this sense, the Hitler-Stalin Pact has remained until today the pivotal point of the Russian-European and the Russian-German relationships.

But beyond this it is important to understand the entire context of this relationship since the time of Peter the Great, a context under the banner of Russia's consistent advancement westward, towards Europe. The end of the Nordic War (1721) resulted in opening the Russian "window towards the West" on the Baltic Sea. During the Seven Years War against the Prussia of Frederick the Great, the Tsarist empire had become a member of the anti-Prussian alliance, and Russian troops for the first time advanced to Eastern Prussia, to the Oder River and temporarily to Berlin.

Decisive for the Russian grope for the West, however, were the three divisions of Poland (1772, 1793, 1795), the territorial lion's share of which became Russia's. The Tsarist empire thus became the immediate neighbor of both Central European monarchies, the Prussia of the Hohenzollerns and the Habsburg empire. In 1815, Russia's western frontier was extended, with the acquisition of "Congress-Poland," to Central Europe. Napoleon's hegemony already could hardly have been destroyed by the rest of Europe without Russian concurrence. As of 1815, the Tsarist empire became a recognized member of the community of European powers. It played a role as a senior partner towards Prussia, based on dynastic connections between the Hohenzollerns and the Romanovs. Its veto in 1848–1849 largely helped to prevent the success of the German Unification Movement of the Frankfurt Paul's Cathedral. In 1848, Tsarist troops saved the Habsburg emperor from revolution, especially in Hungary. Bismarck could only establish the German-Prussian Reich because his diplomacy succeeded in using the weakness and isolation of Russia after the Crimean War. Tsar Alexander II finally put up with Bismarck's solution, but his state chancellor Gortchakov was not at all pleased with the new status in Central Europe of 1871.[2] More and more frequently, voices of the growingly nationalist-oriented public opinion of the Tsarist empire warned against the danger of the new German position of power.[3] Since the time of the 1878 crisis in the Orient, which Bismarck attempted temporarily to solve at the Berlin Congress as the "honest mediator," two things became apparent regarding Tsarist Russia's ambitions in the age of industrialization and imperialism. Firstly, it set out to implement its supposedly "historic rights" to the Bosporus and the Dardanelles, and secondly, it was sure of its responsibility for the "slavic brother nations" in Eastern Europe and in the Balkan region. This was bound to result in the destruction of the Ottoman as well as the Habsburg monarchies: The way to Berlin, as some pan-Slavic instigators said, would be via Constantinople and Vienna. The days of the conservative Holy Alliance of the three empires were succeeded by the option of St. Petersburg for republican France, on whose capital Russia's industrialization became dependent. Also, in the German-Russian relationship, the classical reason-of-state was increasingly replaced by the rough categories of the era of nationalism and social-Darwinist imperialism. On both sides, the irresponsible media increasingly spoke of a "final battle between Germans and Slavs." After the so-called "reinsurance treaty" was not renewed by Berlin in 1890 (leading to Bismarck's resignation), the Russian leaders feared their isolation in Europe and made friends with Paris; Germany, therefore, feared being "encircled" by the "steamroller" of the Tsarist military power, especially after Russia returned its attention again to Europe after losing its war against Japan. Plans for war were developed by both sides. On the German side, German Baltic publicists especially developed an ideology of hatred and fear towards Russia; pan-Slavic and all-German extremism grew alternately. Many politicians and military officers in Berlin believed that Russia intended to overthrow Austria-Hungary and, thus, to become the predominant power in Europe. The assassination of the Habsburg crown prince Franz Ferdinand was interpreted as the trigger for such a scenario.

The decision of the German army and government leaders in 1917 to use Lenin's revolutionaries to overthrow the Tsarist empire and, thus, to end the two-front war was an example of how easily little day-to-day political calculations can produce unanticipated long-term historical consequences. In the peace of Brest-Litovsk (March 5, 1918), pan-German tendencies temporarily surfaced: Russia was to be pushed back to its historical core territory around Moscow, while the Baltic states and the Ukraine were to be cut off from Russia, and Poland was to be reestablished. The victory of the Bolsheviks in the civil war and the German defeat in the West reversed this extreme variant of dismemberment. Poland, which was extended eastward, the Baltic states, and Finland became part of the new European order of states in 1919; and the new Bolshevik regime, weakened by war and civil war, was forced to accept this. As a counterthrust, however, Lenin wanted to carry the revolution to Central and Western Europe. The establishment of Soviet republics in Bavaria and Hungary in 1919 and Communist uprisings in the Ruhr area in 1921 and in Saxony and Thuringia in 1923 were part of this revolutionary strategy that failed when the Weimar Republic stabilized in 1924. Lenin's successor, Stalin, concluded from this fact that the phase of the revolutionary "full-tide" had ended for the time being. A phase of revolutionary "low tide" had now to allow for the "establishment of socialism in one country" in order to prepare for the next phase of the revolutionary world process, which, according to Stalin's Marxist-Leninist convictions, had to emerge out of the "inevitability" of further wars between the capitalist-imperialist states. Stalin's long-term revolutionary strategy was made clear in his speech at the plenary session of the Central Committee of the Soviet Communist Party on January 19, 1925, in which he said,

> The basic and new fact in the foreign political relations . . . is that there has been, between our country, which establishes socialism, and the countries of

the capitalist world, a certain temporary balance of power which marks the current phase of "peaceful co-existence" of the country of the Soviets and the countries of capitalism. What we temporarily considered a breathing-time after the war has become a breathing-time stretching over an entire period. . . . Should, however, war begin, then we will not passively look on—we will have to take action, but we will be the last ones to take action. And we will take action in order to thrust the decisive weight into the scales, a weight that will turn the scale.[4]

This was a draft sketch of Stalin's policy for the following years until his pact with Hitler in 1939: The point was to use the "contradictions" among the imperialist nations stemming from the "monopoly-capitalist interests" for profit as best as he could and to prevent their unified front against the Soviet Union. With a "strategy of the triangle," the Soviet leadership could alternately cooperate with either one of the opposing parties in the "imperialist camp": The Treaty of Rapallo with Germany (April 1922) helped to overcome the Soviet isolation during the first postwar years. Later, Stalin implemented his Comintern strategy against "social fascism," that is, against the social democrats, and, thusly, *de facto* supported Hitler's assumption of power. Stalin apparently expected the speedy outbreak of the "second imperialist war" according to Marxist laws. He told the leading KPD (German Communist Party) functionary, Heinz Neumann in 1931, "Don't you believe, too, Neumann, that if the nationalists (i.e., Nazis; K.-H.) seize power in Germany, they would be exclusively busy dealing with the West such that we can set up socialism without disturbance?"[5] Hitler's vehement revisionary policies towards the Versailles treaty settlement after 1934 made Stalin switch, as a counterweight, to the new Comintern strategy of the "Anti-fascist Front." However, when the Western nations failed to prevent Hitler's advances in Austria and Czechoslovakia, Stalin turned to Hitler as a calculated step to press him into unleashing war and to exploit then the "contradictions of imperialism" (August 23, 1939). With his pact with Hitler, Stalin not only was able to cancel Russia's territorial losses at the end of World War I (eastern Poland, the Baltic region, Finland, Bessarabia); he also gained time to improve his arms buildup and industry. At the end of a war in the West, which Stalin believed would follow the model of the First World War, he expected, at the end of the war a new phase of "fulltide" in the revolutionary process in Europe to begin. The Soviet Union then, at the most favorable time and the most profitable side, would be able to throw its "decisive weight into the scales."[6]

"The Russian-German agreement was the trigger for the Second World War. Soviet historiography has since attempted to deny his causal connection to order to blame Hitler and the Western powers for the war." However, there can be no doubt that the Soviets knew that the pact with

Hitler meant war, and they feared only one thing in the summer of 1939: a postponement of its outbreak.[7]

The Political-psychological Situation
of the Germans since World War II

Depolitization in the Federal Republic of Germany

It is not possible sufficiently to assess—especially abroad—the current situation and possible future perspectives of the German question and the chances for its solution without considering the internal, politico-psychological situation of the Germans. The collapse of 1945 and the subsequent national partition have wrought deep wounds in the German political consciousness; if they did not destroy the German sense of identity, they severely weakened it in various aspects. Also the "political culture" in the two German states, the Federal Republic of Germany and the so-called German Democratic Republic (GDR), has developed rather differently since 1945 based on contrary political-social conditions.

The founding consensus of the Federal Republic was based "on the desire of the large majority of the population to establish, from the ruins of the Hitler-Reich, a free democracy of the Western style, and not to become the subjects of yet another, this time communist party, dictatorship."[8] The option to decide in favor of the West thus meant preferring freedom for the larger part of the country over a unification under the banner of Communism. This decision, however, was taken with the understanding that the economic and political stabilization of the western part of Germany was the first step towards regaining freedom for the *entire* country. Especially the politicians of the new democratic beginning—most of whom had been in political life already in the Weimar Republic—understood the founding of the Federal Republic as an expression of the national and democratic right to self-determination, as a continuation of the German state, and as an act of political and national self-assertion against Soviet expansion. This political desire is expressed in the solemn preamble of the Basic Law (constitution) of 1949:

> Conscious of their responsibility before God and men, animated by the resolve to preserve their national and political unity and to serve peace in the world as an equal partner in a united Europe, desiring to give a new order to political life for a transitional period, (the German people) have enacted, by virtue of their constituent power, this Basic Law for the Federal Republic of Germany. They have also acted on behalf of those Germans to whom participation was

denied. The entire German people are called upon to achieve in free self-determination the unity and freedom of Germany.

Although the fathers of the constitution in 1949 understood the Basic Law explicitly as a provisional constitution "for a transitional period," they set it up as a liberal model-constitution without reference to the national division. In the beginning, the occupation powers took care of external security. Later, membership in NATO served this purpose. Membership in NATO and the German defense contribution were understood as something like an insurance premium for peaceful normality. However, getting accustomed to the protection of the alliance, and the feeling that it was convenient to rest in the shade of the "Big Brother" United States, caused the West Germans to focus their energies primarily on economic reconstruction and the private chase for happiness. The emphasis on individualism and consumption became the most conspicuous new standards of value. A welfare-state democracy developed oriented primarily to domestic policy, social achievements and distribution. The pluralistic interest-bargaining of such a society tends to reduce politics because it denies the insight that every society "has a higher task."[9] Such a society tends to lure the citizen into misusing his freedom instead of reminding him of his duties. It makes egocentrism the standard and undermines, in the long run, the sense of belonging together as a community, particularly with regard to the national issue. The foreign policy of such a welfare state democracy tends, out of its indolence, simply to accept so-called "realities" and to praise itself for such *Realpolitik*. Raymond Aron has branded such consciousness in Western democracies as "loss of sense of reality" especially with regard to foreign political questions.[10] This is particularly true for the Federal Republic of Germany. It is even intensified by the specifically "German" tendency to go from one extreme to the other; i.e., to want to be "more holy than the pope" (a German saying), or else to be "150 percent." This tendency to extremes led from the "obsession with power" during the time of Hitler to the "oblivion of power" of many West Germans today,[11] "from the omnipresence of nationalism to the glorification of everything foreign; from the urge to meddle with things everywhere to the will not to commit themselves anywhere. . . . They (the Germans) have been conditioned such that they begin trembling every time someone even speaks about power—which of course makes them susceptible to any teaching that would weaken them" (according to French author Alain de Bénoist).[12]

In this respect, everything we see today with the so-called peace movement or the "Greens" in West Germany is in no way surprising, because it only continues a certain fundamental mentality in West Germany in the second generation after the war. Here, the protestant-rigorous argument is repeated of (former president) Gustav Heinemann from the time of his debate with Konrad Adenauer in the 1950s about the issue of a German defense contribution: "God struck the weapons out of our hands, we must never pick them up again." And here, the Federal Republic and its Western option are totally rejected "with rage and grief" as the member of the Bundestag, Greens deputy Dr. Antje Vollmer, recently stated in a debate there. Adenauer is being branded the big bogeyman, "a man of the West, a man of big capital and an anti-communist." The Greens' platform is a result of the reverse conclusion: neutralistic distance towards the "monopoly-capitalist" West, a wornout "socialism" inimical to industry, and a united-front policy with Communists while at the same time making the Soviet Union appear harmless. [Some of the Greens and many of the pacifists have raised objections, although perhaps not as vigorously as they should have to just this.] And, of course, guilt and national self-accusation is part of the partner. When Mrs. Vollmer says, "We belong to the daughters and sons of a nation that is the major responsible one for two world wars" (the responsibility of *all* nations for World War I is as little taken notice of as the *joint* conspiracy of both totalitarian dictators against peace in the summer of 1939). Connected to this national self-hatred is a political teaching for salvation of such nature and belief that only oneself possesses the recipe for a durable peace. And all this culminates in the goal to rescue themselves from all the quarrels in this world to an island of neutrality, and, as the rest, to accept the Germany policy of the Soviet Union together with the demand, to recognize all realities "as they came to be in Germany after World War II."

In this political worldview of the peace movement and the Greens (both are largely identical) can clearly and tangibly be noticed the long-term effects of a consumer-oriented indolence that had been accepted in West Germany for years, and the effects of the lack of a sense of history that was often created systematically. This led to the political loss of the sense of reality and to a tendency towards political-national self-destruction. In addition, no few film productions from here and abroad carried this type of one-sided, manipulatory and self-destructive attempt to deal with the past (Vergangenheitsbewaltigung) into every household in recent years via television and repeatedly tried "to make out of the entire German history an album of criminals" (as ex-Chancellor Helmut Schmidt put it in the German Bundestag).

The Discussion on "National Identity" in the Federal Republic.

The picture of the politico-psychological situation in West Germany would not be complete, however, if I did not report on the public debate, going on for several years now, about *who* the Germans actually are, whether they are still a nation and want to be one; expressed in political terms, the question discussed is what this state, the Federal Republic of Germany can really be and wants to be, i.e., also the question of its "all-German" responsibility.

A "disturbed psychological economy," a "block in historical conscious-ness" and "national paralysis of emotion," developed in West Germany after 1945 as a reaction to the dark chapters of Nazism, the political disaster of 1945 and the subsequent division of Germany.[15] It is revealing that this debate today extends from the national-conservative part of the population through the whole political-ideological spectrum, including the deep left beyond the Social Democratic Party. SPD party manager Peter Glotz in a guideline essay in 1980, "On Political Identity," said: "Our full concen-tration, focussed on the material reconstruction of the destroyed country, did not allow us the time to produce something like a new identity. For this reason, there is this helpless turning away of a large part of the young generation. . . . However, in the long run, a well-organized network of goods and services alone cannot keep a society together."[16] Political sci-entist at the University of Frankfurt, Irving Fetscher, wrote, "After many decades of maximum distance to Germany which with some was expressed in socialist internationalism and with others in cosmopolitan consumption-ism, the need, the desire reawoke to be 'oneself', to be also nationally something unique."[17] Even some members of the younger generation who come from the far left former "extraparliamentary opposition" oppose the "tradition of self-accusation" the German leftists often follow: "Germany is being painted in the darkest colors: the whole world is better—only Germany is the perfect horror."[18] The son of Willy Brandt, Peter Brandt, who is substantially farther left than his father and an assistant professor of history in West Berlin, criticized in the same way the numerous substitute-identifications of the past decades which the young generation used: from Ho Chi Minh to Mao Tse-tung to Fidel Castro or today's Daniel Ortega of Nicaragua. Peter Brandt also demands that the current problem in the national identity of the Germans be overcome, especially "in a world of unbroken or rather convulsively awakening national identity."[19] And likewise democratic conservatives criticize particularly the historical vac-uum prevalent in West Germany in which Germans retreat into the "quiet corners of a petty-bourgeois idyll."[20] This national failing is seen as a major cause for rebellion, especially among the academic youth and e.g., for "conscientious objectors."[21] Democratic conservatives, in light of the global correlation of forces, consider Germany's alliance with the Western democracies as inevitable, and they also recognize the ethnic, historical and political points they share. This cannot, however, mean, in their opin-ion, that Germany should surrender her national history with its many positive achievements such as the formation of a constitutional state in Prussia or the modern social welfare state created by Bismarck.[22] In their opinion West Germany must not become an a-historical and faceless subsidiary of the American industrial and consumer society.[23] Instead, Germany should make efforts to combine democracy and nation, a task for a creative synthesis yet to be undertaken. Professor Schwarz demanded that Germany achieve a reasonable medium between the will for peace and the instinct for power: "A country whose government almost exclusively speaks about peace policies and whose public preferably dreams of a world without power, would be doomed . . . in a world full of power politics and misuse of power, or else would be . . . merely . . . a vassal state within the European empire of the Soviet Union."[24] Without regaining such "moral factors" (Clausewitz), the Federal Republic cannot be a stable partner in the alliance, because these factors are more important than the number of soldiers or the amount of weapons—not to mention a policy aimed at a long-term restoration of political unity and the national right to self-determination for the Germans, for which these moral factors are indispensable.

At the left and right fringes of this debate, we find the concepts of neutrality for both German states, or of a neutral reunified Germany to stand between the two power blocs. At these fringes, various resentments breed—be it against the monopoly-capitalist "Reagan-America," on the left side, or against the "servility towards the victors" on the right side, where there is talk about the "reproach of fascism and disturbed self-consciousness."[25] While right-wingers think in terms of a historical concept of a Germany between East and West, as has been the case under Bismarck or for the Weimar Republic, left-wingers pursue the image of a "third way" between capitalism and the Soviet system, usually in the form of a confederation of both German states with a "socialist" order. The majority of the population, however, is aware that it is impossible today "to pull the blanket of neutrality over our heads" (West German president von Weizsäcker) and that a neutral nationalism offers no real prospect for German policy in the near future.

The National Discussion in East Germany and its changes.

The GDR (East Germany) developed out of a deep contradiction: its leadership for decades after the war emphasized national demands and simultaneously supported the Soviet policy of "social change" and the establishment of socialism right after the war despite national separation. Its official founding date is October 7, 1949. But it was already de facto founded on April 21, 1946, when the SED (Socialist Unity Party, the East

German Communist Party) was founded by forcibly fusing the KPD and SPD. This is so, because the eastern European peoples' democracies are under the complete control of their Marxist-Leninist parties. The first constitution of the GDR was based on that of the Weimar Republic and was presented as a constitution of the future German core state. In this respect, it mirrored the Basic Law of the Federal Republic. In 1954 East German leaders still spoke of "the nation as split into two states" and saw the GDR as the model for a future all-German socialist state. In 1957–1958, then SED chief Walter Ulbricht suggested a step-by-step approach of the two contradictory social systems via a "confederation" and called the restoration of the unity of the nation "inevitable." The second GDR constitution of 1968 in its preamble spoke of its "responsibility to lead the way into a future of peace and of socialism for the entire German nation." It called the GDR in its Article 1 "a socialist state of the German nation."

As a reaction to the West German government's Ostpolitik in 1970, the SED leaders changed their course towards greater demarcation: They now strictly differentiated between the "socialist German nation" in the GDR and the "bourgeois German nation" in West Germany. These two had no points in common and their unification was as impossible as that "of fire and water." The continuation of the "German nation in two states" emphasized by the then government of Brandt was now rejected as "nationalistic demagoguery." The continuation of a joint German nation as a foundation for "special relations" of both German states towards each other was now strictly denied. There was no longer, in the viewpoint of the SED, a "German question," "but there are simply two socially contradictory German states independent of one another" (as the member of the East Berlin Politburo Hermann Axen said).[26] And this line was finally anchored in the changed constitution of 1974. The GDR is now referred to as "a socialist state of workers and farmers" (Art. 1) which is "forever and irrevocably allied with the Union of Socialist Soviet Republics" and is "an inseparable part of the socialist community of states" (Art. 6). However, unclear points continued to exist. Did not, in this case, the GDR, the SED, and numerous organizations of the regime such as the "Free German Association of Trade Unions," the "Free German Youth," or the official party paper "New Germany" have to change their names? How did the citizens of the GDR have to fill out the registration forms in hotels abroad? General Secretary Honecker himself had to clear up the matter with the following instruction: "citizenship GDR—nationality German."

In the meantime, the new discussion about the right and future of the nations—which has been ongoing for long in Eastern Europe and the Soviet Union—has also reached East Germany. Politically the GDR leadership still insists on full recognition of its citizenship by the Federal Republic.

However, since about 1980 the SED leaders—evidently because of Honecker's personal initiative—began using the national motive and the "positive traditions of German history" for the "socialist German national state" GDR in place of the ideological forces of integration of Marxism-Leninism that were hardly effective anymore. In this respect the GDR lagged severely behind the socialist brother states of Eastern Europe. East German leaders could study the example of West Germany to see what negative effects the loss of national identity and of history could have on the integrating and legitimizing forces of a country, especially in a situation of division. Slightly before, and parallel to the identity debate in West Germany, the political leadership in the GDR dealt with the same issue. The resort to German history is not limited any more to only the Prussian reformers of 1807–1815 or to the Peasant War of 1525. Even Martin Luther, Frederick the Great (whose monument was returned to the East Berlin government quarters in the avenue Unter den Linden), and Otto von Bismarck are now being integrated into East Germany's account of history. Already earlier, the GDR had much less difficulty in cultivating certain Prussian traditions than did West Germany. The "National People's Army" of the GDR, for example, is in its entire appearance insistently Prussian. Furthermore, substantial amounts of money were made available for the restoration of historically valuable buildings in Berlin, Dresden, Erfurt, Leipzig, etc. There can be no doubt that such ostentatious measures contribute towards strengthening the collective self-consciousness of many citizens even if they reject the regime. Apart from this, many behavioral patterns and values upheld by the people in the GDR now appear much more "German" and often more old-fashioned than those in the Federal Republic, which by bomb-raids, quick reconstruction and its "economic miracle" was thoroughly "modernized" and also Americanized. Charles de Gaulle once spoke of "Prussia and Saxony" when talking about the GDR. As a matter of fact, Prussian discipline and willingness to serve as well as submission to the authorities were joined in a union with Saxon craftsmanship and industrial diligence—a union that offered valuable and characteristic elements for the establishment of a modern "socialist industrial society."[27]

Political culture and national mentality cannot be represented by statistical figures; they are formed and also re-formed by concrete social and political conditions, which between East and West Germany today differ considerably. Contrary to the mostly individualistic people in West Germany, East Germans are much more strongly oriented towards the political and social entirety, even when they withdraw as much as possible into private niches as a reaction to being constantly used socially.[28] Because the people in the GDR, compared to the West Germans, have in many ways had to deal with a more difficult fate, their national feeling has remained much more vivid, and less weakened by individual egoism than that in West Germany. Of course, this new turn towards national history and tradition by the SED regime is opportunistic. However, it also evidences skill in combining regime interests with the needs of the people. In 1981, an SED publication said that "the nation of the GDR was neither capable of existing nor acting . . . without a socialist German national feeling." And it would be wise to see in this new cultural-political course not only a policy for stabilizing and legitimizing the status quo; it is also (according to a "dialectical" approach) an important contribution to a long-term policy of national reunion under the leadership of the "socialist Piedmont" of the GDR. In his speech in Jena in February of 1981, Erich Honecker slightly lifted the veil from such long-term planning when he said in the direction of the Federal Republic, "Be careful! Socialism will one day also knock at your door (strong applause), and when this day comes, when the toilers of the Federal Republik start . . . restructuring . . . the Federal Republic of Germany, then the question of the unification of both German states can be put anew (strong applause). There should be no doubt as to how we would decide at that time" (long applause).[29]

The Jena speech of the General Secretary was an appeal to the doubtlessly strong pan-national feelings in the GDR. They were not only cited in the writings of authors loyal to the system, but also of authors critical of the system who had to leave the "first workers and farmers state on German soil"—authors like Günter Kunert, Sarah Kirsch, Reiner Kunze, and even such a Marxist author as Wolf Biermann. Even within the SED this critical approach was reflected, for example, in the "Manifesto of the Alliance of Democratic Communists," published in 1978, which not only contained fundamental criticism by "secondary rank" Party members of the "dictatorship of the clique of secretary and politburo and of the bureaucracy over the proletariat and the entire people. . . ." The "Manifesto" also proposed the concept of an "offensive national policy which aims at the reunification of Germany, in which Social Democrats, Socialists and democratic communists have the upper hand over the conservative forces."[30] As a precondition for that it mentioned the withdrawal of all foreign troops, leaving the military blocs, peace treaties with both German states, a guarantee for neutrality by the Security Council of the United Nations, complete disarmament and the channeling of the thus saved monies for arms to the Third World. The Manifesto even suggested concrete interim steps such as GDR membership in GATT, its cooperation with the World Bank, convertability of the GDR Mark, unhindered travel between both German states and generous cooperative relations. This program was rounded off with this inner party underground opposition opposing strongly the "colonial system of the red imperialism."[31]

The Solution to the German Question
as Part of a Strategy of Change.

Farewell to the Illusions of Détente.

I should like now to advocate an offensive political strategy. "Strategy of change" is intended to suggest the restoration of the priority of *political* thinking over military-technical concerns. Strategy of change means anticipating an internal peaceful change in the world and not the least in the Soviet system, and to support it however and wherever possible—instead of trying to prevent it by a policy of status quo, via an objective coalition with the *Nomenklatura* class. Such a policy of change is related to the forces of history, because history knows only constant change. Instead of treating the mere symptoms usually via an appeasing détente, a policy of change aims at unleashing the true healing forces, i.e., the real and actual abolition of the *causes* of friction in the world, in Europe, and in Germany.

The Soviet leaders have succeeded in convincing the West of their own interpretation of détente as a measure to secure peace. In fact, however, this interpretation was and is a smoke screen behind which is hidden a policy of expanding the Soviet positions and of changing the global correlation of forces in its own favor.[32] The Soviet Union rigorously misused their interpretation of détente to launch a new wave of expansion from Afghanistan to Africa and Latin America. While Moscow means by peaceful coexistence continuation of "class struggle on the world-level" short of global military confrontation. The West often does not even know that a war is going on at all or that the Soviet Union with this kind of Third World war aims at a "victory without war."

While in the 1970s the Soviet Union expanded its influence to Southeast Asia, Africa and the Middle East and while Admiral Gorshkov set up his worldwide operating fleet, while Moscow was well on its way to endanger the sources of raw material and the sea links of Western Europe (and Japan), left-liberal and socialist media in the West spoke of the Soviets' "fear of being encircled." By manipulating symbols such as "cold war," détente (to which there was "no alternative"), arms race, peace, etc., the Soviet Union engaged in a revolutionary-psychological diversion—the struggle on the "battlefield of consciousness"—which Stalin had first spoken of.

The children of a peaceful, affluent society such as the Federal Republic often seek an easy escape from power politics into the green fields of individual ethics and conscience. In the German situation after 1945—amputated, controlled, physically and psychologically weakened—they docilely listened to the ideology of liberal internationalism and moralism, which appeared in the form of a reeducation program imposed by the victors. Today they tend to search for world harmony. During the social-democrat/liberal coalition of the 1970s; "conflict," under the banner of a renewed ideology of class struggle, was rediscovered in domestic policy; the notion of an "enemy" was increasingly made into a taboo in the foreign and inter-German policy; a mere "perception of threat" replaced the threat itself; and the Soviet Union and the GDR were declared "security partners." The so-called Ostpolitik was overloaded with a moralism under the slogan of "reconciliation."

What will happen to international morale, if it becomes common practice to justify the acquisition of territory best by expelling the inhabitants and with the—irrefutable after 30 years—yet absolutely cynical argument that those who have since been born there also have a legitimate right to a homeland? What will become of the moral substance of a free nation when she must, for practical political reasons, recognize a totalitarian satellite government, and woo it, although it suppresses 18 million of its own fellow countrymen?

Hans-Peter Schwarz posed this important question, and rightfully so.[33] Within the so-called peace movement this moralism is based on ethical claims for the absolute and on the opinion to successfully deal with international and security policy with the mentality and morality of the small group.[34]

The elite in politics, science, media, and education in West Germany have to learn anew that "liberal democracies must secure their independence, their existence and their welfare within a world of nations, which in many places are under the law of power politics."[35] They must learn that peace policies at any price cannot be the alternative to the totalitarian aggression of Hitler. In 1939, the French were talked into the fake alternative of "Hitler, or war"[36] by the disinformation of the Nazis. They got both. Corresponding to that is today's slogan of "rather red than dead." Only responsible power politics can expose today's pseudo-peace policies in order to prevent both the nuclear holocaust, *and* the Gulag Archipelago.

The first task therefore is the necessity for information and, again, information about the history and policy of the nearly 68-year-old Soviet Union, about the reasons for its victories and failures, its political, social and ideological system; about the facts of today's international constellation; the fight of the Soviet Union in Afghanistan, its support of Nicaragua, its sponsorship of Mengistu in Ethiopia and of the PLO, the size of its nuclear arsenal, its armies, that occupy half of Europe and half of Germany, its fleet at anchor in Vietnam and Africa, its military posture just outside

Hamburg. What must be overcome is the often depressing ignorance of West Germans, and of the West at large, regarding East Germany, its political system, its actual social conditions,[37] the various disinformation about the GDR in schoolbooks, in SED-controlled literature in West Germany, together with the harmonizing (or ideologically intended) concessions of publishing houses, schoolbook publishers and authors, radio and television stations, and so on. Besides keeping a military balance, which is indispensable, there must also be realistic information which should correct unrealistic fear as well as emotional illusions and détente euphoria; this information should thus create the preconditions for legitimate and responsible politics that would truly serve peace through the reduction of the *causes* for tension.

Factors and Premises for a Solution to the German Question.

I shall summarize now the above into theses in order to subsequently make several concluding, prognostic statements.

a. The position in Europe today of the Soviet Union, which divides this continent and Germany right at the center, constituting a half-hegemony that would become a full hegemony without the American counterweight—and the Soviet Union is of course continually seeking that full hegemony—is the result of the political collapse of the European system of states at the end of World War II; from a historical perspective it is also the peak of a continual Russian westward expansion in which the will for expansion played a role as large as that of favorable opportunities, e.g., the Polish division in the eighteenth century made Russia the immediate neighbor to Central Europe; another example is the Hitler-Stalin Pact of 1939 which aimed at a new elimination of Poland.

b. The founding of the Federal Republic of Germany in 1949 meant establishing a partial German state in freedom instead of a German unity under Soviet hegemony. But this did not mean that Germans resigned themselves to partition. A close aide to Chancellor Helmut Kohl, Horst Teltschik, described the position of the Federal government as follows, "Millions of Germans are denied human rights and the right to self-determination. The island position of West Berlin, the wall and barbed wire symbolize in the most impressive way the abnormal nature of the division of Germany." Tension and conflicts in Europe and around Germany will therefore exist as long as their *cause*, namely the division, has not been removed.[38]

c. As long as no peace treaty has been agreed on, the German question remains open not only politically but also by international law. The

Western powers in 1952–1954 in Article 7 of the so-called Germany Convention committed themselves to the common aim of a "reunified Germany enjoying a liberal-democratic constitution like that of the Federal Republic and integrated within the European community." The signatory states agreed "that the final determination of the boundaries of Germany must await such settlement."

d. The treaties of West Germany with the Soviet Union, Poland and East Germany 1970–1972 established the *de facto* recognition of the existing German borders and the renunciation by the West German government of the use of force to change them. But this did not at all affect the rights of the victor nations regarding Germany as a whole nor a final settlement in a peace treaty.

e. In the era of detente some leaders in the West attempted to separate the issues of peace from that of the German question. But that was tantamount to treating the symptoms while failing to solve the problem at its roots. The wall and the monstrous "state border west" of the GDR are the visible, material proof for the fact that Germans are not accustomed to the division and that there is no "normality": "As long as the Brandenburg Gate is closed, the German Question is open."[39]

f. To imagine that the German question be not open any more would not only be a sin against the right to self-determination but to the human rights of the German countrymen in the GDR and their future generations. It would also contradict the fact that there has never been a permanent status quo.

g. Today, the German question seems more open than 10 or 20 years ago. The signs of increasing stiffness and deadlock inside the Soviet Union have contributed to this development just as have national movements in Eastern Europe and even in the Soviet Union. We cannot exclude that the national questions will be the question of the twenty-first century and that it will be stronger tomorrow than the question of classes.[40]

h. The current debate in the Federal Republic of Germany about national identity and the efforts of the SED leaders for legitimacy by returning to national history are both consequences of these Eastern European developments; they are also a reaction to the shock experienced at the time of collapse after World War II with its consequences of the loss of history and the tendency to turn away from politics.

i. In order to call the Germans back into history, which is necessary for the solution of the German question, and into a politically meaningful and responsible existence, it is necessary first to overcome the political and national paralysis so rampant in West Germany. The Germans will only be able to take on their historical-political role in Central Europe when they regain natural self-consciousness and renewed patriotism.

The German Potential Developments.

It's not up to a simple historian to step on the field of "Sovietology" with its various and contradictory judgments and prognoses regarding future possibilities of development in the Soviet Union and in Eastern Europe. However, three preliminary judgments seem important to me:

—Different developments in the Soviet sphere also will each imply different possibilities to the solution of the German question;
—This does not mean, however, that the West (including West Germany) would have no influence on the developments there and that they should have to wait passively. Robert F. Byrnes recently pointed out correctly that developments in the West are in correlation to the decisions taken by the Soviet leaders. A weak West and chaotic developments in the Third World for example would not be helpful in making the Soviet Union modify its system or moderate its foreign political ambitions.[41] The connection existing between the mental and social disposition of Western societies and nations and their foreign policies is today often too much overlooked;
—I can only agree with Wolfgang Leonhard and other experts who have pointed out that the stability and "monolithic" character of the Soviet system often have been overestimated in the past 40 years, and that events like June 17, 1953, in East Germany, 1956 in Poland and Hungary and the Prague Spring in 1968 and then again the Polish events since 1980 were "surprises" nobody would have dared to predict.[42] This is a fact that shows how fast internal contradictions within the Soviet system can lead to crisis-like explosions.

Let me now shortly sketch three potential developments—"scenarios" regarding possible changes in the Soviet Union and possible effects of them upon the German question:

—A policy of reforms in the Soviet Union involving economic moderni-zation of the system, the leading exponent of which seems to be the new General Secretary would not assist German reunification. Only a few months after his coming into office he once more pulled out the old concepts of "peaceful coexistence" and détente, as always happened in the past when new Soviet leaders had to cope with severe problems at home and were launching reform plans. In this sense the new General Secretary offered to Bonn "normality" despite the partition of our coun-try and despite the fact that the Soviet Union is dominating about 47 percent of Germany within the frontiers of 1937. In the course of "normality," as the Moscow partocracy sees it, favorable trade relations, credits, and transfer of technical know-how are essential for the Soviets. During such a period of modernization of the system the Kremlin must be extremely interested in stable Western frontiers in Europe and Germany. In case the Soviet Union acquires an authoritarian Russian nationalist system, certain reductions of the present global overcommitment could be expected. However it would not be obvious whether such a system would be willing to abandon its European overcommitment as well. On the contrary, it will more likely uphold Russian imperialist interests and pretensions. In this case much would depend upon the strength of the "peoples liberation revolution" in Eastern Europe and within the Russian empire itself.[43]

—More favorable preconditions for overcoming German partition could develop from a consistent process of democratization in the Soviet Union, such as described by Sakharov and others, with the disappearance of the apparatus of oppression, the creation of free trade unions and parties, the change of the Supreme Soviet into an authentic parliament, etc.[44] In such a case a spontaneous and broad popular movement for national unity might be probable in both parts of Germany. In this situation much would depend upon the insight of the leaders of a democratic Russia concerning Russia's real security interests, in other words, upon their insight that a free, democratic and united Germany, friendly towards a democratic Russia, is a far better guarantee of Russian security than the present situation in Central Europe, which is based on force and on the presence of half a million Soviet troops in this region. In this case, the alliances in East and West could be dissolved, the military presence of Russia and the Western powers on German soil could be abolished. Also a peace treaty with a united and free Germany could be made which ends the confrontation of the two superpowers in Europe and brings back to the continent its real political self-determination. After all, the political and military strength of the two great powers in the East and West would continue and thus they would guarantee the future status quo in Europe based on the reunification of the continent in general and of Germany in particular.

Even, however, were the present Soviet regime replaced by a post-Soviet, democratic Russia within its natural frontiers and the present multinational Soviet empire dissolved into nation-states, Europe would want to have a say in the political formation of Germany. The old problem of the "critical mass" of a united Germany in the center of the continent would reappear which Bismarck had to cope with a century ago. That means the question of how large and strong such a united German state could be without threatening its neighbors. Perhaps other European nations would prefer a so-called "Austrian solution" to the German question in which the present "GDR," would be non-Communist and without Russian occupation, but neutral like Austria today. In any case, France and Poland especially would only agree to a reunified Germany *without* the areas to the East of the Oder and the Neisse rivers.

Hardly anyone in Europe today is likely to savor changing the present German status to that of the prewar status quo. Most thoughtful Germans would be satisfied if a minority statute would be enacted that would permit those Germans—probably not too many—who might want to return to their prewar homelands. At any rate no second expulsion could be envisaged. That of 1945 with its frightening and inhumane injustice was sufficient! "Our hopes for national unity are not directed towards the shifting of frontiers, but they must have the aim of modifying the quality of frontiers"[45]—just as has happened within Western Europe and the European Community.

Future German-Polish relations also are closely connected—as in the past—with the future development of Polish-Russian relations. Indeed, everything is connected with everything in Eastern Europe. For example, why should it not be imaginable that the harbor of Stettin would be utilized both by Poland and Germany? In any case it seems to be important to destroy Stalin's diabolic attempt to produce antagonism between Poles and Germans for all eternity with the Oder-Neisse line.

A successful strategy of change in Eastern Europe and Russia could lead to a renewal of old national conflicts in this region that for decades were suppressed by the Soviet imperial power. But, on the other hand, all parties may have learned the lessons of history. It is, of course, an open question, whether the Western European Common Market would be joined by non-Communist Eastern European nations. Much would depend on whether Western Europe would apply its economic strength selfishly or for the purpose of a reasonable partnership with the free peoples in the Eastern parts of our continent.

Even a successful strategy of change in Europe in the framework of which alone a just solution to the German question seems to be possible will not bring a perfectly ideal order. However, all participants would prefer it by far to the status quo. The goal of individual and national freedom is so valuable that the strategy of timid preservation of an unfree, immoral status quo that is dictated by the totalitarian, imperialistic Soviet power and that insults the honor of peoples, should be replaced by a strategy of change.

Alexander Shtromas correctly said at the conclusion of his book *Political Change and Social Development—The Case of the USSR*: "There is no genuine peace without freedom and there is no genuine freedom in a state of 'peace' imposed by coercion, which only suppresses but does not eliminate genuine, deeply-rooted cleavages and conflicts."[46]

And here we are led back to the preconditions for a successful strategy of change to which I drew your attention at the beginning. I should like to summarize them in the words of George F. Kennan who wrote in his *Memoirs*,

> Much depends on health and vigor of our own society. World communism is like a malignant parasite which feeds only on diseased tissue. This is the point at which domestic and foreign policies meet. Every courageous and incisive measure to solve internal problems of our own society, to improve self-confidence, discipline, morale and community spirit of our own people, is a diplomatic victory over Moscow worth a thousand diplomatic notes and joint communiques. If we cannot abandon fatalism and indifference in face of deficiences of our own society, Moscow will profit—Moscow cannot help profiting by them in its foreign policies.[47]

Notes

1. The literature on the subject is abundant; fundamental seems to be Lothar Ruehl: *Russlands Weg zur Weltmacht* (Russias Road to World Power), Düsseldorf and Wien 1981; compare also: Heinrich Jordis von Lohausen: *Mut zur Macht* (Courage for Power), Leoni 1981.
2. A good summary I find in the Freiburg MA-thesis by Wittigo von Rabenau: "Russland als potentieller Gegner des Deutschen Reiches" (Russia as potential enemy of the German Reich) 1904–1914 (University of Freiburg 1985).
3. See Jean-Baptiste Duroselle: "Die europäischen Staaten und die Grundung des Deutschen Reiches" (The European States and the Foundation of the German Reich), in: Theodor Schieder (ed.): *Reichsgründung* 1870/71 (The Foundation of the Reich 1870/71), Stuttgart 1970 and Eberhard Kolb: "Russland und die Gründung des Norddeutschen Bundes" (Russia and the Foundation of the Northgerman Federation), in: R. Dietrich (ed.): *Europa und der Norddeutsche Bund* (Europe and the Northgerman Federation) Berlin 1966.
4. See J.W. Stalin: *Werke*, Bd. VII (Works, vol. VII), Ost-Berlin 1952, p. 11 compare my article "Peaceful coexistence and détente," in: P. Gutjahr-Löser/ K. Hornung (eds.): *Politisch-Pädagogisches Handwörterbuch* (Political-Pedagogical Manual), sec. enlarged ed. Munich 1985.
5. See Margarate Buber-Neumann: *Kriegsschauplätze der Weltrevolution. Ein Bericht aus der Praxis der Komintern 1919–1933* (Theatres of World Revolution. A Report on the Practice of the Comintern), Stuttgart 1967, p. 332.

6. See Philipp W. Fabry: *Der Hitler-Stalin-Pakt 1939–1941* (The Hitler-Stalin Treaty), Darmstadt 1962; Andreas Hillgruber/Klaus Hildebrandt: *Kalkül zwischen Macht und Ideologie—Der Hitler-Stalin-Pakt: Parallel bis heute?* (Calculation between Power and Ideology—The Hitler-Stalin Treaty: Parallels until today?), Zurich 1980; Bianka Pietrow: *Stalinismus—Sicherheit—Offensive. Das Dritte Reich in der Konzeption der sowjetischen Aussenpolitik 1933–1941* (Stalinism—Security—Offensive. The Third Reich in the Conception of Soviet Foreign Policy), Melsungen 1983 (Kasseler Forschungen zur Zeitgeschichte—Kassel Research of Contemporary History, Bd. 2, vol. 2); Ernst Topitsch: *Stalins Krieg. Die sowjetische Langzeitstrategie gegen den Westen als rationale Machtpolitik* (Stalins War. The Soviet Long-Range Strategy against the West as Rational Power Policy), München 1985.

7. Ruehl (see note 1), p. 346; Stalin negotiated at the same time with Great Britain and France and with Berlin in order to cover his best costs from the German side finally.

8. Richard Löwenthal: "Vom Kalten Krieg zur Ostpolitik" (From Cold War to Ostpolitik), in: R. Löwenthal/K.P. Schwarz (eds.): *Die zweite Republik—25 Jahre Bundesrepublik Deutschland. Eine Bilanz* (The Second Republic—25 Years Federal Republic of Germany. A Balance), Stuttgart 1974, p. 604.

9. John Kenneth Galbraith: *Gesellschaft im Überfluss* (The Affluent Society) München and Zürich 1958, p. 338.

10. Raymond Aron: *Plädoyer für das dekadente Europa* (Plea for Decadent Europa), Düsseldorf 1977.

11. Hans Peter Schwarz: *Die gezähmten Deutschen. Von der Machtbesessenheit zur Machtvergessenheit* (The Tamed Germans. From Obsession of Power to Oblivion of Power), Stuttgart 1985.

12. Alain de Benoist: "In aller Freundschaft. Kritisches über die Duetschen" (In all Friendship. Critical Remarks on the Germans), in: *Criticón*, Munich No. 60/61, 1980, pp. 199 ff.

13. See Klaus Hornung (ed.): *Frieden ohne Utopie* (Peace without Utopia), Krefeld 1983.

14. Dr. Antje Vollmer in the German Bundestag September 29, 1984.

15. Professor Erich Kosthorst: "Stellungnahme in einer Öffentlichen Anhörung des Ausschusses für Innerdeutsche Beziehungen 1976," in: *Die Deutsche Frage in der Politischen Bildung—Zur Sache. Themen parlamentarischer Beratung* Heft 2/1978 (Statement in a Public Hearing of the Bundestag Committee for the Relations within Germany, in: The German Question in Political Education—Topics of Parliamentary Debate No. 2/1978.

16. Peter Glotz: "Über Politische Identität" (On Political Identity), in: *Merkur* (Monthly) No. 12/1980, pp. 1177.

17. Iring Fetscher: "Die Suche nach der nationalen Identität," in: J. Habermas (Hg.): *Stichworte zur 'Geistigen Situation der Zeit'*, Bd. 1: *Republik Nation*, Edition Surkamp Bd. 1000 (In Search for National Identity—Notes on the Intellectual Situation of Our Time), p. 123.

18. Thomas Schmid in: H. Brüggemann (ed.): *Über den Mangel an politischer*

Kultur in Deutschland (On the Lack of Political Culture in Germany), Berlin 1972, p. 112.

19. Peter Brandt and Herbert Ammon (eds.): *Die Linke und die Nationale Fragen* (The Left and the National Question), Reinbek 1981, p. 25.

20. Günther Zehm: "Wie Benjamin Franklin zum Ahnherrn der Bundesrepublik gen den ist" (How Benjamin Franklin became an Ancestor of the Federal Republic *Die Welt* No. 232/Oct. 4th, 1980.)

21. Heinz Karst: "Wider die nationale Erniedrigung der Deutschen" (Against National Humiliation of the Germans), in: G.K. Kaltenbrunner (ed.): *Was ist deutsch? Die Unvermeidlichkeit, eine Nation zu sein* (What is German? The Inevitability being a Nation Herderbücherei INITIATIVE Vol. 39/1980, p. 72.

22. See note 20.

23. Thus already in 1965 the then Chairman of the German Bundestag Dr. Eugen Gerstenmaier (*Welt am Sonntag*, December 27, 1964).

24. Hans-Peter Schwarz s. note 11.

25. Professor Bernard Willms, see note 12.

26. The position of the GDR is represented in the book of Professor Alfred Kosing: Nation in *Geschichte und Gegenwart. Studien zur historisch-materialistischen Theorie der Nation* (Nation in Past and Present Studies in the Historical-Materialistic Theory of the Nation), Ost-Berlin 1976; a fine summary by Jens Hacker: "Das nationale Dilemma der DDR" (The National Dilemma of the GDR), in: B. Meissner/J. Hacker (eds.): *Die Nation in östlicher Sicht* (The Nation in Eastern Perspective), Studien zur Deutschlandfrage, Bd. 1, Berlin 1977 (Studies in the German Question).

27. Hermann Rudolph: *Die Gesellschaft der DDR—eine deutsche Möglichkeit* (The Society of the GDR—a German Possibility?, Munchen 1973.

28. Günter Gaus: *Wo liegt Deutschland? Eine Ortsbestimmung* (Where is Germany Situated?), Hamburg 1983.

29. Thus in the official daily of the German Socialist Unity Party (SED) *Neues Deutschland* (New Germany) February 16, 1981.

30. *DDR—Manifest der Opposition. Eine Dokumentation* (GDR—Manifesto of Opposition. A Documentation), München 1978, p. 21.

31. See note 30, p. 15.

32. See Jean-Paul Picaper: *DDR-Bild im Wandel* (Picture of the GDR in Change), Berlin 1980, p. 15 and Klaus Hornung: "Der Politisch-Revolutionäre Krieg der Gegenwart. Abschied von den Illusionen der Entspannung" (The Political Revolutionary War of Our Time) in: *Herderbücherei INITIATIVE* vol. 13/1976, pp. 94.

33. Hans-Peter Schwarz: *The Tamed Germans*, p. 46.

34. Klaus Hornung: *Peace without Utopia.*

35. Hans-Peter Schwarz: *The Tamed Germans*, p. 171.

36. Wilhelm Ritter von Schramm: . . . *sprich vom Frieden, wenn du den Krieg willst* (Speak about Peace if You want War), Mainz 1975.

37. Jean-Paul Picaper: *DDR-Bild*, p. 167.

38. Horst Teltschik: "Aspekte der deutschen Aussen-und Sicherheitspolitik" (Aspects of German Foreign and Security Policy), in: *Aus Politik und Zeitgeschichte*, Beilage zur Wochenzeitung *Das Parlament* No. B 7/8/1985 February 16, 1985 (Politics and Contemporary History, Supplement to the weekly Das Parlament).

39. Thus the minister (Senator) of the Interior of West Berlin, Mr. Heinrich Lummer, during the last election campaign in West Berlin.

40. Thus the member of the Politbureau of the Federation of Communists of Yugoslavia, Alexander Grlickow, at the Party Convention at Belgrade in Summer 1982.

41. Robert F. Byrnes: "Veränderungen im sowjetischen politischen System: Möglichkeiten und Grenzen" (Changes in Soviet Political System: Possibilities and Limits), in: H.J. Veen (ed.): *Wohin entwickelt sich die Sowjetunios?* Forschungsbericht Bd. 38 der Konrad-Adenauer-Stiftung (Where develops the Soviet Union? Research Report vol. 38), Melle 1984, p. 289.

42. Wolfgang Leonhard: *Dämmerung im Kreml. Wie eine neue Ostpolitik aussehen musste* (Dawn in the Kreml. How a new Ostpolitik should be shaped), Stuttgart 1984, p. 245.

43. Wolfgang Strauss: *Revolution gegen Jalta. Die ungelöste nationale und soziale Frage in Osteuropa* (Revolution against Yalta. The Unsolved National and Social Question in Eastern Europe), Berg am See 1982.

44. Wolfgang Leonhard: *Dämmerung im Kreml*, p. 245.

45. Michael Stürmer: "Die deutsche Frage stösst auf harte Grenzen" (The German question and its disputed borders), in: *Rheinischer Merkur* No. 34/August 17, 1985, p. 3.

46. Alexander Shtromas: *Political Change and Social Development: The Case of the Soviet Union*, Frankfurt am Main—Bern 1982, p. 140.

47. George F. Kennan: *Memoirs 1925–1950*, Boston and Toronto 1967, p. 559.

2

Likely Changes in Post-Soviet Policy Toward the Third World: A Speculative Essay

ROGER E. KANET

The expansion of Soviet activities in the Third World during the past 30-odd years has stimulated in the West a large and growing literature that attempts to chronicle the continuing extension of Soviet involvement, to explain the factors that determine Soviet policy, and to project the implications of that involvement for the long-term interests of the industrial states of the West.[1] However, no consideration has been given in this extensive literature to the impact that a change of regime in the Soviet Union itself—i.e., the collapse of the current system in which a small Communist Party elite, basing its right to rule on the dictates of Marxist-Leninist ideology, dominates all aspects of state power—would likely have on the nature of Soviet policy toward the Third World.

In the present essay I shall attempt to address precisely this question: what impact would a collapse of the present Soviet political system have on Soviet policy toward the developing countries of Asia, Africa and Latin America? Of necessity the discussion that follows will be largely speculative. The speculation will be based on a number of assumptions about the nature of present Soviet policy and the nature of a post-Soviet Russia that will be spelled out in some detail in the initial sections of the essay.

It should be noted that, in the view of the author, the type of major change envisaged in the following discussion is not very likely to occur in the foreseeable future.[2] Despite the vast array of problems currently facing the new Soviet leadership, the probability of fundamental systemic change that would result from either revolution or from radical changes introduced by Soviet leaders themselves is quite low. The author agrees in principle with the assessment of Timothy J. Colton that only a major military defeat or a complete collapse of the economy combined with the outbreak of violent ethnic conflict would provide the type of stimulus necessary for revolutionary collapse of the Soviet regime. Neither of these is a probable development in the near future.[3]

The Nature of a Post-Soviet Russia

Before examining the possible changes in foreign policy that might occur in a post-Soviet Russia, it is essential to try to answer three important questions concerning the nature of a post-Soviet Russia. The first concerns the different processes of change that might lead to the replacement of the present authoritarian and highly centralized Stalinist system (albeit a system in which some of the most repressive elements of "high Stalinism" have disappeared) by some other form of political organization. The second important question concerns the geographic and ethnic makeup of a post-Soviet Russian state. Finally, we must discuss the governmental form that is likely to emerge in a New Russian state. There is no single answer to any of these questions. Change in the system could occur gradually or through revolutionary upheaval. The results of that change could include the continued existence of a single multiethnic state or the rise of a number of smaller political units with New Russia only one among a number of successor states. Finally, New Russia could have a democratic or an authoritarian political structure.

The process of change that eventually might bring about the downfall of the present Soviet system is important for our consideration of the nature of the foreign policy of a post-Soviet Russia, for it is likely to influence the type of political system that replaces the present Communist system. If the present system, based on Marxist-Leninist ideology and dominated by a small Communist Party elite, were to erode gradually through a process of increased incorporation of new (especially non-Russian) elites into the leadership class and a growing pragmatism in which the official tenets of Marxism-Leninism provided little more than a facade for policies determined by other factors, it is possible that a post-Soviet Russia would remain geographically intact. If elites in the non-Russian republics (as well as broader segments of the population throughout the entire Soviet Union) are provided with the opportunity to deal with problems of immediate concern to them—e.g., housing, consumer satisfaction, and related issues—and if crucial decisions, such as those relating to the organization of Soviet agriculture, are made on the basis of rational factors, rather than within the straitjacket of ideological imperatives, then the USSR might evolve over the course of several decades into a political system quite different from the present one. Such evolutionary change, even though it occurred within the framework of a nominally Communist state system, might well result in a de-ideologized Soviet Union in which broader segments of the concerned public were able to have an impact on policy and in which the rights of various population groups—including the non-Russian nationalities and religious believers—were respected. Such a system would remain authoritarian—at least in comparison with the liberal–democratic systems of the West. However, it would also be characterized by a greater awareness of the need for central authorities to respond more fully and effectively to the legitimate needs and demands of the populace.

Were such an evolutionary change to occur, it is quite probable that the new Soviet system would continue to control the territory and population currently incorporated within the boundaries of the USSR—even though central control from Moscow in various areas of public life would likely be reduced. However, should the Soviet leadership continue to ignore the growing evidence of crisis—in the domestic economic sphere, in the non-Russian regions of the country, and among growing numbers of disaffected Soviet citizens of all nationalities, then the process of evolutionary change sketched above will not occur. More likely would be some form of revolutionary upheaval in which the current system would be destroyed. The nature of the system (or systems) that would emerge from such an upheaval would then be much more problematic. It is quite conceivable that in such a revolutionary upheaval the role of resurgent nationalism among non-Russians would be quite important.

The Soviet Union today, as the successor to Tsarist Russia, is a multinational empire in which the Great Russians comprise barely 50 percent of the population. Despite the fact that the non-Russian (especially the non-Slavic) portion of the population has been growing much more rapidly than the Russian, most positions of decision-making importance within the state, party, economic and military apparatus are held by Russians. Moreover, increasing evidence is available, even in the closely guarded Soviet press, of the rise of nationalist orientations among an increasing percentage of the non-Russians within the USSR.[4] Despite the success of Soviet leaders to date in integrating local political elites into the Soviet governing structure, there is absolutely no guarantee that a post-Soviet Russian state that emerged from revolution would be able to retain control overall (or even most) of the territory that currently comprises the Soviet Union. In fact, in his provocative essay, *Will the Soviet Union Survive Until 1984?*, Andrei Amalrik argued that the centrifugal force of revitalized nationalism among key population groups in the Soviet Union would eventually bring about the disintegration of the Soviet system.[5]

It is quite conceivable, therefore, that out of the revolutionary collapse of the centralized multinational Soviet state would emerge a number of smaller, ethnically more homogeneous, political units. The group of successor states could consist of one or more Moslem states in Central Asia, several independent political units in the Caucasus, and independent states in the western territories that now comprise the Ukrainian and the Baltic union republics. In addition, the countries of Eastern Europe that now represent a part of the extended Soviet empire would likely gain full independence from the Russian successor state.

Were such a situation to emerge that deprived a post-Soviet Russia of much of its non-Russian population and most of its border territories (including Eastern Europe), the post-Soviet Russian leadership would be faced with an entirely new series of political, economic and security needs that would, of necessity, greatly reduce its ability to function as a global power. A "balkanization" of the USSR would require the New Russian leadership to devote primary attention to working out relationships with the new states along its periphery. Even assuming that the New Russia incorporated all of the territory presently included in the Russian Republic—i.e., including the vast expanses of Siberia with its raw material riches—the total resource base available, including population, would be greatly reduced. In other words the leadership would be faced with a totally new configuration of relationships—including, in particular, security relationships—while simultaneously being deprived of many of the economic and population resources available to its predecessors. A new Russia that emerged from the collapse of the Soviet system stripped of many of its peripheral areas would, for the foreseeable future, be reduced to the position of a major regional power, concerned primarily with consolidating its control and legitimacy in the territories that it retained and with protecting its contracted borders against potential new enemies (in the other successor states) and old enemies (especially China).

Such a New Russia, even though it would still possess great resources, would not likely be able to continue to play a major role in areas far from Russian territory (regardless of the political orientation of the new leadership in Moscow). Thus, one can assume that a breakup of the Soviet union into its constituent parts would result in a substantial reduction of Russian involvement and influence throughout much of the Third World, for the Third World would be relegated to a position of tertiary importance in Russian foreign objectives.

Another important issue that would likely determine the foreign policy orientation of a New Russia would be the type of regime that replaced the present Communist system. It is sometimes assumed in the West (especially in the United States) that the total collapse (as opposed to the gradual evolution discussed above) of the highly centralized, authoritarian system dominated by a relatively small Communist Party elite would result in the establishment of some form of democracy in the USSR. Yet, virtually all Western students of Russia and the Soviet Union note that neither Tsarist Russia nor its Soviet successor has had a tradition upon which a post-Soviet democratic system could likely be built. As Richard Pipes has argued, the history of both pre- and post-revolutionary Russia demonstates "the intrinsically illiberal, antidemocratic spirit of Russian ruling elites." Moreover, the history of Russia since the emergence of Muscovy in the fifteenth century has been characterized by "the persistent tradition of Russian expansion."[6] In a more recent study, Robert Daniels has detailed the tragic history of a Russia which from the days of the Tsars until the present has fostered a rigid authoritarianism based, in part, on a fear of the outside world and feelings of inferiority in the face of that world.[7]

The major point to be made here is that a liberal-democratic regime would not likely emerge in Moscow after a revolutionary upheaval in which the Communist system had been overthrown. Even in late Tsarist Russia, when some change was occurring, support for participatory democracy was limited to a very small segment of the intelligentsia. The views of so prominent a Russian dissident as Aleksandr I. Solzhenitsyn, who sees in Tsarist Russia and traditional Russian Orthodoxy a model for the future, do not augur well for the establishment of democracy in a post-Soviet Russia.[8] Although recent unofficial polls indicate that about one-fifth of the population of large cities in the Russian republic has a democratic orientation, those same polls show that about sixty percent of the populace is indifferent and the remaining twenty percent is clearly anti-democratic.[9] Given the history of Russia under both the Tsars and the Communists, the essential prerequisites for a participatory democratic system in Russia are lacking.

The Foreign Policy of New Russia

As we have seen, a number of possible scenarios for change in the USSR exist—depending on the nature of the process of change, the size and ethnic composition of a post-Soviet Russia, and the type of political system established. The following major possibilities emerge from the discussion:

1. *Evolutionary change* resulting in a less authoritarian political system in a unified state encompassing all of the present territory of the USSR.

2. *Revolutionary change* resulting in
   a. A unified Russian state incorporating all (or most of) the present
   territory of the USSR
      i. with a liberal-democratic political system.
      ii. with a basically authoritarian system.
   b. A number of successor states in which one would be New Russia
      i. with a liberal-democratic political system.
      ii. with a basically authoritarian system.

Of these possibilities the most likely alternative to occur would appear
to be a New Russia that emerged after revolutionary upheaval with a
"traditional" authoritarian system, but limited primarily to territory populated by Great Russians. However, as has already been argued above, a
truncated Russian state would be so concerned with the demands of its
new position in international affairs—in particular with its relations with
the successor states along its borders—and would have such a reduced
resource base that it would not likely be able to pursue an active policy in
the Third World. Therefore, in order to examine the likely orientation of
a post-Soviet Russia toward the Third World, we shall assume in the remainder of this essay that New Russia would emerge within the present
territorial boundaries of the Soviet Union and with all of the resources of
the present Soviet state. We shall also assume that it would be characterized
by a primarily authoritarian political system in which Great Russians
continued to play the dominant political role.

The type of Russian state envisaged above would remain a global superpower with the capabilities (in particular military) to attempt to influence developments in all areas of the world. Its leaders, although no longer
committed to global sociopolitical revolution, would nonetheless share
much of the worldview of their Soviet and Tsarist Russian predecessors—
a worldview characterized by an almost paranoid concern with security
based in part on a strong sense of inferiority and both an attraction to and
a disdain for the culture and technology of the industrialized West. One
can identify a number of important constants in Tsarist Russian and Soviet
foreign policy; as Daniels has argued:

Stalinism . . . revived, with a new vocabulary, some of the oldest, crudest,
and harshest habits and premises from the Russian cultural heritage. Until
the limited reform efforts of the mid-nineteenth century, the imperial government was a centralized bureaucratic despotism, backward and inefficient;
the Stalinist government was also a centralized bureaucratic despotism, though
vastly more effective both in its reach and its grasp. Imperial Russia was
nationalistic, chauvinistic, and imperialistic; Stalin shed all inhibitions in deal-

ing with the outside world. Imperial Russian society was a hierarchy based originally on service to the state; Stalinist society took the same form and same purpose. Imperial Russia maintained a state religion and discouraged the import of ideas from abroad (except in technology); Stalinist Russia found another, more rigorous basis in Marxism to achieve the same ends.[10]

It is most likely that a New Russian leadership would continue, at least for the foreseeable future, to organize society and to deal with the outside world in ways that appear endemic in Russian history.

It is most important to remember that much, but by no means all, of the international behavior pattern that we currently associate with the Soviet Union has its roots in the Tsarist past. For example, the traditional Tsarist Russian approach to security was characterized—as its Soviet counterpart has been—by the attempt to expand and absorb areas along the Russian periphery, in order to eliminate the sources of potential threat and to extend the line of defense farther from the centers of Russian power. Moreover, Tsarist Russian policy—as that of current Soviet leaders—was committed to the maintenance of military power equivalent to that of all of its potential opponents combined.[11] In another area, the use of international "front organizations," the Tsars developed the technique which was later expanded and improved upon by the Communist government. Throughout the ninteenth century, for example, the Orthodox Church and Panslavism were used by Russian rulers in order to gain foreign support for various foreign policy goals.[12]

More directly related to the topic of this essay is the expansion of Russian involvement into areas of the world that today would be termed the Third World. Russian expansion differed from that of the industrial states of Western Europe primarily because the Russians were extending colonial control into regions geographically contiguous to Russian territory, rather than into overseas territories. However, throughout the latter half of the nineteenth century the Tsars were also strongly drawn toward expansion into southern Asia and the Middle East, and only the presence of the British in India effectively precluded such an extension of Russian power.[13] Even in far-off sub-Saharan Africa the Russians attempted to compete with the other European colonial powers. Throughout the 1880s the Tsars supported several attempts to establish Russian colonies in the Horn of Africa; during the 1890s they supported Ethiopia against Italian and British expansion; and after the Boer War the Tsar even gave serious consideration to supporting an Afrikaaner challenge to British domination in South Africa.[14] As Daniels has noted in comparing Tsarist and Soviet foreign policy: "The Soviets, to be sure, have engaged in some far-flung ventures in recent times—in Latin America, Southeast Asia, Africa. Yet allowing for

a half-century's change in communications technology and in political opportunities, it cannot be said that the communists have done anything
incompatible with tsarist aims and practices."[15]

Before finally turning directly to the topic of the likely policy orientation
of a post-Soviet Russian state toward the countries of the Third World, it
is important to summarize the major aspects of recent Soviet policy toward
developing countries, in order to provide a base from which to project
likely changes in that policy.

The Evolution Of Soviet Policy
Toward the Developing Countries

When Stalin died in 1953 the Western opponents of the Soviet Union
maintained political, economic and military relations with all areas of the
world—much of which was still under European colonial control—while
Soviet international contacts were limited primarily to the countries that
formed their newly created empire in Eastern Europe and to their allies
in China. The Soviet ability to project military—and in most cases political—power was limited to those regions under direct control of the Soviet
army. The United States and its European allies had already become engaged in a process of expanding a network of military bases from Europe
through the Middle East to east Asia as part of the policy of containment.
To counter these efforts the Soviets initially entered upon a policy of
"denial" aimed at ensuring the neutrality of those developing countries—
especially Afghanistan, India and Egypt—which professed a nonaligned
approach to foreign policy and opposed the intrusion of military alliances
into their region. The Soviets sought to expand their ties with these countries in order to prevent the uncontested growth of Western political and
military influence, to ensure that gaps would remain in the U.S.-sponsored
alliance network, and to win the support of the nonaligned states for international political issues of importance to the Soviet Union.[16] Measured
in terms of political contacts, economic relations (including assistance), or
military aid, Soviet involvement in the areas of special strategic concern
along the southern borders of the USSR expanded rapidly.[17] In addition,
however, the Soviets did attempt to take advantage of a number of opportunities in other geographic regions presented, for example, by the civil
war in Zaire (then Congo-Leopoldville) and the radicalization of the governments of Sukarno in Indonesia, Nkrumah in Ghana and Touré in
Guinea.

Although the initial Soviet push toward expanding contacts with the
countries of the Third World was accompanied by optimistic statements

about the prospects for the development of a revolutionary climate in these countries, the immediate Soviet goal was the reduction of Western influence in regions of strategic significance for Soviet security. This at times led to a contradiction between the imperatives of Soviet policy and the USSR's ideological assessments of these countries, since the leaders involved could no longer be depicted as reactionaries who ought to be swept away by the tide of revolution. At the authoritative level, this change in doctrine was heralded at the XX Party Congress in 1956 with Khrushchev's introduction of the concept of the "zone of peace." The nonaligned states were no longer to be regarded as mere outposts of Western imperialism, but as independent proponents of peace and, therefore, worthy of Soviet support and assistance. Thus, despite rhetoric about support for the construction of "scientific socialism" in developing countries, the Soviets were willing to provide support to such evidently nonsocialist countries as monarchical Afghanistan and the Ethiopia of Emperor Haile Selassie in an attempt to undermine Western influence.

By the time of Khrushchev's overthrow in late 1964, however, Soviet policy toward the developing countries was in partial disarray. The optimism of the 1950s was already under attack within the USSR and was being replaced by a growing realism concerning prospects for political and economic developments in most of the Third World. Although the Soviets had ended their isolation from these countries, they had not succeeded in establishing significant influence with them. Where Soviet goals had been partially accomplished—e.g., the reduction of the Western presence in the Middle East—success resulted far more from the initiatives of the developing countries themselves than from Soviet policy. Soviet hopes that many of the emerging nations would be willing to cut or reduce their economic and political ties with the West proved unfounded. Rather than emulate the Soviet Union as an alternative sociopolitical model, the majority of leaders in Asia and Africa chose instead to use the Soviet Union as a means to lessen their dependence on the former colonial powers and give them an additional source of military and economic assistance. Additionally, the USSR's capacity to provide support to their friends—such as Lumumba, Nkrumah and Keita—in periods of crisis was made difficult by its inferior position vis-à-vis the West—particularly by the virtual absence of an ocean-going navy.[18]

Despite their shortcomings, the Khrushchev years were not without successes upon which future Soviet policy could be built. In southern Asia, India had already begun to depend heavily upon the USSR for both military assistance and for support in the development of heavy industrial projects in the state sector of the economy. In the Middle East both Egypt and Syria were now indebted to the Soviets for military and economic assistance, while Turkey and Iran had begun to expand their ties with their northern neighbor as a means of lessening their dependence on the United States. Throughout Asia and Africa the Soviet Union had become a force to be dealt with by the United States and its allies, even though the West still commanded more influence and was able to exert more military capabilities in most areas of the developing world.

The first few years of the regime of Brezhnev and Kosygin saw a continuing reassessment of Soviet attitudes and policies.[19] Confidence in the development of Soviet-type socialist systems and an emphasis on economic "show projects" were replaced by the effort to establish firmly based relations with Third World countries that would begin to provide the Soviets with bases of operation from which they could expand contacts and attempt to increase their activities and build their influence. Even more than in earlier years Soviet leaders focused on countries and political groupings that had inherent importance for their own purposes. First, they reemphasized close ties with those countries along the southern boundaries of the Soviet Union—from India to the Arab countries of North Africa. The importance of this area for the strategic security interests of the Soviet Union is self-evident, as Soviet commentators have repeatedly noted.[20] Support for minor revolutionary groups and for activities in sub-Saharan Africa were generally downplayed in the late 1960s—to the point where some Western commentators mistakenly argued that the Soviets had virtually lost interest in that continent.[21] Since the early 1970s, the Soviets have continued to provide substantial support to political groups or countries of potential importance to their strategic and global interests, despite what seems to be a preference for supporting "progressive" regimes and movements.

In spite of the upsurge of Soviet involvement in sub-Saharan Africa in the past decade, Soviet interest is still concentrated heavily in the arc of countries that border the southern flank of the USSR. Here the Soviet goal continues to be the reduction of Western influence and military capabilities and the concomitant expansion of the military and political capabilities of the Soviet state. This has meant that the Soviets have continued to provide military and political support to such countries as Iraq, Syria and South Yemen. In several cases they have signed treaties of friendship and cooperation with important southern Asian and Middle Eastern countries, such as Iraq and India. In fact, during the 1970s they increased their efforts to improve relations with countries formally allied with the West, such as Turkey and Iran (prior to the overthrow of the Shah) by offering economic assistance and military sales as a means of reducing these countries' dependence on their Western allies—in particular the United States. Another important element in Soviet policy has been the search for access to both naval and airport facilities that would enable them to expand the reach of their military capabilities.

Throughout the last 30 years Soviet policy toward the developing countries has relied heavily on the provision of economic and, especially, military assistance as means of developing and consolidating relations.[22] In general the terms of Soviet assistance are favorable when compared with commercial loans available to emerging nations on the international market, though the Soviets offer virtually no nonrepayable grants, and all aid is provided in the form of credits for the purchase of Soviet goods and equipment. Soviet trade with Asia and Africa has grown rapidly as well, although an important aspect of this trade has been the degree to which it has been related to the provision of economic assistance. With few exceptions (e.g., the sale of military equipment to Libya and the purchase of rubber from Malaysia), trade has resulted from agreements between the Soviet leaders and their Afro-Asian counterparts which include the commitment of Soviet economic and technical assistance. Examples of this type of agreement have been those with Egypt and India which called for the Soviet Union to provide capital equipment on the basis of long-term credits. These loans were to be repaid with the products of the recipient country over a period of 12 years at an interest rate of 2.0–2.5 percent. Such agreements have been especially attractive to those countries which have had problems obtaining the convertible currency necessary to purchase machinery and equipment on the world market needed for economic projects.

By the 1980s, then, the relative position of the two major power blocs in the Third World had changed markedly. The collapse of the Western colonial empires and the ensuing rise of numerous anti-Western political regimes in the developing world, voluntary Western military retrenchment and various other developments had resulted in the contraction of the Western military presence and of Western political influence throughout much of Asia and Africa. At the same time the Soviets had been able to establish a network of economic, political and military relationships that permitted them for the first time in their history to play the role of a global power with worldwide interests and the capabilities to pursue many of those interests effectively. This change in the relative position of the Soviet Union in the international political system has resulted in part from the continued buildup of Soviet military power and the willingness and ability of the Soviet leadership to take advantage of the conflicts between the less developed states and the major Western states.[23] Already in the 1970s the Soviets were able to employ their newly–developed military power, including an oceangoing fleet and long-range transport aircraft, in conjunction with access to port and air facilities in order to support distant and dispersed political and strategic goals. Examples include the use of the Soviet fleet in the Bay of Bengal to demonstrate support for India in the 1971 war with Pakistan, the transport of large numbers of Cuban troops to Angola four years later to support the MPLA and a virtual repeat of this operation in Ethiopia in 1978, and the provision of substantial military supplies to revolutionary groups in Central America in the 1980s.

Today the Soviet Union is truly a superpower with the ability to influence developments in areas far from Soviet territory. Although the primary means available to Soviet leaders in their attempts to accomplish their short- and long-term objectives throughout the Third World has been the provision of various forms of military support, that support has been accompanied by a wide range of other Soviet activities—relations with revolutionary movements and political parties, modest amounts of economic assistance, political support in various international forums and a vast assortment of propaganda activities. After this brief examination of the major trends in Soviet policy toward the Third World we can now turn to a discussion of the likely impact that radical change in the Soviet political system would likely have on that policy. It is important to recall, however, the assumptions that we have already made about the probable nature of a post-Soviet Russian state and the implications that this would have on the foreign policy of that state.

New Russian Policy
In the Developing World

One of the most serious problems facing a post-Soviet government, even one that managed to incorporate all of the territories of its predecessor and was still predominantly authoritarian in nature, would be the concern with establishing a degree of internal legitimacy. In the foreign policy sphere—given the traditional Russian concern with security against external threats—this would most likely result in policies that did not differ significantly, at least in their basic orientation, from those of the USSR. One can assume that the New Russian leaders would continue to give special priority to military-security factors. In keeping with long-standing Russian-Soviet tradition, they would continue to maintain a large military force and would attempt to exert extensive influence over neighboring countries.

In its relationships with the West New Russian policy could follow one of two quite different orientations. On the one hand, one cannot assume that the leadership of a "traditional authoritarian" post-Soviet Russia would automatically establish cordial relations with the United States and the other Western liberal democracies. It is definitely conceivable that the policies of a basically authoritarian, nationalistically oriented New Russia would be characterized by the chauvinism and paranoia concerning the West that has been endemic in Russia for the entire modern era.

Yet, a second possible foreign policy orientation toward the West could evolve in Russia, one based on pragmatic "realism" concerning the inherent weaknesses of the position of Russia in world affairs. Such an approach to relations with the West, while not necessarily based on a substantial coincidence of interests, would recognize the importance of an effective *modus vivendi* with the United States and Western Europe for the New Russia. Reduced political conflict with the West would limit the likelihood of Western support for political or nationalist dissent among the non-Russian population of the extended New Russian state. It would also lessen the likelihood of direct confrontation with the United States and, thus, the need to devote as large a percentage of national resources to security concerns. This, in turn, would provide domestic resources that could be employed to deal more effectively with the long-term structural problems of the economy. Moreover, a reduction of tension in relations with the West would most likely open up to the New Russia new sources of both investment capital and technology from the West.

Whichever of these two scenarios of New Russian policy toward the West were to emerge, it is likely that relations with the developing countries would follow the pattern outlined below. Given the success of their Soviet predecessors in expanding the global influence of the Soviet-Russian state and, for the first time in Russian history, ensuring the virtual inability of a foreign invader to challenge Soviet security, the New Russian leaders would probably continue to pursue an active foreign policy in competition with the United States, Western Europe and China. What would change in that policy would be the elimination of one important element of current Soviet policy—i.e., the involvement with and support for radical, Communist-oriented, leftist governments and movements. However, as we have pointed out above, current Soviet policy in the Third World is also characterized by the establishment of strong ties with a variety of regimes in which ideological affinity plays little or no role—e.g., India, Libya, and Iraq.

The Regional Orientation of New Russian Policy.

The primary focus of post-Soviet policy in the Third World would continue to be placed on areas geographically contiguous to Soviet territory. The Middle East and southern Asia would remain the regions in which the New Russian government would most likely attempt to influence developments—as they have ever since the establishment of an active Soviet Third World policy in the 1950s. Of primary concern would be the prevention of the establishment of a Western or Chinese military presence in areas of critical strategic concern for the New Russian state. The Russians would attempt to take advantage of conflicts between countries in the region and the West, and military-security support would most likely remain the major means available to them to solidify their relationships.

However, several important changes are likely to occur in a New Russian policy in this region. First of all, although the new leadership would not look favorably on the establishment in Afghanistan of an anti-Russian political system allied to the West, it would most probably be willing to work out some type of arrangement for the establishment of a neutral, and independent, Afghanistan in return for firm assurances that Russian security interests would be guaranteed. The establishment of a non-Communist regime in Russia would also have probable implications for relations with a number of other countries in the region—most importantly with Iran. Although it is doubtful that a fundamentalist Moslem regime in Teheran would ever look upon Russia as a friend—especially given the long-standing conflicts between Iranians and Russians—it is probable that the level of hostility in their relations would be reduced. Moscow would no longer be perceived, as it currently is, as the "second Satan." A traditionally oriented Russian state might well be able to benefit more than the present Soviet leadership from the antagonism that currently characterizes relations between Iran and the United States.

Elsewhere in the region, in particular in the conservative Arab states of the Persian Gulf region, the Russians would probably find it much easier to establish relations once they were no longer associated with radical leftist revolutionary elements. In India one can assume that relations would continue more or less as they have developed in the past. Present Soviet-Indian ties are based primarily on the mutual security interests of the two countries. Assuming that the conflicts between China and both India and a New Russia would continue, the basic ingredients for close Russian-Indian relations would remain in place.

The nature of the Russian relationship with Vietnam would likely be modified—assuming, of course, that Vietnam retained its Marxist-Leninist orientation. However, since the basis of that relationship is mutual hostility toward and suspicion of China and the importance of Vietnamese military facilities for the extension of Soviet power in that region, one can assume that a New Russian leadership would continue to provide substantial military-security support for the government of Hanoi. The only factor that would likely lessen Russian support for either India or Vietnam would be a reduction in the level of conflict between a New Russia and the more pragmatic post-Mao China and/or a resolution of the problems with the United States that have resulted in the global competition for power and influence between the two current superpowers. However, since present Sino-Soviet hostility results from a substantial number of sources—not merely ideological conflict between two Marxist-Leninist political parties—a resolution of the conflict cannot be assumed. In fact, it is possible that post-Soviet Russian leaders, who might be even more nationalistic than the current Soviet leadership, would find the resolution of their major differences with the Chinese even more difficult than have recent Soviet leaders.

Throughout the rest of Southeast Asia, the post-Soviet regime might well find it much easier to establish relations than has the Soviet government. This would be especially true in the economic area, should a non-Marxist government in Moscow be successful in solving some of the basic problems that currently plague the Soviet economy. However, an improvement of Soviet relations with the non-Communist countries of Southeast Asia would also depend, in part at least, on the perception of the leaders of those countries of the security threat represented by Vietnam.

It is in Africa that New Russian policy might undergo the most visible changes, since it is in relations with a number of African states and revolutionary movements that the Soviets have established the most important ideologically based ties during the course of the past decade.[24] This is not to argue that the primary motivation or orientation of Soviet policy in Africa has been ideological; here, as elsewhere in the Third World, a prime determinant of Soviet policy has been the attempt to undermine the position of the West and to establish the basis for long-term influencial relationships. However, the Soviets have determined that combining a policy based on military support for revolutionary movements (e.g., the MPLA or SWAPO) or embattled leftist regimes (Angola after 1975 and Ethiopia) along with close party ties with self-proclaimed Marxist-Leninist parties is likely to bring them the most stable long-term benefits. It is the second component of current Soviet policy—the ties with Marxist-Leninist regimes—that would change. Given our assumptions about the overall nature of the foreign policy of a post-Soviet Russian leadership, there is no reason to expect that New Russia would eschew opportunities to increase their involvement and to establish their own positions of influence (including gaining access to military facilities); however, that policy would no longer be based on what has been the Soviet attempt to demonstrate the coincidence of interests between like-minded revolutionary Marxist-Leninist regimes.

In Latin America changes in post-Soviet policy would most likely have a dual result. First of all—assuming no change in the radical political orientation of Cuba—the Soviet relationship with Cuba would of necessity undergo some change. However, since Cuba has been the Soviet Union's most important ally in the Third World since the mid-1970s, one can assume that the Soviets would attempt to maintain strong ties with the government of Fidel Castro.[25] A significant deterioration of Soviet-Cuban relations would have a deleterious effect on Soviet policy in a number of developing countries—including in Nicaragua and among revolutionary groups in Central America. One can assume that the post-Soviet leadership in Moscow would make every attempt to maintain good relations with Cuba—as they most likely would with Vietnam—because of the benefits that they would continue to gain in their expected, continuing global competition for influence with the United States. The major problem that a New Russia would have to work out in relations with Cuba would relate to the probable divergence between the two countries on the issue of support for radical revolution.

One can also assume that a post-Soviet government would also attempt to build on the ties that have already been forged with Nicaragua—in large part for the same reasons that they would attempt to retain their ties with socialist Cuba. However, a New Russia no longer committed to radical revolution might find it much easier to expand the relationships that the USSR has already established with major Latin American countries such as Argentina and Brazil. In addition, assuming that the post-Soviet government would be able to solve the basic problems that currently plague the Soviet economy, one could expect a substantial expansion of the economic relations between a New Russia and the industrializing states of the continent.

In sum, the most dramatic change that a collapse of the present Soviet political system would likely have on post-Soviet Russian policy in the Third World would be to eliminate its role as supporter of Marxist-Leninist revolutionary movements. However, this would most likely benefit Russia in the long run. To date, ideological affinity with Third World regimes has been an important factor in only a very few countries; Afghanistan, South Yemen, Angola, Ethiopia, Cuba, Vietnam, and Nicaragua are the most important examples. In some respects these are what might be termed Third World "basket cases." None of them has a viable independent economy; several require massive Soviet investments in order to subsist; although two (Cuba and Vietnam) have become important regional military powers, their positions would weaken dramatically without constant infusions of Soviet military and economic support. In other words, Soviet "successes" in establishing close, ideologically oriented ties with Third World states have occurred primarily in the least viable of countries.

A New Russian policy that emphasized the other, more pragmatic, side of current Soviet policy—i.e., the establishment of solid state-to-state relations based on mutual interest with the more important Third World regional powers (or potential regional powers), such as India, Nigeria, and Brazil—might well result in stronger long-term relationships and greater overall benefits for Russia. The elimination of the emphasis on radical revolution would most likely enhance the ability of New Russia to establish closer relationships with these countries.

The Instruments of New Russian Policy in the Third World.

As has already been noted, the Soviets have employed a wide array of instruments to accomplish their policy objectives in the Third World. Of primary importance during the past decade have been arms transfers and other forms of military assistance provided to developing countries. However, in addition to military relations, the Soviets have also devoted substantial efforts to expanding economic and political contacts with key Third World states. Economic aid and trade; political relations based on long-term treaties of friendship; support (at least verbal) for important Third World initiatives in international bodies, such as the campaigns for both a New International Economic Order and a New International Information Order; the training of economic and political cadres for developing countries; propaganda, subversion and other types of "active measures"—all of these have been part of overall Soviet policy toward Third World states. In addition, special, ideologically based relations with international front organizations, such as the Afro-Asian People's Solidarity Organization, and direct party-to-party relations have played a role in Soviet relations with a more limited number of developing countries.

One can assume that a post-Soviet Russian state committed to the goal of retaining superpower status, including an influential role in the Third World, would employ most of this broad array of foreign policy instruments. As has already been argued above, ideological affinity has had a relatively limited place in Soviet relations with most developing countries. This is especially true in relations with such countries as India, Iraq, Syria, Libya, Algeria, and Argentina. Military relations with key Third World states would remain an important element of New Russian policy.

One would also expect that economic relations would expand in importance, assuming that the economic base of New Russia improved through the introduction of major reforms of the structure of the domestic economy. Currently, the single greatest weakness of the Soviet Union in attempting to carry out its global competition for influence with the United States is precisely the economic inferiority of the USSR. Although the Soviets have proven to be quite effective in providing military security assistance to

Third World clients faced with serious internal or external security threats, they have been unable or unwilling to provide comparable economic support. Thus, when faced with the problems of economic development and growth, Third World leaders—even those ideologically disposed in favor of the USSR—have been forced to turn to the West.[26] A Russian state with an improved economic base would be in a much stronger position to compete economically with the United States in establishing long-term stable relationships with important developing states.

One cannot assume that the leaders of a New Russia would eliminate the use of the other means of foreign policy implementation employed by their Soviet predecessors, in particular since many of these have been based on long-standing Russian traditions and, moreover, have become an important component of the foreign policy arsenals of all world powers since World War I. The major exception to this statement would relate to the core role played by Marxist-Leninist ideology in Soviet policy. As we have already noted, international front organizations and party-to-party ties with radical leftist political movements would no longer be available to the Russian leaders. In addition, although they would not likely dismantle entirely the vast foreign propaganda apparatus targeted on the Third World, the content of the propaganda effort—which is currently strongly ideological in tone—would change dramatically.[27] Furthermore, support for various forms of radical left subversion and terrorism targeted against both the West and against pro-Western governments in the Third World would most likely be greatly reduced. However, there is no assurance that a New Russian leadership would give up all use of covert means to achieve foreign policy objectives.

Some Tentative Conclusions

In many respects the policies of a post-Soviet Russia toward the Third World would resemble current Soviet policies—if our assumptions about the probable nature of New Russia are correct. This is likely to be true because, to a substantial degree, the policies of the USSR in the Third World during the past three decades have been those of an aspiring superpower attempting to compete for status and influence with an established superpower, the United States. Although Soviet policy has been characterized by a strong Marxist-Leninist ideological component which would disappear in the policy of a New Russia, it has also demonstrated a strong element of pragmatism. Soviet successes in relations with the Third World—at least with the more important of the developing countries— have been based far more on a coincidence of interests than they have been on ideological affinity. The leaders of a New Russia would hardly be likely to eliminate those aspects of Soviet policy which have permitted Soviet Russia to achieve global superpower status.

In many respects a post-Soviet Russia, no longer committed to the reality or the rhetoric of Marxist-Leninist revolution, might find itself in a position to play an even more important role in the Third World than has the Soviet Union. As we have argued, Soviet successes have occurred in relations with two very different types of countries in the Third World. In both cases military-security relations have played an extremely important role in establishing and maintaining Soviet ties with developing countries. However, only in relatively small and unstable countries have they been able to supplement the security relationship with ideologically based ties and exert anything approximating active influence on the policies of the client state. Yet, even here (as the recent case of Mozambique's movement away from the USSR has demonstrated) the inability to supplement military and ideological ties with concrete economic support has created problems for the Soviets.

In relations with larger and potentially more important Third World states the Soviets have had an even more mixed record of success. They have found that countries such as India, Iraq and Libya (not to speak of Egypt) have been unwilling to accept ideologically based Soviet tutelage. Although aspects of Marxism-Leninism—e.g., the Leninist interpretation of imperialism or the organizational aspects of the Communist Party—may be attractive to many Third World leaders, the vast majority of these leaders are unwilling to accept the entire Soviet view of the world or the Soviet interpretation of the flow of historical processes. In other words, Soviet attempts to use ideological affinity as an important instrument in influencing the policies of Third World states have not been overly successful. In fact, they have been detrimental to the establishment or strengthening of Soviet relations with some of the more important developing countries (e.g., the conservative oil-producing Arab states).

A New Russia unencumbered with the ideological baggage of revolutionary Marxism-Leninism might find it easier than the Soviet Union has to establish long-term, stable relationships with the important Third World states. These relations would be based primarily on mutual, reinforcing interests of the New Russia with Third World partners and would not include the objective of restructuring the socioeconomic and/or political structure of the partner state. New Russian policy toward the Third World would likely not suffer from the schizophrenia that has characterized Soviet policy ever since the Bolshevik revolution of 1917—i.e., the attempt to play the role of a traditional power in relations with other states, while simultaneously working to bring about revolutionary change in the very structure of those states. Although this dichotomous nature of Soviet policy—which has been very evident in the USSR's policies toward developing countries—has provided benefits for Soviet efforts to accomplish some foreign policy objectives, it has also posed some serious problems. A post-Soviet Russia would be able to pursue a more coherent and less contradictory policy and, thus, might well discover that its "successes" would be more durable.

Probably the most important points to emerge from the speculation pursued in this essay concern the probable nature of a post-Soviet Russia and the orientation of the foreign policy of a New Russia. First, it is important to reemphasize the point made at the very beginning of this article that the type of major structural change in the nature of the Soviet state assumed throughout is not likely to occur—at least in the foreseeable future. Second, were such a change to occur, the Russia that would emerge would probably be authoritarian and strongly nationalistic in nature. Finally, such an authoritarian and nationalistic Russia would pursue an active policy in the Third World that shared much in common with present Soviet policy. What would change in that policy would be the focus on Marxist-Leninist ideology and ideologically based ties, but not the competition with the West for influence or the role of military-security relations in that competition. In addition, a post-Soviet Russia might well find itself in a position to extend significantly its importance as an economic partner in the developing world.

Notes

1. Reviews of most of the English language books dealing with Soviet policy in the Third World published since 1975 can be found in the review essays prepared by the present author and his graduate students and published on a regular basis since 1977 in *Osteuropa*.
2. For a different view of the likelihood of major change in the Soviet system see Alexander Shtromas's perceptive essay, "How the End of the Soviet System May Come About: Historical Precedents and Possible Scenarios," which is included in this collection. See, also, Alain Besançon (interview), "La Technique du Pouvoir en URSS," *L'Express*, 2–9 December 1978, p. 92.
3. See Timothy J. Colton, *The Dilemma of Reform in the Soviet Union* (New York: Council on Foreign Relations, 1984), esp. pp. 58ff.
4. For discussions of the rise of nationalist sentiments among the populations of Central Asia see Hélène Carrère d'Encausse, *L'Empire élaté: La Révolte des Nations en U.R.S.S.* (Paris: Flammarion, 1978); and Alexandre Bennigsen

and Marie Broxup, *The Islamic Threat to the Soviet State* (London-Canberra: Croom Helm, 1983). See, also, the contributions to *Religion and Nationalism in Soviet and East European Politics*, edited by Pedro Ramet (Durham, NC: Duke Press Policy Studies, 1984).

5. Although Amalrik expected a protracted war between the USSR and China to act as the catalyst for nationalist disruption within the Soviet state, according to the logic of his argument any other serious, protracted crisis could provide the stimulus. See Andrei Amalrik, *Will the Soviet Union Survive Until 1984?* (New York: Harper & Row, Perennial Library, 1971), esp. pp. 44ff.

6. Richard Pipes, "Détente: Moscow's View," in *Soviet Strategy in Europe*, ed. by Richard Pipes (New York: Crane, Russak, 1976), pp. 7, 9. Pipes develops this thesis in great detail in his study of *Russia under the Old Regime* (London: Weidenfeld and Nicolson, 1974). For critiques of Pipes's views see Wladislaw G. Krasnow, "Richard Pipes's Foreign Strategy: Anti-Soviet or Anti-Russian?," *Russian Review*, XXXVIII, no. 2 (1979), p. 189; and reviews of Pipes's book by Donald Treadgold, in *Slavic Review*, XXXIV, no. 4 (1975), pp. 812–814, and Nicholas Riasanovsky, in *Russian Review*, XXXV, no. 2 (1976), pp. 103–104.

7. Robert V. Daniels, *Russia: The Roots of Confrontation* (Cambridge, MA-London: Harvard University Press, 1985).

8. See, for example, Aleksandr I. Solzhenitsyn, *The Mortal Danger: How Misperceptions about Russia Imperil America* (New York: Harper & Row, 1980, 2nd ed.), pp. 1–71; reprinted as "The Mortal Danger," in *The Soviet Policy in the Modern Era*, ed. by Erik P. Hoffmann and Robbin F. Laird (New York: Aldine, 1984), pp. 5–39. See also, Aleksandr Solzhenitsyn, "Letter to the Fourth Congress of Soviet Writers," in Solzhenitsyn, *Critical Essays and Documentary*, ed. by John Dunlop, Richard Haugh, and Alexis Klimoff (Belmont, MA: Wordland Publ., 1973), pp. 463–471; and "Misconceptions about Russia are a Threat to America," *Foreign Affairs*, LVIII (1980), pp. 797–834. For discussions of the revival of strong Russian nationalism see Alexander Yanov, "Na polputi k Leontievu," in Vadim Belotserkovskii, ed., *Demokraticheskie alternativy: sbornik statei i dokumentov*. Achberg: Achbergerger Verlagsanstalt, 1976, p. 193; Alexander Yanov, *Détente After Brezhnev: The Domestic Roots of Soviet Foreign Policy*. Berkeley: Institute of International Studies, University of California, Berkeley, 1977, pp. 43ff,; and Ludmilla Alexeyeva, *Soviet Dissent: Contemporary Movements for National, Religious, and Human Rights* (Middletown, CN: Wesleyan University Press), 1985, pp. 431–448. For an excellent discussion of Western perceptions of the impact of Russian nationalism on the evolution of the Soviet state that criticizes the views of Richard Pipes and Alexander Yanov see John B. Dunlop, *The Faces of Contemporary Russian Nationalism*. Princeton: Princeton University Press, 1983, pp. 274–294.

9. Alexeyeva, *Soviet Dissent*, pp. 455–456.

10. Daniels, *Russia*. p. 21.

11. For a brief discussion of this aspect of Russian military policy see Edward A.

Luttwak, *The Grand Strategy of the Soviet Union* (New York: St. Martin's Press, 1983), pp. 13–16.

12. See Alexander Dallin, "The Use of International Movements," in *Russian Foreign Policy: Essays in Historical Perspective*, ed. by Ivo J. Lederer (New Haven-London: Yale University Press, 1962), p. 31.

13. For a discussion of late Tsarist policy in the Middle East see Firuz Kazemzadeh, "Russia and the Middle East," in *Russian Foreign Policy*, ed. by Lederer, pp. 489–530.

14. For a discussion of late Tsarist involvement in Africa see Roger E. Kanet, "The Soviet Union and Sub-Saharan Africa: Communist Policy Toward Africa, 1917–1965." Unpublished Ph.D. Dissertation, Princeton University, 1966, pp. 8–15; see, also, Sergius Yakobson, "Russia and Africa," in *Russian Foreign Policy*, ed. by Lederer, pp. 453–468.

15. Daniels, *Russia*, p. 22. This view is strongly contested by Michael Karpovich, who has denied that the Tsars had any global aims in their foreign policy. See Michael Karpovich, "Russian Imperialism or Communist Aggression?, *The New Leader*, June 4, June 11, 1951; reprinted in *Readings in Russian Foreign Policy*, ed. by Robert A. Goldwin, *et al.* (New York: Oxford University Press, 1959), pp. 659 ff. Solzhenitsyn is even more outspoken in his criticism of American specialists on the Soviet Union who find in Russian history roots of the present Soviet system. Solzhenitsyn, "The Mortal Danger."

16. Richard Lowenthal, *Model or Ally? The Communist Powers and the Developing Countries* (New York: Oxford University Press, 1977), pp. 185–186.

17. For information concerning the expansion of Soviet military and economic assistance in the 1960s see U.S. Department of State, Bureau of Intelligence and Research, *Communist Economic Offensive Through 1964*. Research Memorandum, RSB-65, August 5, 1965, p. 6 and U.S. Department of State, Bureau of Intelligence and Research, *Communist Governments and Developing Nations: Aid and Trade in 1965*. Research Memorandum, RSB-50, June 17, 1966, pp. 12–19.

18. For a discussion of Soviet policy toward the Third World in the Khrushchev era see Roger E. Kanet, "Soviet Attitudes Toward Developing Nations Since Stalin," in Kanet, ed., *The Soviet Union and Developing Nations* (Baltimore: The Johns Hopkins University Press), 1974, pp. 27–50.

19. For the full development of this argument see Elizabeth Kridl Valkenier, *The Soviet Union and the Third World: An Economic Bind* (New York: Praeger, 1983).

20. Andrei A. Gorshkov, *Ogonëk*, no. 6 (February 3, 1968). For a Western assessment of Gorshkov's major writings see James McConnell, "The Gorshkov Articles, the New Gorshkov Book, and Their Relation to Policy," in *Soviet Naval Influence: Domestic and Foreign Dimensions*, ed. by Michael MccGwire and John McDonnell (New York: Praeger, 1977).

21. See, for example, Roger E. Kanet, "The Soviet Union and the Developing

Countries: Policy or Policies?" *The World Today*, vol. 21 (1975), pp. 344–345.

22. See Roger E. Kanet, "Soviet Policy Toward the Developing World: The Role of Economic Assistance and Trade," in *The Soviet Union and the Developing Countries: Successes and Failures*, ed. by Robert H. Donaldson (Boulder: Westview Press, 1981), pp. 331–357; and Roger E. Kanet, "Soviet Military Assistance to the Third World," in *Communist Nations' Military Assistance*, ed. by John F. Copper and Daniel S. Papp (Boulder: Westview Press, 1983), pp. 39–71.

23. Several recent books examine in detail Soviet involvement in Third World conflicts and Soviet arms transfer policy. See, for example, Stephen T. Hosmer and Thomas W. Wolfe, *Soviet Policy and Practice Toward Third World Conflicts* (Lexington, MA: Lexington Books, D.C. Heath, 1983); Joachim Krause, *Die sowjetische Militärhilfepolitik gegenüber aussereuropäischen Entwicklungsländern* (Ebenhausen: Stiftung Wissenschaft und Politik, 1983); and Bruce D. Porter, *The USSR in Third World Conflicts: Soviet Arms and Diplomacy in Local Wars 1945–1980* (Cambridge-London-New York: Cambridge University Press, 1984).

24. For a discussion of Soviet policy in Africa see Roger E. Kanet, "Security Issues in Soviet African Policy: The Imperatives of Soviet Security Policy in Soviet-African Relations," *Crossroads: An International Socio-Political Journal*, no. 10 (1983), pp. 81–120. For a discussion of the possible implications of the collapse of the Soviet system for Marxist-Leninist regimes in Africa see Lewis Gann, "Would the Marxist-Leninist Regimes in Africa Survive the Collapse of the Soviet Regime?" which appears in this collection.

25. For a discussion of the possible impact of structural changes in the Soviet system on Cuba and Latin America see W. Raymond Duncan, "Implications of the Fall of the Soviet Regime on Cuba and Cuba-Sponsored Revolutionary Regimes and Movements in Latin America," which is published in this volume.

26. See Roger E. Kanet and Sumit Ganguly, "Instruments of Soviet Policy in the Third World: Soviet Economic and Military Relations," *Coexistence*, Spring 1986, forthcoming.

27. For a discussion of Soviet propaganda activities targeted against the Third World see Roger E. Kanet, "Soviet Propaganda and the Process of National Liberation," unpublished paper presented at a conference on "Contemporary Soviet Propaganda and Disinformation," Airlie House, Warrenton, VA, June 25–27, 1985.

3

Would the Marxist-Leninist Regimes in Africa Survive the Collapse of the Soviet Regime?

LEWIS H. GANN

From times immemorial, man has sought reassurance in the present by looking into the future. Statesmen in ancient Greece asked counsel of the Delphic oracle; seventeenth century monarchs and warlords looked to astrologers for campaign forecasts and dynastic advice. Politicians today consult academicians learned in politics, economics, and sociology for predictions concerning the state of the world's population a generation hence, or the future availability of natural resources such as oil and uranium. Forecasting has become an international growth industry, and an impressive array of organizations, administrative and academic, national and international, are in the business of telling us what the future holds in store.

Perils of Futurology

Forecasters, on the whole, are not a cheerful lot. In the nineteenth century economics was described as the "dismal science." Nowadays the futurologists hold the palm among doomsayers. Their predictions are usually gloomy, no matter whether they bear on the fate of any one particular country, or on the destiny of the entire planet. Ever since Arthur Keppel-

Jones, a highly reputable South African historian now resident in Canada, published in 1947 a futurological book, *When Smuts Goes*, scholars in many disciplines have predicted that an inevitable revolution would soon smash the white regime in South Africa. Employing one of several mechanistic metaphors—the clock whose hands perpetually pointed at five minutes to twelve, the powder barrel ever ready to explode, the boiler without a safety valve about to blow up—forecasters committed themselves to predicting what they wanted to see, the overthrow of what they regarded as a racist tyranny. During the 1970s, gloomy predictions also became fashionable regarding the world. The earth's population could continue to increase at a rapid pace; natural resources would deplete in an ever more catastrophic fashion; fresh water would become ever scarcer; oil prices would rocket to the sky, as would the prices of many other raw materials. Swarms of insects immune to chemicals would spread from continent to continent. The plagues of Egypt would be as nothing compared with the wrath to come.

None of these predictions have as yet come true. Scholars, whether liberal or conservatives, have not been particularly successful as prophets; poets and storytellers—men such as Heinrich Heine and H.G. Wells—have in fact done better at inspired guessing than academicians.[1]

Many reasons account for the forecasters' failures. There are too many variables involved in exercises that attempt to predict, say, the future of the world's carrying capacity. Statistics are apt to be incomplete or inaccurate. Hence long-range statistical forecasting through sophisticated computer techniques may not be more accurate than forecasts made in the fashion of antiquity through looking at the entrails of a goat or at the flight of an eagle. Political forecasting is fraught with perils equally great. No political scientists—not even a writer of science fiction—could have predicted, for example, the horrific melodrama of the Third Reich—only the poet Heine did so.

Nevertheless, forecasting is an activity that human beings cannot avoid, either in their private or in their public lives. Whenever someone decides to act, an avowed or unavowed forecast based on past experience has been made. A suitor in love with a woman proposes marriage to her, rightly or wrongly convinced by his past dealings with her that she will make him a kind and loving wife. A bank will grant a loan to an entrepreneur, convinced by his or her credit record and past business performance, that the transaction will prove profitable. A politician will support, or fail to support, an arms program by judging, or misjudging, a hostile neighbor's immediate intentions. A statesman, understanding that nations are forever in flux, seeks to comprehend long-term trends.

Such forecasts are bound to be uncertain. But speculation is by no means useless. While Soviet policy-makers believe that, in the long run, the capitalist system will perish of its own contradictions and that Moscow should seek to hasten this process, it is at least possible to consider the ultimate decline of the Soviet empire. It is conceivable that—at some future stage— the Soviet Union might lose the interest, or at least the capability possessed at present of supporting Marxist-Leninist regimes in Africa, and of leaving them, together with Cuba and other client states, to their own devices. It is also possible at least that, eventually, the Soviet system might collapse, giving way to a military regime. In that case, Bonapartism would turn out to be both the highest stage of Communism and its last.[2] Such forecasts— the point bears repeating—are highly speculative. An expert such as Major General Yosef Avidar denies, for example, that there is a basic division between army and Party in the USSR; he believes that even if a shift in power were to take place, the new rulers would still remain to the outside world "the monolithic Party of Lenin."[3] Nevertheless, planners would do well to consider that history does not run on a single track, and that there may be alternate futures. This paper thus tries to contribute to such a discussion in the spirit of imaginative exercise.

Independence and its Aftermath

The collapse of the British, French, and Belgian empires in Africa owed little to the Soviet Union. Fanatical anti-Communists might explain every independence movement in terms of its real (or alleged) Soviet connections. But in fact, Moscow at first took but little interest in the activities of men such as Kenneth Kaunda in what is now Zambia or Kwame Nkrumah in Ghana. Decolonization, in its initial stages, was occasioned by social and political developments within the metropolitan powers after World War II and by changes within the colonies themselves. The first of the imperial dominoes to fall was the British-ruled Gold Coast which, in 1957, assumed sovereign independence under the name of Ghana. Within the next decade, the Union Jack and the Belgian and French tricolors had ceased to fly anywhere in sub-Saharan Africa.

The new states came to be subject, for the most part, to military dictatorships or to one-party governance. Most of the new political parties share certain characteristics. Their leadership overwhelmingly derived from strong personalities rather than from collegiate control. They suffered from numerous organizational weaknesses associated with factionalism and a fluctuating membership (natural to countries where so many African workmen were migrant laborers). They had to cope with financial stringency (made worse oftentimes by poor record keeping, poor bookkeeping, or by financial defalcations on the part of ill-paid officials). Their ideology was eclectic, owing more to Pan-Africanist writers, to French socialists, or to British Labourites such as Harold Laski than to Marx and Engels. Their propaganda aroused activists and often aroused quasi-millenarian expectations of the spiritual and material benefits to be brought about by liberation.

The new parties claimed to represent the disinherited, the mass of village cultivators and the new urban proletariat. Party leadership, however, did not mainly derive from the ranks of rural and urban laborers, but from "white collar" professions, especially junior civil servants and schoolmasters. The teachers in particular had their own networks of present and former colleagues and students that served well in politics. They brought to their task a peculiarly didactic style and a sincere and lasting commitment to education. Most of these men and women had become involved in the organization of trade unions, civic clubs, welfare societies, and the like before they embarked on a political career. Politics, for many of them became alike an avocation, a way of life, and a source of livelihood. Opponents of, as well as heirs to the colonial tradition, they had strong faith in education as an instrument of social improvement and the power of the state as an engine of reform; and they widely looked to public institutions, the civil service, their party, or "parastatal" organizations to provide for the advancement of educated Africans.

The new parties soon managed to mobilize a mass membership. They skillfully internationalized their struggle and gained support abroad as well as at home. But the new rulers faced tasks of extraordinary complexity. Most of the new states had been colonial creations; only a handful (Ethiopia, Burundi, Lesotho, Botswana, Swaziland) could trace their origins to precolonial kingdoms. For the most part, the new states formed ethnic mosaics without an overriding sense of national consciousness. The new states remained economically backward. Even relatively wealthy states such as Zambia or Zimbabwe had been propelled under colonial auspices from the Early Iron Age to the age of modernity within the space of less than a hundred years. They were politically unstable, and in many ways showed a striking resemblance to the newly independent Balkan states of the nineteenth century described with such mastery by Barbara Jelavich.[4]

The newly independent African states widely followed a similar path. There was widespread graft—not because the new African leaders were personally more dishonest than their colleagues elsewhere, but because the officeholders' ties of kinship and ethnic affiliation usually remained stronger than shadowy obligations to an impersonal bureaucracy or an equally impersonal state. The new rulers compounded their troubles by vastly augmenting the number of public functionaries in the civil service, the "parastatals" (public corporations), and the party. The peacetime strength of the new African armies came to vastly exceed the peacetime military effectives of the new rulers' imperial predecessors. The new men in office were apt to neglect the interests of rural cultivators so as to favor the city-bred. Worse still, cultivators were often discouraged by the operation of marketing boards and other devices that paid cultivators less for their food than they might have been able to obtain on the open market. This is certainly not to say that there was no progress. Countries such as the Ivory Coast, Malawi, and Botswana, by encouraging private enterprise, farming as much as industry, registered particularly noteworthy advances. But by and large, the almost messianic hopes once placed in independence evaporated; most sub-Saharan states increasingly came to depend on food imports—this in a continent that at the time of independence had been able largely to feed itself. Profligate expenditure, combined with falling world prices for raw materials, helped to bring about widespread inflation and great budgetary deficits. By the late 1970s, most of the sub-Saharan states found themselves in the throes of a profound crisis.[5] White-ruled South Africa, much to the African nationalists' anger, remained the military and economic giant of the subcontinent.

The Soviet Challenge

Soviet theory regarding Soviet relations with the rest of the world has always been straightforward. From the beginnings of Soviet rule, the Soviets have regarded themselves in a state of social war with the capitalist world. According to Soviet policy-makers, capitalism and socialism are locked in a fateful struggle in which global victory is destined to go to socialism. The victory of Communism may necessitate temporary and limited alliances between the Soviet state and other capitalist states for specific purposes; the struggle for world Communism equally requires temporary and limited alliances between the world's proletariat, represented by Moscow, and other classes. Coexistence is possible for a time between the Soviet state system and capitalist state systems. But long-term "peaceful coexistence" and "entente" cannot apply to opposing social systems. On the contrary, "peaceful coexistence" is itself an instrument for the intensification of the international class struggle. This class struggle must be waged on many different planes—economic, political, commercial, cultural, ideological or military. But there can only be one outcome—the ultimate triumph for the "forces of socialism" headed by the Soviet Union against its present and future enemies.

The socialist countries, having already managed to shift the international correlation of forces in their favor, must strive to make this change irreversible. Their military supremacy will facilitate the class struggle on a global scale by ultimately denying to the West the very option of military assistance. War is not inevitable; but if it comes, the socialist camp will win. For—as Heinz Hoffman, minister of defense in the German Democratic Republic, and a military thinker in his own right, explains, "we do *not* share the view, put forward even by progressive members of the peace movement, that a just war is no longer possible in a nuclear age, or that a struggle waged with nuclear rockets no longer entails the continuation of politics by other means on the part of conflicting social classes, but only a nuclear inferno—the end of the world."[6]

As they pursue their grand aim, Soviet policy-makers do not look to the automatic breakdown of capitalism. At a time when Western savants forecast permanent stagnation for the Western economies, Soviet scholars have come to very different conclusions. For instance, addressing himself to the problem in 1978, Dr. Nikolai Inozemtsev, the late director of the Institute for World Economics and member of the CPSU's Central Committee, warned his countrymen against underestimating the potential of capitalism. In his view, the gross national product (GNP) of the developed capitalist countries might increase by 100 to 140 percent over their 1978 level by the end of the century while industrial output may go up by about 150 percent. Dr. Inozemtsev was no ordinary scholar and his words carry weight. The fruits of revolution, in other words, will not just drop from the tree; on the contrary, revolutionaries must shake the tree until it breaks.[7]

The Soviets' ultimate aim never varies—even Mikhail Gorbachev has never renounced the international class struggle nor abandoned the hope for a socialist future to unify all mankind. But the Soviets' day-to-day strategy as far as Africa was concerned, Moscow was at first slow in utilizing the new opportunities provided by decolonization in Africa. Stalin, in the wake of World War II, apparently felt convinced—as did the pro-Moscow Communist parties of Western Europe—that Communism would win in Africa as a result of Communist successes in Europe, that the way to Lagos led via London and the road to Dakar via Paris. Stalinist postwar orthodoxy within the Soviet Union entailed an equally rigid approach to the Third World. Moscow believed that newly independent nations such as Ghana had acquired no more than a fictitious independence, that African leaders such as Nkrumah were no more than imperialist lackeys representing the interests of the emergent petty bourgeoisie and the comprador class in Africa. Only the working class could lead the struggle for true independence against the forces of neocolonialism. Soviet faith in the working class went with a profound contempt for what Soviet theoreticians styled "tribalism," a reactionary force skillfully utilized and enhanced by the imperialists as part of their design to divide and rule. Disdain for tribalism was in turn linked to the Soviets' domestic endeavor to bring about the ultimate unification of the Soviet nationalities at home.

After Stalin's death, Soviet policy became increasingly flexible. From 1956 onward, Soviet policy-makers admitted that independence might be attained under middle-class nationalist leadership, that Marxist-Leninists should aim at alliances with the progressive bourgeois forces in Africa, that "united fronts" should be set up to build a "national democracy" as a stepping stone towards socialism. At the same time, Soviet scholars admitted that they had previously held "rigid and dogmatic views" regarding Africa's social problems and its complex ethnic realities; in 1959 the Africa Institute opened its doors in Moscow to improve and coordinate Soviet academic endeavors in the continent. The new policy in Africa dovetailed with a measure of de-Stalinization at home and with a more cautious approach toward the ultimate unification of the Soviet nationalities, an aim now to be accomplished in the distant, rather than the immediate future.[8]

Under the new dispensation, Soviet policy in Africa became more skillful and operated in many different dimensions. The Soviets gave support to a variety of African regimes—especially those wedded to eclectic forms of "African socialism." The Soviets courted leaders such as Kwame Nkrumah in Ghana, Mobido Keita in Mali, Sekou Toure in Guinea, Siad Barre in Somalia, Julius Nyerere in Tanzania, and Idi Amin in Uganda, but not with much long-term success, given the "opportunistic" nature of these regimes, and their unwillingness or inability to set up disciplined cadre-parties following the Soviet model. Moscow also found itself hampered by the Soviet Union's limited capacity at the time of projecting its military might to distant shores and distant skies.

In addition, the Soviet Union worked through conventional Marxist-Leninist parties, and also achieved considerable success in capturing so-called liberation movements. On their own, the orthodox Communist parties achieved little. For instance, in Nigeria, the Socialist Working People's Party (founded in 1963) failed to obtain political influence, though the party managed to gain a strong foothold in the Nigerian Labour Congress (NLC), headed by the Party's presidium member Hassan Sunmonu, who succeeded in sending most NLC trainees to Eastern bloc countries and kept out Western labor organizers. The South African Communist Party (founded in 1921 as the Communist Party of South Africa, the first Marxist-Leninist party on the continent, banned in 1953, refashioned in 1953 as the South African Communist Party, SACP) operated as a well-disciplined organization, completely loyal to Moscow, and ideologically the most sophisticated Marxist-Leninist body on the continent. The party of course had many weaknesses. It worked in exile, an army of officers without men. But the party gained control over the African National Congress (founded in 1912 as an ultra moderate body, but later effectively reduced to the status of a Marxist-Leninist "mass organization," and a convenient transmission belt for SACP orders).

The ANC in turn established an alliance with other liberation fronts, including ZAPU (Zimbabwe African People's Organization), SWAPO (South West African People's Organization), and, more importantly, with FRELIMO and MPLA in the Portuguese colonies. MPLA (founded in 1956) and FRELIMO (created in 1962) had similar origins. Both were liberation fronts with a Marxist-Leninist core. (The framework for MPLA, for example, was laid in 1955 with the formation of the Communist Party of Angola which subsequently joined other groups in the creation of MPLA where Communists held the leading positions.)

During the 1970s, Moscow's position greatly improved in Africa. Great Britain's withdrawal from "east of Suez," the U.S. defeat in Vietnam, a worldwide oil crisis, and the final breakdown of the Portuguese African empire in 1974 (the latter occasioned by a Portuguese officers' coup) all pointed to a weakening of Western resolve. South Africa, the most powerful pro-Western state in Africa, was thrown on the defensive. Rhodesia—reduced after its Unilateral Declaration of Independence in 1965 to a South African client state—could not be defeated by the guerrillas, but equally proved unable to overthrow them. Hence Pretoria concluded in 1976 that black governance had become inevitable in Rhodesia, and the warring parties settled on a compromise. In 1980, a new government assumed power in Salisbury (renamed Harare), a government ostensibly wedded to Marxism-Leninism. The new Zimbabwean government, (based on ZANU, Zimbabwe African National Union), to some extent proved a disappointment to Moscow. ZANU looked askance at the support that Moscow had given to ZAPU, ZANU's uncertain ally in the preceding guerrilla war, but at least ZANU stood committed ideologically to the doctrines of Marxism-Leninism, and turned out to be a determined critic of the U.S. in all international forums. The People's Republic of China, having briefly challenged the Soviet Union's position as the chief supporter of world revolution, turned to a more moderate course, one that reflected China's disillusionment with Maoist militance at home, China's economic weaknesses, and the failure of expensive Chinese aid projects such as the much-heralded Tanzam (Tanzania-Zambia) Railway.

The Soviet Union, at the same time, went from strength to strength. Moscow built a powerful navy and a strong military airlift capacity—both with global range. Communists in various parts of sub-Saharan Africa infiltrated into various trade unions and student groups; they tried to build networks of agents and supporters through local peace groups, cultural fronts, youth leagues, womens' organizations, and the like. The Soviet Union took a leading part in UN debates calling for an end to Western empire in Africa, and denouncing "neocolonialism." Soviet intervention in Africa took many other forms: economic aid to incumbent governments; conventional diplomacy; cooperation between the CPSU (Communist Party of the Soviet Union) and ruling Marxist-Leninist parties in Africa; contacts between the CPSU and nonruling Communist groups; the provision of scholarships to African sympathizers; the supply of expert and organizers to oppositional groups; collaboration on a party level between the CPSU and other African Marxist or left-wing nationalist parties on the other; the use of the Soviet navy to show the flag and to sustain Soviet diplomatic initiatives; massive deployment of Soviet, Cuban, and Eastern European technicians, military advisers, and security officers—made more effective by a "socialist division of labor" between the various Warsaw Pact states in this regard; the formation of joint economic enterprises (particularly in transportation, fishing and mining) between the Soviet Union and African partners; the massive provision of military hardware both to established governments and to guerrillas; and the training of "freedom fighters" arrayed against white-dominated governments. Above all, the Soviet Union and its allies opened a new chapter in revolutionary warfare by the massive deployment of conventional proxy forces (specially Cubans, and—to a lesser extent—East Germans) in Angola and Ethiopia to promote "proletarian internationalism" and extend Soviet influence.[9] By the end of the 1970s, the Soviet Union had made much progress; as a front-page editorial in *Izvestia* put it, Africa was "marching confidently toward total liberation."[10]

In the Horn of Africa, the shift of Soviet support from Somalia to Ethiopia had enabled Ethiopia decisively to defeat a Somali invasion. Ethiopia became a Soviet client and in 1979, the military dictatorship made some attempt to organize a Marxist-Leninist political organization that would supplement army rule. To the Soviet Union, the Ethiopian experiment meant a great deal—not merely on account of Ethiopia's strategic position, but also because Soviet theoreticians saw a striking parallel between their own revolution in 1917 and the revolution in Ethiopia little more than half a century later. They were inclined to equate the Ethiopian emperors with Russia's Tsars, the Ethiopian church and the Ethiopian landed magnates with their own defunct nobility. To the Soviets, the revolution was an extraordinary experiment in setting up a Marxist-Leninist society within the unpropitious context of what they regarded as neocolonialist Africa. This is not surprising, for by the 1970s, the Leninist model had begun to acquire much prestige in many other parts of Africa as a device that might enable any small cohesive group of functionaries to seize and keep power. The very terminology of Leninist party organization itself became fashionable and found acceptance even among a number of non-Marxist parties.

In Portuguese-speaking Africa, the cause of socialism also had advanced. Both MPLA in Angola and FRELIMO in Mozambique had been formed with the aid of Communist cadres who had provided the leadership core for these liberation movements. In 1977 both MPLA and FRELIMO transformed themselves from a "movement" or "front" into Marxist-Leninist vanguard parties, dedicated to the pursuit of "scientific socialism," to "democratic centralism," to the creation of socialist societies and of a "new man." Sustained by a large Cuban military force, MPLA faithfully supported the Soviet Union's foreign policy. FRELIMO in Mozambique, having attained and held on to power without Cuban proxies, was not as dependent on Moscow as MPLA; nevertheless FRELIMO likewise considered the Warsaw Pact countries as Mozambique's national allies, a line not surprising—given the close relations that had long existed between FRELIMO, the MPLA, the CPSU, and also the pro-Soviet Portuguese Communist Party (PCP). FRELIMO and the MPLA in turn also formed part of a wider African party alliance that included SWAPO in Namibia, and the ANC in South Africa. SWAPO guerrillas operated from bases in southern Angola against Namibia; the ANC used bases in Mozambique against South Africa. Both made far-reaching claims as regards the assumed effectiveness of their respective incursions.

In Zimbabwe, the Soviets were not placed in as favorable position as in Angola. Moscow had given more support to ZAPU, ZANU's rival and ethnically a Ndebele organization, than to Robert Mugabe's ZANU, the new ruling party, backed by Zimbabwe's Shona majority. But Mugabe had never made a secret of his commitment to the cause of socialism, his friendship for "liberation groups" such as the PLO, and his hostility to great Britain and the U.S. as Ian Smith's supposed puppet masters.[11] Soviet hopes of being able gradually to enhance Moscow's influence in Harare did not by any means therefore seem unrealistic.

But it was South Africa that held the key to the continent. According to Soviet strategists, the Republic of South Africa occupies a major place in world strategy as a whole because of South Africa's geographic position and partly because of its role as a supplier of strategic minerals, at a time when Western capitalism is undergoing a serious crisis. As *Izvestia* puts it, "the South African question is a special one," partly because of the size of American investments in the country and partly because "South Africa occupies a key position in world communications. Control of South Africa means control of the southern Atlantic and the Indian Ocean."[12] South

Africa, in a wider sense, is regarded as the main Western bastion in Africa; the "liberation" of Africa requires the elimination of the South African bulwark.

Marxism-Leninism at Bay?

By the early 1980s, Marxism-Leninism in Africa had proven a striking success, but also a disastrous failure. As a means of seizing power, Marxism-Leninism had prospered. In countries as far afield as Angola, Benin, the Congo, Cape Verde, Guinea Bissau, and São Tomé and Principe, a similar power structure was in operation. Power rested with a single party. The top party leadership, drawn from the ruling party's politburo and its central committee, filled all key ministerial posts. The ruling party controlled the key institutions within the economy. The ruling party generally set out to eliminate the remnants of the indigenous middle class by a variety of confiscatory devices. The ruling parties received advice from Soviet-bloc parties or other "progressive organizations," created a network of party schools and "mass organizations." Central planning and secret police techniques were adapted for local usage from socialist countries overseas. A new class of party functionaries had come into being, with the politburo as main power center. As a rule, the politburo included the military chiefs, the most senior party officials (with the ruling party's secretary general as the chief of state), heads of the secret police, and similar dignitaries. The rulers of "democratic centralism" strictly limited significant political debates among the party factions, and the politburo's small memberships reduced, though it did not eliminate, internal fragmentation.[13] The writ of the ruling party might not run in remote villages; the ruling party might not be able to crush guerrilla outbreaks in the provinces; but the main cities were firmly under the government's control. Nowhere in Africa was a Marxist-Leninist regime overthrown from within.

Economically, however, the Marxist-Leninist regimes performed poorly, more poorly even than in Europe. Marxist-Leninists had always promised that socialism would resolve the irreconcilable differences that supposedly beset the capitalist system. Socialism would create prosperity and indeed new modes of production. By the latter part of the 1980s, such hopes had almost vanished alike in the Soviet Union and Eastern Europe. Mikhail Gorbachev's economic advisers furnished devastating accounts of the Soviet Union's economic condition; his scientific advisers warned of the parlous condition of Soviet science. In Moscow, Prague, and Wawsaw alike, the truly exciting debates among intellectuals no longer hinged on Marxism-Leninism, but on the role of a market economy, on nationalism, and religion. The intellectual atmosphere in the Soviet Bloc had changed in a manner unthinkable even ten years earlier. Expatriate African students, technical experts, military officers, guerrilla leaders sent to the Soviet Bloc for further training could not be shielded from the impact occasioned by the intellectual crisis of Marxism-Leninism.

Without exception, the Marxist-Leninist regimes in Africa moreover experienced striking economic decline. Mozambique may serve as an example.[14] On assuming power FRELIMO tried to profit from the lessons learned during the war against the Portuguese when FRELIMO had set up cooperative forms of enterprise in the so-called liberated zones. But wartime experience in running remote rural settlements proved inadequate for the purpose of ruling a country. Once in power, FRELIMO attempted to restructure traditional tribal society. The Europeans, beset by a growing sense of personal insecurity, and alienated by the partial confiscation of their property, mostly left, leaving behind a substantial infrastructure of schools, hospitals, railways, hydroelectrical undertakings that FRELIMO was ill qualified to run. FRELIMO attempted to make socialism work by placing about 5,000 of its members into the government, and the provincial administration. Some white experts were reengaged on contracts; Eastern European countries and South Africa alike provided a good deal of technical expertise. But FRELIMO could not prevent a general economic collapse. Some of its senior men were well educated and able. But the ruling party lacked the cadres necessary to run a socialized eonomy. There was a new class of revolutionary profiteers, who filled official posts, who battened on inflated salaries, who were ill qualified for their work, while virtually holding tenure for life. Neither did all of the new expatriates turn out to be satisfactory. Many were ignorant of local conditions; their salaries (higher than those of the Portuguese colonialists) imposed a severe drain on hard currency reserves. In fact President Machel himself was disagreeably surprised at the exacting conditions and salaries required by Soviet technicians. Many of the doctors supplied by North Korea and Bulgaria proved unaccustomed to tropical medicine, while Cuban advisors were unable to avoid, for instance, a near disastrous drop in the 1976 sugar harvest.[15]

FRELIMO's economic performance thus failed to match its aspirations. FRELIMO founded committees and worker production councils to operate the railways, plantations and factories. Workers' control over manufacturing was viewed as the basis for increased production. At its third congress, the party articulated a program of "making the building of heavy industry the decisive factor in breaking with misery and imperalist domination."[16] Unfortunately, the quality of management in no way matched such revolutionary aspirations. By the early 1980s, industrial output may have fallen to less than 50% of its prior level.[17] Soon signs of neglect and deterioration appeared everywhere. Industrial investments almost ceased, as the Portuguese—with their propensity to save—had departed. Beset by high inflation, graft on every level of government, and unwillingness or inability to provide adequate incentives, the Mozambique economy rapidly contracted. Hence many citizens turned to the growing private underground economy, thereby making themselves guilty, in FRELIMO's eyes, of profiteering or economic sabotage, offenses that entailed draconian punishment.

FRELIMO fared no better in farming. From the late 1970s, FRELIMO opted for communal village agriculture, rather than mechanized state farms of the Soviet type. But agricultural output declined drastically, as FRELIMO's social engineering ran against both societal obstacles as well as climactic reverses. At first heavy rains brought devastating floods to the southern regions of the country. Then droughts followed, causing crops to wither and livestock to perish. The worst period of dessication in decades gripped southern Africa, raising havoc with the region's economies. Mozambicans sarcastically complained that "when the Portuguese left, they took the rain." By the end of the 1970s, "guerrilla socialism", as it might be called, had widely come to be recognized as a failure, even among some of FRELIMO's leading cadres. The country's debt burden had greatly increased, despite the constant infusion of foreign aid. The majority of the country's state-owned enterprises kept running up deficits (covered by the Banco de Moçambique, set up in 1975). Private loans from abroad proved difficult to secure, especially after the government, in 1978, nationalized all but one of the country's banks and credit institutions. There was widespread discontent as the grand slogans of the revolution—repeated *ad nauseam*—aroused derision. There was widespread guerrilla warfare. This was inspired in part by ethnic dissensions, and even more so by the cultivators' hostility to the new class of salaried functionaries and their countless exactions. Guerrilla warfare was further facilitated by the existence of arms caches and by habits of violence dating from the anti-Portuguese struggle, and by the infiltration of additional weapons from South Africa.

Angola fared even worse. In an economic sense, Angola—like Mozambique—had experienced its golden age of development during the 1960s and the early 1970s during the last decade of Portuguese governance. Angola then grew the bulk of its own food; some industries had gotten underway. Angola was a major producer of coffee, oil, diamonds, and iron ores. For all its poverty, Angola had a chance. The revolution, however, led to the exodus—both voluntary and enforced—of some 400,000 whites. At a stroke, Angola lost a large portion of its entrepreneurs, technicians, merchants, and advanced farmers—the very people whom most critics of

Table 3–1

	Food aid and Imports (Kilograms per capita)		Annual Average Growth Rate of Agricultural Production per Capita (per cent) (food)
	1978	1982	1970–1982
Ethiopia	2.5	5.5	−0.3
Mozambique	12.3	9.8	−5.1
Angola	2.2	8.4	−2.0

SOURCE: The World Bank, *Toward Sustained Development in Sub-Saharan Africa: A Joint Program of Action.* Washington, D.C., The Bank, 1984, p. 76, 77.

Portuguese rule had previously denounced as functionless parasites. By the early 1980s, something like 80 percent of Angola's enterprises were run by the state, commonly with a great deal of inefficiency. The distribution network was in a state of disarray. Agricultural production had plummeted. Angola had increasingly become dependent on foreign food aid; agricultural production had declined—just as in the other Marxist-Leninist states of Africa. A high proportion of the country's hard-earned foreign exchange went to the military, to maintain the Cuban forces deployed in the country, and to repay Angola's debt to the Soviet Union. [See Table 3.1] A strange partnership continued to operate between commissars and corporate capitalism. Whereas Angola—like Mozambique—had done its utmost to wipe out the local bourgeoisie, Gulf Oil continued to operate as an economic enclave, supplying the greater part of Angola's foreign exchange and much of the wherewithal to pay for Soviet arms and Cuban men. Ethiopia was in an even worse case, and by the mid-1980s, the country was stricken by widespread famines—conveniently, as always, due to droughts rather than to governmental incompetence, public insecurity, widespread guerrilla warfare, and socialist campaigns against "kulaks," compradors, assorted saboteurs, and other putative villains. In addition, the Angolan government had to deal with a new military threat posed by Unita in southeastern Angola, supported by South Africa.

Both Mozambique and Angola tried to deal with economic disasters by introducing new local versions of Lenin's NEP ("New Economic Policy") adopted in the Soviet Union in the 1920s. The new departure went parallel to reformist policies adopted by other Communist governments in countries as far afield as Vietnam and the People's Republic of China, policies designed to give somewhat greater leeway to private traders and small-scale private farmers.[18] In Angola, the new policy entailed some relaxation of socialist controls, concessions to foreign (especially South African) entrepreneurs. But existing ills were hard to repair, and by the mid-1980s, the socialist economies of Africa all remained in disastrous disarray.

Not only had Marxism-Leninism proved a failure in the economic field, Marxism-Leninism had also gravely disappointed its advocates as an instrument of revolutionary guerrilla warfare against South Africa. Ever since the late 1940s, social scientists in the Eastern bloc and the West— Marxist-Leninists, Marxists, liberals—had predicted the inevitable South African revolution. Whole library shelves stood filled with publications that used the same metaphors—the inevitable tide, the coming dawn, the South African clock standing forever at five minutes before midnight, the powder barrel or the steam boiler ready to explode. But the facts of the situation perversely seemed to contradict all such forecasts. In terms of military and economic power, South Africa remained by far the strongest state on the continent. Far from being able to ignite a revolution in South Africa, South Africa's neighbors instead complained of Pretoria's success in destabilizing its neighbors.

In Angola, the MPLA government could not maintain its hold on the outlying provinces. South African counterraids across the Angolan border had immobilized the SWAPO partisans. The Angolan government forces proved unable to stamp out Unita, despite extensive armed support from Cuba. In fact the strain of maintaining large forces proved increasingly onerous for Fidel Castro. (Something like one fourth of Cuba's armed forces were deployed in Africa by 1988.) At the same time, there was some disillusionment in Moscow with regard to its African commitments. (Between 1984 and 1988, the value of arms and military supplies furnished to Angola was estimated at one billion dollars a year.) Aid to Third World countries in general proved unpopular with the Soviet public. (Moscow's own domestic propaganda backfired in this regard, as the Soviet public, quite mistakenly, began to blame consumer shortages at home on the assumed generosity of Soviet assistance to the Third World.) Gorbachev moreover was anxious to promote—at least temporarily—better relations with the U.S. and Western Europe for the sake of pushing domestic reforms. South Africa likewise became anxious to cut its expensive military commitments in Angola—all the more so since the South Africans, by 1988, had lost their former air superiority in the field. In 1988, the contending parties arrived at a compromise whereby the Cubans promised ultimately to withdraw from Angola, while the South Africans prepared to grant independence to Namibia.

South Africa's success in Mozambique was even more striking. South Africa had successfully managed to turn guerrilla warfare to its own benefit. South Africans had done much to assist Remano (or RNM, Resistência Nacional Moçambicana), a rural resistance movement, that made much of

Mozambique's countryside unsafe for the government. Mozambique's position further worsened owing to the country's inability to escape from its economic dependence on South Africa. Angola and Mozambique alike were forced to recognize the realities of South Africa's military and economic power. Under the so-called Nkomati accord of 1984, Mozambique and South Africa vowed that they would no longer support guerrillas operating in each other's territories; the two countries went as far as to conclude a nonaggression pact, with the result that the ANC found itself hamstrung. The Nkomati accord effected southern Africa in a manner similar to Egypt's pact with Israel. The ANC stood in danger of becoming a southern African equivalent of the PLO, by 1984 an unwelcome guest in most Middle Eastern countries. Far from dreading revolution, South Africa—in African terms—had become a superpower, confident in its ability to impose its will on weak and unstable neighbors, convinced moreover that the Soviet tide in southern Africa had begun to recede.

Africa Without the Soviet Bloc?

If some future cataclysm were to destroy Marxist-Leninist domination in the Soviet Union, Russia would certainly continue to play a major part in Africa. Russian interests in the continent are of ancient standing. To give just one example, from the end of the last century, Russia had shown much interest in Ethiopia as a counterweight to British and Ottoman power in a region of great strategic importance. The Russian Orthodox Church had looked with sympathy on the Ethiopian Church. During the South African war, 1899–1902, the Tsarist government had attempted to support the Boers. Assuming that the military were ever to seize the reins of government in Moscow, they might perhaps also seek strategic advantages all over the world, just as their predecessors in office. A nationally minded government in Moscow similarly would seek to strengthen pro-Russian parties in Africa, just as imperial Russia had supported pro-Russian groups in the newly independent Balkan states during the nineteenth century— Moscow would still carry out a frank and unashamed *realpolitik* to strengthen Russian national interests. Russia would presumably seek allies, and sustain with rubles and with guns; the African continent might well continue as an area of great power rivalry similar to the Balkan peninsula in the nineteenth century, but on the other hand, the possibility should not be excluded that a new Russia might seek a genuine accommodation with the West, and agree to peaceful solutions for Third World countries.

The destruction of Marxism-Leninism in the Soviet Union would, however, deal a shattering blow to Marxism-Leninism as a prestigious philosophy. Christianity and Islam might emerge with greater strength. So would traditional African creeds. (It was not for nothing that ZANU, a non-Soviet Marxist-Leninist party, had—unlike the MPLA—drawn on the support of spirit mediums in Zimbabwean civil war, and that the new ZANU government later recognized traditional healers as legitimate practitioners.) The end of Marxism-Leninism would at least compel existing Marxist-Leninist regimes to Africanize their existing styles of goverance.

The end of Marxism-Leninism in the Soviet Union would also strike at the reputation of this philosophy as an instrument of power—this at a time when the magic of central planner and public ownership of the means of production has begun to wane in many parts of the Western world. The Marxist-Leninist and the so-called socialist governments in Africa would no longer be able to draw on a huge reservoir of Soviet and Eastern European experts, planners, advisers, security consultants, party and trade union organizers. There would be an end to "proletarian internationalism"—much to the benefit of the world's genuine working classes. The socialist vocabulary of abuse directed against the so-called kulaks, compradors, and monopoly capitalists would occupy a less prominent place than at present in the parlance of international intercourse. Countries such as Malawi, the Ivory Coast, and Botswana, countries that have encouraged private enterprise and stressed investment in agriculture more than in industry, would gain more public approval than at present for the relative success with which they have managed their economies. Marxist-Leninist countries such as Ethiopia and Mozambique would incur international censure for socialist policies in agriculture that have greatly contributed to widespread and disastrous famines. In the world at large, the Russian economy—deprived of its socialist shackles—would become more prosperous; consumer demands would increase, thereby augmenting international trade, and helping Third World exports.

This is not to say that one-party governance would end in Africa. The Marxist-Leninist governments established in Africa at present all have certain distinguishing features. The new order has created a privileged position for a new salaried class of party functionaries and politicized soldiers. The ruling party is run by "hard cadres" at the top of the hierarchy. But at the foot of the pyramid there is often a lack of discipline; party organization leaves much to be desired; corruption prevails—not because Africans are personally more dishonest than Europeans or Americans, but because ties of ethnicity and kinship are commonly stronger than loyalty to an impersonal organization such as the party or the state. The new Marxist-Leninist regimes give special prominence to the armed forces and the security apparatus. There is a striking discrepancy between the ruling party's economic claims and its achievements. Urban interests are favored over rural interests; cultivators are squeezed through a variety of taxing and marketing devices; agriculture is neglected in favor of urban service industries. Despite the ruling party's nondiscriminatory ideology, there is widespread reliance on particular ethnic groups (such as the Amhara in Ethiopia). A large proportion of the national budget goes to the military. The "second economy" plays an important part in national life; but its very operation introduces an ever-present element of illegality into the most obscure transactions. The edifice is upheld by a powerful coercive machine whose servants shrink from no atrocity to maintain the rulers' privileges.

Marxist-Leninist parties in Africa share many of these characteristics with other African ruling parties. But Marxism-Leninism makes even greater demands on the masses by reason of the "progressive vanguard's" resolve to control every aspect of life for the sake of creating a "New Man." Parliamentary democracy and civil liberty have not fared well in Africa. It was not only Marxist-Leninists who assumed that, in backward countries, the "primitive accumulation of capital" should be at the cultivators' expense. It is not only in Marxist-Leninist countries that man-made famines stalk the land. The end of Marxist-Leninism in the Soviet Union—and even on the entire African continent—would not by itself entail the disappearance of the "new class" of party functionaries and politicized soldiers. At worst, Lenin's legacy might be replaced by the Emperor Bokassa's or Papa Doc's.

How would the collapse of Soviet power affect the existing Marxist-Leninist regimes in Africa? Critics of these regimes, including many conservative critics, are apt to overestimate the effect of their economic failures. Hoxha's regime in Albania, for example, had failed to build up his country's economy. The regime enjoyed no popular support. Yet Hoxha's regime survived through the exercise of massive and ruthless terror. How far could the existing Marxist-Leninist regimes in Africa manage to perform the "Hoxha trick," if deprived of Soviet assistance?

As regards Africa as a whole, some fundamental changes would certainly get under way, changes that would accelerate existing trends. South Africa's position as the continental superpower would probably be enhanced, given the inability of the so-called "front line" states to build up the Southern Africa Development Coordination Conference (SADCC, comprising Angola, Zambia, Botswana, Zimbabwe, Malawi, and Tanzania) as an effective economic counterweight. South Africa's African neighbors would continue as before to depend on their South African neighbor as a source of capital, skills, as a market, and as an outlet for their seaborne trade. Zimbabwe would continue its uneasy coexistence with South Africa; ZANU would continue to seek a privileged status as the country's sole ruling party, though ZANU leadership would presumably de-emphasize its Marxist-Leninist credentials, as would oppositional groups such as ANC in South Africa, and SWAPO in Namibia.

In Mozambique, the ruling party would probably experience great difficulty in maintaining its existing power. The party can rely on a small corps of highly trained functionaries at the top. But the subordinate cadres lack discipline in a Marxist-Leninist sense; there are regional and ethnic dissensions. The armed forces (more important than in conventional Marxist-Leninist regimes) would acquire further importance. The ruling party, in order to stay in power, would increasingly have to become Africanized in its approach, and would have to become more tolerant of traditional African customs and beliefs. South African influence would become even more potent than at present. As Joseph Hanlon, (author of *Mozambique: The Revolution Under Fire* and an avowed admirer of the present regime) puts it regretfully, the Nkomati agreement has dangerously enhanced South Africa's position in Mozambique by giving new facilities to South African entrepreneurs. The MNR would seek at least participation in the Mozambican government—this with South African support. As Hanlon puts it, even now the *retornados* and MNR exiles coming back to Mozambique from South Africa could form the basis of "the first-ever political opposition to FRELIMO inside the country." This opposition would be reinforced by surviving members of the African middle class, and by those Portuguese (including Portuguese farmers) who had not fled the country, all the more so as the U.S. might seek to strengthen the forces of capitalism in Africa through restructured U.S. aid policies that benefit the private rather than the public sector. As Hanlon sadly indicates, FRELIMO has already modified existing socialist policies. At its fourth party congress in 1983, FRELIMO agreed on a new program of favoring consumer goods for rural areas, higher prices for cultivators, and more support for private business. Mozambique, unable to pay its mounting debts to foreigners, had agreed to join the IMF. As Hanlon sees it, FRELIMO now faces the destruction of the socialist dream.[19] Without Soviet backing, the socialist system in its present form would perhaps disintegrate in Mozambique, or become totally Africanized.

In Angola, the ruling party would face problems even more severe than those encountered by FRELIMO in Mozambique. Whereas FRELIMO had come into power on its own, without the overt intervention of Soviet proxy forces, the MPLA could never have seized control in 1974 without the aid of Cuban soldiers. MPLA can rely—like FRELIMO—on a small corps of highly trained "hard cadres" at the center. By the mid-1980s, party organization, discipline, and cohesion in the lower ranks left much to be desired. The discipline of "democratic centralism" remained hard to enforce in a country where ethnic, communal, and kinship loyalties remain strong. Deprived of foreign (including East German and Cuban) experts in the field of security and organization, the party would have to modify existing social policies. During the independence struggle, MPLA had emphasized the need to do away with "tribalism," missionary religion, and "fetishism" (that is to say traditional animistic beliefs). The peoples of Angola were to be fused into a single nation, a revolutionary republic one and indivisible. This approach (acceptable to the many Portuguese-speaking men and women of mixed ancestry within the party cadres) would have to be greatly modified.

At the same time, Angola would have to change its economic policies, policies that had led to a striking decline of Angola's economy since independence. By the late 1970s already, the government had attempted a few cautious reforms. For instance, in 1979 new legislation was put on the statute book to ease the foreign lenders' lot. In addition, the authorities tried to give some encouragement to domestic cultivators. Nevertheless, Angola's ability to feed itself progressively declined. (By 1981, Angola supplied no more than 56 percent of its own domestic food requirements as opposed to about 90 percent at the end of the colonial era.) Worse still, from the government's point of view, Unita consolidated its hold, and put forward a constructive program for a mixed economy.[20] No one can be certain what will happen to Angola, if the 50,000 or so Cuban soldiers were to depart from Angola, together with the Soviet and East German advisers deployed in that country. (The Cubans might try to evade the 1988 agreement in a variety of ways, for instance by causing Cuban soldiers to take out Angolan naturalization papers, and remaining in the country in the guise of Angolan citizens.) But if all foreigners were actually to leave, the MPLA would probably be forced to seek a compromise with Unita, granting Unita a share in the government. Angola would then follow a neutralist course in foreign policy. (The original provisions for Angolan independence had in fact looked to a coalition government which the Portuguese and the resistance movements had agreed to set up in the days preceeding Angolan independence. Angola might then be restructured as an ethnic confederation, and the country would be spared the destruction and the enormous military expenditure incurred through ongoing civil wars.

In Ethiopia, Colonel Mengistu Haile Mariam in 1984 had convened the founding congress of the country's new Marxist-Leninist ruling party, the Workers' Party of Ethiopia, an event attended in a "fraternal spirit" by the presidents of Zambia, Angola, Zimbabwe, and South Yemen, as well as Gregory Romanov, a leading member of the CPSU's Politburo. Party organization and discipline, by the mid-1980s, left much to be desired. Effective power remained in the hands of the Provisional Military Admin-

istrative Council (PMAC) whose leading members all secured represen-
tation in the ruling party's Politburo and its Central Committee.
Widespread fighting, however, continued in many parts of Ethiopia—in
Eritrea, in Tigre, and elsewhere. The Eritrean Resistance Movement
(ELF), the Ethiopian People's Democratic Movement (EPDM), and the
Tigrean Liberation Front (TPLF) continued as viable organizations, and
even Mengistu admitted at the Congress that "a rather bitter struggle"
continued against the country's assorted reactionaries and secessionists.[21]
The bulk of the Cuban expeditionary force had been withdrawn after
Ethiopia's victory over Somalia, but Ethiopia continued to rely on Soviet
military advisers, and Soviet equipment to keep the country's vast military
establishment in fighting trim.

Deprived of Soviet assistance, Ethiopia would surely continue as a military dictatorship; the Amhara would continue to form the country's dominant ethnic community; Ethiopia would strive to maintain its territorial
cohesion, and continue the battle against Somali, Eritrean, and Tigrean
opposition. Ethiopia, deprived of Soviet help, would increasingly revert
to the traditions of the old empire that the revolutionaries had overthrown.
Ethiopia, by the mid-1980s moreover, remained in a parlous economic
condition, one much aggravated by the economic and social policies
adopted by the new regime. State farms and "resettlement" of discontented
peasants had led to disaster. The country's distribution system had been
disrupted through the destruction of small traders and through the official
campaign against "hoarding" and "speculation." Famine stalked the land,
and the future seemed grim. Shorn of Soviet aid, the Mengistu dictatorship
would undoubtedly be forced to make more concessions to its ethnic
minorities, and conceivably find a way out through a confederal constitution. The rulers would probably cease their hitherto unsuccessful attempts to turn Marxism-Leninism into a trans-ethnic bond. The Amhara
might be tempted to revert to their ancient Christian traditions; but the
historical struggle between Christians and Moslems in the Horn of Africa
would still continue.

Overall, the disappearance of Marxism-Leninism in the Soviet Union
and its allies would not do away with Africa's manifold problems. They
might, however, be easier to resolve.

Notes

1. L.H. Gann, "Futurology: An Inexact Science," *South African Journal of
   African Affairs*, v. 9, no. 1, 1979, p. 2–7. My own record of forecasting in

the African field may, I believe, have been perhaps somewhat better than that of my liberal colleagues in academia. Between 1959 and 1961, at the time of decolonization—a time when liberal Africanists mostly assumed that the new African states would be democratic, progressive entities wedded to a policy of "nation-building," "mass mobilization," and economic progress— my co-author, Peter Duignan and I considered that the new African states would be mostly one-party or army dictatorships, and that wealthy ethnic minorities would be in danger of persecution. We considered that British liberalism, based on the model of Great Britain in the nineteenth century, would have no applicability to South Africa. In our opinion, the problems of South Africa resembled far more those of eastern and south-central Europe, where class conflicts had been overlaid by insoluble ethnic conflicts. In 1960 we were alone among Africanists in the U.S. in believing that a French defeat in Algeria might be followed by the expulsion of Europeans from Algeria. We emphasized, in 1960, the Communist element in the Angolan revolt, and we foresaw that none of the guerrilla organizations active at the time would be in a position to effectively control Angola in the event of a Portuguese withdrawal. After the Unilateral Declaration of Independence, at a time when nearly all experts expected a rapid Rhodesian collapse, I believed that white Rhodesians would hold out much longer than their critics assumed, a view that I reiterated in the early 1970s.

These examples of successful forecasting must be balanced against various errors. Peter Duignan and I assumed in 1960, for example, that a French withdrawal from Algeria might be followed by a revolt of the French army and the installation of a semi-Fascist regime in Paris; we did not anticipate de Gaulle's role. We thought in 1961 that South Africa might be forced by an unwise Western policy into a neutralist position; such a possibility as yet remains. Our worst mistake in 1960 was to assume that the Portuguese would not fight a long war for their colonial empire—but they did. After UDI in Rhodesia in 1965, while believing that the white Rhodesians would hold out, I failed to foresee the sudden breakdown of Portuguese power in Mozambique, and the decisive effects of the Portuguese collapse on Rhodesia's ability to prevent guerrilla infiltration along its extended eastern border.

2. M.S. Bernstam and L.H. Gann, "Will the Soviet Union Stay Communist?", *Intercollegiate Review*, Spring/Summer 1984, p. 13–22.

3. Yosef Avidar, *The Party and the Army in the Soviet Union*. (Jerusalem, Magnes Press, 1983), p. 324.

4. Barbara Jelavich, *History of the Balkans: Eighteenth and Nineteenth Centuries*, v. 1, (Cambridge University Press, 1983), p. 298–299.

5. For statistical details, see for instance, The World Bank, *Accelerated Development in Sub-Saharan Africa*, (Washington, D.C., The Bank, 1981), and *Toward Sustained Development in Sub-Saharan Africa*. (The Bank, 1984). Peter Duignan and Robert Jackson, eds., *Politics and Government in African States 1960–1985*, London, Croom Helm, Stanford, Hoover Institution, 1986.

6. General Heinz Hoffmann, cited in Klaus Ehring and Martin Dallwitz,

Schwerter zu Pflugscharren: Friedensbewegung in der DDR, (Hamburg, Rowoholt, 1982), p. 120.

7. Nikolai Inozemtsev, "Capitalism Over the Next Two Decades," *World Marxist Review*, v. 22, no. 10 (October 1979), pp. 36–39. There will, however, be a shift within the capitalist world as the relative importance of the United States will decline and the relative importance of the Western European countries and Japan will increase.

8. See L.H. Gann and Peter Duignan, *Burden of Empire: An Appraisal of Western Colonialism in Africa South of the Sahara*, 1967, (Stanford, CA, Hoover Institution Press, 1984 reprinting). David Morison, *The U.S.S.R. and Africa*, (London, Oxford University Press, 1964). Arthur Jay Klinghoffer, *Soviet Perspectives on African Socialism*. (Fairleigh Dickinson University Press, 1969). William H. Friedland and Carl G. Rosberg, eds., *African Socialism*, (Stanford, CA, Hoover Institution Press, 1964).

9. For general surveys, see for instance, Thomas H. Henriksen, ed., *Communist Powers and Sub-Saharan Africa*. (Stanford, CA, Hoover Institution Press, 1981). Richard E. Bissell and Michael S. Radu, eds., *Africa in the Post-Decolonization Era*, (New Brunswick, Transaction Books, 1984). L.H. Gann and Peter Duignan, *Africa South of the Sahara: The Challenge to Western Security*, (Stanford, CA, Hoover Institution Press, 1981).

10. *Izvestia*, 10 April 1979, cited in *Yearbook on International Communist Affairs*, (Stanford, CA, Hoover Institution Press, 1980), p. 89.

11. See Robert Mugabe, *Our War of Liberation: Speeches, Articles, Interviews 1976–1979*. (Gweru, Zimbabwe, Mambo Press, 1983).

12. *Izvestia* (July 13, 1976).

13. Michael S. Radu, "Ideology, Parties and Foreign Policy in Sub-Saharan Africa", in Richard E. Bisell and Michael S. Radu, eds., *Africa in the Post-Decolonization Era*. (New Brunswick, Transaction Books, 1984, p. 24–25).

14. See Thomas Henriksen, "Lusophone Africa", in Peter Duignan and Robert Jackson, eds., *Africa Since Decolonization*, (1984), for details.

15. Keith Middlemas, "Independent Mozambique and Its Regional Policy", in John Seiler, ed., *Southern Africa Since the Portuguese Coup*, (Boulder, CO, Westview Press, 1980), p. 220.

16. See *Central Committee Report to the Third Congress of FRELIMO*, (London; Mozambique, Angola, Guinea Information Centre, 1978), p. 48.

17. See René Pélissier, "Economy" in the entry on "Mozambique", *Africa South of the Sahara*, 1983–1984, p. 593.

18. See for instance, *Economist* [London], 13–19 October 1984, p. 78, 84, 98–99.

19. Joseph Hanlon, "Stealing the Dream", *New Statesman* [London], 19 October 1984, p. 21–22.

20. UNITA, *The Angola Road to National Recovery*, (Jamba, Angola, 1983).

21. *Africa Research Bulletin*, [London], September 30, 1984, p. 7370–7373.

4

Implications of the Fall of the Soviet Regime on Cuba and Cuban-Sponsored Revolutionary Regimes and Movements in Latin America

W. RAYMOND DUNCAN

Speculating about the implications of the fall of the Soviet regime on Cuba and Cuban-sponsored revolutionary regimes in Latin America is a useful intellectual exercise. First, it stimulates thought about the current Third World context within which Soviet-Cuban relations are played out and how Soviet-Third World conditions might affect Moscow's perceptions of its Cuban ties under a non-Soviet regime. Second, it leads naturally to an exploration of the nature of the Soviet-Cuban relationship, especially as it might be seen by a post-Soviet government in Russia as well as by those individuals governing the Havana regime. Third, it leads us into the domain of current Cuban foreign policy toward revolutionary regimes and movements in Latin America and how major alterations in Soviet-Cuban relations would likely generate changes in Havana's foreign policy.

Probing this three-dimensional problem is fascinating, but difficult. We cannot be certain how, and in what ways, tomorrow's leaders will alter today's priorities, or how old drives behind Soviet and Cuban foreign policies may find new forms. While predicting these outcomes is hazardous, we can suggest alternate future scenarios depicting how a shift in Moscow away from Marxism-Leninism might affect the Soviet-Cuban relationship and Havana's sponsorship of revolutionary regimes and movements in Latin America. This offers a useful avenue of investigation, used in previous studies of how leadership perceptions affect a country's foreign policy and international relations.[1] To develop future scenarios, we first need to understand current Soviet and Cuban intentions, perceptions and images of the world—best approached through a number of working assumptions and hypotheses.[2]

Assumptions and Hypotheses

To begin, Soviet foreign policy reflects the quest for global power status and equality with the West. It is shaped at minimum by two central belief systems: Marxism-Leninism and Russian nationalism, both of which are conditioned by Russia's legacy of the past.[3] Both contain a sense of universal mission and expansionist drives.[4] Should Marxism-Leninism pass away, Russia's leaders probably will retain some form of Russian nationalism with its various images: defense against an axiomatically hostile world, commitment to empire, sense of universal mission, and belief that power is the means to international recognition and material rewards.

Hypothesis one: The passing of Marxism-Leninism would leave Russian nationalism as a major belief system shaping Soviet foreign policy toward the Third World and Cuba. While this does not mean that Soviet foreign policy will pursue the same Third World opportunities regarding global power status, it does suggest that Russia will remain an ambitious country with great power interests. Russian nationalism will continue to motivate Soviet foreign policy, albeit without the expansionist imperatives wrought by Marxism-Leninism. How this perception will affect Cuban foreign policy remains to be seen.

A second assumption is that a future non-Marxist-Leninist foreign policy will retain an interest in a strong Third World posture. For it is Russia's Third World presence that has provided enormous geostrategic and geopolitical benefits, allowing the Kremlin to break out of its continental isolation of the early 1950s.[5] Compared to the mid-1950s, when the USSR first began to court Third World countries under Nikita Khrushchev's leadership, the Soviets have used the Third World to transform themselves from a continental-based power into a global superpower. They have played the game of power politics rather successfully over the years in pursuit of opportunities to project power and gain a measure of equality in global decision making with the United States.

Moscow's new global reach is imprinted within the Third World of the

1980s in several respects.[6] Expanded airlift and naval facilities, intelligence-gathering capabilities, diplomatic contacts with a wide variety of Communist and non-Communist developing countries, commercial relations, and academic scholarships attest to its world class power status.[7] Soviet relations with Cuba and Vietnam provided Moscow with considerable leverage vis-à-vis its major global rivals: The United States and China.[8] Ties with Syria and Libya have promoted Soviet interests in the vital Middle East.[9] And in the strategic border country of Afghanistan, the Soviets have established a strong, albeit incomplete, foothold for geopolitical security.[10] The collapse of the Portuguese empire has yielded major strategic gains in southern Africa during 1975–1979, when Cuba, in advancing its own priorities, has helped the Soviets promote their interests—in Angola, Ethiopia and Mozambique.[11] These pro-Soviet countries, along with Nicaragua in the Caribbean basin, offered some hope for an expanding pro-Soviet world socialist system and weakening of U.S.-led imperialism and capitalism as called for in Moscow's "correlation of world forces" ideological script for the unfolding drama in world politics.

Commercial relations with the non-Communist developing countries have become an especially important aspect of Soviet great power politics. Trade with the non-Communist Third World provides markets for Soviet products and sources for the purchase of major commodities such as fish, food, and minerals. Weapons sales yield critical hard currency earnings as well as additional sources of oil and gas as partial payment for weapons. Should the Soviet economy increasingly decline in oil production and continue its need for Third World resources, commercial relations with the Third World will likely play a critical role in Moscow's perceptions of its interests in the developing countries.

Hypothesis two: The Third World will remain an arena of great power interest and opportunism for future Russian leaders. Interest in the Third World does not necessarily mean that Soviet ties with Cuba will remain intact. It does suggest, however, that Moscow's future leaders will make foreign policy decisions regarding Cuba in the context of its Third World posture. This is so because Cuba has served as an important proxy in complementing Soviet interests in the Third World, as vividly demonstrated by Cuba's fighting on behalf of the pro-Soviet Movement for the Popular Liberation of Angola (MPLA) in Angola (1975) and in support of the pro-Soviet Mengistu Haile Mariam regime in Ethiopia during 1977–78. Cuban policies in Grenada (1979–1983) and Nicaragua (after July 1979) have further advanced Soviet interests.[12]

A third assumption is that Moscow will face mounting burdens of consolidating its past gains in the Third World. Soviet gains in the developing countries are offset by serious negative trends which do not bode well for the Soviet empire.[13] The spate of Soviet gains—in terms of helping pro-Soviet clients achieve power, as in Angola and Ethiopia, or in helping clients immediately after they came to power, as in Grenada and Nicaragua ended in 1979. Soviet military intervention in Afghanistan in 1979 symbolized the end of a period of Soviet expansionism through collapsing colonial empires and the beginning of a period of trying to manage old relations and consolidate past gains.

Since the invasion of Afghanistan, the burdens of empire have become more pronounced within their military, economic, and political dimensions. The Soviets are bogged down in Afghanistan against a persistent opposition, face mounting difficulties of conducting a counterinsurgency war for which they are ill prepared, rising morale problems among their troops, and increasing international disapproval with their brutal conduct of the war which has produced several United Nations condemnations for violation of human rights in Afghanistan. Nor is their Afghanistan posture popular among the Third World countries, where Soviet claims as the Third World's "natural ally" frequently meet with cynicism or suspicion. Afghanistan is the classic example of Moscow having become less a defender of national liberation movements, for which it claims leadership, than the fighter of counterinsurgency battles against national liberation movements. Soviet opposition to the UNITA forces in Angola and against the Marxist-oriented Eritrean People's Liberation Front in Ethiopia illustrate this problem.[14]

The economic dimension of Soviet-Third World relations faces equally difficult problems. In essence the economic burden is two-dimensional. First, the Soviet economy itself has been experiencing declining productivity. Behind this situation lies an inefficient economic system, excessive bureaucracy, corruption, worker absenteeism, and heavy defense spending which drains investments away from consumer goods. Oil production has begun to fall, as easily extracted oil declines, while Soviet domestic, Eastern European, Cuban and Vietnamese demands for Soviet oil remain high.[15] Second, the Third World economies supported by the USSR are inefficient; Cuba and Vietnam are notable cases in point. Other Third World clients supported by the Soviets strive for increased economic aid, a goal that has not been attained. Mozambique's turning toward the West for developmental assistance and Nicaragua's unhappiness with the level of Soviet economic aid highlight this problem.

Hypothesis three: Future Russian leaders will assess carefully the costs as well as the benefits of their extended Third World presence. When future Russian leaders make this analysis, the costs, as well as the benefits of supporting Cuba will become a major consideration in determining whether or not to continue the huge Soviet economic outlays (around $4 billion annually during the mid 1980s) and free military aid. The Cuban economy is notoriously inefficient, and continues to be a source of major discord between Moscow and Havana officials.[16]

A fourth assumption centers on the Soviet-Cuban relationship as essentially one of each country pursuing compatible foreign policy interests through cooperative actions. So long as each country's interests remain compatible, relations will remain strong. To the extent interests become less compatible, relations will become strained. Predicting future scenarios is best served by understanding the relationship as one of two countries in pursuit of their foreign policy goals through cooperative action, rather than the Soviet Union controlling or dominating Cuba's destiny, or Havana pursuing its interests through its influence on the Soviet Union.[17]

In this context, it is helpful to conceive of Cuba as a country with its own foreign policy agenda as distinct from strictly serving Soviet foreign policy goals as ordered by Moscow. Cuba's priorities include national security (especially with regard to the U.S.), economic development, survival of the revolution, projecting Cuban power abroad in support of Third World revolutionary movements and "internationalist duty," and a search for international status.[18] These motivations are complimented by Castro's own charismatic personality, his sense of revolutionary activism, and his pronounced global aspirations.[19]

When looking at the Cuban motivations in foreign policy, the forces of Marxism-Leninism and Cuban nationalism merit our attention. While Cuban Communism appears more prominent, nationalism should not be underestimated. Nationalist forces take many forms inside Cuban decision making: (1) Castro's 26th of July Movement followers occupy prime positions in the political hierarchy, (2) Cuban identity, unity and purpose is stressed in political socialization and public pronouncements, (3) defense of the patria or fatherland has been strongly emphasized in defense policy, (4) the Cuban population is infused with a nationalist as well as internationalist ethic of work and struggle for the people and homeland, and (5) the government has striven to forge in Cuba's population a sense of pride, not only in domestic policies, but also in foreign affairs as Cuba entered its new brand of twentieth century diplomacy following the revolution of 1959.[20]

Hypothesis four: Future Cuban reactions to shifts in Soviet foreign policy will be a product of Cuban nationalism and national interests as well as its ideological orientation to Marxism-Leninism. This hypothesis suggests a degree of greater flexibility in Cuban foreign policy, than might be assumed were the country driven more strictly by Marxist-Leninist orientations. What directions Cuban nationalism might take the country, should its Russian patron drop its own Marxist-Leninist orientation, remains in question. Yet the roots of adaptability exist, stemming from Havana's own national interests and nationalist forces.

A fifth assumption concerns the nature of Cuban economic and military dependency on the USSR. Without free Soviet military assistance, Cuban security would be greatly reduced. Without Soviet economic aid, Cuba could not survive. Soviet military and economic aid admittedly make possible Cuba's foreign policies, which serve interests in both Havana and Moscow. A future Russian regime may determine that continued military and economic aid will provide benefits that outweigh costs. One of those costs would be continued adversarial relations with the U.S., should Cuba continue its support of revolutionary regimes and movements in Latin America. But should Russia's military or economic aid be severely reduced, Cuba's security, economy and current support of revolutionary regimes and movements in Latin America would face substantial vulnerabilities and limited options.

Hypothesis five: Cuba's economic and military dependence on the USSR make Havana's foreign policy highly vulnerable to sharp reductions in aid from Moscow. Should a future Russian regime determine to cut either its economic or military support to Cuba, Havana would be forced to think through its current support of revolutionary regimes and movements in Latin America. Soviet reductions in low-priced petroleum supplies or in the purchase of Cuban sugar above the world market price would force Cuba to look for economic support from other sources. A cut in military supplies would leave Cuba extraordinarily vulnerable in the Caribbean Basin, most notably vis-à-vis the U.S. Either type of sharp reduction would likely force the Cubans toward a less distinct forward strategy in support of revolutionary movements and regimes in Latin America and toward a more accomodative posture with the U.S.

A sixth assumption in constructing alternate scenarios is that distinct Soviet and Cuban foreign policies operate in Latin America. While their policies converge in many respects (anti-imperialism, efforts to weaken the U.S., voicing opposition to a possible U.S. intervention in Nicaragua, supporting the Contadora process for regional negotiations of disputes in Central America), they reflect distinct goals and priorities. Moscow perceives its Caribbean and Central American policies in the context of East-West relations; Havana stresses the North-South struggle for development. Moscow has emphasized peaceful change and the primary role of pro-Soviet Communist parties within "united fronts" as the path to change in most of Latin America; Cuba more often has advanced the armed struggle road to change and identifies more closely with regional leftist guerrillas—some Marxist-Leninist, some less so. The Soviet Union has been more cautious and conservative, wishing to avoid a direct confrontation with the

U.S.; Cuba has demonstrated a willingness to take higher risks and has periodically demonstrated discontent with Moscow's more reserved manner in backing revolutionary regimes and movements, especially with economic assistance.[21] Limited Soviet economic aid to Nicaragua under the Sandinistas is a case in point.

Hypothesis six: A non-Marxist-Leninist Russian government would be more inclined to back away from direct support of revolutionary regimes and movements in Latin America than Cuba. This hypothesis is not meant to suggest that Cuba is incapable of following a policy adapted to peaceful state-to-state relations when pressed to do so. This is precisely what happened from the late 1960s to the late 1970s, when it became clear that guerrilla warfare in Latin America was not working, and when Soviet economic pressures within Cuba and from the USSR forced Castro to move away from his previous emphasis on armed struggle in the western hemisphere as the primary road to change.[22]

By the mid-1980s, moreover, Castro was following a two-track policy in Latin America. On the one hand, Castro has been pursuing peaceful state-to-state relations with a wide range of states in the western hemisphere; expanding bilateral commercial, cultural and political relations with most Latin American countries; stressing the Contadora process in Central America; and seeking widened diplomatic support in Latin America to offset the possibility of a direct confrontation with the U.S., following its October 1983 intervention in Grenada. But on the other hand, Castro has continued to support the revolutionary government of Nicaragua with approximately 7–8,000 Cubans, of which about 3,500 are military personnel; training and advising guerrillas in El Salvador (although direct weapon flows through Nicaragua to El Salvador apparently have been cut back compared to 1980–81); and diplomatic backing of other guerrilla movements operating in Chile, Colombia and Guatemala.[23]

So long as Castro is in power, he is highly likely to wish to pursue guerrilla struggle—the model of Cuba's revolution—when opportunities exist. Should the new Russian government determine to back away from its present support of revolutionary regimes and movements, while Fidel Castro was still in power and revolutionary opportunities remained in Central America and the Caribbean, Havana's pursuit of clandestine revolutionary activities would be more difficult. But activities of this type cannot be completely ruled out, given Castro's perception of revolutionary change in Hispanic America as the best long-range source of security for the Cuban revolution.[24] It was Castro's view of armed struggle and support for the Sandinistas that likely forced the USSR to change its thinking about guerrilla warfare in 1979, lest they be left behind Castro's lead. And Castro continues to demonstrate support for guerrilla groups in Central and South

America, when the Soviets are pursuing more pragmatic tactics in state-to-state diplomacy.[25] Castro's own pragmatic adaptability should not be underrated, but neither should his commitment to armed struggle.

A seventh assumption focuses on Caribbean and Central American opposition to Cuba's support of revolutionary regimes and movements in the region. Dating back to the mid-1960s, when the Castro government strongly advocated armed struggle in Latin America, the larger hemispheric governments have by no means been sanguine about Cuba's revolutionary activities.[26] As Cuba's backing of armed struggle and revolutionary regimes in the Caribbean basin escalated again following the revolutions in Grenada (March 1979) and Nicaragua (July 1979), the more powerful regional actors demonstrated their discontent. By 1982 Cuba's relations had soured with Colombia, Ecuador and Peru—and with the smaller countries of Costa Rica, Jamaica (under Eduard Seaga) and Panama.[27] Even Mexico, Cuba's old staunch ally, was becoming sensitive to the mounting regional conflict. This trend led Mexico to play a more powerful role in attempting to negotiate a political settlement of the various aspects of regional discord emanating from El Salvador and Nicaragua. Venezuela, meanwhile, cut off crude oil deliveries in 1982 to Nicaragua, when the Sandinistas did not pay their bills.

Hypothesis seven: Regional actors in the Caribbean and Central America, who oppose Cuban support of revolutionary movements and regimes, will serve as a major deterrent to Havana's guerrilla warfare policies should Russian economic and military aid decrease. Without low-priced energy supplies and military weapons from Russia, the Cuban government will become highly dependent on regional sources of petroleum and extremely vulnerable to those regional actors who oppose violent change. Cuba's vulnerability to economic sanctions from regional actors stems from its notorious economic deficiencies. Cuba has recently been unable to meet its export commitments to the Soviet bloc. It suffers from low productivity, misplaced investment priorities and unrealistic budgeting. Its trade with the West has slipped from about 40 percent to 13 percent, and it has an approximately $3.2 billion debt to the West—on top of a $9 billion debt with the Soviet Union. Without Soviet oil and sugar purchases, oil from Ecuador, Mexico and Venezuela become all-important. Hence Castro's perception of the benefits and costs of conducting guerrilla warfare activities and supporting revolutionary regimes like Nicaragua must be calculated in the context of regional actor reactions.

Assumption eight gets at the other major obstacles facing both Soviet and Cuban efforts to support revolutionary regimes and movements in Latin America. These obstacles have been discussed elsewhere, but they bear identifying here. First, economic constraints abound. Neither the

Soviet Union nor Cuba is capable of extending the quantity and quality of capital and technology required for revolutionary regimes to meet their economic development needs. This problem results from both the economic weaknesses of Moscow and Havana and of their chief recipients, as demonstrated by Grenada (before October 1983) and Nicaragua. Nicaragua (and Grenada before the U.S. intervention) is inundated with economic difficulties: approximately 50 percent inflation in 1984, a rising external debt, steady decline of GDP growth, declining exports, and reports of corruption in upper levels of government.[28]

Second, political constraints confound Soviet and Cuban efforts to gain influence in revolutionary regimes and movements. Nicaragua is experiencing popular discontent, draft resistence, the defections of previously committed supporters (Jose Arturo Cruz), personal disagreements among the Sandinistas.[29] El Salvador reflects a decline in popular support for the Cuban-backed insurgency, frictions within the guerrilla movement, and general weakness in the guerrilla offensive following the March 1985 elections.[30] The Communist parties of Latin America remain weak, divided by personalities, disorganized, and challenged by other parties, such as the recently elected APRA party of Peru. Guerrilla movements and revolutionary regimes face opposition from the Hispano-Catholic Church, as in Nicaragua, while the political culture of personalism tends to make difficult the attainment of permanent unity in revolutionary movements. Nationalism throughout Latin America tends to limit the power of external forces to control internal events.

Hypothesis eight: Limits to both Soviet and Cuban influence over revolutionary movements and regimes in Latin America will restrict Cuban capabilities more sharply should Soviet aid to Cuba be reduced. The constraints to Soviet and Cuban influence have been operative for years. Should Cuba be forced to go it alone in the western hemisphere, the previous balance between united Soviet-Cuban capabilities and regional obstacles would be shifted dramatically toward the power of the latter, given the power lost from potentially reduced supply and diplomatic links with the Soviet Union. Alone, Cuba simply faces huge obstacles in trying to back revolutionary regimes and movements in Latin America.

Assumption nine takes note of the personality differences in Cuba's ruling elite. The elite includes three key individuals: Fidel Castro, his brother, Raul, and the old-line Communist leader, Carlos Rafael Rodriguez. Of the three, Fidel is the more committed to revolutionary struggle and direct support for revolutionary regimes and movements in the Third World. Raul, as defense minister trained in the USSR, is probably most close to Soviet counterparts, but somewhat less noted for the charismatic revolutionary zeal of his brother. Carlos Rafael is an economic pragmatist, concerned with efficiency of economic management and the overall economic development of Cuba.

Reactions of a future Cuban leadership to shifts in the Soviet connection will hinge in part on who is in charge in Havana at the time. Should Fidel still lead the government, the perception of revolutionary opportunism—set against the operative assumptions and hypotheses noted above—will constitute a key variable. Still, Castro has demonstrated tremendous flexibility in foreign policy in the past, and we do not suggest here that he would predictably pursue a relentless support of armed struggle and revolutionary regimes should Soviet ties be cut. Raul is another kind of actor. His inclination might lean more toward deep concern for Cuban defense—rather than revolutionary adventures—in face of reduced Soviet ties. A Carlos Rafael at the helm would likely demonstrate deep sensitivity to Cuba's economic needs, rather than a concern for projecting a Cuban revolutionary enthusiasm abroad. This would mean devising any number of possible options for diversifying Cuban trade patterns toward the West and Japan.

Hypothesis nine: Cuban reactions to a shift in relations with Russia will depend in part upon who is minding the store at the time. Castro will continue to be interested in projecting the Cuban experience abroad, albeit under altered conditions. Raul's focus will center on defense of the homeland—and foreign intervention, if possible, under a new Russian regime. Carlos Rafael will remain committed to the economic development of Cuba and how to best maximize the available options for Cuba's economy under sustained or altered ties with the USSR.

Our last assumption stresses the role of third-party actors in affecting Cuba's reactions to changes in its Soviet connection. In trying to understand how the Cuban regime will react to an altered situation with the Soviet Union in the future, we must assume that its leaders will need to assess their relations with other countries. This is especially so if another actor is geographically proximate, as is the U.S. Just as the current Soviet-Cuban relationship is affected by Soviet and Cuban perceptions of U.S. foreign policy, so too will future Soviet and Cuban foreign policies be conditioned by the U.S.

Hypothesis ten: Cuba's reactions to shifts in future relations with the Soviet Union will be shaped by Havana's leadership perceptions of U.S. foreign policy. Political realities of the quarter century Soviet-Cuban-United States triangular relationship will be instructive to Cuba's future decision making. Since the early 1960s, Cuba's ties with the USSR have been perceived in the United States as the major destabilizing force in the western hemisphere. Havana's relations with Moscow have shaped U.S. views of subsequent revolutionary movements, leading the United States toward a determination to prevent "another Cuba"—as in El Salvador, Grenada, Guatemala or Nicaragua. A Marxist-Leninist Cuba in the Soviet embrace has created a sense of vulnerability in the United States, a deep concern with U.S. physical security that has triggered a defensive posture historically associated with the Monroe Doctrine. Certainly, Cuba's ties with the USSR have shaped U.S. perceptions not only of Cuba itself, but also of the USSR as an intractable enemy unamenable to pragmatic problem solving and bent upon Third World domination.

The key point is that Cuba's ties to the Soviet Union have greatly shaped East-West relations, thus contributing to the Cold War. They have complicated the management of U.S.-Soviet adversarial relations, undermined detente between the two super-powers, and made most Cuban actions highly suspect. The net effect of past Cuban ties with the USSR has admittedly provided some benefits to Cuba, such as providing a natural outside enemy against which the Fidelistas could urge popular unity, a work ethic of struggle for development against heavy odds, and a symbolic enemy against whose opposition Cuba might earn additional international dignity and prestige from other Third World countries. But U.S. opposition to a Soviet-tied, Marxist-Leninist Cuba in its "strategic backyard" has been heavy: huge economic sanctions from Cuba's most logical aid and trade partner, security threats which have diverted scarce resources away from Cuba's economic development, and perpetual opposition against most of Cuba's development model and foreign relations. These costs and benefits would likely be assessed in any future Cuban decision making brought about by altered ties with Moscow.

Alternate Future Scenarios

Based upon these assumptions and hypotheses, three alternate scenarios are possible in future Cuban support for revolutionary regimes and movements in Latin America should the USSR move toward a non-Marxist-Leninist regime. Each is contingent upon a different type of future Soviet-Cuban relationship and its impact on Havana's perceptions and foreign policy decision making. These three types of relationship are: (1) a complete break in relations between the USSR and Cuba (about a 40 percent probability), (2) a partial reduction in Russian economic aid and military assistance to Cuba (around a 50 percent probability), and (3) little or no change in present levels of Soviet economic and military support (approximately a 10 percent probability). Utilizing the assumptions and hypothesis outlined above, it is possible to construct probable Cuban reactions to each of these conditions.

Scenario one: A complete break in Soviet ties with Cuba

A first distinct possibility in future Russian-Cuban relations is a complete break in Moscow's ties with Havana. This scenario is based upon hypothesis three, which emphasizes Moscow's enormous costs in maintaining its present Third World empire and the projection of those costs into the future. It assumes that although the new Russian leaders would likely retain an interest in the Third World as an arena of great power competition, new priorities would require implementation. These conceivably would include a mix of: (1) concentrating on more geographically proximate regions where national security is paramount, e.g., southern Asia and the Middle East, (2) dumping politically weak and economically inefficient Marxist-Leninist clients, including Cuba (despite its geographic proximity to the U.S.), and (3) establishing more favorable diplomatic state-to-state relations with the United States.

Scenario one is based upon the assumption that future Russian leaders will concentrate on several key priorities. These include minimizing the costs of their Third World activities, easing the Cold War and moving toward renewed detente with the United States in order to open new trade options, reduction of military spending and the risk of nuclear war through arms control, and trying to lessen the unity of a NATO aimed at the Russian heartland. These aims and ambitions might include severance of Cuban ties. This scenario presupposes, however, that the new Soviet regime would probably have to justify to the Russian military its giving up a key strategic gain in Cuba and the possible loss of a valuable base of operations vis-à-vis the United States.

Despite the positive attributes for Soviet-Third World policies provided by Cuba, Havana is not completely cost free. First, future Russian leaders may calculate that their extraordinary levels of aid to Cuba inhibit their capacity to lend to other developing countries. A new Russian regime, without the Marxist-Leninist ideological perceptions, may determine to extend more extensive assistance to non-Communist, lesser developed countries, arrange more lucrative trade credits, or purchase additional food and raw materials from the developing areas.

Second, the direct Soviet connection with Cuba—and Havana's presence in Third World settings (especially in Africa and the Caribbean Basin)— has raised fears of Soviet-Cuban power projection on the part of other Third World countries. A new Russian leadership might conclude that Cuban ties constitute an obstacle to more effective economic and political relations with the non-Communist Third World.

Third, the Soviet-Cuban connection has directly contributed to United States perceptions of the USSR as a threatening adversary. The Soviets are perceived by many in the United States as a destabilizing force in southern Africa, the Middle East and, especially, in the Caribbean Basin, and Moscow's ties to Cuba have contributed to a sense of vulnerability in Washington's own backyard. This set of perceptions has tended to undermine détente relations between Moscow and Washington since its inception in the late 1960s, has deeply affected United States beliefs about the USSR as an intractable enemy unamenable to pragmatic problem solving, and has contributed to the huge U.S. military buildup—directed against the USSR. These connections between Soviet-Cuban relations and the East-West conflict would likely not escape future Russian leaders.

Fourth, economic strains currently affect the Soviet-Cuban relationship. By 1984–85, owing to problems in the Soviet economy, Moscow's oil supplies to Havana were beginning to slip from previous levels, and the Soviets were increasingly demanding that Cuba fulfill its commitments to supply sugar to Soviet bloc nations. These Soviet demands reportedly forced Havana to spend $100 million buying sugar on the world market in 1985 to meet its Soviet commitment, and by mid-1985 Havana was embarked upon numerous austerity measures in their own economy. Other economic strains may have been at work behind Castro's refusal to attend the June 1984 COMECON meetings in Moscow, especially the Soviet-led CO-MECON insistence that Cuba continue to be a chief agricultural supplier to COMECON members rather than being allowed to press ahead with industrial diversification as desired by the Cuban leadership. Notably, Fidel Castro also failed to attend Chernenko's funeral in March 1985, and he did not sign the book of condolences at the Soviet embassy in Havana. Castro had attended the funerals of Chernenko's two predecessors, Yuri Andropov and Leonid Brezhnev. Raul, Castro's brother and Cuban defense minister, attended Chernenko's funeral.

Fifth, other major economic strains in the Soviet-Cuban relationship suggest the possibility of scenario one. Soviet supply of petroleum to Cuba at below the world market price, coupled with sugar purchases at above the world market price, represent substantial hard-currency losses to the Soviet economy. With Cuba costing the Soviet leaders approximately $4 billion per year, when the Cuban economy remains enormously inefficient (about which the Soviets have registered frequent complaints), future Russian leaders may simply determine that the economic cost of "carrying" Cuba is simply not worth the benefits.

What would be the likely impact of a total break in Soviet-Cuban relations on Havana's sponsorship of revolutionary movements and regimes in Latin America? Drawing upon hypotheses five through eight, the most probable outcome of a total cut in Soviet-Cuban relations would be a virtual cessation of Cuban-sponsored revolutionary regimes and movements. Owing to Havana's need to look elsewhere for aid, trade and markets, the

Cubans would likely be pressed toward a more accomodative relationship with the United States. That the Cuban leaders are pragmatically capable of such a shift in policy has been demonstrated in the past, when external and internal pressures convinced Castro that it was in his interest to so. His shift away from support of armed struggle in the hemisphere toward peaceful state-to-state relations in the late 1960s is a classic case in point.

Here it should be noted that Castro has always been nervous that the Soviets might sell him out in order to get a deal with the United States. These fears would undoubtedly be strengthened in case of a change of regime in Moscow, especially if it involved an end or sharp reduction of Soviet aid. On the other hand, his fears of the United States might be significantly lessened if a change of regime in Moscow brought a United States perception that Cuba (and others) were no longer tied to a world revolutionary mission. These perceptions might make Castro's ability to adapt all the easier.

A complete downgrading of Cuban support for revolutionary regimes and movements in scenario one likely would take several forms. It would include sharply reduced military, paramilitary (intelligence training and organization, state police) and political-organizational training for regimes in power, e.g., the Sandinistas, and support for guerrilla movements, as in El Salvador, Guatemala, Chile and Colombia. Second, the Cubans would likely be forced to restrict their free development aid to Third World countries in the form of teachers, doctors, paramedics, agronomists and construction workers in countries like Nicaragua. Where these services are paid for, however, as in Angola, they would probably continue as a needed form of hard-currency earnings.

Should this eventuality occur, it would in turn impact sharply on revolutionary regimes in place, such as the Sandinistas of Nicaragua—insofar as they depend so heavily on the Soviet Union and Cuba for security assistance to keep the current leaders in power. Without Soviet and Cuban assistance providing Nicaragua's national security needs—weapons, training and operating the police and intelligence services—the Sandinista military buildup and support for guerrillas in El Salvador would be sharply restricted. This in turn conceivably would have the impact of encouraging the Sandinistas more toward some form of power sharing (through possible elections) with the opposition, although by no means guaranteeing an abrogation of power. It would probably produce increased disunity among El Salvador's guerrillas, but not necessarily an end to their resistance, given the culture of power, struggle, and personalism in Latin American politics. Admittedly, should Fidel Castro still be in power, he conceivably would continue his interest in guerrilla struggle. But without Russian economic and military aid, his capabilities to project Cuban power—in the face of

Caribbean Basin, Central American and U.S. opposition—would be severely diminished.

As to other revolutionary movements, it is likely that the already weak Latin American Communist parties would be shattered without Soviet or Soviet-Cuban aid. In contrast, indigenous revolutionary movements might be helped by being rid of ties to outside revolutionary movements, especially if the United States becomes less worried about them as a result of the Soviet demise.

One major caveat must be appended to this scenario. Should Cuba be able to procure the same, or higher, levels of economic and military aid from another Communist country, the effects of lost Soviet assistance could be overcome. The one country which might try to fill the bill is mainland China, although China's interest in playing the "U.S. card" against the USSR suggests that China would eschew the Cuban gambit. Still, a Communist Chinese-based assistance program would offset Soviet losses and make possible the continuance of Castro's support of revolutionary regimes and movements in Latin America.

Interesting questions are closely associated with this scenario. Would a new Russian regime seeking to differentiate itself from its Soviet predecessor bring pressure on former Soviet clients, like Cuba, to change their ideological orientation? Would the loss of Soviet support erode Fidel Castro's political base, generating discontent and a need for Castro to explain why he had tied himself to a loser? Would Castro—ever the revolutionary—revert to a kind of traditional Latin American caudillo and try to continue to play the role of revolutionary leader, this time not tied to the Soviet Union?

Scenario two: A partial downgrading of Soviet economic, military and political support for Cuba.

A partial downgrading, rather than complete break, is a second possibility as suggested by hypotheses one and two. A new Russian regime, embued with preset images of past Russian imperial ambitions, security threats from abroad, great power aspirations, and a current Third World presence in place, might determine to retain its Cuban connection if possible. This scenario suggests that the new Russian leadership would perceive distinct advantages in trying to hold on to key clients, whose own policies help check U.S. power, e.g., Cuba and Vietnam, which occupy geostrategic positions close to the other global competitors with Russian superpower goals—the United States and China.

In this scenario, the Russians might likely pursue a number of policies designed to improve their international security setting: (1) promotion of a nationally oriented (as opposed to Marxist-Leninist) form of detente with the United States, including arms control, (2) pursuit of some form of accomodation with China, (3) trying to reach some type of code of conduct for Russian-U.S. relations in the Third World, and (4) easing, but not breaking, ties with Cuba. The latter might conceivably include a reduction, but not complete cut-off, in weapons transfers, reduced economic aid, strong encouragement for Cuba to diversify its trade links into the Western economies, and pressure on Cuba to cease its guerrilla warfare activities in Latin America.

The Cuban reaction to a partial reduction in Soviet economic and military aid is more difficult to predict than a complete severance of ties with the Soviet Union. But given Havana's nearly complete economic and military dependence on Moscow, any major cuts in Soviet aid would likely propel Havana in the same direction as the first scenario, out of the need to acquire supplemental forms of aid, trade and markets. The Cuban economy is simply so heavily dependent on Soviet aid, and is so in need of external ties in order to raise its productivity, that Havana's leaders would probably court foreign investment alternatives—as in scenario one. The Cuban government already has a 1982 foreign investment law on the books, so the ground has been laid for options in this direction. A corollary option is increased emphasis on tourism, an industry which the government is currently building.

In order to meet the demands of economic growth, Cuba would presumably cut back on its direct forms of assistance to revolutionary movements and regimes. This would include those direct military, paramilitary, political-organizational activities in Nicaragua, El Salvador, Chile, and Colombia. But unlike scenario one, the Cubans might still be able to continue their nonmilitary developmental support of revolutionary regimes, as in sending teachers, agronomists, construction workers, doctors and paramedics to Nicaragua. Havana would probably continue its more indirect diplomatic and political support of revolutionary regimes and movements, as through radio broadcasts, meetings of guerrillas in Cuba, and propaganda. Again, alternate forms of aid from another Marxist-Leninist country, China, to offset Soviet losses, would provide the means of a more complete package of Cuban revolutionary, security and developmental support to revolutionary regimes and movements.

A partial cutback in Cuban (and Soviet) support for the revolutionaries of Latin America would likely have different effects in different arenas. In Nicaragua, as in scenario one, it would probably produce increased security vulnerabilities, with the possible outcome of greater willingness to share power with the opposition. El Salvador's guerrillas would conceivably react along the lines of scenario one, and the guerrillas elsewhere in Chile and Colombia would probably be little affected.

Scenario three: Little change in current levels of Soviet support for Cuba.

A third scenario is one in which, owing to hypotheses one and two, a new Russian leadership would opt for little shift in its current levels of support to Cuba. Should this outcome occur, Cuba's activities vis-à-vis revolutionary regimes and movements would continue in the present direction. Yet, this direction reflects a turndown in Soviet energy and other aid transfers to Cuba, Soviet displeasure with Cuban economic inefficiency, and differences of opinion between the two countries regarding their roles in Latin America—notably in Central America and the Caribbean.

These differences had by no means produced a significant reduction in either country's military support for Nicaragua by the mid-1980s. (Outside of the reduction of 100 Cuban military personnel in early May 1985). Indeed, in a report to Congress in May 1985, President Ronald Reagan said that there were about 200 Soviet and other bloc advisers serving with the Sandinista military. He also stated that Russian officers were identified serving with Sandinista combat troops fighting against the contra forces on Nicaragua's northern frontier.[41] But Cuba's economic inefficiencies, Nicaragua's debilitated economy, Soviet domestic economic problems, and General Secretary Gorbachev's economic improvement program at home might be leading toward reduced Soviet aid to Cuba and only marginal aid to Nicaragua—relative to its developmental needs. In this event, Cuban capabilities to support revolutionary regimes and movements conceivably might be circumscribed even before any termination of Marxism-Leninism in Russia. Indeed, as the Gorbachev leadership attacks economic problems and stresses efficiency inside Russia, one could project increased strains with Cuba. For in that country, inefficient economic management has long been a problem for the Soviets. The effects of increased strains on Cuban foreign policy under the Soviet shadow may tell us which of the above scenarios is the more likely under a non-Marxist-Leninist regime.

Notes

1. See, for example, Robert Jervis, "Hypotheses on Misperception," in Klaus Knorr, ed., *Power, Strategy, and Security* (Princeton, N.J.: Princeton University Press, 1983).
2. *Ibid.*
3. See Seweryn Bialer, "Soviet Foreign Policy: Sources, Perceptions, Trends," in *The Domestic Context of Soviet Foreign Policy*, ed. by Bialer (Boulder, Colorado: Westview Press, 1981), pp. 409–441.
4. *Ibid.*
5. Roger E. Kanet, *Soviet Foreign Policy in the 1980s* (New York: Praeger Special

Studies, 1982), Chapter one. W. Raymond Duncan, *Soviet Policy in the Developing Countries*, ed. (New York: Pergamon Publishing Co., 1980), Chapter one.

6. See *The Soviet Union and the Third World: A Watershed in Great Power Policy*, Report to the Committee on International Relations, House of Representatives, Congressional Research Service, Library of Congress (May 8, 1977); and *Soviet Policy and United States Response in the Third World*, Report prepared for the Committee on Foreign Affairs, House of Representatives, Congressional Research Service (March 1981).

7. See Joseph G. Whelan, *The Soviet Union in the Third World, 1980–1982: An Imperial Burden or Political Asset?* Washington, D.C.: Congressional Research Service, The Library of Congress, December 1984.

8. W. Raymond Duncan, *The Soviet Union and Cuba* (New York: Praeger Publishing Co., 1985).

9. Adeed Dawisha and Karen Dawisha, eds., *The Soviet Union and the Middle East* (New York: Holmes & Meier Publishers, 1982).

10. See Richard Bernstein, "Remaking Afghanistan in the Soviet Image," *The New York Times Magazine*, March 24, 1985, p. 30 ff. Also, Henry Bradsher, *Afghanistan and the Soviet Union* (Durham, N.C.: Duke University Press, 1985).

11. David E. Albright, *Communism in Africa* (Bloomington and London: Indiana University Press, 1980).

12. Robert S. Leiken, "Eastern Winds in Latin America," *Foreign Policy*, No. 42 (Spring 1981), pp. 94–113. Jiri Valenta, "Soviet and Cuban Responses to New Opportunities in Central America," in Richard E. Feinberg, ed. (*Central America: International Dimensions of the Crisis* (New York: Holmes and Meier, 1982), Chapter 6. W. Raymond Duncan, "Soviet Interests in Latin America: New Opportunities and Old Constraints," in *Journal of Inter-American Studies and World Affairs*, vol. 26 (May 1984), pp. 163–198.

13. Charles Wolf, Jr. *et al., The Costs of the Soviet Empire* (Santa Monica, the Rand Corporation, 1983), R–3073/1–NA. Also Peter Clement, "Moscow and Southern Africa," *Problems of Communism* Vol. 34 (March–April 1985), pp. 29–50.

14. Clement, *op. cit.*.

15. *The Christian Science Monitor*, April 3, 1985; also *The Costs of the Soviet Empire, op. cit.*.

16. See *The New York Times*, November 19, 1984. Castro has denied any difficulties between the Cubans and Soviets, as in his interview with Robert MacNeil of the Public Broadcast Service's (PBS) "McNeil, Lehrer Newshour, in Havana. See Federal Broadcast Information Service, 20 February 1985.

17. Scholars differ on the precise nature of the Soviet-Cuban relationship. Some see Cuba as strictly a Soviet surrogate, dependent on and politically controlled by the USSR. See statement by Professor Luis E. Aquilar, Department of History, Georgetown University, *Impact on Cuban-Soviet ties in the Western*

Hemisphere. Hearings Before the Subcommittee on Inter-American Affairs, House of Representatives, May 14, Washington: U.S. Government Printing Office, 1980, p. 98; Leon Gouré and Morris Rothenberg, *Soviet Penetration of Latin America* (Miami: University of Miami, Center for Advanced International Studies, 1975, pp. 63–69; James D. Theberge, *The Soviet Presence in Latin America* (Crane, Russak & Co., Inc., 1974), pp. 65–66; David Rees, *Soviet Strategic Penetration of Africa.* Conflict Studies, No. 77, London: Institute for the Study of Conflict (November 1977), pp. 1–21. Others see Cuba more as an autonomous actor in pursuit of its own policy and having substantial influence over the USSR within the Soviet-Cuban bilateral relationship. See Nelson P. Valdes, "Revolutionary Solidarity in Angola," in Cole Blasier and Carmelo Mesa Lago, eds., *Cuba in the World* (Pittsburgh: University of Pittsburgh Press, 1979), pp. 110–113; also testimony of William M. LeoGrande, School of Government and Public Administration, American University, *Impact of Cuban-Soviet Ties in the Western Hemisphere* (Spring 1980), *op. cit.,* pp. 94–95; and Mark N. Katz, "The Soviet-Cuban Connection," in *International Security* Vol. 8, No. 1 (Summer 1983), pp. 88–112. A third interpretation of the Soviet-Cuban relationship quite logically has evolved which views Soviet-Cuban diplomacy as something between the first two polar positions. It argues that Moscow-Havana ties are more complex, involving mutual interests, costs and benefits for both sides, and with limits to the complete control by either party over the other. See Edward Gonzalez, "Cuba, the Soviet Union and Africa," *Communism in Africa* ed. by David Albright, (Bloomington, Indiana: Indiana University Press, 1980), pp. 147–165; Jorge I. Dominguez, "Cuban Foreign Policy," *Foreign Affairs* (Fall 1978), pp. 91–95, 98, and W. Raymond Duncan, *The Soviet Union and Cuba: Interests and Influence* (New York: Praeger, 1985).

18. On Cuban foreign policy objectives, see Jorge Dominguez, "The Armed Forces and Foreign Relation," in Blasier and Mesa-Lago, *op. cit.,* pp. 53–86; and W. Raymond Duncan, *The Soviet Union and Cuba op. cit.,* Chapter two.

19. Gonzalez, "Institutionalization and Political Elites," in Blasier and Mesa-Lago, *op. cit.,* p. 19.

20. On the nationalist force in Cuban foreign policy, see Ramon Eduardo Ruiz, *Cuba: the Making of a Revolution* (Amherst: The University of Massachusetts Press, 1968).

21. On Castro's faulting the Soviets for their weak and indecisive responses to U.S. policy toward Nicaragua, see *The Washington Post,* March 24, 1985. On the nature of limited Soviet aid to the Sandinistas, see *The Wall Street Journal* April 3, 1985.

22. See Jacques Levesque, *The USSR and the Cuban Revolution: Soviet Ideological and Strategic Perspectives, 1959–77* (New York: Praeger Publishers, 1978); D. Bruce Jackson, *Castro, the Kremlin, and Communism in Latin America* (Baltimore: The Johns Hopkins Press 1969); Andres Suarez, *Cuba: Castroism and Communism, 1959–1966* (Cambridge, Mass.: M.I.T. Press, 1967), pp.

178–79; and Edward Gonzalez, *Cuba Under Castro: The Limits of Charisma* (Boston: Houghton Mifflin Co., 1974).

23. See *The Washington Times*, April 18, 1985. On Soviet-Cuban relations in Central America, see Jiri Valenta, "Soviet Policy in Central America," *Survey*, 27, 118/119 (Autumn–Winter 1983), pp, 287–303; and Valenta, "The USSR, Cuba, and the Crisis in Central America," *Orbis*, 25, 3 (Fall 1981), pp. 715–745.

24. William Leurs, "The Soviets and Latin America: A Three Decade U.S. Policy Tangle," in *The Washington Quarterly* (Spring 1985).

25. The Nicaraguan revolution led the Soviets to revise their previous emphasis on "peaceful change" through united fronts in Latin America toward a new attraction to armed struggle—which Castro had long advocated and which had so divided the Cubans from the Soviets during much of the 1960s. Following the Nicaraguan revolution, Soviet writers began to assert that the "armed road . . . is the most promising in the specific conditions of most Latin American countries" and that "only the armed road has led to victory in Latin America." See Nicolai Leonov, "Nicaragua: Experiencia de una Revolucion Victoriosa," *America Latina* 3 (1980): p. 37; Sergei Mikoyan, "Las Particularidades de la Revolución en Nicaragua y sus lareas desde el punto de vista de la Teoria y la Practica de Movimiento Librador", *America Latina* 3 (1980), pp. 102–103. This shift in Soviet tactics has been well covered by Robert Leiken, *Soviet Strategy in Latin America*. Published with the Center for Strategic and International Studies, Georgetown University, The Washington Papers/93, v. 10 (New York: Praeger, 1982). On evolving Soviet relations with Latin America, see Cole Blasier, *The Giant's Rival: The USSR and Latin America* (Pittsburgh, Pa.: University of Pittsburgh Press, 1983). Also Augusto Varas, "Ideology and Politics in Latin America-USSR Relations," *Problems of Communism* 33, 1 (January–February 1984), pp. 35–47.

26. See G. Pope Atkins, *Latin America in the International System* (New York: The Free Press, 1977), pp. 332–34.

27. See W. Raymond Duncan, "Soviet Interests in Latin America: New Opportunities and Old Constraints," *Journal of Inter-American Studies and World Affairs*, 26, 2 (May 1984), pp. 163–98. Soviet opportunity seeking in Latin America is discussed by Pedro Ramet and Fernando Lopez-Alves, "Moscow and the Revolutionary Left in Latin America," *Urbis* 28, 2 (Summer 1984), pp. 341–63.

28. On Nicaragua as a revolution in search of answers to economic and other dilemmas, see Mario Vargas Llosa "In Nicaragua," *The New York Times Magazine* (April 28, 1985), pp. 37 ff.

29. *The Washington Post*, March 24, 1985.

30. *Ibid.*

5

Russia and China: *Realpolitik* Scenarios

PETER BERTON

Russia and China are neighbors who share a border of thousands of miles and a history of over three hundred years. Now they are also Marxist-Leninist states who share a common ideology, however differently it may be interpreted in both countries and indeed however differently it may have been interpreted in each country during different periods. They are also Leninist party-states who practice centrally planned economies. There may be some argument about how totalitarian or authoritarian the two regimes are or have been in the past, and how rigidly or loosely they have adhered (or in the case of present-day China, how it is adhering) to the standard model of a centrally planned economy. but for better or worse (and in my judgement for worse), Russia and China have gone through a Leninist and a Maoist revolution, respectively, and are today a part of what we call the Communist world. The two neighbors are also bitter enemies.

What would have been the relationship between these two neighbors had they not shared common Marxist-Leninist values, similar techniques of wielding political power, and similar economic systems? This is an intriguing question which I will attempt to answer in this essay.

My plan is first to review the sources of the present Sino-Soviet conflict, and then to proceed with an analysis of the record of the Russo-Chinese relationship, as well as of the international environment and the balance of power in the area prior to the 1917 revolution in Russia (and, of course, before the 1949 revolution in China). I will then construct two scenarios and, finally, attempt to answer the question posed above: namely, what would the Russo-Chinese relationship have been in a *Realpolitik* situation unencumbered by revolutionary-ideological factors?

The conflict between the Soviet Union and China was initially called an ideological dispute. This is understandable because, as noted above, the two countries share Marxist-Leninist ideology and, as Leninist regimes ruled by Communist parties, have communicated not at the state-to-state level but rather through their respective Communist parties. As a result, the Sino-Soviet dialogue has been conducted in highly abstruse and esoteric Marxist jargon, giving the outside world the impression that differences in ideology were at the root of their disagreements. But Russia and China are also neighboring states with a long history of official and unofficial interactions, trade caravans, and bitter conflicts over territory.

How much of the Sino-Soviet dispute is ideological, directly linked to the two regimes' revolutionary nature? How much of the dispute is experiential, caused by Soviet actions in China that angered and affected the lives of top Chinese Communist leaders, including Mao Tse-tung; and conversely, how much has been brought on by Chinese actions that caused anguish and consternation in the Kremlin? How much of the dispute is personal, reflecting the differing perceptions, status, and personalities of Soviet and Chinese leaders? How much is territorial, involving treaties concluded by the two countries (some, China claims, under duress, and hence perhaps renegotiable) and border areas claimed by both countries under the existing treaties? How much of the dispute is racial and historical, arising from past conflicts between Imperial China and Tsarist Russia? And, finally, how much is military and geostrategic, reflecting power politics?

Sources of the Sino-Soviet Conflict

Let us briefly analyze the sources of the Sino-Soviet dispute from these seven perspectives: ideological, experiential, personal, territorial, racial, historical, and military and geostrategic.

Ideological Issues

The ideological differences between Communist Russia and Communist China go back to XX Congress of the Communist Party of the Soviet Union (CPSU) in February 1956, when the then Soviet leader Nikita

Khrushchev enunciated a number of radical changes in standard Soviet theory and practice, changes which could be said to have contradicted the basic ideas of Marx, Lenin, and Stalin.[1]

The first issue was the question of war and peace. In his desire to promote what he called "peaceful coexistence" between states with different social systems (which later became known as the first detente with the United States), Khrushchev proclaimed that war was not fatalistically inevitable. This was certainly contrary to Lenin's dictum that as long as capitalism and imperialism existed, war was inevitable. And Communist China at this time was not a status quo power; it could not accept the notion that no resort could be made to force. It was, rather, a revisionist power that faced a rival Chinese Nationalist government and did not want to weaken its implied threat of force to "liberate" Taiwan. In fact, a year later in late 1957, Mao overestimated the significance of the successful Soviet missile test and the Sputnik, and declared that "the East Wind prevails over the West Wind," setting the stage for his unsuccessful attempt to take over Taiwan the following year, in what became known as the 1958 Taiwan Straits crisis.

The second issue was the road to power: how could the Communist parties seize power and become ruling parties? While Marx postulated that power could only be obtained through violence and revolution, Khrushchev now proposed that revolution was not the only way and that Communist parties could conceivably come to power peacefully, through parliamentary means. In other words, revolution was not a *sine qua non*; evolution was now possible. But the peaceful road to power was only possible in open, democratic societies. The Chinese Communist Party (CCP) had come to power through long-term guerrilla warfare in a totally different society, and could not conceive of or condone attempts by other Communist parties to adopt evolution and reform.

The third issue involved the concept of different roads to Communism, which was contrary to Stalin's insistence on the primacy of the Soviet experience for all Communist parties, including Communist party-states. On the face of it, the concept of different roads to Communism should have been something that the Chinese Communists would be happy to support, because it would have legitimized their own unique road to victory in the civil war and their own internal policies after coming to power. But Mao was not satisfied to be only the leader of China. As one of the most important figures in the Communist world, he had aspirations toward sharing leadership of the entire Communist empire with the Soviet Union, even though he was only its junior partner at the moment. Given these ambitions, the last thing Mao would want was the weakening of the Communist bloc, and he feared that Khrushchev's policies would lead in that direction.

Mao was, of course, right; and the disturbances in Poland as well as the Hungarian revolt a few months later, in the fall of 1956, underscored this point very graphically.

Space limitations preclude a full discussion of the ideological differences between the two Communist superparties, and besides, the focus of this essay is on the nonideological differences between Russia and China. It must be noted, however, that for years the conventional wisdom among Western scholars of Communism said that the two Communist powers would be brought together should outside pressure be applied to the Communist world. Thus, the American escalation of the war in Vietnam was thought to be a development that would help heal the rift between the two Communist protagonists. But, in reality, their different approaches to the Vietnam War further exacerbated the conflict between them. Mao was opposed to the idea of a united Sino-Soviet front against the United States in Vietnam and preferred to oppose both superpowers. (A decade later, in the 1970s, this policy was ideologically codified into the so-called "Three Worlds Theory.")

We might conclude this discussion of ideological differences between China and the Soviet Union by observing that for years the Chinese have accused the Soviets of being "revisionist" and of taking "the capitalist road," i.e., of not being true to the teachings of Marx, Lenin, and Stalin; and the Soviets have reciprocated by calling the Chinese "dogmatists" who blindly follow ideological tenets without regard for contemporary reality. It is somewhat ironic to note that in the post-Mao era, the pragmatic Chinese leadership can reverse the charges and say that the Soviets are clinging to outmoded ideological economic positions, as the Chinese plunge ahead in their "market-oriented" internal reforms and Open Door policy toward the capitalist world. And it is the Soviets who can now, with some justification, point to the Chinese as "revisionists" taking the "capitalist road." (How things change in just four years. M.A.K., 1989)

Experiential Issues

We turn now to experiential factors for both the Soviet and Chinese leadership. To what extent was the Sino-Soviet dispute caused or exacerbated by bitter memories of real or imagined harm done by the other side?

Although they involve events which took place some 60 years ago, the veteran Chinese Communist Party leaders have bitter memories of the united front with the Kuomintang Nationalists in the 1920s, which the Soviet leaders imposed on the fledgling Chinese Communist Party through the Communist International (Comintern) and which ended in the decimation of the Chinese Party. Even after this disaster, the Comintern continued to meddle in CCP affairs and, in fact, supported their own candidates for leadership. Mao came to power against Joseph Stalin's wishes, and the latter did very little to help the Chinese Communists during their long stay in the Yenan wilderness in the northwest. In April 1941, Stalin concluded a neutrality treaty with Japan—a psychological blow to both the Chinese Communists and Nationalists—and in August 1945 he negotiated a treaty with Generalissimo Chiang Kai-shek's government, on conditions that were rather favorable to the Soviet Union. The 1945 treaty with the Chinese Nationalists restored the Tsarist spheres of influence in Sinkiang and Manchuria (including the Russo-Chinese Railway, the commercial port of Dairen and the naval base at Port Arthur) and forced China to recognize the "independence" of Outer Mongolia (the so-called Mongolian People's Republic) from China.

Every Chinese leader, whether Nationalist or Communist, must have deeply resented the Soviet removal of all industrial equipment from Manchuria following the Red Army's occupation of that region in the final days of World War II. While the Soviets justified this on the grounds that it was Japanese property and, as such, the legitimate spoils of their war against Japan, it was obviously a serious setback to the postwar industrialization of China.

It is of course impossible to tell whether Stalin welcomed the establishment of a Communist regime in China, coming as it did right after Tito's insubordination and the Soviet Union's inability to reassert its dominance over the small Balkan country of Yugoslavia. Stalin may well have preferred a weak Nationalist China on his borders, rather than a Leninist Communist regime intent upon unifying all of China (including the areas under Soviet influence) and creating a strong industrialized state. When he had a chance to negotiate with Mao and the new Chinese Communist leadership in late 1949 and early 1950, he insisted on reconfirming the special Tsarist Russian privileges obtained in 1945 from the Nationalist government, including those in Manchuria and Mongolia.

The new Chinese leaders also must have resented the relatively small amount of economic aid given by Stalin to the newly established neighboring fraternal state. Although the Sino-Soviet treaty negotiated after weeks of wrangling in Moscow is called the Treaty of Friendship, Alliance, and Mutual Assistance, the Soviets provided a loan of only $300 million over a five-year period, or an annual stipend of ten cents per person. (By way of comparison, American Marshall Plan aid to Western Europe was estimated to be over $20 billion.) The Soviets also imposed onerous joint stock companies upon China, which the Chinese regarded as economic exploitation and which they managed to cancel after Stalin's death.

Until 1955, the Soviet Union subscribed to the "Two Camp Theory" articulated by Andrei Zhdanov, which held that there were only the "socialist" and the "imperialist" camps, implying that there were no nonaligned nations. This was somewhat akin to Secretary of State John Foster Dulles' black-and-white view of the world and his notion that neutrality was immoral. In 1955, however, following the previous year's Geneva Conference which supposedly inaugurated the "Spirit of Geneva," the Soviet Union discovered the Third World and inaugurated policies that would allow the manipulation of these underdeveloped countries for Soviet foreign policy goals. One such policy was the granting of economic and technological aid to selected Third World countries, most notably Egypt (the Aswan High Dam) and India (a steel complex), in return for support of Soviet foreign policy positions in the United Nations and elsewhere. Inasmuch as the Soviet Union possessed limited economic resources, these grants of economic aid and credits probably were not welcomed by Peking, which badly needed more and more economic aid from the Soviet Union. The Chinese Communists would have preferred that these finite resources first be made available within the Soviet bloc to fraternal countries, such as China.

The Korean War (1950–1953) provided another area of discord between China and the Soviet Union. It involved asymmetrical and unequal contributions of the two Communist neighbors to the prosecution of the war: while the Chinese had to intervene militarily, and as a consequence suffered heavy casualties, the Soviets provided only material aid. And, if we are to believe the Chinese, this aid had to be, and was, paid for by the Chinese.

The People's Republic of China (PRC) was officially proclaimed on October 1, 1949, but Manchuria (informally claimed by Stalin, in his negotiations with the Chinese Nationalist government, to be in the Soviet sphere of influence) was under Communist control a few years earlier. This was partly the result of the Red Army turning over surplus weapons to the Communist guerrillas in the region, and partly reflected the weakness of the Nationalist government in Manchuria, in spite of American efforts to airlift Nationalist troops to the area. Thus, a provisional regional Communist government was in place in Manchuria before the formal establishment of the Chinese People's Republic in Peking, and this regional government negotiated agreements directly with the Soviet authorities. It is, therefore, very significant that the first purge in the PRC in the early 1950s involved the Communist "warlord" of Manchuria, Kao Kang, who had extensive contacts with the Soviet authorities across the border, a fact which no doubt was one of the main reasons for his purge. This purge of pro-Soviet elements in the CCP must have contributed to friction between the two parties.

Finally, even though Mao probably temporarily accepted the role of junior partner to the Soviet Union in the formulation of the Communist bloc's world strategy, he probably counted on some division of labor and some special area, such as Southeast Asia or southern Asia, which would be assigned to China as its sphere of influence. Yet it seems that the Soviet Union did not want to share spheres of influence with China. One of the first foreign trips that Khrushchev undertook (with his traveling companion Marshal Nikolai Bulganin) was to Afghanistan, India, and Burma—all countries bordering on China—followed somewhat later by a trip to the largest and most important country in Southeast Asia—Indonesia—and a repeat visit to India.

Personal Issues

The death of Stalin, the unquestioned leader of the Soviet Union and the international Communist movement, and the ascension to power of Nikita Khrushchev clearly affected Mao's relationship with the new Soviet leaders. Although in 1949–1950 Stalin treated Mao pretty shabbily and kept him in Moscow for two months before the two delegations agreed on the text of the alliance treaty (there were rumors in Peking at the time that the Chinese leader was being held prisoner), Mao must have had a grudging admiration for Stalin for his decisive, if ruthless, role in the collectivization of agriculture, forced industrialization, and victory over Germany. Like Mao, Stalin belonged to the generation of revolutionaries who participated in the seizure of power in their respective countries. But Khrushchev was a second-generation Communist leader who became a member of the Soviet Party's Politburo only in 1939, on the eve of World War II.

It was only natural, then, that with Stalin gone, and considering the importance of the Chinese Communist Party, Mao probably saw himself as the senior leader in the international Communist movement. (Ho Chi Minh was also a senior Communist personality who knew Lenin in the 1920s. But in 1953, when Stalin died, the Vietnamese leader had yet to win his decisive victory over the French colonialists; and besides, North Vietnam was only a middle-sized Communist country.) Mao's inflated self-assessment must have adversely affected his relationship with Khrushchev.

Mao's personal relationship with Khrushchev deteriorated further when, for domestic political reasons, Khrushchev had to dissociate himself from Stalin. This he did in a dramatic secret speech at the CPSU XX Party Congress, denouncing Stalin for his crimes and setting the stage for the de-Stalinization campaign. (The "secret" speech was not so secret, for the U.S. government somehow got a copy of the text and made it public.) Whatever mixed feelings Mao may have had about Stalin, it is clear that he understood that debunking the myth of a departed supreme leader in a closed society is politically dangerous. And while the most extreme features of the Mao cult were still a decade away from fully blossoming in the so-called Great Proletarian Cultural Revolution, he obviously had to worry about his own "cult of personality" (as the de-Stalinization campaign was termed in the Soviet Union). There was also the matter of confidence and loss of face. Whatever the startling proposals Khrushchev may have wanted to make at the CPSU XX Congress, he should have at least taken Mao into his confidence before the event. But, far from discussing them, Khrushchev did not even inform Mao of the radical doctrinal changes he would be announcing at the congress, especially the debunking of Stalin and the start of the campaign against "the cult of personality." A simple notification would have spared the CCP much embarrassment, since their pre-congress greetings to the CPSU (along with those of the other Communist parties) were full of praises for the departed leader.

Early Sino-Soviet polemics were couched in esoteric Marxist-Leninist jargon, followed by indirect attacks on proxies (Yugoslavia and Albania); only in mid-1963 did both parties directly accuse each other. But by the following year, 1964, the polemics took on a personal character: the Chinese directly attacked Khrushchev and the Soviets directly attacked Mao Tse-tung. Khrushchev likened Mao to Hitler,[2] while the Soviet poet Yevgeny Yevtushenko wrote in a poem that Mao reminded him of Genghis Khan. The Chinese began to describe Soviet policy as "Khrushchevism," and after the Soviet leader's overthrow they referred to "Khrushchevism Without Khrushchev."[3]

Territorial Issues

The territorial dispute is perhaps the most explosive of all current issues between the Soviet Union and China, but it is not the most fundamental. It is quite ironic that both Communist parties subscribe to the fiction that under Communism "state borders will gradually lose their former significance."[4] As the Sino-Soviet, Vietnamese-Cambodian, and Sino-Vietnamese hostilities attest, the most prevalent border skirmishes and outright hostilities are between Asian Communist states and not between Communist and non-Communist nations.

When the territorial issues between the two countries were made public in September 1963, the Soviet Union warned China that it should not be forgotten that in the past territorial disputes and claims were a customary source of acute friction and conflicts between states, a source of inflamed nationalistic passions. That territorial disputes and frontier conflicts were used as a pretext for predatory wars is common knowledge.[5]

The warning came in response to Chinese complaints of Soviet subversion in the westernmost Chinese province of Sinkiang (bordering on the Soviet Union), and more specifically, the coercion of "several tens of thousands of Chinese citizens" into crossing the border to the Soviet Union.[6] Of course, "Chinese citizens" in this case referred to Uighurs and people of other non-Chinese nationalities, who fled to join their brethren across the border in the Soviet Union in the aftermath of the man-made and natural disasters brought on by Mao Tse-tung's radical Great Leap Forward policies. The Soviets, in turn, accused the Chinese of thousands of violations of the Soviet border by Chinese servicemen and civilians.[7]

In early 1964, Sino-Soviet negotiations aimed at solving the border issues began in Moscow and promptly ended without any agreement. However, routine contacts between official delegations continue, in order to regulate transportation, navigation on boundary rivers, and border control. In the 1980s, Soviet offers to resume border talks met with unenthusiastic Chinese response.

What is the territorial dispute between China and the Soviet Union all about? To begin, there are three problem areas:[8]

(1) Chinese claims to territories which now constitute part of the Soviet state. These, in turn, can be divided into (a) territories north of the Amur River and (b) territories east of the Ussuri River, both in the east; and (c) territories east of Lake Balkhash, including the northwestern part of the Ili Valley in the west.

(2) The entire area of Mongolia. This, in turn, can also be divided into (a) the buffer state of Outer Mongolia (the so-called Mongolian People's Republic), which is essentially a client state of the Soviet Union, (b) the Buriat (Mongolian) Autonomous Republic of the USSR, and (c) the Inner Mongolian Autonomous Region of the People's Republic of China.

(3) The Tsarist (and Soviet) spheres of influence within the present boundaries of China. These include Manchuria in the northeast and the Sinkiang province in the northwest.

How serious are these territorial claims and counterclaims? The two areas in the east listed in the first category (north of the Amur River and east of the Ussuri River) did not have any Chinese population when they were colonized by the Russians in the second half of the nineteenth century, and there are no Chinese there now. The areas in the west have been made Chinese by conquest, rather than by settlement and colonization, and the population (like that in the areas to the east under Chinese sovereignty, in the province of Sinkiang) is neither Russian nor Chinese, but largely Uighur, Kazakh and Kirghiz ethnically, and predominantly Moslem by religion. The Soviet position on all three of these areas is nonnegotiable. Barring a Chinese victory in some future Sino-Soviet war, it is unthinkable that any of these territories would revert to China.

Turning to the Mongolian issue, we first can easily dispense with the Mongolian areas inside the USSR and China (the Buriat [Mongolian] Autonomous Republic and the Inner Mongolian Autonomous Region). These areas have been firmly incorporated into the Soviet Union and China, respectively, and the Chinese in fact now outnumber the Mongols in the Inner Mongolian Autonomous Region. As for Outer Mongolia, Tsarist Russia attempted to separate it from Chinese control in the aftermath of the Chinese revolution of 1911. In 1921, the Soviet Union finally succeeded in establishing an informal protectorate over a nominally independent Mongolian People's Republic which, as noted above, was formally recognized by Nationalist China in 1945 and by Communist China in 1950. (In the late 1930s, Mao Tse-tung told Edgar Snow that Mongolia should be returned to China, so we know how the Chinese Communists viewed the detachment of Outer Mongolia from China.)

We must note the strategic importance of Mongolia. Soviet troops and missiles stationed in Mongolia outflank the protruding northern Manchurian salient and are also very close to the Chinese capital. (Soviet forces successfully attacked the Japanese Kwantung Army in Manchuria in August 1945, in a pincer movement coming from two locations: the Maritime Province in the east and Outer Mongolia in the west.) The Soviets are therefore unlikely to give up their position in this client state. Furthermore, genuine independence is unlikely from the Mongol point of view, and given the choice of patrons, they would most likely choose the Soviets. The latter are not only less of a threat in terms of colonization (Inner Mongolia, as noted above, is already demographically dominated by the Chinese), but can also offer more in terms of economic and technological aid.

The Soviet spheres of influence inside the present boundaries of China were pretty much eliminated by the mid-1950s with the return of the Chinese Eastern Railway, the commercial port of Dairen, and the naval base of Port Arthur, as well as with the dissolution of joint Chinese-Soviet stock companies in Sinkiang. But have the Soviets accepted these losses? In the polemics over the territorial issue, Moscow rather ominously announced in 1964 that not all lands lost to China in 1689 under the Treaty of Nerchinsk were recovered under the treaties of Aigun and Peking in 1858 and 1860, respectively.[9] Does this mean that at some future date the Soviet Union might present China with a territorial counter-claim with regard to some Chinese territories south of the Amur River and east of the present Sino-Soviet border in the west? In 1912, an ambitious Russian general argued for drawing a straight line from Tashkent to Vladivostok and annexing all lands north of the line. This would have included the northern half of Manchuria, all of Outer Mongolia, and the northwest part of the Chinese province of Sinkiang.

But in the last quarter of the twentieth century, in contrast to 1912 when there were hardly any Chinese in Manchuria, this region is now predominantly and heavily populated by Chinese. (As noted above, the Inner Mongolian Autonomous Region also has a Chinese majority by now.) The Chinese areas in Sinkiang are still vulnerable because the indigenous population there outnumbers the Han Chinese, and because the province, in contrast to Manchuria, is very far from Chinese-populated areas.

From the Chinese point of view, there are essentially two kinds of territorial disputes between the two countries. The first involves territories taken by Tsarist Russia under the "unequal treaties" in the nineteenth century, described above. These territories are now settled, however sparsely, by Russians or other constituent nationalities of the USSR, and are not now seriously claimed by China. To be sure, the Chinese would like the Soviets to admit that these territories were taken by force; *that* would presumably settle the issue, at least for the moment. What China might claim if, in some unforeseen future, it were to emerge victorious in a war against Russia, is another matter.

The second dispute involves territories occupied by Russia or the Soviet Union beyond what was specified in the "unequal treaties," and problems arising from the demarcation of the Amur and Ussuri boundaries in the east (especially problems involving possession of islands in the middle of these rivers). With goodwill and compromise on both sides, the solution of this second dispute is not impossible.

Racial Issues

In its fourth condemnatory comment (made public in October 1963) on the CPSU's "Open Letter" of July 14, 1963, the CCP accuses the Soviet Party of peddling the "theory of racism," "clearly aiming at inciting racial hatred among the white people in Europe and North America," and raising "a hue and cry about the 'Yellow Peril' and the 'imminent menace of Genghis Khan'." Indeed, the British historian Arnold Toynbee wondered at the time whether a global "race war" might pit the whites against the colored peoples.[11]

There are definitely racial overtones in the relationship between the two Communist neighbors. The Chinese consider themselves the proud descendents of the Middle Kingdom and have treated the Russians, like other foreigners, as barbarians. They have pejoratively called the Russians "big noses." The Russians cannot forget the Mongol yoke, which lasted two and a half centuries, and they have been apprehensive of the "Yellow Peril." Indeed, the word "Asiatic" (*Aziat*) has a pejorative connotation in Russian; mothers tell their misbehaving children to stop behaving like

Asiatics. In a poem composed in March 1969, just after the armed clashes along the Sino-Soviet border, Soviet poet Yevgeny Yevtushenko wrote of a new Battle of Kulikovo, referring to the first victory of the Russians over their Asian overlords in the fourteenth century. During the same period and later, in conversations with Americans (who have always been portrayed in Soviet literature as anti-Negro and racist), Soviet scholars have often tried to portray the Soviet-American-Chinese relationship as one of whites against yellows.

Historical Issues

Beyond the territorial and racial issues, as well as the experiential factors involving Soviet attempts to force United Front tactics on the Chinese Communists in the 1920s (which obviously have historical dimensions), there is a whole range of historical issues which have arisen between China and Russia during three centuries of relations. This historical record includes a number of armed conflicts, beginning with the war that led to the Treaty of Nerchinsk in the late seventeenth century (basically on Chinese terms); a number of treaties regulating trade relations between the two countries; Tsarist Russian participation in the "unequal treaties" forced upon China by Western powers, led by Great Britain, in the mid-nineteenth century; Russian machinations with regard to outright annexation of Chinese territories, as well as Russian attempts at establishing exclusive spheres of influence in China (described above); and, finally, at the beginning of this century, Russian collusion with the imperialist powers, primarily Japan, at the expense of China. These issues will be dealt with in a brief survey of relations between the two countries (see below).

Military and Geostrategic Issues

One can also look at the Sino-Soviet dispute and ask a very simple question: would the Soviet Union want to have on its doorstep a first-class industrial and military power? China is seen by the Soviet Union as a revisionist non-status quo power that harbors irredentist claims to Soviet territory, and that demographically overshadows eastern Siberia and the Soviet Far East by a margin of a hundred to one. (Some analysts argue that power and population are related and that the latter finds its own level, especially in areas of a power vacuum.)

China, on the other hand, fears Soviet collusion with other powers directed against it. For example, Khrushchev's first attempts at "peaceful coexistence" with the United States (known as the Spirit of Camp David) in the late 1950s were seen by China as a threat, as was the obvious Soviet neutrality in China's border disputes with India. (Around the same time, Khrushchev pulled all Soviet technicians, working on numerous industrial projects, out of China.) The tripartite Partial Nuclear Test Ban Treaty, signed by the Soviet Union with the United States and Great Britain in mid-1963, was likewise, and with much truth, seen as an attempt to prevent China from obtaining its own atomic bomb; four years earlier the Soviet Union had torn up a secret agreement to provide China with nuclear technology. This move was in retaliation for Chinese refusal to grant the Soviet Union naval and other bases on Chinese soil, or to place its fleet under Soviet command.

With the escalation of anti-Soviet rhetoric, especially during the Cultural Revolution, the Soviet Union began to strengthen its forces against China. The Soviets moved a number of divisions (including tank divisions) and missiles into Mongolia and significantly increased the number of divisions on their border with China. A crisis in Sino-Soviet relations was reached in March 1969 when a series of armed clashes on the border threatened to plunge the two countries into war. Three months later, Brezhnev called for the formation of an Asian collective security system, which was correctly seen in Peking as an "anti-China encirclement scheme." The proclamation of the so-called "Brezhnev Doctrine of Limited Sovereignty" in the aftermath of the Soviet invasion of Czechoslovakia posed a direct challenge to China, because Soviet troops had entered a fraternal country allegedly to protect socialism. At the time, some American analysts did not preclude the possibility of limited Soviet military action aimed at taking out Chinese nuclear facilities and, in the process, at lopping off some areas of China inhabited by national minorities whose cousins lived across the border in the Soviet Central Asian republics. Although the war scare had subsided by 1970, and especially after China's rapprochement with the United States and Japan in 1972, minor incidents along the border occasionally continued to occur. Most of the incidents, however, were probably unprovoked.

By the 1980s, the Soviets had increased the number of their divisions on the Chinese border to over 50, and had targeted China with at least 1,000 nuclear missiles. In late 1986, over 175 SS–20s were stationed in the eastern part of Siberia. An impartial observer would conclude that all this buildup is far beyond any legitimate Soviet need for self-defense. China cannot keep up with this quantitative and qualitative increase in Soviet forces. At the very least, the Soviet Union wishes to freeze the status quo vis-à-vis China, preserving its territory and its military advantage.

A Brief Overview of
Russo-Chinese Relations

Before discussing the history of Russo-Chinese relations, we must place them in the context of international relations in eastern Asia, which automatically involves the nature of Imperial China's relations with the outside world. Generally speaking, the two-and-a-half centuries from the beginning of the seventeenth century (when Russia began its interactions with China) to the mid-twentieth century can be seen as consisting of three periods in Chinese foreign relations:

(1) the period of Chinese dominance through its tributary system, which lasted roughly until the end of the eighteenth century;

(2) a transitional period of a weakening China, corresponding roughly to the first half of the nineteenth century (though this was not recognized by Russia and the Western powers at the time); and

(3) the period of the "unequal treaties" (forced upon China by Great Britain and the other Western powers in the aftermath of the Opium War), in which China was treated as an object of international rivalry rather than as a legitimate actor on the international scene, and which covered roughly 100 years from the mid-nineteenth to the mid-twentieth century.

The Chinese tributary system was based on the notion of Chinese superiority and Sinocentrism—China was seen as the center of the universe culturally, economically, and therefore politically. China's neighbors were presumed to be less civilized "barbarians" who were expected to pay tribute to the Chinese Emperor, a ruler whose powers were supposed to rest upon the "Mandate of Heaven."[12]

Pre-1917 Russo-Chinese relations have also gone through three periods:

(1) the period from the first contacts in the early seventeenth century until the Treaty of Nerchinsk (1689)—a period of an uneasy balance of power,

(2) the period from the Treaty of Nerchinsk on through the Treaty of Kiakhta (1728) and into the mid-nineteenth century—a period of real or perceived Chinese power, and

(3) the period from the mid-nineteenth century (when the Chinese tributary system disintegrated) and, more specifically in the Russian case, from the Aigun and Peking treaties (concluded in 1858 and 1860, respectively) until 1917—a period of Chinese weakness.

During the first period, Russian expansion in Asia went on rather smoothly, from the crossing of the Ural Mountains in the late sixteenth century to the reaching of the shores of the Sea of Okhotsk 50 years later. There was a vacuum of power, except for the region of the Amur River where the Russians encountered the Manchus, who had just conquered China. Skirmishes between the Russians and the combined Manchu-Chinese forces grew in intensity in the third quarter of the seventeenth century, eventually leading to large-scale hostilities. The first round in the Russo-Chinese dispute was won by the Manchu-Chinese forces, culminating in the Treaty of Nerchinsk in 1689 which effectively barred Russian settlement of the entire Amur River basin.[13]

It might be noted that this defeat has deflected Russian expansion in Asia toward the northeast. This took the Russians into the Kamchatka peninsula, from which one line of advance eventually resulted in the acquisition of Alaska and in Russian settlements in northern California, while the other led southward toward the Kurile Islands and attempts to open Japan.

If we turn to the international environment during this period, we find that it would consist of four actors or sets of actors:

(1) China as the dominant power,

(2) Russia as the unsuccessful challenger,

(3) Western powers as weak economic actors, and

(4) the Mongols and other "barbarian" tribes in the areas between China and Russia who were treated as objects of Chinese and Russian expansion, but who attempted to play the two neighboring powers against each other.

The second period (from the Nerchinsk treaty to the Aigun and Peking treaties) was an era when the Chinese had, or were perceived to have had, the upper hand, although the relationship can be characterized as primarily consisting of trade interactions under a special system codified at Kyakhta in 1828. The Treaty of Kyakhta not only regulated trade relations, but also delineated a portion of the Russo-Chinese frontier, prescribed that fugitives and deserters were to be extradited to their country of origin, and allowed for the establishment of a Russian ecclesiastical mission in Peking.

The international environment during the second period was more complicated:

(1) China was still the dominant power, gradually in decline;

(2) the challengers were now the Western powers, notably Great Britain;

(3) Russia was China's trading partner, gradually being overtaken by the Western powers in terms of economic activity, but beginning to assert its position vis-à-vis the dominant power; and

(4) Mongolia and the other buffer areas were gradually being brought primarily under Chinese suzerainty, and secondarily under Russian control.

The third period of Russo-Chinese relations, from the Aigun and Peking treaties (and the establishment of the Russian port and naval base of Vladivostok in 1860) to 1917, can in turn be subdivided into two shorter periods according to the areas and types of Russian expansion in China, which can be characterized as

(1) penetration and acquisition of territories that at the present time constitute part of the Russian state, and

(2) attempts to carve out spheres of influence in the areas that are today under Chinese jurisdiction.

During the first subperiod, Russia took advantage of China's defeats at the hands of the Western powers to acquire the area north of the Amur River (1858), the Maritime Province east of the Ussuri River (1860), and the area east of Lake Balkhash (the 1860s and 1870s). (For a short time Russia also controlled the entire Ili Valley).

During the second subperiod, which began in the 1890s, Russia concluded a secret agreement with China (allegedly to help the latter against Japanese encroachments), and acquired rights to construct a railroad across northern Manchuria. Later in this subperiod, Russia occupied Manchuria southward to the warm-water port of Dairen and the naval base of Port Arthur, in the wake of the Boxer Rebellion; fought and lost a war against Japan over the latter's interests in Korea and Manchuria; and eventually came to terms with Japan over the division of spheres of influence in Manchuria and Mongolia.

The international environment during the third period was radically different from that of the other two periods:

(1) Britain was now the dominant power;

(2) Other Western powers (including Russia) and Japan were middle powers, although Japan began to emerge as the next potential hegemon;

(3) China was the object and arena of great power competition; and

(4) peripheral regions of the Chinese Empire, such as Outer Mongolia, Manchuria, Sinkiang, Tibet, and Taiwan (as well as former tributary states, such as Korea) fell under the influence of outside powers (including Russia).

From an area hegemon, China became a helpless object of great power competition, and barely escaped total partition and loss of even nominal independence. Russia, on the other hand, first expanded, then was checked by China, then expanded again and was again forced to retrench, this time by other powers. The peoples in the peripheral areas between Russia and China at times played independent roles, but mostly had to submit to one or the other of these powerful neighbors or, when the latter were weak, to other powers in the area, most notably Britain and Japan. The other powers were all, with the exception of Japan, intrusive powers with metropoles on other continents.

Post-1917 Scenarios

We begin our imaginary scenario in mid-1917, assuming that only the March 1917 democratic revolution took place in Russia and that there was no successful Bolshevik revolution in the fall. In this scenario, Russia is likely to have continued to participate in the anti-German allied coalition and is likely to have been one of the victorious powers at the Versailles Peace Conference.

Historically, one of the more vexing problems at Versailles was the disposition of the former German sphere of influence in northern China. Japan, as an ally of Great Britain, almost immediately joined in the war against Germany and occupied the German possessions in China. Japan's declaration of war against Germany was done, however, not because of any obligation Japan may have felt to its ally, but rather for its own selfish reasons. In fact, Great Britain and especially its dominions, Australia and New Zealand (as well as British residents in China), fearing that Japan's participation in the war might unduly strengthen its position in China as well as in the Far East generally, wanted to prevent Japan's entry into the war against Germany. At Versailles, the Chinese delegation unsuccessfully tried to regain from Japan the former German possessions in China. But Japan regarded German territories in China as spoils of war, and refused to return them to the Chinese government.

What would have happened had Tsarist or democratic Russia been present at Versailles? To answer this question, one must first look at Russia's relations with Japan during the period under review. Russo-Japanese relations had been strained over Korea and Manchuria ever since Japan's victory over China in the Sino-Japanese War of 1894–1895, and especially after the Triple Intervention of 1895 in which Russia, France, and Germany conspired to deny Japan a foothold in Manchuria. The Russo-Japanese dispute over Korea was first resolved in a condominium, with Russia's sphere of influence in north Korea and Japan's sphere in south Korea. (It is ironic that the demarcation line between the two spheres of influence was the notorious thirty-eighth parallel, made famous as the dividing line between Soviet and American forces occupying the Korean peninsula at the end of World War II, and still roughly the boundary between the Republic of Korea in the south and the People's Democratic Republic of Korea in the north.)

After the conclusion of the Anglo-Japanese Alliance in 1902, relations between Japan and Tsarist Russia deteriorated over the continued Russian occupation of Manchuria, which began in the aftermath of the Boxer Rebellion. It should be pointed out that its alliance with Great Britain was only one of the options open to Japan at the time; some Japanese statesmen argued for better relations with Russia. Frustrated by Russian intransigence, and reassured that the Anglo-Japanese Alliance would restrain Russia's ally, France, from joining the war, the Japanese attacked the Russian naval base at Port Arthur and declared war on Russia in early 1904. After months of hostilities, the war ended with Japanese victory and the Treaty of Portsmouth mediated by President Theodore Roosevelt in 1905.

After the war, Japan's policy toward Russia took two forms: on the one hand, Japanese armed forces continued to be on guard, fearing Russia's revenge; but on the other, Japanese diplomacy attempted to find a commonality of interests with this former enemy. That common interest was China, and more specifically Japanese and Russian spheres of influence in Manchuria and Mongolia. In 1907 the two countries signed a treaty of commerce and navigation, a fisheries convention, and two political agreements, only one of which was made public. The secret convention divided Manchuria into two spheres of influence, and recognized Japan's position in Korea and Russia's special interests in Outer Mongolia, which was, of course, part of the Chinese Empire at the time.[14] In 1910, 1911, and 1912, both countries considered but decided against annexing their respective spheres in southern and northern Manchuria. In 1912, however, they signed another secret agreement which extended the demarcation line of 1907 and thus divided Inner Mongolia into two spheres along the Peking meridian, acknowledging Japanese interests in the east and Russian interests in the west.

In 1915, when Japan presented its infamous "Twenty-one Demands" to China, Russia did nothing to protect China from Japan's encroachments. In fact, Russian diplomats saw opportunities to strengthen their own sphere of influence in China; for Japan was primarily interested in central and south China, the Yangtze valley, and Fukien Province, while Russian interests were concentrated in Mongolia, Sinkiang Province, and the Altai, Ili and Tabargatai regions. The following year, 1916, Russia and Japan concluded yet another agreement, this time a military alliance, which constituted a warning to Germany (the common enemy of the two countries during the First World War which was raging at the time), the United States (against interfering with the two signatories' plans for territorial aggrandizement), and China (against whom Russia and Japan had been colluding for a decade).

To return to the question of what may have happened at Versailles, it is quite possible that Japan would have been supported by Russia against Chinese claims. Furthermore, had friction developed between Russia and Britain over the division of spoils in the Near East, especially in view of the decreasing popularity and effectiveness of the Anglo-Japanese Alliance, it is probable that a Russo-Japanese bloc could have crystallized in the Far

East to counter the developing Anglo-American coalition. Quite conceivably, Japan could have avoided being isolated at the Washington Conference in 1921–1922, and therefore could have held on to the former German possessions in China.

Thus, projecting Chinese weakness for a few decades following World War I (not an unreasonable assumption, given the fragmented state of Chinese government and the continued "unequal treaty" privileges of the Western powers and Japan), previous Russo-Chinese relations would have continued, with Russia attempting to exploit China and, in cooperation with Japan, to expand the Russian spheres of influence in China. After all, a Russian foreign minister thought in 1915 that "fifty years from now there won't be any China."[15]

Post-1949 Scenarios

In a Rand Corporation study later published as an article in the *Journal of International Affairs* in 1972, Thomas Robinson discusses six different possible types of regimes which could arise in post-Cultural Revolution China.[16] These are:

(1) an ultra-left/Red Guard-dominated regime,
(2) a Maoist regime,
(3) a military-dominated government,
(4) a "muddle-through" regime,
(5) a pragmatic government, and
(6) a weak government or a "warlords" situation, which prevailed during and shortly after World War I.

Yung-hwan Jo and Ying-hsien Pi, in a study of Sino-Soviet relations,[17] compress Robinson's six categories into three:

(1) a radical regime,
(2) a "muddle-through" regime, and
(3) a pragmatic regime,

and posit three possible variant regimes for the Soviet Union:

(1) a hard-line regime,
(2) a middle regime, and
(3) a soft-line regime.

By combining these six categories in a nine-cell matrix of possible combinations of Chinese and Soviet regimes, Jo and Pi draw some useful conclusions as to the likelihood of conflict given this or that combination of regimes in the two neighboring countries.

What kind of hypothetical regimes can we devise for post-1949 China, excluding the Communist Maoist dictatorship which actually emerged?

Table 5.1
Likelihood of Conflict by Regime Type

China Russia	strong/ democr.	strong/ autocr.	weak/ democr.	weak/ autocr.
strong/democr.	M	G	L	G
strong/autocr.	G	VG	VG	G
weak/democr.	L	VG	VL	G
weak/autocr.	G	G	G	M

LEGEND:	VG	(VERY GREAT)
	G	(GREAT)
	M	(MEDIUM)
	L	(LITTLE)
	VL	(VERY LITTLE)

Would this typology also apply to Russia? Rather than simply suggest certain typologies for China and Russia in this hypothetical situation, it seems better to identify some variables and then try to construct possible regimes based on these variables. Such variables could include:

(1) the effectiveness of the central government (centralized, semicentralized, or decentralized),

(2) the type of regime along the civil-military continuum,

(3) the type of regime according to political participation (the open society-closed society continuum),

(4) the type of regime according to economic organization (capitalist, mixed, or socialist ownership of the means of production), and

(5) the power projected by the regime toward the international system.

Since trying to incorporate all these variables (important as they may be) would result in almost astronomical permutations when then trying to construct a matrix for two regimes, I have selected two of the above— outside strength of the regime (strong or weak) and the nature of the political system (democratic or autocratic-totalitarian)—to construct a 16-cell matrix. I shall try to apply to each cell one of five possibilities of conflict (very great, great, medium, little, and very little).

In assigning these variables to my matrix, I am assuming on the basis of general historical evidence that conflict is more likely to occur under the following two conditions (among others):

(1) when there is a discrepancy of power between the antagonists, and (2) when one or both of them are autocratic or totalitarian regimes lacking the constraints implicit in a pluralistic democratic society. Historically, Russia and China lacked democratic traditions and most of the time there was a discrepancy of real or perceived power between them. Thus, if this matrix is reasonable, and the past record is projected into the future, the likelihood of conflict between Russia and China is rather high.

Conclusions

We come now to answering the question posed at the beginning of this essay: what sort of relationships could have emerged between Russia and China had there never been a Bolshevik or a Maoist revolution?

Perhaps we could start with an examination of the issues in the Sino-Soviet dispute, to see which ones would be irrelevant and which ones still operative. Obviously, the whole range of ideological issues would not be applicable in the absence of Marxist-Leninist regimes in the two countries. Nor would what I have called "experiential" issues be operative, because these are largely based on events that took place in the period from the 1920s to the 1950s, between the Soviet Union or the Comintern and the Chinese Communist movement or regime. Also not applicable would be personal or personality issues, because presumably the two countries would have had different types of leaders.

On the other hand, the territorial, racial, historical, and military-strategic issues would have remained. The territorial dispute might not be an immediate issue if China were much weaker than Russia, but the potential for a serious conflict in the future would have remained. When two neighbors are of different races and share a history of conflict (aggravated by territorial irredenta), current relationships are almost always tinged with memories of the unpleasant past, and hence remain burdened.

Given this background, it is clear that the military-strategic issues between Russia and China, namely, the balance of power between the two neighbors and the power and alignment of the other actors in the area, are the most crucial. The relationship between Russia and China would still have been one of competition, friction, and conflict over the border and buffer areas had there never been a Bolshevik or a Maoist revolution. The one exception would be caused by the presence of a third power (such as Japan, Great Britain, or the United States) posing a threat to both of them. Yet even in this situation, when the United States actually did emerge as the enemy of both countries, this did not prevent them from getting bogged down in a serious conflict of their own. Of course, we can posit an international environment in which the outside powers, as well as the buffer states and regions between Russia and China, are all aligned against the two neighbors, in which case a Russo-Chinese entente would be possible. But the buffer states and regions, which played a significant role in the balance of power in the past, are by now so sufficiently drawn into the Russian or Chinese state or sphere of influence (in some instances even populated by significant numbers of Russians or Han Chinese) that they are unable to play an independent role in the regional international system. Our *Realpolitik* scenarios also corroborate the conclusion: Russia and China are likely to remain antagonists with a high probability of conflict in the geopolitically crucial Eurasian landmass.

Notes

* I would like to thank Randall Houston of the USC School of International Relations for timely research assistance.

1. In discussing the causes of the Sino-Soviet dispute, I am drawing some material from my chapter on Sino-Soviet relations in James C. Hsiung (ed.), *Beyond China's Independent Foreign Policy: Challenge for the U.S. and Its Asian Allies* (New York: Praeger, 1985), Chap. 2, "A Turn in Sino-Soviet Relations?" pp. 24–54.

2. Peter Berton, "The Territorial Issue Between Russia and China," *Studies in Comparative Communism*, Vol. 2, Nos. 3 and 4 (July/October 1969), pp. 130–148, at p. 136.

3. *Ibid.*, p. 137.

4. *Ibid.*, p. 131.

5. *Statement of the Soviet Government, September 21, 1963* (New York: Crosscurrents Press, 1963), p. 32, as cited in Berton, "The Territorial Issue," p. 133.

6. *The Origin and Development of the Differences Between the Leadership of the CPSU and Ourselves: Comment on the Open Letter of the Central Committee of the CPSU, September 6, 1963* (Peking: Foreign Languages Press, 1963), p. 47, cited in Berton, "The Territorial Issue," p. 132.

    The entire exchange from June 14, 1963 to November 21, 1964 is available in *The Polemic on the General Line of the International Communist Movement* (Peking: Foreign Languages Press, 1965). See also Peter Berton (comp.), *The Chinese-Russian Dialogue: A Collection of Letters Exchanged Between the Communist Parties of China and the Soviet Union and Related Documents* (Los Angeles: University of Southern California, School of International Relations, Vol. I: 1963, Vol. II: 1964) and John Gittings, *Survey of the Sino-Soviet Dispute* (London: Oxford University Press, 1968).

7. *Statement of the Soviet Government, September 21, 1963*, p. 31, cited in Berton, "The Territorial Issue," pp. 132–133.

8. The following analysis broadly follows, but in some respects expands on, my article on the territorial issue between the two countries, cited in note 2.

9. Berton, "The Territorial Issue," p. 147.

10. *Apologists of Neo-Colonialism—Comment on the Open Letter of the Central Committee of the C.P.S.U., No. 4, October 21, 1963* (Peking: Foreign Languages Press, 1963), p. 31, cited in Berton, "The Territorial Issue," p. 133.

11. Arnold J. Toynbee, "Will a Global 'Race War' Pit the Whites Against the Colored Peoples?" *The New York Times*, October 2, 1963, p. 11.

12. For studies of the Chinese tributary system, see John K. Fairbank (ed.), *The Chinese World Order: Traditional China's Foreign Relations* (Cambridge, Mass.: Harvard University Press, 1968).

13. Some of the more important recent books on Russo-Chinese relations include R. K. I. Quested, *Sino-Russian Relations: A Short History* (London: George Allen & Unwin, 1984); O. Edmund Clubb, *China and Russia: The "Great Game"* (New York: Columbia University Press, 1971); Mark Mancall, *Russia and China: Their Diplomatic Relations to 1728* (Cambridge, Mass.: Harvard University Press, 1971); and *idem, China at the Center: 300 Years of Foreign Policy* (New York: The Free Press, 1984).

14. The narrative of Russo-Japanese relations after the Russo-Japanese War follows Peter Berton, *The Secret Russo-Japanese Alliance of 1916* (Ann Arbor: University Microfilms, 1956), pp. 438 Summary: "Russo-Japanese Relations during the First World War," in *Transactions of the International Conference of Orientalists in Japan*, No. 5 (1960), pp. 95–101. See also V. A. Marinov, *Rossiia i Iaponiia pered pervoi mirovoi voinoi (1905–1914 gody): Ocherki istorii otnoshenii* [Russia and Japan Before World War I (The Period of 1905 to 1914): Essays on the History of Relations] (Moscow: Izdatel'stvo "Nauka," 1974).

15. Quoted by the American ambassador in Petrograd, George Marye (State Department Files), cited in Madeleine Chi, *China Diplomacy, 1914–1918* (Cambridge, Mass.: Harvard University, East Asian Research Center, through Harvard University Press, 1970).

16. Thomas W. Robinson, "Future Domestic and Foreign Policy Changes for Mainland China," *Journal of International Affairs*, No. 2 (1972), pp. 192–215.

17. Yung-Hwan Jo and Ying-hsien Pi, *Russia Versus China and What Next?* (Lanham, Md.: University Press of America, 1980).

6

Relations between East and West during a Regime Crisis and after Regime Change

MORTON A. KAPLAN

During a regime crisis in the Soviet Union, there will be conflict in the West between those who will want to use the crisis to dismantle the Soviet empire and those who fear either setting off a nuclear war or dampening the prospects for a non-Soviet outcome. Of course, such a dichotomous statement oversimplifies the choices that will be available. However, insofar as the choices will be contextually meaningful only with reference to concrete scenarios, there are no practical alternatives to gross oversimplification or an exhaustive examination of an almost infinite variety of contexts. For reasons of economy, I prefer the defects of the first approach to the costs of the latter.

For instance, if the Soviet Union goes through a prolonged internal crisis, one can expect the forces that once backed Solidarity in Poland again to attempt to seize power and, in the absence of a credible capability on the part of the Soviet Union to intervene, to be able to secure the support of some Polish army divisions against the security police, which will be the only reliable forces in support of the regime. In such circumstances, given the overwhelming support of the American public for the Polish opposition, I would not expect a reprise of 1981 when Secretary of State Haig talked tough but reacted like a pussycat.

Nonetheless the risk of war with the Soviet Union would be present and more prudent forces in the administration would attempt to cloak American support for the Polish opposition with other measures designed to assure the contending forces in the Soviet Union that no assault on the national interests of the Russian national system would ensue. Unless the Soviet regime was well on the road to disintegration, this might well mean a "hands off" policy to Ukrainian or Byelorussian independence movements.

Dr. Petro, who commented on another paper of mine in this volume, may regard this as part of a status quo policy that discounts progressive peace-loving forces in Russia. I do not deny that a "go for broke" policy might work. But the world already would look quite good; and the risks of the "go for broke" policy would be inordinate under these circumstances. Furthermore, after reviewing the history of American interventionary efforts, I am less than convinced that such a policy would be carried out skillfully.

The risk that we might unite potentially dissident but patriotic elements with a faltering regime or trigger a war, even if not staggeringly high, in my opinion would not be worth running. After all, even dissident and peace-loving Russians might not interpret our policy as benignly as we might wish. Even if they disbelieve Soviet propaganda, they have no framework of reference other than that presented in the Soviet media. I will never forget the response of a Ukrainian lady in Australia after she was asked her how she liked that country. She said that it would be a good country except for England's imperial control. When told that Australia was an entirely independent country, she said that she came from the Ukraine and knew better.

If the Russian empire suffers the loss of Poland, other desired changes are likely in any event to occur eventually. Therefore a response that runs the risk of underestimating the likely favorable response to American encouragement of democratic change in Russia seems preferable. Our recent intervention in the Philippines was resented by many, although it was legitimated in the minds of even more Filipinos by our historic association. And the scenario that worked in the Philippines depended upon a host of particulars that are unlikely to be matched except in Poland and possibly Hungary and Czechoslovakia.

The other place in which trouble is likely to occur at an early stage is Lithuania. But Lithuania does not seem to capture the imagination in the United States; and little assistance is likely to go to it.

The European response to a disintegration of the Soviet system likely would be quite different from the American. Europeans would be more likely to fear the emergence of a united Germany that would dominate Europe and, thus, would be less likely to contribute toward a rapid breakdown of Soviet control in Eastern Europe than would the United States. They have convinced themselves in any event that there is no Soviet threat.

And although this analysis may result partly from psychological denial of their fear of the Soviet Union, the early stages of a convulsion in the Soviet Union are not likely to lead to a reversal. Europeans are likely to pressure the Americans towards a "hands off" attitude that is far more cautious than I would advocate.

Furthermore, I do not share the Europeans' fear of a reunited Germany. It is true that in the absence of further moves toward economic unity in Europe Germany might become the dominant economic power in Europe. But a breakup of the Soviet empire, and a return to market economies in Eastern Europe, would permit the emergence of a new Europe that in time would not be dominated by Germany and that could counterbalance Russia, the United States, Japan, and a future China.

The myths of the nineteenth century concerning national power have been demolished. It is now clear that national power rests on internal productivity and not on military strength. German irredentism is a possibility, but a minor one in my opinion. Those who were displaced in the aftermath of World War II are dead or of quite mature age. The bulk of the German descendants of the displaced Germans have no living memory of their parents' homes. And, unlike the Palestinians, who were kept in camps by the Arab countries, they live productively in their own nation. Irredentism is more likely to play a role in the smaller nations of East Europe.

Because of the complexity of the transition process, and its dependence on the concrete details of alternative scenarios, the preceding discussion is more of a mind-stretching exercise than a display of either social scientific or historical expertise. Even a discussion of post-Soviet relations between East and West will have some of this quality. However, I believe that some of the constraints on the world order that will emerge from the transition to a non-Soviet regime in Russia can be discussed with somewhat more assurance—or at least with not as great a lack of assurance—than in the case of the transition process.

If one believes, as I do, that the maintenance of the Soviet empire, and its outward expansion, is directly related to the requirements of a failed economic and ideological system in the Soviet Union, then the removal of that system, and of the threat to the control apparatus in Russia from the effects of contagion, will also be removed.

Many see current Soviet policy merely as Tsarist policy in new guise in response to permanent Soviet national interests. But, in my opinion, this is a mechanical projection that fails to incorporate the lessons of the twentieth century concerning national power. Others see a continuity in Tsarist policy, as well as in Bolshevik policy from Lenin and the early Stalin through Gorbachev, that is rooted in ideology. But this is also mechanical and neglects a change in the driving motivation behind the policy from one of imposing a dominant Slavic model on Europe in the case of the Tsars, and on the world in the case of the Bolsheviks, to one of preserving the privileges of an elite by removing subversive examples and by strengthening the myth that the system is unassailable and on the route to inevitable victory, thus disheartening potential oppositionists.

I am aware that I have somewhat overstated the case to make a point and that considerations of ordinary national interest also influence current Soviet policy. I also concede that several contributors to this volume, who argue that post-Soviet policy toward the United States may be highly competitive, particularly with respect to the Third World, in the end may turn out to be correct, for real changes in the world will have little, if any effect, if they are not perceived by those who make policy. And unlike Dr. Petrov I believe that most Russians do take pride in Russia's emergence as a great world power despite their resentment of foreign aid. There are those, particularly in the intelligentsia, who do think differently; but they are no more characteristic of Russia than American intellectuals are of the United States.

A lot will depend on American policy during and after the transition period, assuming that the Soviet system is replaced, an assumption that is less than self-evidently correct, although Dr. Shtromas has made an excellent case for it. To understand what motivating spirit must lie behind a transformative American foreign policy, we must first understand that there are no fundamental conflicts of interest among the major nations of the world, or of their populations, except those that are driven by Leninist organization. Furthermore, the major problems the great powers face— the coordination of economic policy to prevent destructive trade rivalry; the international control of destructive environmental changes, including possible greenhouse effects; the generation of educational systems that will permit all individuals to participate productively in the postindustrial world; and so forth—will not be possible if national security rivalries among them are perpetuated.

Conflicts of interest will continue to exist, but they are like to be relatively weak when contrasted with the commonalities of interest that will demand cooperative solution. And although these solutions obviously will not be compatible with autarchic sovereignty, they can be fully compatible with national independence and dignity. The recent demands placed upon Japan, for instance, that she expand domestic consumption or increase overseas productive investment (as contrasted with bond buying) as a means of reducing the enormous favorable trade balance she enjoys can hardly be regarded as onerous. Such changes in policy are less concessions to external demands than assumptions of civic responsibility; and in the end they are to Japan's advantage as well.

A post-Soviet Russia should be assured that NATO will be dissolved as soon as the WTO and bilateral security treaties between Russia and the Eastern European nations are dissolved and the Brezhnev Doctrine, or some variant of it, renounced. That Russia could be invited to issue, consonantly with an American declaration of the same kind, a unilateral guarantee of support to any European state that is attacked by some other state. Russia should also be assured of membership in the OEEC as soon as it adopts a market economy. It should also be assured of technological transfers regardless of the form of its economy as soon as it adopts the security measures suggested above and agrees to massive mutual reductions in armaments.

A new diplomatic forum should be created outside of the United Nations with the United States, Russia, China, Europe, and Japan as members that will consult on any outbreak of violence among smaller powers and in which an attempt will be made to reach joint policies to dampen the conflict. Both Russia and China, thus, would be assured that they would not be frozen out in the effort to prevent quarrels among unstable states from threatening the peace of the world.

Some may argue that this would disvalue the United Nations and would be a move away from international democracy. But that is nonsense. Democracy rests on a consensus of values and not on simple majority voting; otherwise it is mere majoritarian tyranny. No such international consensus exists. Furthermore, the UN fora are essentially irresponsible, for voting power is held by states that would not be required to implement decisions or to deal with the costs of mistakes. This suggested new council would combine influence with responsibility and it would utilize those states with the greatest interest in international stability, for they would have the most to lose if it were upset. This might not be an ideal system but it likely would fit world conditions better than other practicable alternatives.

I would also propose a global Democratic community consisting of all states with democratic systems. Because I do not believe the world, or even the democratic nations, is ready for a parliament, this body best would be composed of representatives of the executives of the participating nations. The object of this organization should be to promote democracy throughout the world. It should periodically characterize the situation in other nations with respect to progress towards democracy. For instance, the Aquino presidency in the Philippines has restored, at least prospectively, formal democracy in the Philippines. But large elements of an oligarchy still exist, along with private armies. The rule of law cannot be applied successfully in some parts of the Philippines. And most of the citizen body does not possess sufficient independence of means to provide for effective democracy. A global Democratic community acting on behalf of all democratic nations could publicize such defects, suggest changes, and assist them in a way not likely to stir the same kind of resistance that a single nation such as the United States likely would.

Under the global Democratic community should be a court of human rights, a court of political rights, and a police force. The two courts should have jurisdiction over all member nations and over such other countries that accept its jurisdiction. For instance, potentially unstable states or states that could be taken over by small armed forces such as the Caribbean island states might accede and agree to forgo all armed forces except for small police forces. Thereafter if human or political rights were violated in any of these states the relevant court might issue an order that would be enforced by the community police force to restore the violated rights if voluntary compliance did not ensue.

In cases of irredentist claims, the court of political rights could supervise elections in which a particular region, even if not contiguous, could join a different state provided only that the receiving state is willing and the election result is decisively strong or after repeated favorable election results. For instance, in principle, Quebec could join France, New Mexico Mexico, or Sonora the United States. This might provide an incentive for political reform in Mexico lest all of northern Mexico be lost to the United States. It would also permit a fair solution to the problems of Taiwan and Hong Kong.

I think that these suggestions make good sense. But politicians in office are unlikely to embrace the full package. Nonetheless, at least the more minimal of the suggestions—elimination of the blocs; large arms reductions; expanded economic cooperation; and major power consultation to control small state irruptions; and some form of all-European organization—are surely negotiable provided foresightful statesmanship is available.

Even, however, should my minimal suggestions not materialize, there likely would be no vital conflict of interest between the democracies and the new Russia. A post-Soviet Russia would still be concerned about China. Dismantling the empire might be a small price to pay for technological exchange and assistance in reaching a *modus vivendi* with China for a new elite, even if authoritarian Russia, that does not have to fear subversive contagion and that will be able with such cooperation also to raise the standard of living of the peoples of the new state system.

I hear the arguments of the other contributors about Third World conflicts. But who needs influence in Ghana or Uruguay, for instance, if there is no vital geostrategic contest? Who needs the expense? How interested would the United States be in Nicaragua if it did not fear for Mexico and for a diversion of its attention from Europe to the lifelines that alone permit resupply of Europe in an emergency? Am I being singularly dense is seeing no point to such a contest in a post-Soviet world?

Nonetheless a post-Soviet regime might be more competitive in terms of national security policy than my analysis suggests. This is more likely to be the case if we attempt actively to interfere in the succession struggle, to dismember the empire, or Soviet Russia, or even if we fail to assure Russia of our neutrality during a crisis. Even if we do what I regard as "all the right things," it is possible that a succession struggle will occur in such a way that the more xenophobic forces in Russia are among the victorious coalition. It is even possible that they may combine with some of the more conservative forces in the Communist Party in putting together an authoritarian system that jettisons Communist ideology and central planning while preserving the empire and the privileges of large elements of the Soviet elites and the predominance of Russia in the new multinational union. It is even possible that a new and authoritarian regime may be so fearful of the external world and of possible anarchy that it recognizes no alternatives to the constant struggle for power and influence.

The possibilities that may ensue in any of these cases have been explored in a number of the papers for the conference that are included in this volume. There is little point in adding to those comments, particularly as these matters are context determined and, thus, will depend upon the specific details of actual courses of events. The one thing that we can be sure of is that some surprises will be in store.

There is one point that I would like to stress above all others before ending this essay. Beyond the heuristic value of such excursions, there is the much greater value of becoming aware of the alternative types of worlds toward which our policies may point us. The recognition that the main objective is less that of coming out ahead in a particular contest than in helping to build a better world is the key matter. We surely often will be wrong about probable directions of change and of the impact of alternative policies upon them. In any event, we will understand these matters much better as events unfold, for the actual, rather than the infinitely possible, particulars will be available to us, despite our imperfect ability to discern them even when directly confronted by them.

We must also understand that it will be too late effectively and desirably to influence the shape of the future world if we wait until a crisis is upon us. Then our attention will be focused on the crisis and how it affects us in a rather immediate way. And our efforts will be focused on reacting to it. We must train ourselves to think of the relationship of policy to world system outcomes if we wish to be able to link policy at times of crisis at least partly to such considerations and not merely to relative advantage in particular outcomes.

Thinking in terms of alternative world outcomes is not an easy task in the best of circumstances. The relationship between action and outcome is remote and indirect. Moreover, we are not used to observing such invisible systems. Even most scholars of international theory see only anarchy rather than a social system with an equilibrium that is dependent upon boundary conditions, system characteristics, and types of behavior.

The image that nations are in a state of nature with each other is one of the chief sources of this intellectual mischief. But there is a social order just as there is in a pride of lions, even though no central government exists in either case. And ethologists could not conduct their investigations if they did not recognize this. Only theorists of international relations can talk of the international realm as one of anarchy and be listened to respectfully.

We must learn that there is an international social system and that it can be maintained under some conditions and not under others. If conditions are such that it cannot be maintained or that it is both possible and desirable to change it, there are alternative ways in which it can be changed. If statesmen can recognize this and if they can gain support for policies that are formulated with such considerations in mind, then the odds that a desirable outcome can be obtained have been improved. But this will be possible only if we learn to think in these terms.

7

Post-Soviet Russia and the West: Prospects for East-West Reconciliation Viewed from a European Perspective —A Commentary on Chapter 6

ALEXANDER SHTROMAS

One of the most important conclusions Professor Morton A. Kaplan reaches in his paper is that "there would be no vital conflict of interest between the democracies and new Russia." Entirely agreeing with this proposition, I would venture to add that even at present authentic Russian national interests do not clash with any of the national interests of either the U.S. or Western Europe. Russia has no territorial disputes with any of the Western powers, is not involved with the West in any trade wars or other competitive economic pursuits, and, as far as "influence zones" are concerned, these were delineated by the postwar settlement to Russia's more-than-full satisfaction and have never been seriously challenged by the West since.

The present East-West confrontation is rooted, not in the conflict of national interests of whatever kind, but in the irreconcilable differences between the USSR and the West in their respective conceptions of the common foundation for a universal world order, which is to say that the substance of this confrontation is in essence ideological and global and, as such, does not allow for compromise or a lasting settlement.

The USSR, seeking to establish a congenial Communist world order, is committed to the revolutionary expansion of the Soviet-type Communist system, whereas the West resists such attempts on the part of the USSR, aspiring—though without formulating this as its policy objective—for the replacement of the Soviet system in Russia by another system which, being more congenial to the West's own system, would stop threatening the basic security and stability of the West through engineering its Communist transformation. To sum it up, one could say that in the present East-West confrontation the main issue at stake is on what universal foundations— Communist-totalitarian or liberal-pluralistic, and these are incompatible— the future world order is going to be based.

The contention about the ultimate goal of the USSR's policy being the establishment of a Communist world order is treated by most analysts of international relations with certain scepticism and disbelief. These analysts, to quote Kaplan, prefer to "see current Soviet policy merely as Tsarist policy in new guise in response to permanent Soviet national interests," thus mechanically projecting old concepts onto new circumstances and, as a result, failing "to incorporate the lessons of the twentieth century concerning national power." The mechanical projection of Tsarist Russia onto the USSR is wrong however not only because of such general considerations, but also because it is inconsistent with the plain facts. From the eighteenth century onwards (more precisely, after the conclusion of the Nystad treaty in 1721), Tsarist Russia was a normal member of the European community of nations which, as every other member of that community, when driven by her authentic national interests and objectives, was capable of establishing genuine alliances with, as well as engage in wars and other conflicts against, her counterparts in that community.

Before the Bolsheviks seized power in Russia in 1917 there was no such thing in the world as an East-West confrontation. Whenever there were conflicts between Russia and some other European powers, these centered around peripheral matters (such as distribution of "zones of influence" or colonial possessions) and never challenged, either on the part of Russia or her adversaries and allies, the existence or the traditional order of any of the powers involved, with the one exception of the Napoleonic wars which were, again, ideological in nature.

Throughout its history, Tsarist Russia was never involved in any conflict at all with the U.S. These main political adversaries of the present day before 1917 always maintained a perfectly friendly and cooperative relationship exemplified by the U.S.'s unequivocal support of Russia in the Crimean War and Russia's consequent (in 1868) voluntary concession to the U.S. (disguised as sale for the symbolic price of 7.5 million gold dollars) of Alaska and other North American territories. After the collapse in 1871 of the French Second Empire, a perfectly friendly relationship was established on permanent grounds also between Tsarist Russia and France. And as a result of the deal struck by Disraeli and Gorchakov at the Berlin Congress in 1878, all the major conflict-fostering problems between Tsarist Russia and Britain, the main competitors for colonial possessions in Central Asia, were successfully resolved too. In all conflicts between the Central and Allied powers, Russia was always on the side of the latter, i.e., U.S., Britain and France, considering these nations to be her genuine and permanent allies, not, as in the case of the USSR during World War II, enemies turned into temporary allies of convenience.

Could then, in view of these facts, the anti-Western policy of the USSR be seriously interpreted as a mere continuation of international policies of Tsarist Russia? Apparently not, but to scholars who are virtual prisoners of pragmatic political philosophy, which strictly prohibits an assessment of international political endeavours in terms other than expedient power interests, territorial gains, national security deals, economic gains, strategic advantages, and the like, no other interpretation is practically available, and they have to stick to it, however inconsistent with the facts such an interpretation may be. To admit and explain the actual drastic discontinuity between Tsarist Russia's and the USSR's international politics one has to be able to overcome the narrow horizon of the empiricist dogma and realize that the USSR is not a mere nation-state, which Tsarist Russia certainly was, but a Communist clique-state, identifying itself not with any particular nation (e.g., Russia), but with a globally conceived ideological cause and, accordingly, with the proponents of that cause, organized in sectarian groups within every single nation and proliferated around the globe. In his rejection of the "projectionist view" embraced by most experts on international politics, Kaplan has done exactly that. For him the USSR is doomed to pursue its anti-Western policies, as these policies are best suited for safely keeping in power and preserving the privileges of the Soviet ruling elite.

Although I entirely agree with Kaplan that today this is indeed the main driving motivation behind Soviet policy, I do not share his view that, because of this being so, Soviet policy has lost at present its initial Bolshevik ideological identity and orientation, and has thus effectively stopped pursuing its ultimate goal of Communist world control. Kaplan himself admits that the way in which the Soviet ruling elite—an elite, I would like to add, whose only claim to power is based on their being the "high-priesthood" of the Bolshevik ideology of Marxism-Leninism—can preserve its position and privileges is "by removing subversive examples and by strengthening the myth that the system is unassailable and on the route of inevitable victory, thus disheartening potential opposition." But can it, being stranded with its Marxist-Leninist identity, successfully perform such tasks without relentlessly and with utmost determination seeking to establish a Communist world order? I doubt it. The whole non-Communist world is for the Soviets nothing else but a "subversive example" which "must be removed"; and without proving the Soviet system's ability successfully to proceed with such a "removal," the Soviets can hardly strengthen "the myth that the system is unassailable."

The most salient among such "subversive examples," representing a lethal challenge to the Soviet ruling elite, is of course untamed Western Europe flourishing just on the other side of the boundary of the Soviet realm of rule. This sets for the people inhabiting the Soviet realm a practical model for an economically, socially and spiritually superior way of life, which, if unsuppressed, will sooner or later cause the subjects of the Soviet Party-state e.g., the Russians, to follow suit. Hence, in order to preserve its power the Soviet ruling elite must not simply maintain the USSR's Communist identity, but remain committed to Communist expansion on the same scale as in the heyday of the Bolsheviks' genuine Communist zeal. Although Third World countries are more convenient targets for exercising Communist expansion with impunity, they represent only the side product of the relentless Soviet expansionist drive, the main objective of which has always been and always will remain a Communist Europe.

These inherent Communist-ideological interests and objectives of the USSR are at variance with, moreover in direct opposition to, the authentic national interests and objectives of Russia. Communist expansion gives Russia no economic advantage. On the contrary, it imposes upon her an increasingly unsustainable burden of expenditure which never stops growing since, in addition to the costs of expansion itself, Russia also has to bear the cost of maintaining in solvent condition the dwindling socialist economies of the ever-expanding number of her client states. The strategic advantages with which Communist expansionism is supposed to provide Russia are also more than problematic. Even if assuming that Russia sees her national goal in world domination and for this purpose needs to get a strategic advantage over the West, such an advantage bought at a price that high is bound, in the long run, to turn into a major strategic disadvantage. The problem here is that the peoples of Soviet client states are far from being thankful for Russia's care. On the contrary, in the course of getting the experience of the socialist way of life, even those of them which previously bore no prejudice against Russia are becoming her most implacable potential enemies, ready to join forces with the West against the USSR at the first available opportunity. Since with every expansionist success Soviet policing capacity wears thinner, while Western resolve to contain the USSR grows stronger, such an opportunity may eventually present itself in the not too distant future, spelling the demise of the USSR and, in the long run, the breakdown of the Soviet Empire altogether. The Soviet Union stands no chance of winning a prolonged confrontation with the West on any grounds—political, economic or military—but by pursuing an active anti-Western policy of Communist expansionism, it risks to lose even those gains which in a different situation the West would never even have thought of challenging.

Hence, in order to ensure her long-term security and render her position of a dominant regional and thus also a world power immutably stable, Russia badly needs to establish and foster most carefully a truly cooperative and harmonious relationship with the West. For that sake Russia would have to stop sponsoring Communist movements and regimes around the world and, ultimately, to renounce Communism as the foundation of her policies altogether. There is nothing for Russia to lose from such a radical move, and everything to gain. This move, in other words, would be in the interests of the West as much as it would be in Russia's own national interests.

In the climate created by Russia's renunciation of Communism and the ensuing East-West reconciliation, the fact that the presently Soviet-ruled non-Russian nations would regain the right of freely choosing and shaping their sociopolitical and economic systems, thus becoming entirely sovereign or genuinely autonomous, would by no means impair any true Russian national interests. Under the new peaceful circumstances, where there would be no more Western anti-Russian or Soviet-led anti-Western camps left, Russia's closest neighbours would remain naturally bound to Russia, as Latin America is naturally bound to the U.S., with the remaining mutual tensions and suspicions gradually receding and being superseded by mutual interests in economic exchanges and regional cooperation. Furthermore, only in cooperation with the West can Russia ever aspire effectively and promptly to overcome her inherent economic backwardness and thus reliably sustain her status as world power. Large-scale Western technological assistance is only one necessary condition for Russia's fulfilment of that goal. Another one is Western provision of generous credits enabling Russia to import immediately and on a massive scale the widest range of Western high-quality consumer goods. These have to be made available to the Russians in order to induce them to work conscientiously and try hard to earn good money. There are simply not enough locally produced goods to go around and their quality and assortment are insufficient to create the necessary incentives.

It follows from the above that while a world order universally based on liberal-pluralistic foundations and Russia's cooperation with the West would be lethal to the USSR, its establishment is in the best national interests of Russia. This would provide her with the only real hope for peace, security, economic progress and, ultimately, prosperity. A new post-Soviet Russia, albeit not yet necessarily a liberal democracy, will do her utmost to put the artificial East-West confrontation to a definite end.

I believe that for the settlement between Russia and the West to be mutually satisfactory and fully acceptable to the West, it should be drawn up along the following lines:

1) Russia's total withdrawal from Africa and Central and Latin America;

2) Russia's withdrawal of support from, and full break with, the Communist and related parties and movements throughout the non-Communist world, providing reliable guarantees of Russia's noninterference in the internal affairs of respective countries;

3) The reunification of Germany and conclusion with the new democratic government of a united Germany of the long-awaited peace treaty, guaranteeing the national security and other long-term interests of all parties and thus establishing the foundations of a universally acceptable European order;

4) Western guarantees of noninterference with Russia's national interests in Central and Eastern Europe, Caucasus, Central Asia, Mongolia and China should be given in exchange for Russia's granting the right of self-determination to all nations presently living in the Soviet realm of rule. These nations would include the present union republics of the USSR in these areas and would involve, as a prerequisite, the unconditional withdrawal of Russian troops from wherever they are stationed outside Russia's borders.

A settlement along these lines, by having transformed East-West rivalry into partnership, will, no doubt, be able to lay the necessary foundations for the evolution of a new peaceful and cooperative world order which Kaplan so imaginatively and convincingly depicts in his essay.

Kaplan rightly argues that under the conditions of East-West reconciliation whatever conflicts of interest among nations will still remain, "they will be relatively insignificant when contrasted with the commonalities of interest that will demand cooperative solutions." Indeed, most of the major problems the modern world faces cannot be adequately resolved by institutions of autarchic national sovereignty acting either separately or even collectively through various international agencies which possess no sovereign rights that supersede those of the institutions of national sovereignty.

There are two kinds of such problems:

1) Those with which institutions of national sovereignty do not deal at all, as these problems are outside their scope, and which international agencies, if and when they deal with them, cannot do so effectively. Among such problems the following ones should at least be mentioned: prevention

of armed conflicts, authoritative international conflict-settlement, and peacekeeping generally; supervision over, and enforcement of, international agreements and treaties, e.g., those on human rights; world ocean and the international seabed, outer space, international territories, and other similar issues which are treated by international law at present as unmanaged areas of "equal opportunity" for all nations); and 2) those with which the institutions of national sovereignty, along with the existing, weak international agencies, try to deal but are unable to do so in a satisfactory manner, as these problems are in their scope and nature either regional or global (among such problems the following ones should at least be mentioned: economic aid and development, and the whole task of bridging the so-called North-South divide generally; protection of the natural environment and solution of other problems related to human ecology; protection against famine, epidemic diseases, natural calamities, and similar disasters; development, management, and regulation of safety in the fields of nuclear, solar and laser energy; regulation and management of demographic problems, e.g., rational use of manpower resources; coordination of and supervision over some globally vital areas of scientific research).

The necessity of properly tackling these problems in the collective interest of all nations requires appropriate supra-national bodies of global and/or regional authority that together would provide the foundation for a global commonwealth. In the disproportionately developed and highly interdependent twenty-first century's world, the establishment of a global commonwealth on such foundations, while to some extent reducing national sovereignty and instituting on an overriding level areas attributed to the sovereignty of mankind as a whole, will enhance the security and prosperity of each nation so substantially that the partial loss of national sovereignty will not count for much, provided it equally applies to all nations.

In this respect I find Kaplan's idea about establishing a global democratic community as a nucleus for an evolving global commonwealth to be most incisive and brilliant, as is, in my view, also his other idea about setting up outside the UN a "diplomatic forum," consisting of the U.S., Russia, China, Europe, and Japan, for performing the peacekeeping function by effectively preventing and, when they occur, stopping the outbreaks of violence among the world's smaller powers.

There are here, however, a couple of problems that remain unresolved. One of them concerns Europe which, not being, at least as yet, a single political entity, could hardly be represented in the projected "diplomatic forum" as such. Another, which is also closely related to European interest, concerns the practicality of Kaplan's idea, as the experience of history shows that very few effectively functioning political institutions and arrangements have been created in accordance with preconceived theoretical blueprints. Most such institutions and arrangements evolved, in fact, under the pressure of emerging new situations and circumstances with which political leaders had to come to grips; and since, once evolved, political institutions and arrangements acquire a life of their own, they tended, though with some adjustments, to persist, however imperfect or ill-conceived they were.

Because of the existing correlation of forces, a genuine settlement of East-West relations may automatically produce a world jointly dominated by the U.S. and Russia, the two most powerful nations on both sides of the present East-West divide, before the international institutions of the type conceived in Kaplan's essay ever materialized. The resulting Russo-American condominium over the rest of the world would be very difficult to change or even modify, as both superpowers would be bound to be extremely proud of, and satisfied with, their new role. Not only would they thus become the unchallenged masters of their respective geopolitical environments but, by having acquired in addition also the unprecedented capacity of jointly imposing and enforcing settlements of local conflicts wherever they occur, they would also gladly and without hesitation assume the function of the policeman of the world. Initially, the world under a Russo-American condominium might indeed become a more peaceful and secure place, but in the long run this condominium would be bound to engender deep disaffection among all nations other than the Americans and Russians. Resenting the loss of their previous freedom of action on the international scene and driven by a sense of inferiority with regard to the two "big brothers," these nations might try to do their utmost to undermine the Russo-American condominium. The world thus could be plunged into an even bigger chaos of constant cleavages, strifes, and wars than before, when all parties to local conflicts were able to use to their particular advantage the conflicting interests of the superpowers.

On the whole, a truly peaceful and harmonious world order is impossible without fair distribution of national sovereignty among all nations of the world, as the problems besetting our planet at present clearly demonstrate. Only very few among the 180 or so sovereign nation-states are ethnically homogeneous political territorial entities, among which some (e.g., the members of the Soviet bloc) are sovereign only nominally and some are artificial divisions of fully homogeneous nations (e.g., East and West Germanies, and North and South Koreas). Bearing in mind that our planet is inhabited by about 1800 nationalities, it is only natural that the majority of the extant so-called nation-states are multinational entities with, in most cases, only one of the cohabiting nations, and in some none of them (as in many African states), is the real carrier of national sovereignty. There are at present about 1600 known national movements of stateless nations struggling for a sovereign, or at least truly autonomous, status. None of these movements shows any signs of receding or reconciling with their nations' dependent status quo. On the contrary, all of them are steadily growing in strength and constantly intensifying their struggle. One could conclude from this with a certain assurance that these national movements will not relent until their goal is achieved, unless the nation on whose behalf the struggle is conducted was meanwhile dispersed or otherwise annihilated by its ethnically alien rulers.

The Hungarian revolution of 1956; the attempt in 1967–1970 at creating the Ibo nation-state, Biafra, and splitting up Nigeria on ethnic-territorial grounds; the actual splitting of Pakistan and creation in 1972 of the new state of the Moslem part of the Bengali nation, Bangladesh; the continuous struggle for a sovereign nation-state by the Palestinians, the Sri-Lankan Tamils, or the Timore people in Indonesia, are just highlights of the ongoing worldwide process of reconstruction of the present system of nation-states along genuinely ethnical lines which, now in more, now in less conspicuous forms, continues unabated.

No system of world order, whether the East-West confrontation continues or not, can be just and, as a consequence, reliably peaceful and stable without the present nation-states having undergone the process of fission (first of all in such openly multinational settings as the USSR and Yugoslavia, but also, perhaps, South Africa, Nigeria, Czechoslovakia, Spain, Belgium, Canada, etc.), fusion (in the cases of Germany and Korea), and reshufflement (for example, in order for the Kurds to establish their nation-state, they have to amalgamate Kurdish territories, taking them from Iran, Iraq, Turkey and the Caucasian republics of the USSR; similar territorial reshufflements between Ethiopia and Somalia are necessary for solving the Ogaden problem; the same applies to the USSR and Iran housing the Azeris; or Pakistan, Iran, Afghanistan, Punjab in India, and the USSR, housing the Baluchis; as well as of course to most African states, inclusive of South Africa).

The Russo-American condominium over the world, while not being able to solve any of these problems (it could only temporarily suppress them by enforcing "for the sake of peace" the status quo) would, by reducing quite significantly the independence of all the sovereign nations, only greatly exacerbate them. The Russo-American global settlement would inevitably reduce to a minimum the American commitment to Western Europe. As a result, Russia, by the sheer logic of geopolitics, would become the sole dominant European power. Russia might substantially reduce its grip on Eastern Europe, but it would at the same time extend its prevalent influence over the European continent as a whole, East and West alike.

Hence, "Finlandization" might become the equal fate of all European nations, irrespective of what their geopolitical situation in the present world is.

At the same time Europe is in a uniquely strong position to ensure its full independence from both America and Russia and thus also to prevent the possibility of a Russo-American condominium over the rest of the world from ever being translated into political reality. For this Western Europe should evolve its unity much beyond the present arrangement of economic convenience, as represented by the EEC, and become a single political entity speaking on the international stage with one voice and possessing a united military force. Neither the U.S. nor Russia would be able to push around such a united Europe, which would thus become a superpower in its own right.

A thus enhanced Western European unity would hardly be, however, a sufficient guarantee for Europe to be able properly to assert itself against strong joint Russo-American pressure or to make its voice, when it is raised in opposition to the joint voice of the U.S. and Russia, effectively heeded. To put itself really on a par with a Russo-American alliance, Europe would have to become the champion and protector of the rights and interests of the non-West European nations, too, enlisting thus their support for European causes. To a united Western Europe this role of spokesman for the rights and interests of so many nations would come naturally and easily, as acting on behalf of the specific and collective interests of a multiplicity of nations is exactly the European community's basic substance and cause.

To protect its nations from all sorts of eventualities (such as "Finlandization" or joint superpower manipulation) and to be able to assure for them, under the conditions of East-West reconciliation, adequate independence and freedom, Western Europe must consolidate and further build up its unity here and now. It should without procrastination and delay develop new, and endow with more power the extant, all-European political institutions; establish, first within NATO and subsequently independently of it, a joint European military command; intensify all aspects of European relations with the U.S., seeking to become indispensable to vital American interests under all circumstances. Kaplan's proposed global democratic community should be taken up by Europe with the view of making it into the basic foundation stone for the permanent coupling of Western Europe with the U.S. It is in the pursuit of these objectives that Western Europe may become sufficiently united and strong to be able to withstand the Russo-American alliance and properly to defend from a joint Russo-American dictate its own nations, as well as the nations of the rest of Europe and the world at large. It is thus through the agency of a united Western Europe that the principle of fair distribution of national sovereignty may be practically and irreversibly implemented into the newly emerging universal world order, assuring its lasting peacefulness and developing harmony.

If Kaplan's global democratic community is effectively to serve as the nucleus and a model for a global commonwealth—and I firmly believe it to be the best possible actor for playing this role—it has to adopt as a criterion for a state's membership the assurance by that state of national freedom alongside all other democratic rights. The demand to surrender some elements of national sovereignty to institutions representing the sovereignty of mankind as a whole can be justifiably made only if this demand equally applies to all the nations of the world or, in other words—if the sovereignty of mankind is established on the basis of fair distribution of national sovereignty and, conversely, equality of its limitations with regard to all nations.

I believe that Kaplan's ideas on the future post-Soviet world are of crucial importance. They provide in my view the clearest and so far the most farsighted vision of the world's future union. In the above remarks I have sought to endorse this vision, elucidating some aspects of it and making a few additional points, the most important of which are:

1) As long as the USSR is a Communist clique-state, the East-West confrontation is bound to continue unabated, making the establishment of a stably peaceful world order impossible.

2) The replacement in the USSR of the present regime by a Russian national government of whatever description is the prerequisite for bringing the purely ideologically motivated East-West confrontation to an end and laying the foundation stone of a stable peaceful world order.

3) A stable, peaceful world order may properly develop and be consolidated under the conditions of fair distribution of national sovereignty among all the nations of the world.

4) The stable, peaceful world order, thus developed and consolidated, would be able to evolve a global commonwealth—a complex of institutions embodying the sovereignty of mankind as a whole and thus endowed with the necessary authority effectively to deal with supranational issues, which increasingly acquire an overriding significance for the survival of mankind.

Notes on Contributors

Peter Berton is Professor of International Relations at the School of International Relations, University of Southern California

Hsi-sheng Ch'i is Professor of Political Science at the University of North Carolina

W. Raymond Duncan is at the State University of New York at Brockport

Lewis Gann is Senior Fellow at the Hoover Institution, Stanford, California

David Gress is a Senior Research Fellow at the Hoover Institution, Stanford, California

Klaus Hornung is Professor of Political Science at the University of Freiburg, West Germany

Roger E. Kanet is Professor of Political Science and Department Head at the University of Illinois at Champaign-Urbana

Morton A. Kaplan is Professor of Political Science at the University of Chicago

William R. Kintner is Emeritus Professor of Political Science at the University of Pennsylvania

Joseph L. Nogee is Professor of Political Science at the University of Houston

R. Judson Mitchell is Professor of Political Science at the University of New Orleans

Nicolai N. Petro is Assistant Professor of International Studies and Director of the Center for Contemporary Russian Studies at the Monterey Institute of International Studies, Monterey, California

Otto Pick is Emeritus Professor of International Relations at the University of Surrey, Guildford, UK

Alexander Shtromas is Reader in Politics and Contemporary History at the University of Salford, UK

Peter S.H. Tang is Professor of Political Science, Boston College, Chestnut Hill, Massachusetts

William R. Van Cleave is Professor and Director of the Defense and Strategic Studies Program, University of Southern California

Peter Vigor is Consultant and former Director of the Soviet Studies Research Centre, The Royal Military Academy Sandhurst, Surrey, UK

Jerry F. Hough is professor of political science and director of the Center of East-West Trade, Investment and Communications at Duke and senior fellow at the Brookings Institution.

Index